ARCHAEOLOGY
OF THE
DREAMTIME

The story of prehistoric Australia and its people

JOSEPHINE FLOOD

This book is dedicated to the
Aboriginal people of Australia.

Front cover: The late Nipper Kapirigi at the
Kunawengayu Rock-shelter, Arnhem Land.

Angus&Robertson
An imprint of HarperCollins*Publishers,* Australia

First published in Australia by William Collins Pty Ltd in 1983
Reprinted 1984, 1988
Revised edition 1989
A&R edition 1992
Revised edition 1995
Reprinted in 1996
by HarperCollins*Publishers* Pty Limited
ACN 009 913 517
A member of the HarperCollins*Publishers* (Australia) Pty Limited Group

HarperCollins*Publishers*
25 Ryde Road, Pymble, Sydney, NSW 2073, Australia
31 View Road, Glenfield, Auckland 10, New Zealand
77-85 Fulham Palace Road, London W6 8JB, United Kingdom
Hazelton Lanes, 55 Avenue Road, Suite 2900, Toronto, Ontario M5R 3L2
and 1995 Markham Road, Scarborough, Ontario M1B 5M8, Canada
10 East 53rd Street, New York NY 10032, USA

National Library of Australia Cataloguing-in-Publication data:

Flood, Josephine.
Archaeology of the dreamtime.
[New ed.].
Bibilography.
Includes index.
ISBN 0 207 18448 8.
1. Man, Prehistoric—Australia. [2]. Aborigines, Australian—Antiquities.
3. Australia—Antiquities. I. Title.
994.01

Cover photograph by George Chaloupka
Cover and internal design by Russell Jeffery
Printed in Hong Kong

9 8 7 6 5 4 3 2   96 97 98 99

Josephine Flood was born in Yorkshire and came to Australia in 1963, having completed her BA at Cambridge. She began lecturing in archaeology at the Australian National University soon after her arrival and has since gained her MA and Ph.D. from the university.

Dr Flood has participated extensively in field work in most States and Territories in Australia, her most recent research being on rock art and archaeology in the Northern Territory. She has published widely on Australian prehistory and is the author of three other books: *Four Miles High* (the story of two women's mountaineering expeditions to the Himalayas of India and Nepal, 1966), *The Moth Hunters* (the first account of Aboriginal prehistory in the Australian Alps, 1980) and *The Riches of Ancient Australia: A Journey into Prehistory* (a guide for exploring prehistoric Australia, 1990 and revised edition in 1993).

Dr Flood worked as Director of the Aboriginal Environment Section of the Australian Heritage Commission in Canberra from 1978 to 1991, when she retired to devote herself to full-time research and writing. She has two sons and a daughter, and her major recreational interest is mountaineering.

Contents

PART I ORIGINS

PART II THE RISING OF THE SEAS

List of Illustrations

LIST OF COLOUR PLATES

All scales are in centimetres unless otherwise stated.

LIST OF BLACK AND WHITE PLATES

LIST OF FIGURES

Preface

This is a book about the archaeology of prehistoric Australia. It examines both what we know about Aboriginal prehistory and how we know it, with the emphasis being on the tangible remains left by Australians of the distant past.

Archaeology of the Dreamtime was first published in 1983, some minor revisions were incorporated in a revised edition in 1989, and a thorough revision and update has now been completed for this new edition to take account of the many archaeological discoveries over the last decade.

In particular, many new ice age (Pleistocene) sites have been discovered. The age of the earliest habitation sites found in Australia has been pushed still further back, with recent finds of occupation in the Top End of the Northern Territory in excess of 50 000 years old. New early sites dating between 30 000 and 40 000 years old have been excavated in North Queensland and Western Australia, where in one rock-shelter, Mandu Mandu Creek in the Pilbara, a magnificent shell necklace has been found (see colour plate 7). Tasmania's southwest has given up yet more ice age secrets, with the discovery of more than twenty Pleistocene habitation sites, including three art sites and several caves with occupation dated between 30 000 and 35 000 years old. The world's oldest rock art has been dated in the Olary region of South Australia, and the number of Australian sites that are more than 30 000 years old has more than tripled.

Other exciting developments are the new dating and forensic techniques now being widely applied in archaeology. Analysis of DNA is shedding new light on human origins, and identification of residues on the working edges of stone and bone tools is revealing their functions. Of special significance is the finding of blood that has been identified as belonging to human or animal species, including that of extinct megafauna. For example, blood of a *Diprotodon*, an extinct marsupial resembling a rhinoceros-sized wombat, has been found on the blade of a stone tool in a newly discovered, 30 000-year-old camp site (Cuddie Springs in New South Wales), alongside bones of *Diprotodon* and extinct giant kangaroos, lending strong support to the interpretation of this camp site as being Australia's first proven megafaunal kill site.

This book has been written for the general reader, for Aborigines interested in learning more about their own heritage, and for secondary and tertiary students. Every effort has been made to avoid jargon and unnecessary technical terms, but, at the same time, to maintain scientific integrity. Feedback since the original publication has led to some significant changes in this new edition. *Archaeology of the Dreamtime* is being used so widely in the educational field that it seemed desirable to expand the glossary, references and date list to make them adequate for students' needs. The chapter end notes aim to give the most recent or comprehensive reference on a topic or site, whilst unpublished reports have been omitted as they are inaccessible to the general public.

Australian prehistory has become such a large subject that this book is, of necessity, highly selective — since Angus&Robertson was not enthusiastic about a two or three volume work! One topic that has been almost completely omitted is the prehistory of Papua New Guinea and Melanesia, as this is well covered in Peter

White and Jim O'Connell's *A Prehistory of Australia, New Guinea and Sahul*, published by Academic Press in 1982. Although this is now out of print, some accounts are included in Peter Bellwood's books on Southeast Asia, Melanesia and the Pacific, and I understand that Jim Allen is also in the process of writing a general prehistory which will include Melanesia. The history of Australian archaeology and a detailed description of Aboriginal stone and bone tools have also been omitted, because these topics are likely to receive comprehensive coverage in the new edition of *The Prehistory of Australia* by John Mulvaney and Johan Kamminga, currently in preparation. Finally, the subjects of Aboriginal custodianship, heritage and cultural resource management are so important that they merit several separate books devoted solely to them; so far do they exceed the scope of this book that they receive barely a mention. However, I have tried in the section on further reading to point the interested reader to some relevant works on these and other topics that I have been forced to omit for want of space.

There are only two sources of knowledge about the really distant human past of Australia: archaeological evidence and Aboriginal oral traditions passed down as stories abut the Dreamtime. The Dreamtime is the era of creation, the time of the great Spirit Ancestors, who have profoundly influenced the traditional pattern of life as Aborigines know it today. The myths tell the story of human origins in Australia, of which much has been substantiated by scientific investigation. Oral traditions about events that took place many thousands of years ago have endured: the eruption of volcanoes, the rising of the seas, and the change from lush vegetation to desert in the heart of Australia.

The human story has been unfolding for over 50 000 years in Australia, and for 99.5 per cent of Australia's human history, it is Aborigines who have been on the stage. Yet the recording of their past has been woefully neglected. A number of books have described Aboriginal life as it was at the time of first European settlement, but so far only three general books have been written about Australian prehistory: the two mentioned above and Geoffrey Blainey's *Triumph of the Nomads*, published in 1975. The focus of my book is on the distant rather than the recent Aboriginal past, and hence on archaeological rather than historical evidence. It therefore covers events long before the period of European settlement. It also encompasses topics not dealt with by the other prehistories, such as Aboriginal oral traditions.

For most of Australian prehistory, meagre archaeological evidence is our only source of information. Part I examines this in some detail in relation to the earliest period of human occupation in Australia, the Pleistocene. Part II covers the last 10 000 years of prehistoric culture, from the rising of the sea at the end of the ice age up until the dramatic impact of European colonisation. There is so much information available elsewhere on this more recent period that my coverage has been more selective.

Within the chronological framework adopted, the book's organisation is partly by topic, such as art, human origins or megafaunal extinction, and partly by region. For example, two chapters are devoted to Tasmania, basically one to the Pleistocene and one to the Holocene, although there is some overlap, especially regarding sites that span both periods. (Reference to the comprehensive index should overcome any problems in this respect.)

There are no easy answers to questions such as, 'When did people first come to Australia?', 'Where did they come from?', 'Why did the giant marsupials become extinct?'. In these cases, the evidence and theories are summarised and then the readers are left to make up their own minds. The further reading section and the end notes for each chapter also give the reader the opportunity to pursue particular topics or the prehistory of a particular region in greater depth. A list of radiocarbon dates for major archaeological sites is also included, and this has been much expanded and laboratory codes added for reference purposes, since such a list is not available in any other current work. Dates for sites outside Australia and for human skeletal remains and rock art are included in full in the text where appropriate.

Finally, archaeology is such a rapidly developing field that the information in a book of this type needs constant updating; it would therefore be much appreciated if new information or corrections could be brought to my attention so that I can incorporate them into the next edition.

Josephine Flood
PO Box 26
Ainslie
Canberra ACT 2602

and

Ffynnon Bedr
Llanbedr-y-Cennin
Conwy
Gwynedd LL32 8YZ
United Kingdom

March 1994

Acknowledgments

I would like to express my appreciation to all those who have aided in the production of the original book and of this new edition. The encouragement and support of my husband, Nigel Peacock, has been invaluable, particularly in making available that most precious of all commodities, time. My three children, Adrian, Michael and Nadine, have continued to be an inspiration.

The enthusiasm and helpfulness of Alison Pressley, the Publisher of Angus&Robertson, brought about this new edition. Editing was carried out inhouse by Siobhán O'Connor and Bronwyn Sweeney, whom I thank for their meticulous work, patience and unfailing good humour, for coping with the vagaries of Australia Post and my idiosyncratic computer disks . . .

In relation to this new edition, I particularly appreciate the information and/or new photographs supplied by Jim Allen, Jane Balme, Bryce Barker, Peter Bellwood, Sandra Bowdler, Peter Brown, John Chappell, Annie Clarke, Bruno David, Iain Davidson, John Dodson, Ron Dorn, Neale Draper, David Frankel, Natalie Franklin, Judith Furby, John Head, Tom Loy, Isabel McBryde, Kate Morse, Michael Morwood, Margaret Nobbs, Bert Roberts, Andrée Rosenfeld, Robin Sim, Claire Smith, Michael Smith, Peter Veth, Grahame Walsh, Alan Watchman and Stephen Webb.

Special thanks go to my research assistant, Stuart Huys, an Honours graduate in prehistory from the Australian National University, who both acted as a critical sounding board and helped in the last desperate throes of updating references, tables of dates and megafauna in November 1993. I would also like to thank the staff of University House and the Australian Institute of Aboriginal and Torres Strait Islander Studies for their assistance during this period, and again in February and March of 1994.

The manuscript of the original book was improved by the comments of Alex Barlow, Sandra Bowdler, Rhys Jones and Nigel Wace, who read the whole, and of Jim Bowler, John Chappell, Charles Dortch and Jeannette Hope, who read certain parts. I am especially grateful to Sandra Bowdler for her detailed, constructive suggestions. Any errors are, of course, my own responsibility.

Illustration is a necessary and important part of any book on archaeology and I am grateful to all who have provided photographs or drawings — individual acknowledgments are given in the captions — but I should record the generous response of all those archaeologists whose assistance was sought. The maps, drawings and photographs are by the author, unless indicated otherwise.

The Australian Heritage Commission and, in particular, Chairpersons David Yencken, Kenneth Wiltshire and Pat Galvin, and Directors Max Bourke, Colin Griffiths and Sharon Sullivan, were generous with support until my retirement in July 1991. In addition, I would like to acknowledge my great debt to John Mulvaney, Jack Golson and Rhys Jones, who have been a continuing source of advice, information and encouragement since I first turned to Australian prehistory.

Finally, my sincere thanks go to those who have expressed encouragement for and appreciation of this book. I have been particularly delighted by the favourable reaction of Aboriginal people, to whom this book is dedicated.

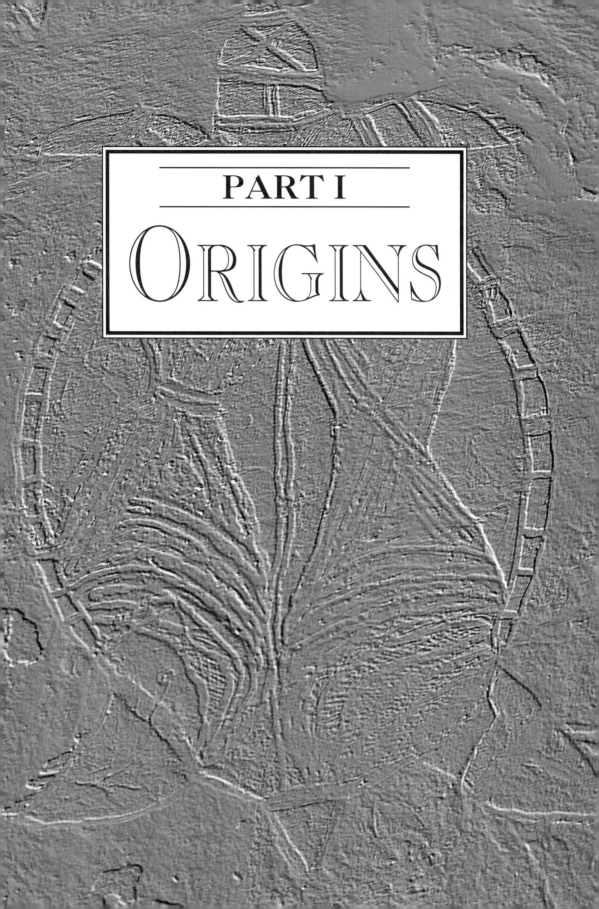

PART I

ORIGINS

Documents of Stone and Bone

Archaeology is the study of human cultures in the past. In Australia this means that most archaeologists recover and analyse the material evidence of past Aboriginal activity, although a growing number of historical archaeologists concentrate on the traces of early European settlement. The human story in Australia is generally divided into two periods, prehistoric and historic, prehistory being the period before the use of written records. Because there are no written records about prehistoric Aboriginal Australia, knowledge of the distant past comes from archaeological evidence and Aboriginal oral traditions handed down from generation to generation.

While Aborigines have sometimes said that they see no need for archaeology for they already know what happened in the past, they also acknowledge the value of scientific evidence showing the tremendous length, continuity and complexity of Aboriginal culture in Australia. If the time scale of human occupation of Australia were represented by one hour on a clock, Aboriginal society would occupy over fifty-nine and a half minutes, European society less than half a minute. Yet most Australian history books devote barely a chapter to the Aboriginal past.

What archaeologists try to do is to discover the patterns of past culture history, past lifestyles and the processes of culture change. Culture is the distinctive and complex system developed by a group of human beings to adapt to their environment. It includes ways of getting food, social organisation, religion, artefacts, dwellings and the like. And because the environment is always changing, in small or large ways, so too culture is continually adapting and changing.

Australian Aboriginal traditional culture is no exception, but because the changes are less obvious than those in many other parts of the world, even as late as the 1920s Aborigines were categorised as 'unchanging man in an unchanging environment'. The first real archaeological excavation in Australia was not carried out until 1929,[1] and the first university post in Australian archaeology not established until the 1960s.[2] Since then there has been an amazing acceleration in archaeological studies and it has now been well established that Aboriginal culture has changed and evolved over more than 50 000 years. Moreover, Aboriginal society has the longest continuous cultural history in the world, its roots being back in the ice age or Pleistocene (the period from about 2 million years ago to 10 000 years ago), when the Australian continent was both larger and greener than today.

Australian Aborigines have been called by world-renowned anthropologist Claude Levi-Strauss, 'intellectual aristocrats' among early peoples. Outstanding features of traditional Aboriginal society include sophisticated religion, art and social organisation, an egalitarian system of justice and decision-making, complex far-flung trading networks, and an ability to adapt and survive in some of the world's harshest environments.

Traditional Aboriginal society as it existed 200 years ago has been recorded by anthropologists, who study living human societies. Their data can then be used by archaeologists to provide analogies in the interpretation of prehistoric culture. Such ethnographic analogies are particularly useful in Australia because of the long continuity of Aboriginal culture, although they must always be used with caution, since amid the vast prehistoric continuities there are also fundamental changes.

It is fortunate that there is such a rich ethnography (writings about local indigenous people) concerning traditional Aboriginal society, for the archaeological record is largely restricted to stones and bones. These data, the results of field surveys and excavation, serve as the documents from which we piece together the jigsaw of prehistory. Stone tools are the most lasting items, surviving in the soil under almost all conditions, but organic substances, such as bone, wood and shell, tend to perish after a few hundred years under normal Australian conditions. In a few remarkable exceptions, however, conditions have remained constantly wet or dry over many millennia. The waterlogged peat bog of Wyrie Swamp in South Australia preserved wooden boomerangs for 10 000 years, bones of giant kangaroos dead for more than 20 000 years have been found in constantly dry desert sand, and bone tools of a similar antiquity have been found at Devil's Lair in Western Australia and in other limestone caves.

Although the material traces of the distant past are usually fragmentary and confined to only the most lasting materials, archaeologists, in their detective hunt to piece together the events of the past, are aided by scholars from other disciplines.

Geologists, by studying the sediments and landforms associated with ancient camp sites, contribute to discovering past environments and climate. Palynologists, from their analysis of pollen grains and charcoal contained in cores drilled out of lake beds, can establish what prehistoric vegetation was like and how much burning took place. Palaeontologists and palaeobotanists identify respectively the animal bones and plant remains from prehistoric sites, producing important information not only about past fauna, vegetation and environment, but also about prehistoric human diet.

Human remains are the province of the physical anthropologist, who finds out about the appearance of prehistoric people and their physical links with other human groups. By a careful study of the form of human skulls — the most durable part of a skeleton — the age and sex of the dead person can be determined, together with their physical affinities with other human populations. Finally, physicists and chemists have developed methods of dating organic materials, such as charcoal and shell, from prehistoric sites.

The archaeologist's particular role is to study artefacts, the material traces of past behaviour. An artefact is 'anything which exhibits any physical attributes that can be assumed to be the result of human activity'.[3] Artefacts thus include stone or bone tools, butchered animal bones, and rock engravings. There is both continuity and change in Australia's prehistoric tool kit (figure 1.1). Stone tools have been in use from the beginnings of humankind in Australia until the twentieth century. Some, such as adzes and scrapers, were tools to make tools, so they tended to be in use continent-wide and to change little over the millennia. Other more specialised types, such as stone spear points, were in fashion more briefly and more regionally, so they can be used as cultural markers, diagnostic of a particular time and place in the prehistoric world.

In general in Australia, there had been a progression from large, heavy stone tools to lighter, smaller ones, and from simple hand-held, general purpose tools to more specialised forms, including composite ones.[4] Composite tools involve mounting or

Making a flake from a stone core

Using a hammer-stone to detach a flake from a core. When a blow is struck on flinty rock, a cone of percussion is formed by shock waves rippling through the rock. Fracture of this type is called conchoidal (shell-like).

A flake showing conchoidal fracture. The inner surface of the flake bears the bulb of percussion.

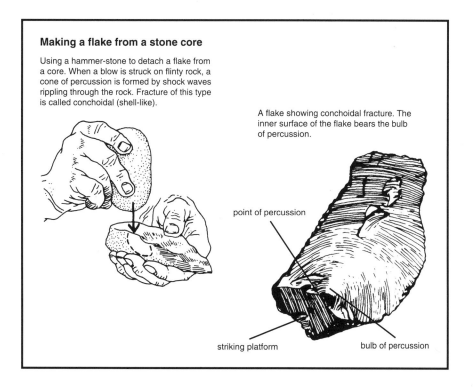

point of percussion

striking platform

bulb of percussion

Chopping: use of pebble tools and horsehoof cores

A pebble tool, unifacially worked. The speckled area is the original surface (cortex) of the stone.

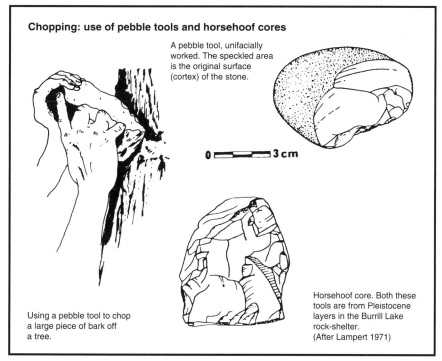

0 ▭▭▭ 3 cm

Using a pebble tool to chop a large piece of bark off a tree.

Horsehoof core. Both these tools are from Pleistocene layers in the Burrill Lake rock-shelter.
(After Lampert 1971)

**Figure 1.1 This page and overleaf. The manufacture and use of stone tools.
(Drawn by R. O'Brien)**

Woodworking with scrapers

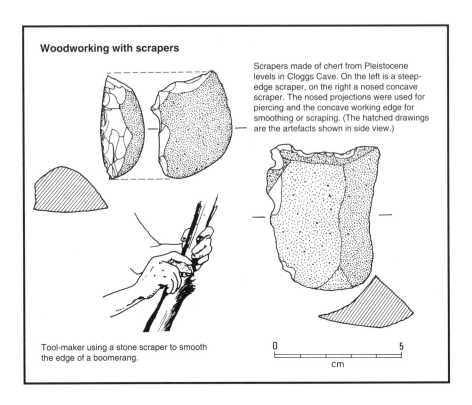

Scrapers made of chert from Pleistocene levels in Cloggs Cave. On the left is a steep-edge scraper, on the right a nosed concave scraper. The nosed projections were used for piercing and the concave working edge for smoothing or scraping. (The hatched drawings are the artefacts shown in side view.)

Tool-maker using a stone scraper to smooth the edge of a boomerang.

0   5
cm

Chopping with ground-edge axes

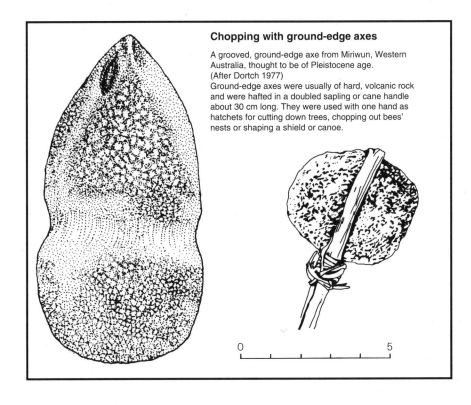

A grooved, ground-edge axe from Miriwun, Western Australia, thought to be of Pleistocene age.
(After Dortch 1977)
Ground-edge axes were usually of hard, volcanic rock and were hafted in a doubled sapling or cane handle about 30 cm long. They were used with one hand as hatchets for cutting down trees, chopping out bees' nests or shaping a shield or canoe.

0   5

hafting tools on a handle for greater leverage. In nineteenth-century Aboriginal Australia, most stone tools were hafted, but the widespread adoption of hafting had been a relatively recent occurrence in Australian prehistory.

While a remarkable amount of information may be derived even from a single isolated artefact found lying on the ground, the most valuable find is a site with a number of artefacts in their cultural context. A site is any place containing traces of past human activity: it may be a scatter of a few stone artefacts on the ground surface; a mound of shells, or 'midden'; the remains perhaps of a single meal; or a cave containing debris from thousands of years of human occupation.

The archaeologist carefully records the location of all artefacts in a site. If the site is stratified, with more than one layer of occupational debris, an excavation may be carried out, and the precise position of each artefact recorded. It can thus be determined which artefacts are associated with each other and to which layer or archaeological horizon they belong. When a site has been excavated, it should be possible to say which artefacts belong together and which are the younger ones.[5]

The relative age of artefacts is established by the 'law of superposition', the principle that the lowest occupational debris in a site is older than that accumulated on top of it. The absolute age can be established by radiocarbon dating, if there are sufficient organic remains present, such as charcoal or shell. Radiocarbon dating is based on the fact that the percentage of the radiocarbon isotope carbon 14 (C-14) in living organisms is equal to that in the atmosphere. When the organism dies, its C-14 begins to disintegrate at a known rate (one half every 5730 years, but its half-life was originally calculated by W. F. Libby as 5568 years, and this value is still utilised in calculating radiocarbon ages). The age of an organic object can thus be calculated by measuring the amount of C-14 left in any gram of organic material and comparing this with what is normally present in a modern sample or standard. Since the initial quantity of C-14 in a sample is low, samples more than about 40 000 years old hold too little for dating, although efforts are now being made, with some success, to extend the limit of detectability back to 70 000 years and beyond.

Radiocarbon dating does not give a precise date as to when the death of an animal or shell occurred, or exactly when a tree was cut down and used as firewood, producing the charcoal that is the most common material to be dated by this method. Thus radiocarbon years do not precisely equal calendar or solar years. When a date is received from a radiocarbon dating laboratory, it will bear a statistical plus or minus factor and will be expressed in 'years BP', which means 'before the present' — the *present* being 1950, when this dating method was first developed. For example, in the date 4000 ± 200 BP, the 200 years represents one standard deviation and means there are two chances out of three that the reading is between 4200 and 3800 years BP. However, there is a further complication: radiocarbon dates do not calibrate exactly with dates obtained from tree-ring dating, because the amount of C-14 in the atmosphere has fluctuated over time. Since radiocarbon dates can only be corrected over the last 8000 years by comparison with tree rings, no C-14 dates in Australia have been calibrated, which means that they will generally be a few hundred years too young. In any case, all C-14 dates are approximate, but without them Australian prehistory would be virtually undated.

Dating is only one of the archaeologist's tools in unravelling the past and reconstructing prehistoric lifeways. Analysis of artefacts can tell us a great deal about past cultural systems, prehistoric people's level of technological skill, diet, settlement patterns, seasonal movement, trading partners, cultural groupings and even religious and social systems. And by studying remains from different periods, the archaeologist can also uncover cultural changes through time, such as changes in diet or artefact types. The next step is to explain why such changes took place and what they meant, in other words the process or mechanisms by which cultures change.

Archaeology is both a science and an art, utilising scientific data and methods to produce the art of prehistory. Field work, such as a survey for prehistoric surface sites or excavation of a stratified cave deposit, is only the beginning. Then comes analysis of the data, placing of the artefacts and site records in the appropriate museum, and finally publication of the archaeologist's findings and their significance in the general context of Australian prehistory.

To give an idea of the whole process, the rest of this chapter is devoted to description of the discovery, excavation and study of one ice age cave. In the whole of mainland southeastern Australia, only one cave has been found so far with Pleistocene human occupation and good preservation of bone. This is Cloggs Cave in eastern Victoria.[6]

People sometimes ask, 'How do you find sites?'. The answer is that field work usually starts in libraries, reading what has already been written about the region in question: not only the ethnography, but also accounts of the area by geologists, foresters, historians, bushwalkers and cavers. The next step is to seek from local people information about where caves or rock-shelters are located or where some stone tools have been ploughed up. In the case of Cloggs Cave, a combination of these approaches, plus a little luck, led me to the site.

I had chosen the southeastern highlands for a regional archaeological study, for there is a fatal fascination and challenge about an area completely blank on the archaeological map. The likelihood of finding any early human occupation in the Snowy Mountains area seemed remote, and everyone said that I would find nothing. Fortunately, they were wrong. Not only did I find a great deal of evidence concerning the last few thousand years of highland prehistory, but I also discovered one major ice age site.

I was looking for a cave in, or as close as possible to, the Snowy Mountains to find out how early the highlands were occupied. I therefore drew on a map a series of concentric circles from the top of Mount Kosciusko, Australia's highest mountain with a height of 2228 metres, and explored every likely cave within each ring. This is not as difficult as it may sound, for most States now have guidebooks that list and describe caves of interest to speleologists. These are usually confined to limestone caves and do not include sandstone and granite rock-shelters, but it was limestone caves in which I was particularly interested, because they have the best preservation conditions for bone tools and faunal remains.

It emerged that there are few caves or rock-shelters suitable for human occupation in the southeastern highlands, and those I tried, such as Yarrangobilly, proved apparently barren. However, in the outermost concentric circle lay Buchan, a region of over 200 limestone caves in eastern Victoria at the foot of the Victorian Alps, 76 metres above sea level and 37 kilometres inland from the present coast. Through consultation with the Victorian Speleological Association I was able to eliminate many of the 200 caves as being too wet, steep or rocky for human occupation. Then, reduced to a 'short list', I began visiting the possible candidates one by one.

I was driving down the Buchan to Orbost road on my way to another cave when I noticed a dark cleft in a cliff near the top of a hill (plate 1). This meant that it was likely to be a dry cave, instead of having a river running through it like so many others, so I abandoned my previous plans and headed across the paddocks up to the cliff, even ignoring what looked suspiciously like a bull!

Cloggs Cave, for such it was, proved to be just what I had been looking for. Outside the cave entrance was a rock-shelter with the roof blackened from the smoke of many campfires. A short, rocky passage led into a dimly lit inner cavern, with a high cathedral-like roof. I had feared there would be a rockstrewn floor; instead the earth floor was soft and dry, perfect for prehistoric and indeed modern campers. The back of the cave is higher than the entrance, which means that cold air drains out but warm air remains inside, simply rising to the back of the cave where there is a narrow passage, but no exit. In fact, in every way it was a perfect prehistoric residence. Even had there been no traces of prehistoric occupation, I would have done a test excavation, but there were some small artefacts and mussel shells on the surface of the rock-shelter floor.

The first step in organising the excavation in 1971 was to obtain permission from the landowner. (Nowadays one would need to carry out full consultation with the relevant Aboriginal custodians or traditional owners and with the State authority with statutory responsibility for Aboriginal sites, but in 1971 there were no local Aboriginal organisations nor had the Victoria Archaeological Survey come into being.) Then a team of student diggers was arranged for what was to prove the first of three seasons of excavation at the site.

Plate 1 Cloggs Cave, Buchan, Victoria. The small black overhang on the right protects the rock-shelter and the high cleft leads into the inner chamber.

The Cloggs Cave project began with making detailed maps of the site, with both plan and profile views. When a full record had been made of the site before excavation, digging commenced both in the rock-shelter and the inner chamber of the cave.

The digging was a slow, painstaking process. No tools larger than a trowel were used, and everything was screened through a fine mesh sieve. At times dental tools and soft paintbrushes were used to prise or gently brush the covering off artefacts and bones so that they could be identified, photographed and fully recorded in position before removal. Only small areas were dug at any one time and the deposit was sieved, so that if any small artefacts were found during the screening rather than during the digging, their original position could be established reasonably accurately.

There are varying views on how much of a site should be dug. In the past it was the custom to excavate the whole, or at least most, of a site. This total approach has the advantage that one can see how various parts of the site were used for activities such as tool-manufacturing, sleeping or cooking. It has been done very effectively in some overseas sites, especially in France, but there most of the caves were completely dug out in this total approach in the nineteenth century.

In Australia, prehistory is still in its infancy, little is known of the vast continent, and there are far more known sites than archaeologists available. It is therefore more practical to carry out a large number of small-scale digs to gain a preliminary idea of Australia's archaeological resources, rather than to spend twenty years on a single site. The main reason for doing small test excavations is that, by only digging a small pit in a site, the rest of the site is left for the future, when scientific methods will have advanced so that even more information can be gained from the site than at present.

Why then dig at all? There are several good reasons. One is the need to answer specific questions about people in the past, to test carefully formulated hypotheses about prehistoric life. These may be fairly general questions, such as, 'How long have people lived here?'; 'What did they eat?'; or 'What were their tools like?'. Or they may be very specific. Such research is an important scientific pursuit in its own right. And before we can protect the prehistoric past, we must know what is there and how important it is. This necessitates survey and sometimes excavation. For example, Cloggs Cave lies in an area containing minerals and good-quality limestone that is being extensively quarried for building material. If its archaeological importance had not been established, it might have been inadvertently destroyed.

The increase in knowledge that each excavation brings (finding nothing can tell you something!) helps to predict the location of other important sites. When enough research has been done in a region, it becomes possible to predict with reasonable accuracy how many and what types of site will be present in other unsurveyed parts of the region. Finally, much of the archaeology being done nowadays is salvage archaeology: excavation of sites that will be destroyed because they stand in the way of developments such as mines, reservoirs, pipelines or housing projects.

The size of an excavation depends on many factors. The minimum size pit that it is practicable to work in is 1 metre square, and if the deposit is deep, a larger pit will be needed. The usual technique in excavating a rock-shelter is to put a trench at least 1 metre wide from the back wall right out beyond the edge of the shelter down the slope below, which often contains occupational debris. In this way the excavation may pick up traces of perhaps a sleeping area against the rock wall, then perhaps a stone-tool manufacturing area sheltered from the elements, cooking hearths near the front of the overhang, and occupational debris such as food refuse thrown or fallen down onto the slope.

The Cloggs Cave rock-shelter divided naturally into two zones: the area under the smoke-blackened overhang and the area outside the entrance to the inner chamber. A small excavation was carried out in both these zones. The overhang area proved to be a chipping floor. Thousands of small stone chips and flakes showed that this had been a tool manufacturing area. Only a few definite implements were present and they were all small tools, including backed blades and small flattish scrapers. Radiocarbon dates from the basal layers of this occupation showed that it belonged to the last 1000 years.

Outside the cave entrance a similar small tool industry gave way lower down to something quite different. The floor was a jumbled mass of huge limestone blocks interspersed with earth, dust and rubble. It was not a promising deposit and the diggers' enthusiasm was flagging when we came across the first large pebble tool, with an encrustation of carbonate testifying that it had been in the ground for much longer than the fresh-looking small tools above. Our efforts redoubled, and eventually this area of 5 square metres outside the cave entrance yielded three pebble tools and eight steep-edged scrapers, all of them carbonate encrusted.

Meanwhile excavation had also commenced in the inner chamber, where a pit of 4 square metres was opened up against the far wall of the lower cave. There were no artefacts on the surface and the top 20 centimetres of dusty earth yielded only two small tools. This might have discouraged some, but I was convinced that if Pleistocene people used any caves in southeastern Australia for shelter, they would have used Cloggs, for who could resist such an ideal piece of prehistoric real estate? I was right, for below the sterile surface layer we came across an occupation layer of consolidated ash and charcoal from ancient hearths. This layer eventually proved to be 8000 years old. And it was only the youngest occupation! When the sterile surface layer from the area between the pit and the entrance was removed, we found that the hearth level continued right across this lower part of the cave floor. (This area has now been covered up again with plastic sheeting and the surface earth replaced, to await possible future excavation.)

The hearth layer consisted of a series of fireplaces containing ash, charcoal and burnt bones, surrounded by hearth stones, river pebbles blackened and cracked by heating. These probably resulted from the use of 'ground ovens', which were recorded by such observers as Richard Helms as being in use in southeastern Australia in the nineteenth century. According to Helms, a fire was made in which stones were heated, then game was placed on top of the heated stones, covered first with bark and green bushes, and then with hot ashes, and left to cook.

The burnt bones in the hearth layer may be merely the result of lighting fires on top of cave earth already containing a lot of bone. They cannot, therefore, be assumed to be human food debris. In fact, in this situation it is virtually impossible to distinguish between the remains of human meals, animal predation and natural death in the cave. However, at least we know which species were present in the late Pleistocene period. The fauna included possums, gliders, koalas, bandicoots, kangaroos, rock and swamp wallabies, rats, marsupial mice, wombats and a wide range of birds. No fish bones or shellfish remains were present, so if these foods were exploited, they were not brought back to the cave for cooking.

There were a few stone artefacts in the hearth layer and, as digging progressed downwards, more artefacts and a great deal of bone were recovered. Indeed, parts of the deposit could be described as a bone bed. The bones found close to the rock wall were more numerous and smaller than those in the centre of the cave. Two cubic metres of deposit from a square adjacent to the rock wall yielded 11 368 grams of bone, of which 10 906 grams, or almost 90 per cent, were from small mammals. Yet the same volume of deposit in a square further away from the wall produced only 4487 grams, of which 2244 grams, or only 50 per cent, were from small mammals. Why the difference? If the same sort of animal bones were found in both areas but just in different quantities, it would seem that the bone had simply fallen or been swept against the cave walls. However, the much larger proportion of small creatures found near the cave wall made me examine the wall closely. I found projecting ledges where birds could sit. What seems to have happened is that owls brought their prey to the cave, sat on the ledges, ate their catch and then regurgitated the remains of their dinner onto the floor below. Bones derived from the regurgitated pellets of owls show the following characteristics: the bones are generally unbroken and whole skulls may be present; the animals represented are small (the largest is about the size of a bandicoot) and the larger-sized animals are represented by juveniles. The small mammal bones found close to the walls of Cloggs Cave show all these characteristics, so they are almost certainly derived from owl predation.

The mass of bone was analysed by palaeontologist Jeanette Hope, the species were identified from their jaws, and the minimum number of each species present in each level of each square of excavation was established. This was done by counting

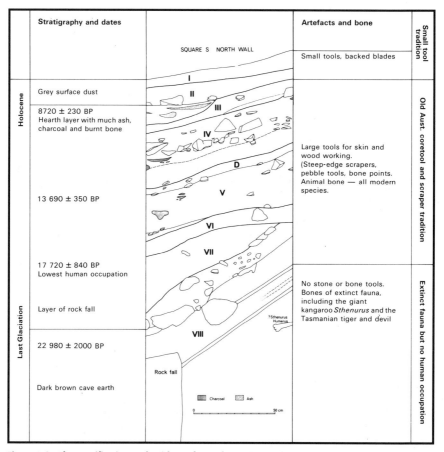

Figure 1.2 The stratification and evidence from Cloggs Cave, Victoria.

for each species the number of left and right mandibles and left and right maxillae, and then taking the number of jaws in the largest of these four categories as the minimum number for the species. Twenty-nine species of mammals were found in Cloggs Cave, representing a minimum of 1350 individual animals.

A column sample was also taken from the cave. This involved taking a 50 × 50 centimetre pillar of the deposit layer by layer, putting the deposit of each layer into a plastic bag and taking them all back to the laboratory for detailed analysis. Analysis included 'flotation', a process in which each bag of the column sample was immersed in water, causing bone, seeds or any other organic matter to float up to the surface. Using this technique, we were able to recover enough charcoal to obtain a whole series of dates for the deposit. We also found organic matter, such as 12 000-year-old leaves and coprolites, the fossilised faeces of animals. Further analysis of the contents of the coprolites told us what grasses animals were eating 20 000 years ago.

As we dug on downwards, it became clear that the occupation was very old. The colour of the bones changed from white at the top to dark orange at the bottom. The bones of locally extinct species also began to appear, such as *Pseudomys higginsi*, the long-tailed rat which now frequents rainforests in Tasmania. At a depth of 2 metres, no more artefacts were found, but below the lowest traces of human occupation was the jaw of a giant extinct kangaroo, *Sthenurus orientalis* (colour plate 1). Also from this lowest layer came teeth of the Tasmanian tiger and the Tasmanian devil. Some of the associated bone bore teethmarks, which indicated that the cave may have been a lair of one of these carnivorous predators 20 000 years ago.

Huge limestone blocks which could not be removed had fallen from the roof, so further digging was prevented. However, the cave floor could not have been very far below the lowest excavated level, because near the bottom of the pit we kept encountering stalagmites, the limestone formations that grow up from a cave floor as the result of water dripping from the roof.

Excavations at Cloggs Cave allow us to reconstruct its prehistory with a reasonable degree of certainty (figure 1.2). Before humans first occupied the cave, it was at times a lair of both the Tasmanian devil (*Sarcophilus*) and tiger, or thylacine (*Thylacinus cynocephalus*), at other times a home for rock wallabies. Outside the cave, the landscape was similar to today's, with grassland and dry sclerophyll woodland bordering the river, but the climate was considerably colder and rather wetter than at present. Giant marsupials, such as the large kangaroo, still inhabited the area, but gradually died out as the climate became more arid.

Then, some 17 000 years ago, humans began to use the cave. At first they used simple flakes and pebble tools of local quartz, but gradually their tool kit expanded to include scrapers of chert and jasper. They only visited the cave occasionally, but drips from the limestone roof slowly built up stalagmites, and from time to time the small stalactites fell from the ceiling into the soft earth floor. Occasionally a large stone block also crashed down.

Use of the cave increased between about 13 000 and 9000 years ago, as it became warmer at the end of the glacial phase. During the daytime, the rock-shelter was used — the rock ledges provided warm sitting places and a good vantage point out over the valley. At night, fires were lit on the cave floor from *Eucalyptus* wood. The group gathered round, heating hearth stones and cooking food items collected during the day, whittling with scrapers to make wooden spears and boomerangs, and rubbing hides with smooth river pebbles until they were pliable enough to sew together as cloaks. With sharp quartz flakes, the possum or kangaroo skins were trimmed to size, holes were pierced with a bone point — its tip ground and polished to needle-like sharpness — and kangaroo tail sinews were chewed until supple enough to be used as thread.

About 8500 years ago, the climate warmed and the inner chamber of Cloggs Cave was apparently vacated. Only the rock-shelter was used as a camping place by later hunter–gatherers. Over the last thousand years, occasional groups camped there, manufacturing small, backed blades and quartz flakes, and eating freshwater mussels from the river. Then came European settlement. Aborigines and Europeans coexisted in the Buchan Valley from the 1830s to 1860s, and the hunter–gatherers learned the use of clay pipes and steel axes. But measles and other epidemics decimated the Aboriginal population of Gippsland, and the cave was abandoned to the bats, and later bushwalkers and speleologists. Now it has been placed on the Register of the National Estate by the Australian Heritage Commission, and the archaeological remains are protected against vandals by a steel grille, through which it is possible to peer but not disturb the site. Control of the site is now in the hands of the local Aboriginal community, the Moodgi Aboriginal Cooperative in Orbost, who have decided not to permit public access nor further excavation.

The significance of Cloggs Cave is the long sequence of artefacts and fauna that it revealed, which enabled reconstruction of the cultural and environmental history of the region over 20 000 years. Radiocarbon dates provide a firm chronological framework for changes in tool technology and fauna, and in particular for the presence of megafauna (large extinct animals). There are very few indisputable dates for megafauna in Australia, so the Cloggs Cave evidence is of particular importance. So, too, is the evidence that megafauna and humans were *not* associated, in view of the controversy about the part played by humans in the extinction of the megafauna (see chapter 12).

Artefacts at Cloggs Cave are not numerous, but the few found are significant (see figure 1.1). The first evidence that bone tools went back into the ice age was found there, and this has since been confirmed by evidence from Devil's Lair and a few other sites. The Cloggs Cave Pleistocene tool kit also bears a close resemblance to that from the 8000-year-old levels at Rocky Cape Cave in northern Tasmania and from newly discovered Pleistocene caves in the southwest. This similarity strongly supports the theory of the derivation of Tasmanian culture from the mainland in the Pleistocene by means of the land bridge that then spanned Bass Strait. Cloggs Cave is still the only ice age site in the southeastern corner of mainland Australia in which both bone and stone tools are preserved, and it provides a valuable reference point with which to compare the new finds described from other Pleistocene sites.

The First Boat People

*T*he truth is, of course, that my own people, the Riratjingu, are descended from the great Djankawa who came from the island of Baralku far across the sea. *Our spirits return to Baralku when we die. Djankawa came in his canoe with his two sisters, following the morning star which guided them to the shores of Yelangbara on the eastern coast of Arnhem Land. They walked far across the country following the rain clouds. When they wanted water they plunged their digging stick into the ground and fresh water flowed. From them we learnt the names of all the creatures on the land and they taught us all our Law.*

That is just a little bit of the truth. Aboriginal people in other parts of Australia have different origins and will tell you their own stories of how the mountains came to be, and the rivers, and how the tribes grew and followed the way of life of their Spirit Ancestors.

The huge Wandjina, makers of thunder, rain and lightning, soared over the sea to Western Australia. Their faces stare at us from the cave walls of the Kimberley Ranges and the spears that fought their giant battles are still in the sands on the coast north of Derby. The giant Rainbow Serpent emerged from beneath the earth and as she moved, winding from side to side, she forced her way though the soil and rocks, making the great rivers flow in her path, and carving through mountains she made the gorges of northern Australia. From the Rainbow Serpent sprang many tribes, and tales about her are told all over Arnhem Land — over to Western Australia, in central Australia and even to New South Wales. Our paintings on rocks illustrate this true story about one of our Ancestors ...

In Queensland Giroo Gurrll, part man and part eel, rose out of the water near Hinchinbrook Island and named the animals, birds and all the places there, while the great Ancestor Chivaree the Seagull paddled his canoe from the Torres Islands down the western coast of Cape York to Sandy Beach where his canoe turned into stone.[1]

Many Aboriginal oral traditions about origins, like this one recounted by Wandjuk Marika, agree with scientific evidence that the Aborigines came to Australia from across the sea. There are innumerable stories about the beginning of Creation in the Dreamtime, but in northern Australia one of the major themes concerns the arrival of the Great Earth Mother, symbol of fertility and creator of life. Amongst the Gagadju (Kakadu people of the Alligator Rivers region), the great ancestress was called 'Imberombera'. Imberombera came from across the sea and arrived on the coast of Arnhem Land. Her womb was filled with children and from her head were suspended woven dilly bags in which she carried yams, bulbs and tubers. She travelled far and wide, she formed the hills, creeks, plants and animals, and left behind her many Spirit Children, giving a different language to each group.

The Gunwinggu people of Arnhem Land tell a similar story about the Mother, Waramurungundji, who came across the sea from the northwest, the direction of

Indonesia, to land on the northern Australian coast at the beginning of Creation. Not only did these Dreamtime ancestors come from across the sea, but they also came by canoe.

Some Aborigines have always believed that their ancestors came from across the sea in canoes in the Dreamtime, and now scientists have come to the same conclusion from archaeological and other evidence. In the same way that archaeology has revealed material traces of the oral traditions enshrined in Homer's *Iliad* and *Odyssey* or the Old Testament stories of the Bible, it has uncovered evidence for some of the historic events remembered in the rich body of Aboriginal 'myths'.

The human history of Australia encompasses the time since the first migrant stepped ashore — which we now know from archaeological evidence from the Northern Territory was in excess of 50 000 years ago. There is no possibility that human evolution occurred in Australia independently of the rest of the world, for the ape-like ancestors from which *Homo sapiens* — the modern human race — developed in Africa have never been present in Australia. Where, then, did the Australian Aboriginal race originate? The first migrants could not have walked to Australia, but must have come across the sea. Since people have been in Southeast Asia for more than a million years, it would theoretically have been possible for Australia to have been colonised at any time during this period (figure 2.1). There was, however, one serious barrier to cross — water.

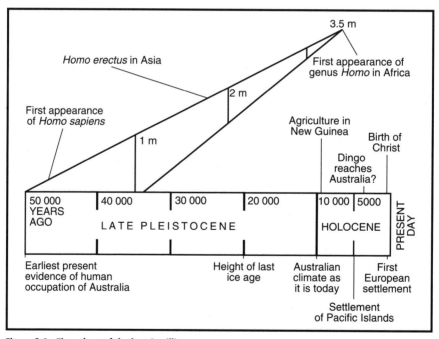

Figure 2.1   Time chart of the last 3 million years.

At no time during the last 3 million years has there been a complete land bridge between the Asian and Australian continents. And before then the gulf was even wider. We know from geological evidence that until some 50 million years ago, Australia was part of the great southern continent of Antarctica, well removed from the Asian mainland. It had by then evolved a marsupial fauna. About 35 million years ago, the Australian continent drifted northwards, acting as a Noah's Ark for the marsupials. Australia was isolated until about 25 to 15 million years ago, when it approached the southern fringes of the island chain of the East Indies. Australia is still, in fact, a continental raft drifting northwards, but will take some time to reach Asia at the current rate of less than 5 centimetres a year.

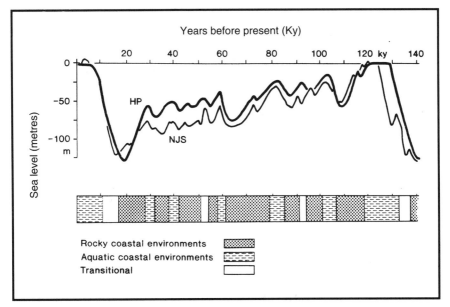

Figure 2.2 **Changes in sea level over the last 140 000 years. (ky = 1000 years, HP = Huon Peninsula curve (Chappell & Shackleton 1986) and NJS = temperature-corrected isotopic sea level curve (Shackleton 1987).) Bottom: Alternation of rocky and aquatic (coral lagoon and mangrove) coasts in response to sea level changes. Relatively low levels occurred around 18 ky (c. –140 metres), 70 ky (c. –68 to –75 metres), 90 ky (c. –45 to –55 metres), and 110 ky (c. –60 metres). (Chappell 1993[2])**

The lack of Asian animals in Australia is evidence that for many millions of years there has been a significant water barrier between Asia and Australia, which prevented them spreading southwards. For the last 2 million years (the Pleistocene or ice age), the sea gap isolating Australia from Asia is thought never to have been less than 90 kilometres wide.

The world's sea level has fluctuated dramatically during the last million years as the result of a series of glacial periods. During these glaciations, the mean annual temperature dropped by as much as 6 to 10 degrees Celsius, much of the world's water was frozen into ice sheets at the poles, and vast glaciers made large areas of the northern hemisphere uninhabitable. The huge amounts of water locked up in ice sheets caused a drop in sea level of as much as 130 metres (figure 2.2).[3] This turned the 2.5 million square kilometres of continental shelf around Australia into dry land and added onto Southeast Asia an area the size of the Indian subcontinent.

When the drop in sea level was only 60 metres, the continent of Greater Australia stretched from the equator to latitude 43 degrees south and encompassed an area of 10 million square kilometres. It included not only New Guinea and Tasmania, but also the present Gulf of Carpentaria and northwest shelf (figure 2.3). It was possible to walk from Burma to Bali, from New Guinea to northern Australia, and from

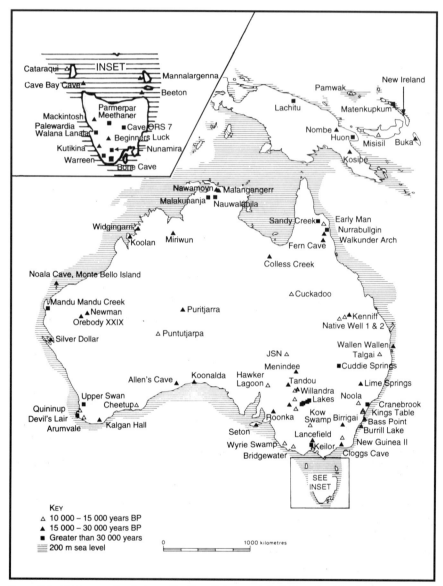

Figure 2.3 Pleistocene sites in Australia, New Guinea and the Melanesian islands.

southern Australia to Tasmania, but the gap between the Australian continent and Asia remained a substantial water barrier.

The Australian continental shelf is known as Sahul Land; that fringing Asia, as Sunda Land. Sunda Land includes islands on the continental shelf of Asia, such as Java, Sumatra and Borneo. The edge of the Sunda shelf marks the southeastern boundary of the oriental faunal region. The Sahul shelf marks the boundary of the Australian faunal region. In between lies a zone of thousands of islands, usually termed Wallacea, after the nineteenth-century geographer Alfred Russel Wallace. Wallacea is not a distinct fauna zone, but includes many different regional sets of fauna.[4]

Beyond the islands of Wallacea, there was still a wide stretch of sea to cross to Australia. Humans managed to cross this in early prehistoric times, but the only other mammals, apart from birds and bats, that made the crossing were rats, mice and dingoes. Evidence suggests that dingoes were brought to Australia by humans, but the Asian ancestors of Australian rodents arrived unaided, probably carried across on logs or 'rafts' of vegetation more than 2 million years ago.[5]

ROUTES TO AUSTRALIA

We tend to imagine that the first migrants would have taken the shortest and most logical route from Asia to Australia. But we must constantly remind ourselves that the shape of the continent was different then and that these people had no maps, did not know that Australia existed, and even after arrival would have had no idea that they had reached a continent rather than another small island.

The routes by which the first migrants may have arrived in Australia were examined in great detail by Professor Joseph Birdsell and have recently been reanalysed by economic historian Professor Noel Butlin in the light of new, much more detailed maps of the sea beds between Australia and Asia (figure 2.4).[6] In particular, it has emerged that at a sea fall to –60 metres below the present level, there would have been a long chain of small islands on the edge of the Sahul Shelf, parallel to and visible from Timor, reducing the open sea voyage across the Timor trough to a visible destination only 90 to 100 kilometres away. There would also have been broken tongues of land extending out from the coast of northwestern Australia to the west and east of Joseph Bonaparte Gulf. Between the outer chain of islands

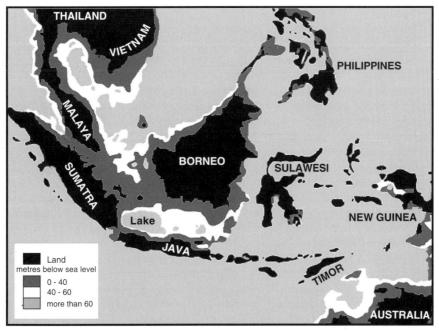

Figure 2.4 Sea depth contours between Southeast Asia and Australia. (After Butlin 1993, based on United States National Oceanographic and Atmospheric Administration computer tape records)

and the two arms of land there would have been a large variety of 'stepping stones', such as Ashmore Reef, Cartier Islet, and Marie and Troubadour Shoals.

The new archaeological evidence suggesting that humans had reached Arnhem Land by 53 000 or more years ago (see chapter 7) presents a riddle for those like Birdsell who thought that humans would have reached Australia at a time of very low sea level. The two major lowerings were at 18 000 years ago — much too late — and 140 000 years ago, which most archaeologists consider much too early. Whilst it is rash to argue from negative evidence, no sites of or near this age have been found in Australia or nearby Sunda Land,[7] and such an early date for the arrival of *Homo sapiens* in Australia does not fit with the evidence of physical anthropology (described in chapters 4 and 5).

One likely time for human entry would now seem to be around 70 000, when the sea level was about –75 to –68 metres. Birdsell suggested the most favourable route would have been a northerly one through Sulawesi to New Guinea, but Butlin's research has shown that, in distance terms, the Timor to Australia route would have been no more difficult, for both would have involved crossing a maximum of about 90 to 100 kilometres of open sea. Butlin, after considering innumerable factors, such as visibility of the target destination, wind direction, likely possession of watercraft, directional control and sailing capability, makes a strong case that 'the Timor–Australian route was the more likely ancestral and long-sustained path to Australia'.[8]

His arguments in favour of the Timor route were, in summary:

1. 'Contrary to prevalent understanding, it seems likely that Australia received substantial migrant flows from Timor at a relatively early stage and more persistently than by other routes. Flows via New Guinea may have become more prominent with the development of directional skills in sailing.'
2. 'Means to travel by sea from Timor did not depend on very advanced maritime technology.'
3. 'With quite minimal watercraft, lowering sea levels (and hence reduced sea distances) were not as generally dominant an issue in opening opportunities for transfer as has often been suggested; on the other hand, the facility to travel directly from Timor to Australia was determined by comparatively small sea level changes and by the shape of the Australian Shelf.'

Points in favour of migration *not* being confined to times of lowest sea level have recently been pointed out by John Chappell,[9] who thinks times of rising or even high sea level are equally likely. Firstly, high sea level would be more conducive than low sea level to northwest monsoonal winds, which would blow voyagers from Wallacea southwards and eastwards towards Greater Australia. Secondly, rising sea levels generally enhance aquatic food resources by enlarging lagoons and favouring coral reef development and diversification of reef environments. Such 'aquatic coasts' are likely to have reached their maximum extension at or near the end of each sea level rise, whereas 'rocky coasts' less favourable for aquatic food gathering tend to characterise falling sea levels.

People who constantly cross coral lagoons and mangrove estuaries to collect shellfish and other marine foods typically use rafts or canoes, for example in New Guinea today. This use of watercraft on aquatic coasts in all probability extends back into the distant past. It may well be then that the first voyagers to Australia were coastal dwellers who not only used watercraft such as simple rafts to gather shellfish and other sea foods, but also could already make substantial sea voyages utilising winds and currents.

In order to make successful landfalls across more than 90 kilometres of open sea, the colonists would have needed buoyant and sturdy watercraft. No archaeological evidence of Pleistocene watercraft has been found or is likely to be found in Australia, since such perishable artefacts are most unlikely to survive and most Pleistocene coastal sites have now been submerged.

None of the watercraft known from prehistoric Australia seems a likely candidate for Pleistocene voyages. The Tasmanian Aborigines used either simple driftwood logs for crossing rivers or watercraft made from three bundles of paperbark or stringybark lashed together. These craft were generally not taken more than 5 to 8 kilometres off the coast, as the bark became waterlogged after a few hours.[10]

The bark canoes used in southern mainland Australia were more rigid, but likewise unsuitable for long sea voyages. In northern Australia, much more seaworthy sewn-bark canoes were up to 5.5 metres long and 0.5 metres wide and could carry six to eight people. A sewn canoe is recorded as having made a 32-kilometre, open sea voyage off Arnhem Land from the Sir Edward Pellew Islands to Macarthur River, but generally trips of over 10 kilometres were rare. Evidence of such canoes has been found only in the Australian tropics and, on the analogy of other items found only in the tropics, they may have been a relatively late introduction to Australia.

Plate 2 Mangrove log raft, Western Australia. A Worora youth paddles this raft on George Water, Glenelg River district. (Photo by H. Basedow 1916, in the Basedow Collection, National Museum of Australia, Canberra)

It is possible that the earliest colonists were tide-riders, using rafts like the *kalum*, a light, triangular, mangrove-wood raft of double construction, used until recently by four tribal groups on the northwestern coast of Australia (plate 2). This raft was paddled and was normally used over a distance of 8 to 16 kilometres along this coast, one of the most dangerous and inhospitable in the world. Its tides are among the world's highest, fluctuating 9 metres, and its currents attain a speed of 10 knots, swirling among numerous islands and coral reefs.

The Kaiadilt of Bentinck Island in the Gulf of Carpentaria used similar rafts made of mangrove or driftwood to exploit the rich seafood around their low, barren islands. Their log rafts did tend to become waterlogged, they did not undertake long sea voyages and the death rate on even medium-length voyages was extremely high. Two recorded sea voyages of about 13 kilometres each made by the Kaiadilt on rafts resulted in an average death rate of 50 per cent.[11]

The tide-riders of northern Australia may be the best model for Pleistocene voyagers from the Sunda to Sahul shelf, who no doubt were aided by the northwest monsoon winds. Bamboo may have been used for their rafts or canoes. Cordage would have been required to lash the bamboo tubes together, but ropes could easily have been made from the rich Asian flora. Bamboo shafts are coated in silica and thus are impervious to water and extremely buoyant. Bamboo would have grown in areas of high rainfall all along the northern migration route, and at least as far as Java on the southern route. An experimental bamboo raft based on contemporary ethnographic rafts in South China was built (in two hours) and sailed by Alan Thorne, who found it 'surprisingly easy to steer' and achieved a speed of four to five knots. Data from this raft voyage were used to set up a computer simulation experiment, which showed that during the monsoon nearly every raft (without sails) blown away from the coast of Timor would end up on the Australian coast sooner or later, most within a week or ten days. These results were obtained at present sea level; at times of much lower sea level 'it appeared literally impossible for such a raft to miss Australia'.[12] Fire would probably have been taken on deliberate voyages to keep warm and cook fish. A clay hearth could be made in the bottom of the boat; this was the custom among Tasmanian Aborigines.

Once in Australia, the voyagers would have been virtually 'trapped' by the lack of bamboo, for only a few relatively thin-stemmed species (such as *Bambusa arnhemica*) grow in isolated pockets in the northern coastal plains.

TRIGGERS TO MIGRATION

Distant smoke from natural bushfires on the Sahul shelf should have been visible from some Indonesian islands, perhaps providing an incentive for deliberate voyages to Australia. The vegetation on the shelf at the time is likely to have been semiarid savanna woodland, which is prone to fires caused by lightning. Even small fires in this type of vegetation produce billows of smoke rising to 1000 metres or more above sea level, and smoke from large bushfires commonly reaches 5000 metres. Smoke plumes 1000 metres high could have been seen by people standing at sea level up to 110 kilometres away.[13] When the sea was at its lowest level, smoke could have been visible ahead on any route to Australia. And at any time during the ice age, the smoke and glare of bushfires on the Australian shore should occasionally have been visible on such Indonesian islands as Timor, Roti, Tanimbar, Seram and Gebe. Likewise, as amply demonstrated by later Polynesian navigators, the flight of birds would have been a good indicator of land ahead. There was also a continual stream of 'travel information' from Australia to Timor and from New Guinea to Sulawesi in the form of seasonal migrations of birds, including the vividly coloured, noisy 'dollarbird', which is eaten in Indonesia today. As well as being a source of food, such birds imply the presence of fresh water, vegetation, and probably fish and other game.

In addition to the 'pull' of the possibility of new land and food resources, 'push factors' also probably operated to encourage migration. After detailed consideration of the economic and demographic issues, Butlin identified problems of population pressure and food scarcity as prime candidates for the most likely ways of explaining the migration process. He argued for population growth in mainland Southeast Asia during the last glacial period on the grounds of adequate resource supplies, new technological developments and other factors, and 'the implied population growth could then have led gradually to increasing group size, unmanageable groups and splintering'. Such splintering would have led to dislocation, either through long-distance movements or by short, 'shuffling' migrations, herding competing groups south and east. The glacial period was a time of considerable environmental fluctuation. It is generally believed that in the tropics of Southeast Asia, the glacial cold spells caused the habitable area of land to expand during times of very low sea level, with a decrease in the extent of rainforests in favour of more food-rich savanna and open woodlands, leading to population growth. When the sea rose again, the habitable area would have shrunk within a few thousand years, leading to stress, possible conflict and intensified migration as people tried to find substitute locations.

Butlin thought that 'there were pressures potentially leading to a more or less persistent and rising flow of migration to Australia at least from around 65 000 BP and possibly earlier, even though there may have been some interruptions to this flow'. However, he suggested that the last great sea fall of the last glacial maximum (about 18 000 BP) might have actually decreased pressures to migrate because of the vast expansion in the Sunda and Sahul shelves. When the rising post-glacial sea reintensified pressure on land and resources, a new solution may have been found in the form of increased sedentism and the development of horticulture and agriculture, as seen in the highlands of New Guinea around 11 000 years ago.[14]

NEW GUINEA

Throughout most of human history the island of New Guinea (comprising Papua New Guinea and Irian Jaya) formed part of the same land mass as Australia. This has been called 'Greater Australia'. New Guinea also lay on the route from Asia to Australia. To a coastal, maritime-adapted people from tropical islands clad in rainforest, the coast of New Guinea would have offered a familiar environment. Exciting new evidence suggests that the human settlement of New Guinea goes back more than 40 000 years.

The Huon Terraces (in the vicinity of Fortification Point) are one of the best sets of relict Pleistocene coastlines anywhere in the world.[15] The terraces rise like a giant flight of steps out of the sea: each 'tread' is an ancient coral reef now raised up high above modern sea level. Massive earth movements, earthquakes and volcanic eruptions to which New Guinea is subject have raised the coral reef formed at the shoreline 120 000 years ago to 400 metres above sea level. On one of the lower terraces 80 metres above sea level, twenty-four weathered axes were found.[16] These 'waisted axes' (colour plate 2) are large, heavy stone tools with a flaked cutting edge.

A notch flaked out of each side edge gives them a 'waist' or hourglass shape. The notches are not just to provide a grip on hand-held stone tools, since some of them are too wide apart for a hand to stretch across. The notches were probably made to aid hafting — the attaching of a handle. Wear marks, obvious even to the naked eye, show that the groove must have been for a cane or vine binding.

These waisted stone tools are highly significant because they reflect the very great antiquity of the concept of hafting, which involves binding a tool to a handle for greater efficiency and leverage. A total of over seventy large, heavy, waisted stone axes have been found either buried or as surface finds by Les Groube, Jo Mangi and others.[17] Groube has argued persuasively that they were used for forest clearance, 'taming' the rainforest for food plant promotion:

> *Restricted natural stands of food plants such as aerial yams, local bananas, swamp taro, and such tree crops as sago and Pandanus, could be promoted by judicious trimming, canopy-thinning and ring-barking, and perhaps, with the aid of fire, some minor felling.*[18]

Even today in Papua New Guinea, bananas are cultivated in the middle of rainforests simply by axing back enough vegetation cover for sunlight to reach a banana clump.

One extremely weathered stone axe was found with some other stone tools under 2 metres of volcanic ash in a layer dated to about 40 000 years ago. It was sandwiched between ash layers firmly dated by the thermoluminescence method to between 37 000 and 45 000 years. This makes it the earliest hafted stone axe in the world.

These waisted stone tools resemble the 26 000-year-old tools from Kosipe, the earliest site previously known in New Guinea. The discovery of Pleistocene occupation at Kosipe, a 26 000-year-old campsite,[19] was a surprise, for it lies in the southeast corner of New Guinea, at least 1400 kilometres from the western ice age coastline and, even more surprisingly, in the highlands at 2000 metres above present sea level. It seems clear that humans were paying at least seasonal visits to the highlands of southeast New Guinea 26 000 years ago, when the snowline was only about 1000 metres above the camp site and the temperature would have been about 6 degrees Celsius lower than at present.

The Kosipe artefacts, although few in number, are important because they demonstrate not only the use of hafting, but also the concept of edge-grinding, in which the working edge of a tool is ground to a chisel-like form for better cutting properties (see figure 1.1). Until these discoveries at Kosipe by Peter White of Sydney University, it was thought that the techniques of stone-grinding and of hafting were developed in Australia only during the post-glacial period. Kosipe revolutionised ideas about the early technological history of the Australian region and lent support to surprising discoveries made in mainland Australia (see chapter 7).

Kosipe lies adjacent to a pandanus swamp, where Geoff Hope has recovered evidence from pollen analysis for firing and forest clearance 30 000 years ago.[20] Kosipe may therefore have been a focus for at least the seasonal collection of pandanus fruits. Seven other major Pleistocene sites have been found in the New Guinea highlands.[21] The two oldest sites are Kosipe and Nombe, both occupied by at least 25 000 years ago. Nombe is a rock-shelter at 1720 metres above sea level, some 400 kilometres northwest of Kosipe and more than 100 kilometres from the nearest coast. Nombe produced, in an early level, a stemmed axe resembling the waisted tools from Kosipe and other highland sites, together with exciting evidence of the coexistence of humans and megafauna. In the same 25 000-year-old layer were found stone tools and the bones of extinct *Protemnodon*, *Dendrolagus*, thylacine, and an unidentified, pig-sized *Diprotodon*. It is unclear whether humans were hunting and scavenging these big animals, but they were certainly familiar with them.[22]

In a (1983) review of these eight highland sites, Jack Golson, Jim Allen and Geoff Hope came to the conclusion that Pleistocene settlement occurred mainly in mid-montane forests accessible to 'a vast altitudinal spread of resources extending downwards into lowland valleys'.[23] This finding did not support an earlier prediction that Pleistocene occupation of the highlands would concentrate in the ideal hunting grounds of the forest grassland ecotone, where alpine grasslands lay just above the tree line.[24]

A Pleistocene date of 35 360 ± 1400 BP has recently been obtained for basal occupation in the limestone Lachitu rock-shelter on the north coast in West Sepik Province, by Paul Gorecki, Mark Mabin and John Campbell of James Cook University.[25] Whilst the evidence of Pleistocene occupation of New Guinea is still sparse, we now know from this rock-shelter and the Huon Terraces that migrants had reached the island's north coast by 40 000 years ago, and were exploiting rainforest resources in the highlands by 25 000 years ago.

OUT TO THE GREATER AUSTRALIAN OUTLIERS

There is growing evidence for an explosive spread of the modern human race, *Homo sapiens*, across Southeast Asia and the western Pacific rim in Upper Pleistocene times. Early occupation including stone artefacts has been found in the limestone cave of Lang Rongrien in peninsular Thailand (c. 37 000 BP); Kota Tampan in Perak, peninsular Malaysia (c. 31 000 BP); Niah Cave in Sarawak (c. 40 000 to 35 000 BP); the cave of Leang Burung 2 in Sulawesi, Indonesia (c. 31 000 BP); Tingkayu in Sabah, Malaysia (c. 28 000 BP); and, in the Philippines, Pilanduk Cave (c. 28 000 BP) and Tabon Cave on Palawan Island (c. 26 000 BP).[26]

The next step, however, was the major one. The seemingly insignificant sea straits between Sunda Land and the Sahul Shelf created immense barriers to mammalian fauna; it was only humans with their boatbuilding skills who managed to cross Wallacea. Pleistocene boat use is undocumented anywhere else in the world until the end of the Pleistocene, and Iain Davidson and William Noble have argued that 'the first colonisation of the Greater Australian region, Sahul, is the oldest evidence for the expression of behaviour that is distinctively human ... Language is necessary for the building of a boat and for the emerging picture of the symbolic and representational abilities of the earliest people in the Australian region.'[27]

There is now abundant evidence for systematic sea voyages before 28 000 years ago to the permanently separated islands northeast of New Guinea, at the eastern end of Greater Australia and the western end of the Melanesian island chain of the Pacific Ocean. Since 1985, the then only known island Melanesian site of Pleistocene age (Misisil Cave on New Britain, with 11 000-year-old occupation) has been added to by seven others, through the work of Jim Allen of La Trobe University, and others. The oldest Melanesian island sites discovered so far are the coral limestone caves of Matenkupkum (basal date between 32 000 and 33 000 BP) and Buang Marabak (basal date about 32 000 BP) on New Ireland (one of the Bismarck Group),[28] and the limestone rock-shelter of Kilu on Buka Island in the northern Solomons, first occupied about 29 000 years ago.[29] The other Pleistocene sites are Panakiwuk and Balof 2 in the north of New Ireland, first occupied around 14 000 BP;

Matenbek (adjacent to Matenkupkum), with a basal date of some 20 000 years;[30] and the recent find of Pamwak Cave on Manus in the Admiralty Islands, where Matthew Spriggs and Wal Ambrose have recently excavated 2 metres of cultural deposit below a radiocarbon date of 12 500 BP.[31]

Both the oldest sites show a strong coastal dependence with a focus on reef resources, especially shellfish. Indeed, the world's oldest marine fish bones were discovered in a deposit of marine shells going back 32 000 years at Matenkupkum. None of the fish bones present belongs to deep or open sea species, which would suggest the use of hook and line; they are mostly shallow reef dwellers, probably captured in fish traps on the reef platform or by netting, spearing or poisoning.

Even more surprisingly, the world's earliest direct evidence of the use of root vegetables was found in the 28 000-year-old layer of Kilu Cave, in the northern Solomon Islands, when Tom Loy identified the genus of the starch grains and crystalline raphides found in residues on the working edges of stone artefacts there.[32]

The emerging picture is of highly mobile, broad-spectrum hunter–gatherers, exploiting a wide variety of marine and terrestrial resources. Shellfish came from both the intertidal reef zone and coastal-fringing mangroves, and the earliest levels of occupation at all the New Ireland sites contain bones of snakes, lizards and rats, with Matenkupkum also having birds, and Panakiwuk and Balof 2 bats. Later in the Pleistocene — around 19 000 to 20 000 BP — a phalanger, *Phalanger orientalis* (the marsupial cuscus) was added to the fauna of at least southern New Ireland. This seems to have been a deliberate import to increase the food resources.[33] Another introduction at the same time (to Matenbek) was obsidian, derived from New Britain, a straight line distance of 350 kilometres away. Transport of a mineral resource over such a distance 20 000 years ago is truly remarkable.

Overall, Melanesian Island Pleistocene prehistory presents an example of a maritime, coastal-adapted people colonising oceanic islands with a restricted range of natural resources. Their stone tool kit was too generalised and amorphous to be a good indicator of affiliation to any particular prehistoric group, but it seems likely that they voyaged to New Britain, New Ireland, the Solomons and even the Admiralty Islands from Sahul Land. From New Guinea, two sea voyages — both under 50 kilometres — were needed to reach New Ireland. The crossing to the northern Solomons would have involved, for the first time since leaving Southeast Asia, a 'blind' crossing, requiring voyagers to leave one landmass before the next was in sight. Reaching the Manus Islands, however, was a quantum leap, for they required an open-sea crossing of at least 200 kilometres even at times of lowest sea level, out of sight of land for 60 to 90 kilometres. If occupation in Pamwak Cave proves to be of similar antiquity to the caves in New Ireland and Buka, a drastic revision will be required of traditional Western thinking on the ocean-voyaging capabilities of Pleistocene migrants!

The first Australians were the world's earliest ocean voyagers. New finds in Australia suggest that people had reached the necessary technological level to cross substantial bodies of open sea and adapt to a new continent more than 53 000 years ago. The settling of Australia marked the first human expansion beyond the single landmass comprising Africa, Europe and Asia, for settlement of the Americas seems to have come rather later. This adaptation to a strange, new continent at such an early date must be counted as a major achievement in the world's human story.

CHAPTER THREE

Life and Death at Lake Mungo

The first migrants to the Australian continent encountered a favourable environment. Once they penetrated inland, most of the fauna would have been unfamiliar, but would have presented little threat to the new arrivals. There are few carnivorous predators in Australian fauna. Those that existed then in mainland Australia were the native cat (*Dasyurus*), the Tasmanian 'tiger' or 'wolf' (*Thylacinus cynocephalus*), the Tasmanian 'devil' (*Sarcophilus*) and the marsupial 'lion' (*Thylacoleo*), a leopard-sized carnivore, which may have been a predator or may have eaten only carrion. There would also have been crocodiles in the tropical rivers and some poisonous snakes, fish and insects, but these would have been familiar dangers to migrants from Asia.

In addition, a number of giant animals and birds (megafauna), which are now extinct, existed over much of Australia until the last phase of the ice age, which ended some 10 000 years ago. These included huge flightless birds and giant animals, such as a donkey-sized wombat, kangaroos 3 metres tall and the marsupial *Diprotodon*, which was the size of a rhinoceros. Some of these animals were relatively slow-moving herbivores and would have fallen easy prey to hunters. However, their extinction may have been caused by climatic change rather than by human overkill, or been a combination of both (see chapter 12).

The tropical environment in coastal and riverine northern Australia would have provided the human colonists with largely familiar fish, shellfish, birds and plant foods. The arid-adapted flora further south would have been quite new, together with the marked seasonality of rainfall. Australia is also the world's driest inhabited continent; on over 75 per cent of its surface, rainfall is exceeded by potential annual evaporation. This was not always the case, for great changes in the Australian climate occurred during the ice age. One of the key areas where both climatic changes and early human occupation are documented is the semiarid belt of western New South Wales. As most of the earliest Australian skeletal remains, together with very early habitational debris, come from this region, it seems appropriate for our survey of the early human fossil record to begin here.

In 1968, Jim Bowler, a geomorphologist at the Australian National University, was studying the nature of sediments to establish the pattern of climatic change over the past 100 000 years. His work was focused on the Willandra Lakes in western New South Wales, a series of interconnected lake basins carrying the waters of a tributary of the Lachlan River to the Murray (figure 3.1), and the following account is based on his research findings.[1] The Willandra 'lakes' have been dry for the past 15 000 years, but once they had a surface area of more than 1000 square kilometres of fresh water.

During the Pleistocene, there were long periods when western New South Wales, and Australia as a whole, had much more standing water than occurs today, and the Willandra Lakes were full of water, mainly because of the much lower evaporation

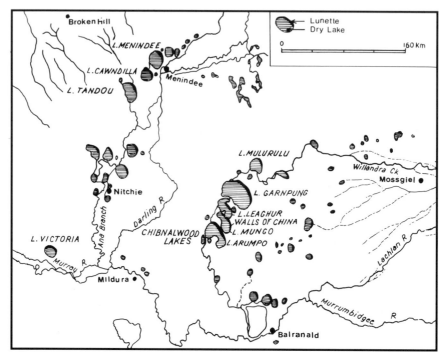

Figure 3.1 The Willandra Lakes region, western New South Wales.

rate caused by lower temperatures. The present barren landscape of the Willandra Lakes would have been very different 40 000 years ago, with lakes full of fresh water and teeming with large fish. The now dry bed of Lake Mungo would have been 20 kilometres long and 10 kilometres wide, with a depth of some 15 metres. On its eastern side, sand dunes provided sheltered campsites by the lake shore.

Most research in the fossil lake system was concentrated on Lake Mungo, which has suffered extensive erosion of its lunette, the crescent-shaped dune formed on the lake shore, exposing 600 hectares of its core and partially exposing much of the rest of the lunette (colour plate 3). The Mungo lunette is 25 kilometres long and was, before deflation, up to 40 metres high. It is visible from several kilometres distant as a long, low, white hill among the flat, brown plains. Erosion has sculpted the lunette into such spectacular shapes that it was named 'the Walls of China' in the 1860s, possibly by Chinese workers from local sheep stations.

The earliest sediments in the area, called the 'Golgol sediments', were laid down before 120 000 years ago, when the lake was full. From about 120 000 to 60 000 years ago, the lake was dry and the lake floor was covered with soil and vegetation much as it is today. No evidence of human presence has ever been found in the Golgol sediments, and it seems that people did not begin to camp at Lake Mungo until the latest full-water phase. This commenced about 55 000 BP and, by about 50 000 BP, the lake was full, as a result of increased runoff from the Lachlan River catchment flowing down Willandra Creek and filling the Willandra Lakes. This full-water period has been named by Bowler the 'Mungo lacustral phase' (figure 3.2). Freshwater shellfish and other aquatic fauna inhabited the lake, and many large trees grew around its margins; outlines of their branching roots have been fossilised and

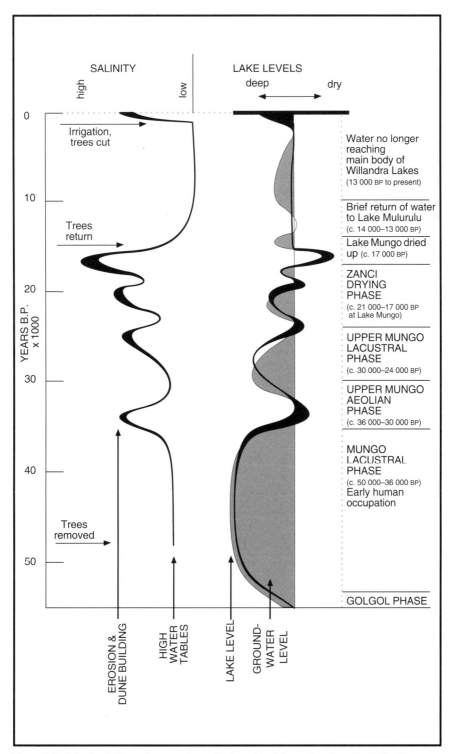

Figure 3.2 Lake levels in southeastern Australia, based mainly on data from the Willandra Lakes. (Based on Bowler et al. 1976, as revised by Bowler 1992)

preserved by calcium carbonate. Waves driven by the westerly wind created a crescent-shaped sandy beach (a lunette) on the eastern lee shore. This dune consists of the Zanci, Mungo and Golgol units, named after local pastoral properties (colour plate 3).

About 36 000 years ago, the water level fell (but never completely dried up) in both Lake Mungo and Outer Lake Arumpo. Expanses of saline mud were exposed, which blew away to form clay-rich dunes. This episode has been called the 'Upper Mungo aeolian phase'. Increased salinity in the lakes may have weakened fish, which became easy prey for those camping around the shores. This period was short-lived and soon the lake was again full of fresh water. Then, about 25 000 years ago, there was another drop in water level and another phase of lunette building which covered earlier beach deposits. From 25 000 to 21 000 BP, the water level varied, but was never as deep as before.

Then, around 21 000 BP, the 'Zanci drying phase' began — the lakes gradually dried, and Lake Mungo disappeared about 17 000 years ago. The wind built up dunes of gypsum and saline clay on lee shores, with a period of maximum dune-building between 17 000 and 16 500 BP. There was a brief resurgence of water between about 14 000 and 13 000 BP at Lake Mulurulu in the northern end of the Willandra system. Thereafter, water never again flowed into the Willandra Lakes, and people and animals moved to use the more permanent channels of the Murray, Darling and other rivers as their new lifelines.

HUMAN REMAINS

Among the stark residuals and shifting sands of the massive eroding dunes, Bowler came across the first exciting hint of early human presence at Mungo. Eroding out of a small midden in the upper part of the Mungo sediment, he found some stone artefacts and mussel shells bearing an encrustation of carbonate. The presence of large freshwater mussel shells in the dune and their association with artefacts is difficult to explain except by invoking human transport. Radiocarbon dating of these shells gave an age of $32\ 750 \pm 1250$ BP.

Bowler later noticed some burnt, carbonate-encrusted bones protruding from a low hummock on the dunes that clearly belonged to the Mungo sediments. He marked the site and left it intact for future archaeological excavation. A group from the Australian National University inspected the site in March 1969, and immediately suggested that the bones were human.

The bones were contained in a quarter of a metre square calcrete block, which was only 15 centimetres thick and was fragmenting; many wind-eroded, broken pieces were scattered around. The features of the site were plotted, photographed and fully recorded; the loose bones were numbered and collected. Then the central carbonate block was undercut and removed in order to take the whole block back to the laboratory for closer analysis. The most secure container available was Professor John Mulvaney's suitcase, which he nobly emptied out to transport the precious finds safely back to Canberra.

The archaeologists returned to the site fully prepared for a major excavation just one week later, only to find that a freak rainstorm had totally changed the scene. If they had left the Mungo skeleton there, it might have been washed away. But the storm had revealed hitherto hidden stone tools in the same area, and 200 carbonate-encrusted stone tools were collected.

Also exposed were fifteen patches of black deposit. They were roughly circular or oval in shape, 60 to 90 centimetres in diameter, and 5 to 10 centimetres deep. The black deposits contained charcoal, burnt animal and fish bones, freshwater mussel shells, emu eggshells and, in four places, stone artefacts. The black deposits seem to have been hearths, and their contents the discarded remains of human meals and tools associated with food collection and preparation. The human bones had lain about 15 metres away from the nearest hearth, and the whole area appears to have been a camp site on the lake shore. Here the ancient inhabitants camped, and roasted and ate their food. They used stone tools and burnt their dead on the sandy dune and beach a few yards from the shingle of the high freshwater lake shore.

The people also collected raw material for tool-making and ochre pigment, consolidated earth made up of clay and hydrated oxide of iron. The ochre did not occur in the Mungo area, but must have been brought there from at least 10 kilometres away.

Back in the laboratory, physical anthropologist Alan Thorne had begun the painstaking removal of the concrete-hard carbonate crust from 'Mungo Man', as the bones had been named. Reconstruction of the skull was a massive task, since it was broken into 175 small fragments. When Mungo Man finally emerged from this process, 'he' proved to be a 'she'. Mungo I, or Willandra Lakes Hominid (WLH) 1 as she is now called, was a young adult female of slender build and small stature; she was 148 centimetres tall (4 feet 10 inches). Her head is very round in shape and her eyebrow ridges are small compared with the heavy, beetling brows of some archaic Australian skulls. Nonetheless, she is one of the oldest human beings so far discovered in Australia.[2] Radiocarbon dating of burnt bone from WLH 1 gave an age of 24 710 +1270/−1100 BP (lab. no. ANU-618B, acid insoluble residues). Later accelerator mass spectrometer dates on the humic acid fraction in further samples of

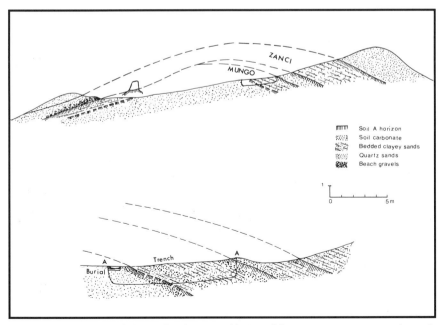

Figure 3.3 Section through the eroding lunette at the sites of the Mungo I (WLH 1) cremation and Mungo III (WLH 3) burial. (After Bowler and Thorne 1976)

WLH 1 burnt bone gave dates of 25 120 ± 1380 BP (NZA-230) and 24 745 ± 2400 BP (NZA-246). These dates confirmed the age of the remains, which Bowler had worked out from their position in the Mungo sediments (figure 3.3), as between 24 500 and 26 500 years old.

Careful analysis of the surface and fractures of the bones tells us that the corpse was first cremated, then the burnt skeleton, especially the face, was thoroughly smashed, and finally the ash and smashed bones were gathered together and deposited in a small depression beneath or adjacent to the cooled funeral pyre. This method of disposal of the dead was still in use among Australian Aborigines in historic times in eastern Australia and Tasmania.

The WLH 1 site has provided the oldest evidence of ritual cremation in the world. It is interesting that it is a woman who was cremated. Although no conclusions can be drawn from a sample of one, it at least shows that 25 000 years ago women were considered worthy of complex burial rites. What emotions inspired those rites we will never know, but this cremation shows a concern for the deceased that is the essence of humanity.

The presence of pellets of red ochre suggests the use of this pigment for ritual, art or decoration, and another nearby site has shown that ochre was used in funerary rites 30 000 years ago. This is the site of another burial, but this time of a male, who was placed in a grave with his body thickly coated with red ochre. This Mungo III (now WLH 3) burial was discovered 500 metres east of the WLH 1 cremation site (figure 3.3). (The name WLH 2 is reserved for a very fragmentary, burnt, probably male hominid at the WLH 1 site.)

In 1974 Bowler was examining an eroded area of the Mungo stratigraphic deposit[3] when the slanting rays of the late afternoon sun highlighted a small, white object protruding 2 centimetres above the surface. It was part of a human skull. Heavy rain had made it erode out of the lunette, and rapid excavation was essential because of the great fragility of the bones and the possibility of further rainstorms. Again, archaeologists from the Australian National University rushed to Mungo, and there was elation when excavation gradually revealed not just fragments of bone or a skull, but a whole skeleton (plate 3). Finds of complete skeletons are extremely rare, and archaeologist Wilfred Shawcross recalls the excitement of the find. 'Two to three people worked flat out for two days. All the time you felt it couldn't go on; but it did. A neck appeared, then a rib. Normally you are lucky to get a skull; in Africa they are lucky to get a jaw. But this was a whole skeleton.'[4]

Excavation revealed a fully adult man, on his side in a shallow grave, with hands clasped. The bones and surrounding sand were stained pink; the pink colour, derived from ochre powder scattered over the corpse, clearly defined the size and shape of the grave. The burial lies within the Mungo sediments (figure 3.3), and its age has been estimated by Bowler and Thorne on geomorphological evidence and its stratigraphic association with WLH 1 to be between 28 000 and 32 000 years old, so the midpoint of 30 000 years is adopted here. This is the only reasonably complete skeleton in Australia soundly dated beyond 20 000 years old. WLH 3 resembles WLH 1 in gracility according to Thorne, but is more fragmentary than plate 3 suggests and awaits full description.

Meanwhile, Stephen Webb's recent study of 130 Willandra Lakes hominids (described in chapter 5) revealed that WLH 3 had most unusual tooth wear on his molars. Webb suggests these distinctive striations 'could be the result of the stripping of some sort of plant fibre with sharp inclusions (quartzose grains or phytoliths) (T. Loy pers. comm.). It is tempting to suggest that these were fibres for fishing nets, baskets or dilly bags.'[5] This fits very well with the evidence described below from the study of fish remains that people were using nets to catch fish in Lake Mungo in that time period.

WLH 3, who was probably about fifty at the time of death, had severe osteoarthritis in his right elbow, initially suggestive of 'spear-thrower elbow', but Webb concludes that its cause is uncertain, and it may have been an infection exacerbated by spear-throwing, with or without a spear-thrower.[6] (This may therefore be used as evidence for the use of spears 30 000 years ago, but not of spear-throwers, the antiquity of which is still uncertain.)

WLH 3 had also lost his two lower canine teeth simultaneously when he was much younger.[7] (Likewise, WLH 22 had lost his two lower central incisors many years before his death.) This pattern of loss is most unusual and may indicate that the teeth were removed in the rite of tooth avulsion. Among Holocene Aborigines, including Tasmanians, the removal of two front teeth formed a common part of initiation rites of young men, but it was two top teeth rather than lower ones which were removed.[8] If these are actually cases of tooth avulsion, in a slightly different form from that practised more recently, this is the oldest instance of the practice anywhere in the world, for WLH 3 is dated to around 30 000 years old. It would also be further evidence for the great antiquity of Aboriginal religious beliefs.

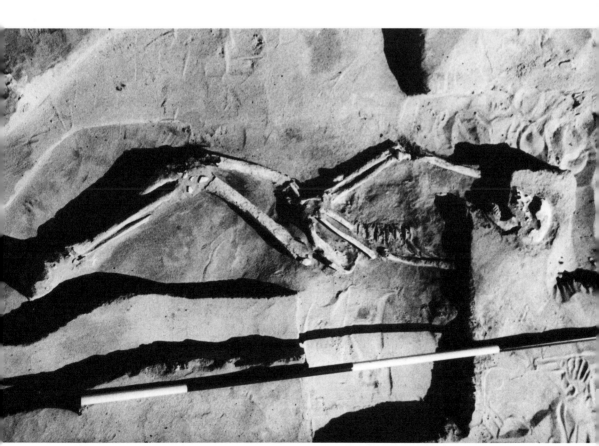

Plate 3   Mungo III (renamed WLH 3) burial during excavation. Red ochre was scattered over this corpse during his burial. (The scale is marked in 20-centimetre sections.) (A. Thorne)

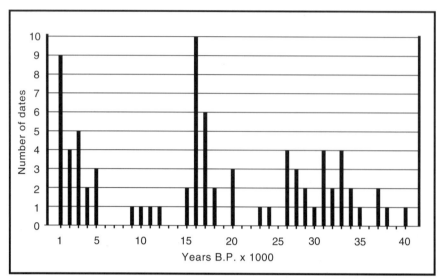

Figure 3.4 Radiocarbon dates from the Willandra Lakes, showing human occupation over the past 40 000 years. (After P. Clark 1987; S. Webb 1989)

The significance of this ochred burial is that it shows that such burial rituals go back at least as far in Australia as in other parts of the world, such as France, where ochred burials have been found in Grimaldi Cave at a similar time. In fact, at Mungo, red pigment was in use even earlier, for lumps of ochre and stone artefacts were found deep below the ashes of a fire lit 32 000 years ago. As the ochre did not occur naturally at Mungo, it must have been deliberately carried there from some distance away. Similar lumps of pigment, some of them showing signs of use, have been found in Pleistocene levels in other widely separated sites, such as Kenniff Cave in Queensland, Cloggs Cave in Victoria, Miriwun and Devil's Lair in Western Australia, and several Arnhem Land rock-shelters.[9] Ochre has no utilitarian functions, such as medicinal use; it is simply a pigment used (at least in the recent past) to decorate rock walls, artefacts, dancers' bodies in ceremonies, and corpses during some burial rites.

Many camp sites, hearths and middens (prehistoric refuse heaps) have now been excavated in the Willandra Lakes region, and more than a hundred radiocarbon dates obtained. Many of these dated occupation sites are between 10 000 and 30 000 years old, but a considerable number also belong to the last 5000 years. No trace of human presence has been found in the Golgol sediments, so it looks as if humans only came to camp by these inland lakes when they last filled with water around 50 000 years ago. From then until about 25 000 years ago, occupation was intensive and the rich resources of the freshwater environment were fully exploited.

Analysis of more than a hundred radiocarbon dates from hearths and shell middens in the region has revealed its continuous use during the last 40 000 years, with seventeen dates in excess of 30 000 years from around Lakes Mungo, Garnpung and Arumpo, and the Prungle Lakes (figures 3.1 and 3.4).

Continuing multidisciplinary work in the Lake Mungo area by archaeologists, geomorphologists, palaeontologists and others has added considerably to these discoveries, although regrettably little of this work is yet published. Mungo has also become a National Park, with excellent displays set up in the Visitors Centre by

Peter Clark, Harvey Johnston and other archaeologists. In 1980 the Willandra Lakes region was entered in the World Heritage List as a place of outstanding universal value on the basis of both its natural and cultural heritage.[10] Major excavations (so far unpublished) of potential human habitation sites were carried out in the 1970s by John Mulvaney, Isobel McBryde, Michael McIntyre and Wilfrid Shawcross from the Australian National University.

In 1973 Mulvaney opened up a large trench in the southern end of the Mungo lunette, not far from the WLH 1 cremation site.[11] Below the light-coloured sediments of the Zanci unit lay the deep-brown, 2-metre thick Mungo unit, in which a hearth was located. This gave a radiocarbon date of 31 100 BP +2250/–1750 BP. Sealed beneath this hearth were small pellets of ochre, which must have been carried to the site. And 1.8 metres below the hearth, in a gravel layer at the base of the Mungo sand unit, were a number of water-rolled stone flakes. A small sample of shells associated with these gave a radiocarbon date of about 40 000 years (ANU-1203).

The problem with the radiocarbon dating method is that 40 000 years is its theoretical limit; the carbon-14 in any samples older than that is indistinguishable from background. At this order of magnitude, contamination is a major problem and even the best charcoal samples are only 70 per cent pure carbon. The relationship between carbon-14 activity and age is logarithmic; beyond 30 000 years, a small difference in carbon-14 activity can produce a large difference in age. This means that the reliability of radiocarbon ages beyond 30 000 BP is open to question, and they may well be too young.

In this situation, Mulvaney's date of 40 000 BP for shell associated with artefacts at Lake Mungo was set on one side, in spite of the sample's impeccable stratigraphic context, but now, in view of the similar or older dates from the Northern Territory, New Guinea and elsewhere which have been obtained more recently by other dating methods, it seems eminently credible that humans were camping by Lake Mungo 40 000 or more years ago.

Early dates of other nearby sites support this view. The shell from a thin, stratified midden of mussel shell, ash and charcoal on Lake Outer Arumpo, excavated by McBryde in 1975, was dated to about 36 000 years, although dates on the soil sediments gave a very different result. This midden (Top Hut III) was exposed in a gully wall, buried under 5 metres of lake shore sediments.

A remarkable find at Lake Mungo, 5 kilometres northeast of the WLH 1 and WLH 3 sites, was a group of five fireplaces 26 000 or more years old. The oldest fireplace was a typical Aboriginal oven — a shallow depression that was filled with ash and charcoal, with several lumps of baked clay on top. This oven was dated to 30 780 ± 520 BP.

A surprise furnished by these fireplaces was the evidence they gave concerning palaeomagnetism: the phenomenon of fossil magnetism of archaeological material such as baked earth and clay from ancient fireplaces. The first Australian evidence for deviations in the earth's magnetic field was found in the early 1970s by Michael Barbetti.[12] His research revealed that 30 000 years ago magnetic north had swung right round 120 degrees to the southeast. This magnetic 'reversal' or 'excursion' lasted for about 2500 years, after which the direction of magnetisation reverted to normal again. This major magnetic reversal is now known as the Mungo excursion, and is one of the youngest and best-documented examples of such changes in polar magnetic direction. When such reversals in magnetism are found in other archaeological sites, they can be dated by comparison with the Mungo and other reversals. A series of thermoluminescence dates has been done on baked clay in Aboriginal fireplaces at Mungo. The thermoluminescence dates come out consistently older than the radiocarbon dates, and it appears that *all* radiocarbon dates on charcoal, at or earlier than about 30 000 BP, may be about 4000 years too young. Dates on freshwater mussel shell are the most reliable, but finely disseminated charcoal is often contaminated by younger organic material moving down through the sandy sediments, giving younger radiocarbon ages than samples of shells in the same layer.[13]

Similar cooking methods seem to have persisted in Aboriginal society for over 30 000 years. Two types of Aboriginal fireplace were in use in the nineteenth century in the Willandra Lakes region: 'hearths' and 'ovens'. Hearths are small areas of blackened earth resulting from an open fire. They were probably used for roasting small animals and do not contain cooking stones. Ovens consist of a shallow depression or pit containing a band of ash and charcoal and cooking stones or lumps of baked clay. The use of such ovens in the region was described by the explorer Edward Eyre in his *Journals of Expeditions of Discovery*, published in 1845 (vol. 2, p. 289):

> *The native oven is made by digging a circular hole in the ground, of a size corresponding to the quantity of food to be cooked. It is then lined with stones in the bottom or clay balls where stones are unavailable, and a strong fire made over them so as to heat them thoroughly, and dry the hole. As soon as the stones are judged to be sufficiently hot, the fire is removed, and a few of the stones taken, and put inside the animal to be roasted if it be a large one. A few leaves or a handful of grass, are then sprinkled over the stones in the bottom of the oven, on which the animal is deposited, generally whole, with hot stones ... laid on top of it. It is covered with grass, or leaves, and then thickly coated over with earth, which effectually prevents the heat from escaping.*

TECHNOLOGY

The artefacts recovered from the Willandra Lakes area give us some idea of the technological level that these Mungo people had attained. Very few bone tools have been found, but it is difficult to know whether this is because they were not present or because they have rotted away. Since the alkaline soils have preserved both large and small animal bones, it is unlikely that bone tools were numerous.

Only three bone tools were found in the first decade of archaeological work at the Willandra Lakes. These are three pointed bone implements, all less than 10 centimetres long. Two were found at the WLH 1 site, on the Walls of China, and one on the Lake Mulurulu lunette. One has been worked to a sharp point at both ends. It is possible that such bipoints were used as lures to catch the large Murray cod, bones of which were found at the same WLH 1 site. In the nineteenth century, Aborigines often caught Murray cod by attaching a fishing line to the middle of a bipointed bone and then pulling it rapidly through the water so that the bone looked like a small darting fish. These bone lures, or fish gorges, were called 'muduk' by Aborigines of the Murray River. This name has been adopted by some archaeologists for bone points, but is inappropriate since it is not certain that all, or even any, of the prehistoric bone bipoints and unipoints were used as lures.

A recent study of use-wear (wear produced on the working edge of a tool from use) on Pleistocene bone tools has identified the function of bone points as the piercing of dry skins in 'sewing', the scraping of skin, spearing of mammals and use as clothes toggles.[14] In historic times, the uses were similar: spear tips, awls for piercing holes in animal skins being sewn together into cloaks, nose pegs, and pins for fastening cloaks.

Stone tools were far more plentiful than bone ones in the Willandra Lakes region. Most are made from silicified quartzite, a hard, fine-grained stone available locally. The major tool types are choppers and flakes (figure 3.5). Choppers are large, heavy tools made from lumps of rock, and they have a flaked cutting edge. They are used for heavy woodworking, such as chopping down trees. A flake is a piece of stone formed when a lump of rock is struck with a hammer-stone (see figure 1.1). The force of the percussion blow detaches a flake of stone that has sharp edges and can be used to cut or scrape flesh, sinew or fur. Sturdy, steep-edged flakes were also used for woodworking, such as scraping, sawing, incising and chiselling.

These smaller tools are traditionally called scrapers, although they were not necessarily used for scraping. They may be made on a flake or on a core, a lump of rock from which flakes have been struck. Some rather specialised scrapers found at Mungo have deeply notched, concave working edges suitable for use as spokeshaves for smoothing wooden shafts such as spear shafts. The large tools made from lumps or nodules of rock are generally termed core tools. Some of them have a flat base, an overhanging, step-flaked edge and a high, domed shape like a horse's hoof, hence they have been called horsehoof cores.

The tool kit from the Mungo cremation site has been described by Rhys Jones of the Australian National University as the 'Australian core tool and scraper tradition'. This term has now been adopted Australia-wide for the early Australian stone industry. Its main characteristics are the presence of large core tools, steep-edged, chunky, high-backed scrapers and concave, notched and 'nosed' working edges. Flatter, convex-edged and round scrapers also occur, which may have been used to make skins pliable for use as cloaks.

These tools were used for the manufacture and maintenance of wooden tools rather than to extract food from the environment. In general, this industry is typologically similar to late Pleistocene and early Holocene tool kits found at the base of such sites as Kenniff Cave and Mushroom Rock in Queensland, Capertee and Burrill Lake in New South Wales, Ingaladdi and Malangangerr (but lacking the ground-edge axes) in the Northern Territory, and New Guinea highland sites such as Kafiavana. The tools also resemble both Pleistocene and Holocene industries of Tasmania, although the upper levels of some Pleistocene sites there, such as Kutikina, Nunamira and Bone Cave, are dominated by tiny thumbnail scrapers (see chapter 9).

Where river or beach cobbles were available, they were often made into chopping tools, termed 'pebble tools', but with the same function as the Mungo-type horsehoof cores. Similar industries based on flakes and pebble tools have been found at about 40 000 BP in Southeast Asia, Sulawesi and at sites such as Tabon Cave in the Philippines and Niah Cave in Borneo.

The Australian core tool and scraper tradition, although often amorphous and generalised, is nonetheless distinctive when compared with the stone tools of the rest of the world.[15] In Australia, there is no Levalloisian nor typical Mousterian technology, nor any signs of the Upper Palaeolithic revolution, except perhaps in the Holocene small tool tradition (described in chapter 15). Why are Australian Pleistocene industries so different? Was the tool kit of the earliest migrants into Australia a package from a source area? If so, where?

These major questions remain to be answered by further research both in Australia and Asia. Sandra Bowdler has recently been comparing the cultural content of the earliest dated cultural sites from both Greater Southeast Asia and Greater Australia, and concluded:

> *There certainly appear to be resemblances between the stone artifacts at the different sites from both regions. It seems possible to suggest that these assemblages can be construed as being part of a common tradition, with local variation due to different environments, site usage and raw material availability. In the light of earlier opinion, it is interesting to note the general low frequency of pebble tools and other large core tools, with the exception of the Huon Terrace waisted tools. Otherwise these industries may be characterized as somewhat amorphous, comprising ad hoc flake tools. There are however some types which occur in several sites, in both the Sunda and Sahul provinces, namely small steep edge-scrapers and thumbnail scrapers.*[16]

Over the millennia, new tools were invented to suit new uses in response to environmental change. The drying-up of the Willandra Lakes was accompanied by

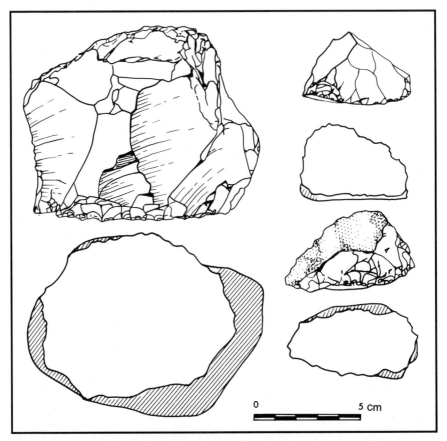

0   5 cm

Figure 3.5 Stone tools from Lake Mungo. The Australian core tool and scraper tradition is exemplified by such tools (made of silicified quartzite): horsehoof cores on the left and steep-edged scrapers on the right. Below each tool is shown its plan view from the base; the hatched areas indicate overhanging areas. (Drawn by Joan Goodrum)

an eventual change from a reliance on freshwater resources to an economy based on the exploitation of wild grass seed. The small, hard grass seeds were crushed to make flour by means of large, flat millstones or mortars. Considerable human activity continued in the region after the lakes had dried up, but it was not related to lake exploitation.

Seed grindstones have been distinguished by Michael Smith from other types of grindstones on the basis of his extensive archaeological work in Central Australia.[17] He identified the following varieties as seed grinders:

1. *Millstones*: flat surface slabs with shallow grooves worn on the grindstone face used as lower grinding surfaces for the wet milling of seeds.
2. *Mullers*: the upper grindstones used in the same process.
3. *Mortars*: flat surface blocks with a shallow oval or circular depression ground in one or both faces, used for preliminary pounding and crushing of hard seeds.

Until recently it was believed that seed-grinding technology was introduced into the area about 15 000 years ago as a response to the decrease in aquatic resources from the drying of the Willandra Lakes. This theory was based on the apparent association of grindstones with sites of 15 000 years or younger, and their absence on older sites. However, re-examination of the archaeological evidence by Harry Allen and Jane Balme has shown that: (a) some of the grindstones are not seed-grinding stones; (b) there is an effective absence of seed-grinding stones *in situ* on the Pleistocene sites; (c) it is most likely that seed-grinders were introduced into the region in the early Holocene; and (d) seed-grinding was not a direct response to increasing aridity.[18] However, a flat grindstone bearing use-polish and siliceous starchy residues has just been found in a 28 000-year-old layer of the Cuddie Springs site in New South Wales (described in chapter 12). It seems likely that the starch grains are from grass or wattle seeds, according to archaeologist Richard Fullager. Whether or not archaeological evidence shows the occasional use of grass seeds in the Pleistocene, the extensive and intensive use of this food seems to belong to a much later period, of only a few thousand years ago.

ECONOMIC LIFE

The Willandra Lakes have provided evidence for the Pleistocene exploitation of a freshwater environment more than 35 000 years ago. As well as 'base' camps containing remains of many different creatures, 'dinnertime' camps have been found containing the remains of a lunch. The Top Hut III midden is probably the remains of a single meal eaten by a small group around 35 000 years ago. Another such site, on the Lake Tandou lunette, has only the remains of 500 yabbies, a small freshwater crayfish. This dinnertime camp is dated to 25 000 years ago. And one Tandou site has been identified by Jeanette Hope as a frog kill site!

The number, size and species of fish remains in sites have been identified by Jane Balme and others by comparing their otoliths, or ear bones, with those of modern fish in the same region.[19] Seventy per cent of fish caught in the Pleistocene Willandra Lakes were golden perch (*Plectroplites ambiguus*). The large numbers of perch at the sites, which dated between 22 000 and 26 000 BP and were each believed by Balme to result from a single event, came from tightly restricted size ranges, which strongly suggests the use of gill nets at some sites and traps at others. Fishing with fixed gill nets is a highly selective process: it tends to catch fish of the

Figure 3.6 A reconstruction of life at Lake Mungo about 30 000 years ago. (Drawn by Giovanni Caselli, in *The Evolution of Early Man*, by Bernard Wood (Cassell, 1977), by courtesy of Professor B. Wood, University of Liverpool)

same species and age. Nets were probably set at the time of a spring spawning run, when the fish migrate up the rivers in large numbers. Golden perch are difficult to catch by other means, such as spearing, lines or poisoning, and if such methods had been employed, there would be a far greater age range among the fish remains.

On the Darling River in the nineteenth century, Aborigines used to set nets 100 metres long about 20 metres offshore to catch golden perch. These nets were made from bulrush fibre (*Typha*) and had wide mesh in which to catch the fishes' gills. Other fishing methods were probably used for larger fish. Some bones have been found in middens of huge Murray cod (*Maccullochella macquariensis*), which were estimated to weigh as much as 15 kilograms. These were probably speared or caught with line and lure.

The diet of the hunter–gatherers at Lake Mungo was varied and rich in protein. As well as fish and mussels, they ate the rat kangaroo, the western native cat, the brown-haired wallaby, the hairy-nosed wombat and various other small animals and birds. Remains of these creatures have been found in ancient fireplaces, together with numerous broken emu shells. Their presence indicates that people were camping at Lake Mungo in the spring, when emu eggs hatch. In the heat of summer, people would have stayed close to the plentiful fresh water and shellfish of the lakes. In the cooler winter, they probably spread out away from the lakes onto the arid plains and hunted land animals, thus conserving the lake's food supplies for the harsh summers. Such a pattern of exploitation and seasonal movement is characteristic of Aborigines in arid regions, and was observed in the Willandra Lakes region in the nineteenth century.

Recent research by archaeologist Harvey Johnston of the New South Wales National Parks and Wildlife Service has shown that the Willandra shell middens are small, and the magnitude and importance of Pleistocene shellfish collecting there may have been overestimated.[20] Plants and land animals may have played a more important role than previously thought, for Loy's analysis of residues on some stone flake tools from the southern end of Lake Mungo has shown they were used for stripping meat from bone and for cleaning tubers, probably the native sweet potato, *Ipomea polpha*.[21] Very few bones of extinct animals have been found in the Mungo region, and none in association with remains of human occupation. The few bones of the giant kangaroo, *Procoptodon*, found so far do not suggest big game hunting.

THE SIGNIFICANCE OF MUNGO

The Mungo evidence documents the most distant dispersal in the world of *Homo sapiens sapiens* and their achievement in adapting so successfully to a freshwater but semiarid environment. One of the most remarkable finds is the evidence that sophisticated fishing methods employing nets and traps were used in Australia as long as 25 000 years ago. An important implication is that the people fishing at Lake Mungo had the knowledge to make cordage out of plant fibres by this time period. The use-wear on the molars of Willandra Lakes hominid 3 (WLH 3), dated to around 30 000 years ago, supports this view. It is not now too far-fetched to suggest that their ancestors may have brought knowledge of plaiting fibres into ropes, string and even large mats for sails with them when they crossed the water barriers of Wallacea into the Australian continent more than 50 000 years ago.

The Mungo sites also provide early evidence of intellectual life. The deliberate transport and use of coloured pigment more than 32 000 years ago parallels its contemporary use in Europe, indicating very early development of an aesthetic sense. This was to flower into the rich decorative and ritual art for which Aboriginal Australia is renowned.

The elaborate cremation of a young woman 25 000 years ago is the earliest evidence for this rite in the world, and shows not only complex ritual concepts and respect for the dead, but also respect for women. Women have always held an important place in Aboriginal society as gatherers of most of the staple food for the community. At Mungo, shellfish were clearly one of the most important foods, available all year round, and gathering shellfish was traditionally women's work.

The archaeological evidence from the Willandra Lakes also reveals great cultural continuity in Aboriginal society from the Pleistocene to the present day. The ritual, symbolic and aesthetic concepts of modern Aboriginal society have their roots in the remote past. Methods of disposal of the dead such as cremation and inhumation have been used from at least 25 000 years ago right through to the ethnographic present. Not only is this complex culture found on the shores of Lake Mungo important in understanding the development of *Homo sapiens* in world prehistory, but it endows Aboriginal society with the dignity and respect it has often been denied.

There has been much debate concerning the gracility of the Mungo human remains, which contrast so strongly with the heavy build of most other Pleistocene and modern Aborigines. Indeed, it was very fortunate that the pelvis and femurs (thigh bones) of Mungo 3 survived, because they clearly showed that the remains, although so gracile, are definitely male. The differences between these gracile Mungo people and the robust Murray Valley population described in the next chapter cannot therefore be explained just by sexual dimorphism, the differences in size and shape between males and females which occur naturally in any population.

The gracile form is not confined to the Willandra Lakes region; the skeleton of another adult woman with a very delicate, thin-walled skull was found by Ken Page and Tony Dare-Edwards in 1988 eroding from a sand quarry in the lunette on dry Lake Urana, some 350 kilometres southeast of Lake Mungo.[22] Thermoluminescence dates on the sediments containing the remains give an age between 20 000 and 30 000 years, when Lake Urana would have been full of fresh water. This find extends the distribution of the gracile Pleistocene physique to the eastern margin of the riverine plain of southeastern Australia. Lake Urana is in Wiradjuri country, and the remains have now been reburied by the Wiradjuri Regional Land Council.

Further new discoveries from Mungo are described in chapter 5, but first let us examine the first fossil skulls to be found in Australia, and the questions and controversies raised by such extraordinary early finds as Kow Swamp man.

CHAPTER FOUR

Australoids

The question of the origin of Australian Aborigines has long fascinated scholars. Ever since their distinctive appearance was described by early European voyagers in the seventeenth century and named 'Australoid', many theories explaining Aboriginal origins have been advanced. In the next two chapters, the fossil evidence from Australia is described, basically in order of discovery, and current theories concerning Australoid origins are discussed.

TALGAI

The first Australian Pleistocene human skull was found in southern Queensland in 1884. This is the Talgai skull, which was found by a contractor, William Naish, when it was exposed in the banks of a billabong after an exceptional flood on the Darling Downs. Naish gave the skull to the Clark family, who kept it for the next thirty years in their homestead at East Talgai. In 1914 it came to the attention of the Australian geologist Sir Edgeworth David, of Sydney University. He was shown the precise find-spot of the skull by Naish, then aged 76 and crippled with rheumatism, who was carried to the site.

The Talgai skull was purchased by Sydney University. When found, it was covered by a massive encrustation of calcium carbonate, but once this was chipped away an archaic, robust type of skull was revealed. All Australian human remains so far found belong to the youngest form of the human race, *Homo sapiens sapiens*, but this skull looked remarkably rugged and archaic.

In 1948 Professor Macintosh, of Sydney University, became interested in the Talgai skull and embarked on what was to become an outstanding twenty-year-long detective hunt to find its precise original location and age.[1] He examined all the written records and then began the search for a local contact who could guide him to the spot. Despite false trails, destroyed evidence and conflicting testimony, in 1967 he at last found one of the men who had carried Naish to the site in 1914: 70-year-old Charles Fraser of Pratten. The long search for a first-hand witness to Naish's identification of the site was over. The site to which Charles Fraser guided Macintosh and geologist Edmund Gill accorded very well with the descriptions of David and Naish.

Analysis of the fragmentary, crushed and distorted Talgai skull has shown that it was that of a boy of about 15, who died as the result of a massive blow to the side of the head. The skull had been 'rolled', that is, transported by water along a watercourse. The generally accepted dating is now between 9000 and 11 000 years old. Although the canine teeth and palate are remarkably large, Talgai does fit within the range of variation of the Australian Aboriginal population.

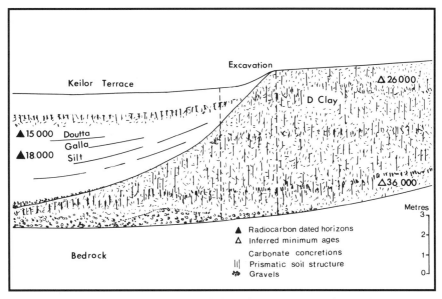

Figure 4.1 Diagrammatic cross section through the Keilor site, Victoria. (After Bowler 1976)

COHUNA

The next significant skull to be found was Cohuna, a well-preserved cranium and facial skeleton, unearthed in 1925 by a plough on the northwestern edge of Kow Swamp, southeast of the town of Cohuna (figure 4.2). No means were available to find the age of the skull. The teeth and palate, whilst typically Aboriginal, are much larger than the Australian average. The outstanding feature of Cohuna is its great size and robustness, far exceeding both the average Aboriginal cranium and Talgai. The forehead has been artificially flattened, as discussed below in relation to Kow Swamp.[2]

KEILOR

In 1940 another major fossil find in Victoria was made near Keilor. This skull was discovered by an alert quarry worker, James White, who unearthed it whilst digging into soft terrace silts being removed to make fine mouldings. Swinging his pick while standing on the quarry floor, he felt it enter something hard. He dug out the object, washed it in the river, and found he had put a neat hole into a fossil skull!

The site, which lies near the junction of Dry Creek and the Maribyrnong River, 2.5 kilometres north of Keilor and 16 kilometres north of Melbourne, was then investigated by a number of workers. Among them was Edmund Gill, then curator of palaeontology at the National Museum of Victoria. He showed that the cranium was contemporary with fauna remains embedded in the Keilor Terrace.

The skull was encrusted with a 2-millimetre thick layer of carbonate, but when this was removed, a yellow loess-like silt was found trapped inside the cranium. This was identical to the upper part of the silt comprising the Keilor Terrace (figure 4.1). Moreover, the carbonate encrustation on the skull could only be accounted for if the skull came from a zone of secondary carbonate deposition in the silt.

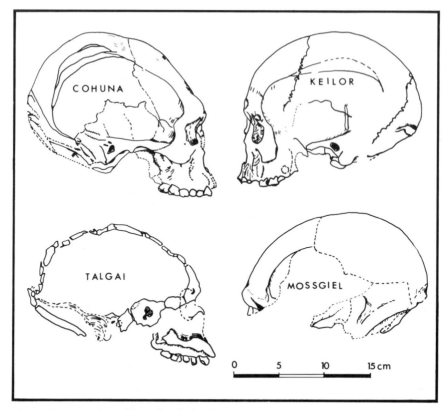

Figure 4.2 Comparison of the Keilor skull with more robust skulls from Cohuna, Talgai and Mossgiel. (All are male.) The forehead of the Cohuna skull has probably been flattened by artificial deformation. (After Macintosh 1965)

The cranium did not belong to a burial intruding into this layer from above, but showed evidence of wear, indicating that it was a 'rolled skull', which must have been rolled into position by the water from a distance upstream, at a time roughly contemporary with the deposition of the sediments. The chemical composition of the skull and other fauna remains from the terrace were found to be similar, which suggested that the skull was *in situ*.

Radiocarbon dates from the femur and skull itself have provided an age of about 13 000 years. The (male) skull is characterised by a full and rounded forehead, and lack of the prominent eyebrow ridges and projecting jaw of Talgai and Cohuna. Thorne, Freedman and Lofgren describe it as gracile, Brown as robust.[3]

Many excavations have been conducted in the Keilor Terrace, but particular mention should be made of the work of Alexander Gallus, a Hungarian archaeologist based in Melbourne, who has concentrated on the oldest deposits.[4] In the base of the D clay, he has uncovered separately both the remains of extinct megafauna and some undoubted stone tools. Many pieces of stone and bone claimed to be tools by Gallus have been rejected by other archaeologists. Indeed, after a conference in 1971, a large group of scientists visited Keilor, filled with scepticism after seeing Gallus's 'tools', only for Jim Bowler to find an indisputable flake implement firmly embedded in the D clay. There is thus at least some evidence of human activity in the oldest deposits at Keilor. Many radiocarbon dates have been obtained on charcoal particles and burnt earth, and 'a conservative age estimate of the lower levels of the D clay would place it at 36 000 BP whilst an age of 45 000 BP is indeed possible'.[5] Gallus's claims of an antiquity of not less than 75 000 to 100 000 years for the earliest chopper industry remain to be substantiated.

It was generally thought in the mid-1960s that the Talgai and similar fossil skulls represented an archaic form of *Homo sapiens*, bearing some resemblance to the fossil skulls of Java, whereas Keilor was a younger, more evolved form. However, discoveries at Mungo and Kow Swamp soon considerably complicated the picture.

THE ENIGMA OF KOW SWAMP

The remarkable discoveries at Kow Swamp stemmed from an outstanding piece of detective work by Alan Thorne. In August 1967, he was examining the human skeletal collections held in the National Museum of Victoria in Melbourne when he came across a museum drawer containing a partial skeleton of remarkably archaic appearance. The bones were heavily mineralised and carbonate-encrusted, and the skull was reminiscent of the Cohuna cranium. From a police report of the location of

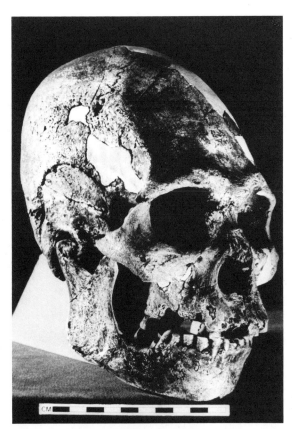

Plate 4   Kow Swamp skull 5 (male), Victoria, showing the massive and archaic features of this group of robust, early Australians. The burial is about 13 000 years old.
(D. Markovic, courtesy A. Thorne)

the find, he traced the skeleton back to the exact find-spot, which was not far from where the Cohuna skull was found. Excavation began in 1968 and revealed part of the same skeleton still *in situ*, including the other half of one of the bones in the museum drawer.

The skeleton was called Kow Swamp 1, since it lay on the shore of Kow Swamp in northern Victoria. Within a few months of the excavation of Kow Swamp 1, additional burial areas were found around the swamp by an interested local resident, Gordon Spark. By 1972 the remains of at least forty individuals had been excavated.

Most of the human remains were located along the eastern shore of Kow Swamp in a narrow belt of lake silt, partially overlain by a low crescentic sand dune. Radiocarbon dates, obtained from bone and charcoal samples associated with the burials, showed that the burials span a period of at least 3500 years, from about 13 000 to 9500 BP.[6] The graves had been dug into relatively soft silt and sand. Carbonate mineralisation of the skeletons after burial had enhanced their preservation, leading to an encrustation up to 1 centimetre thick. Although many burials had been disturbed by earth-moving when an irrigation channel was constructed through part of the site, these disturbed skeletons could be reassembled

Plate 5 Kow Swamp skeleton 14 (male), during excavation. Quartz stone artefacts and freshwater mussel shells were included in the grave fill. (A. Thorne)

fairly easily, because differential mineralisation had rendered the bones of each individual a slightly different colour.

Twelve undisturbed graves were excavated, in which the bodies were orientated in a variety of positions. Three were laid out horizontally and fully extended, two on their backs, and one on its left side. Others were in a crouched position, including one facing forward and downward, with the knees drawn up under the chest and hands placed in front of the face (plate 5). Tightly flexed burials, with the knees brought up to the chest, were also present; the body laid on the left side or on its back. At least one instance of cremation was also found. As in more recent traditional societies, a great variety of burial styles were practised.

The skeletons found at Kow Swamp included men, women, juveniles and infants. This burial complex is at present the largest single population of the late Pleistocene epoch found in one locality anywhere in the world. Kow Swamp is thus of great importance not only for Australia, but also for world prehistory.

The enigma of Kow Swamp is that the skulls, although younger than Keilor and only half the age of WLH 1 and 3 described in the last chapter, appear much more archaic (plate 4). The people buried at Kow Swamp had large, long heads with exceptionally thick bone, up to 13 millimetres thick. Their faces were large, wide and projecting, with prominent brow ridges and flat, receding foreheads. Seen from above, the skulls show pronounced inward curvature behind the eye sockets, which makes the skull look rather like a flask. The jaws and teeth are huge, indeed some mandibles are more massive than those of Java Man (*Homo erectus*, previously known as *Pithecanthropus*, from the Middle Pleistocene).

Teeth are not generally well preserved at Kow Swamp, and few teeth survive with their enamel crowns intact. In addition to damage from postmortem erosion of teeth and disturbance to the site, all adult individuals have suffered pronounced tooth wear. The use of grinding stones to grind up seeds and hard fruits was probably responsible for producing gritty foods, which led to heavy wear on the molars. Only one individual is of advanced age, yet almost every adult's first molars show such a high degree of wear that the roots have been exposed and worn down halfway to their ends. This led to the chronic periodontal disease evident in many individuals.

The rugged, heavy, archaic-looking Kow Swamp remains suggest a population physically similar to those of Cohuna and Talgai, contrasting with the more modern-looking, gracile Keilor and WLH 1 and WLH 3 people. In particular, the gracile group lack the marked eyebrow ridges, flat receding foreheads, thick bone, and massive jaws of the robust Kow Swamp skulls (figure 4.2).

Grave goods were found with several of the Kow Swamp burials. These were ochre, shells, marsupial teeth and quartz artefacts, and one body was laid to rest on a bed of mussel shells. As at Mungo 20 000 years earlier, ochre was powdered over a corpse, which shows the long continuity of such customs.

The presence of grave goods may simply mean that the corpses were being buried with the normal equipment of everyday life, but there are indications that special nonutilitarian regalia were also sometimes included. One body buried at Kow Swamp some 12 000 years ago wore a band of kangaroo incisor teeth around the head. Traces of resin on the teeth showed that they had been stuck together in a band. Similar headbands of kangaroo teeth, plant fibre and resin were worn by Central Desert Aborigines, both men and women, in the nineteenth century.

One of the most spectacular finds of this kind was the huge pierced tooth necklace slung from the neck of the man buried in the lunette of the relict Lake Nitchie in western New South Wales (plate 6).[7] No fewer than 178 pierced teeth of

Plate 6 Necklace from the Lake Nitchie burial, New South Wales. The Lake Nitchie man wore a necklace of 178 pierced Tasmanian devil teeth, taken from at least forty-seven different animals. Each tooth is pierced by a hole that was ground and gouged out. (The Australian Museum)

the Tasmanian devil made up the necklace. The teeth must derive from a minimum of forty-seven individual animals, which are now extinct on the Australian mainland. Indeed, if such necklaces were common, it is not surprising that Tasmanian devils became extinct! Each tooth is pierced by a hole that was ground and gouged — a tremendous labour. This necklace is unique both in present Aboriginal culture and in prehistoric Australia.

The Nitchie burial has other important features. The skeleton was compressed downwards into a shaft-like pit, there were ochre pellets in the grave, and he lacked his two central upper front teeth. This indicates prehistoric tooth avulsion, the widespread practice in male initiation rites of knocking out one or two of the novice's upper incisors. If so, this ritual practice goes back at least some 6500 to 7000 years, the age of the Lake Nitchie burial (6820 ± 200 BP bone collagen date). The skull was originally placed by Thorne in his robust group of prehistoric Australians, on the basis of large size and rugged appearance, but Howells, Freedman, Lofgren, Habgood and Brown consider it belongs in the gracile group. Macintosh claimed from the length of the femur that the man was 1875 millimetres (6 feet 1½ inches) tall, but this has now been revised to 1733 millimetres (5 feet 8¼ inches).[8]

COSSACK SKULL

A skull with extreme 'robust' characteristics was found near Cossack in the northwest of Western Australia, almost 5000 kilometres from Lake Nitchie and Kow Swamp. The remains lay at the base of an eroding coastal dune, which on geomorphological grounds cannot be more than 6500 years old, when the sea reached its present level and formed the dunes. The skull was that of a man about 40 years old, and of a large powerful build (plate 7).[9] The cranial bones are very thick, and the forehead has a marked backward slope. In fact, Cossack man has the most sloping forehead and is the most long-headed (dolichocephalic) Aborigine yet found in past or present Australia. He also had his right upper front tooth missing long before death, probably indicating its removal in initiation rites.

Cossack is similar to Kow Swamp man, but differs markedly from recent male Aborigines in Western Australia. The importance of this find is that it demonstrates that the robust type of Aboriginal physique was not confined to the east, but was widespread over the continent, and lasted into post-glacial times.

The long, sloping foreheads (known as extreme frontal recession) of skulls such as Cossack, Cohuna and Kow Swamp prompted the suggestion that the skulls might have been artificially flattened and deformed. Deformation by bindings or by strapping boards to children's heads has occurred in various parts of the world, for example among the Maya of Mexico and in some of the Melanesian islands north of Australia, but it was rare in Aboriginal Australia.

Among Australian Aborigines, only three groups are recorded as practising intentional head deformation, and there are no artificially flattened skulls in museum collections. These are groups from northern Victoria, Cape York and Mabuiag in Torres Strait. There is no record of what type of deformation was used in Victoria, but the other two societies practised infant head-pressing rather than binding. In Cape York, an observer in 1852 recorded that: 'Pressure is made by the mother with her hands ... one being applied to the forehead and the other to the occiput, both of which are thereby flattened, while the skull is rendered proportionally broader and longer than it would naturally have been.'[10]

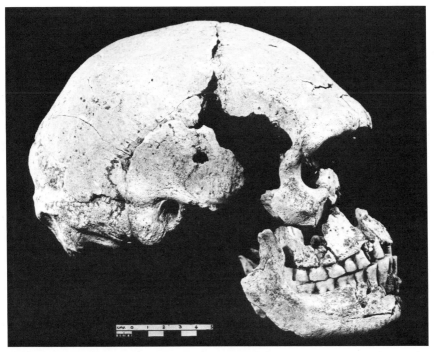

Plate 7 Robust skull from Cossack, Western Australia, about 6500 years old. (L. Freedman and M. Lofgren, with permission from Academic Press, London)

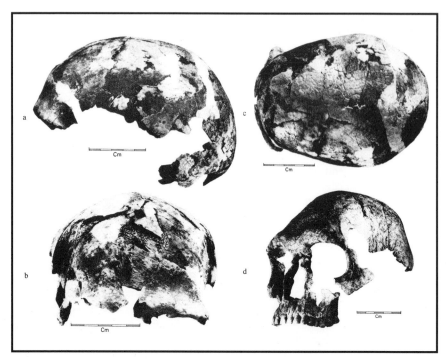

Plate 8 Gracile skull from Lake Mungo, New South Wales, compared with Kow Swamp 1. Three views of WLH 1 cranium A: left lateral; B: frontal; C: vertical; D: Kow Swamp 1. The thin bone, rounded forehead and lack of brow ridges of WLH 1 are characteristic of gracile early Australians. (Photo by D. Markovic; reproduced from A. Thorne 1971 with permission from editors of *Mankind*)

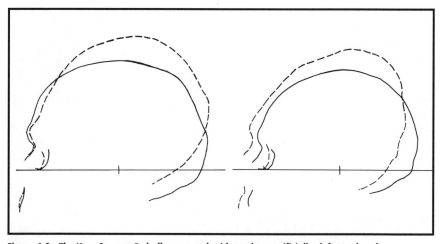

Figure 4.3 The Kow Swamp 5 skull compared with modern artificially deformed and undeformed skulls. Left: Midline cranial contours of Kow Swamp 5 (dashed line) and a modern Murray Valley male Aborigine. Right: Midline cranial contours of an artificially deformed Arawe male (dashed line) and an undeformed male from northern New Britain. (After Brown 1981)

Colour plate 1 *Sthenurus* jawbone *in situ*, Cloggs Cave, Victoria. The remains of this species of kangaroo lay at a depth of 2 metres in a layer older than 21 000 years.

CM

By a comparison of deliberately deformed Arawe (of southern New Britain) male skulls with other Melanesian male skulls that were definitely not deformed, physical anthropologist Peter Brown was able to identify the changes produced by deformation (figure 4.3). He then compared a series of skulls from Victoria, including Kow Swamp and Cohuna. Brown's study sought to establish that Cohuna and some of the Kow Swamp and other robust skulls were artificially deformed. However, according to Thorne, an alternative explanation for the peculiarities of some robust skulls such as Kow Swamp and Cossack is that they reflect the admixture of the robust and gracile populations. Similar high, flat, sloping foreheads are seen on some contemporary Aborigines living in Central Australia, who were certainly never subjected to head-binding or pressing.

LAKE TANDOU

Another Pleistocene skull was found in 1967 by Duncan Merrilees, of the University of Western Australia, at Lake Tandou, 150 kilometres northwest of Lake Mungo in the Willandra Lakes region. It lay on the surface of the lake's lunette, closely associated with a shell midden. A sample of shells from the midden gave a date of 15 210 ± 160 BP (SUA-1805).[11]

After an exhaustive study, Leonard Freedman and Marcel Lofgren of the same university concluded that:

The skeleton probably comes from a male individual 20–25 years of age. The cranium is similar to that of Lake Nitchie and Keilor in overall 'size' and 'shape' ... The analysis made also suggests that Kow Swamp 1 is markedly different in 'shape' to the Lake Tandou, Lake Nitchie and Keilor crania but that the four fossil crania differ strongly from a recent Murray Valley sample in 'size' and 'shape' in about equal proportions ... Tandou fits the 'gracile' group well but its cranial vault bones are very thick, as are those of the so-called 'robust' crania.

KING ISLAND, TASMANIA

In 1989 an Aboriginal skeleton was found in a cave on King Island in Bass Strait off the northwestern tip of Tasmania by Robin Sim.[12] This was studied *in situ* by Thorne (with the permission of the Tasmanian Aboriginal Centre) before being reburied. Charcoal adhering to some of the skeletal remains gave a date of 14 270 ± 640 BP (ANU-7039). At that time of lower sea level, King Island was linked by land to both Tasmania and the mainland, and the cave would have been about 20 to 25 kilometres inland, on the side of a raised plateau overlooking a wide coastal plain.

The method of burial seems to have been secondary disposal, the bones being gathered together in a small pile and covered with jagged rocks forming a small mound within the cave. There were no artefacts, but small pieces of ochre were found on the cranium and femur. The ochre must have been brought from elsewhere, and may either have been added to the human remains or may reflect that

Colour plate 2 This waisted axe from Papua New Guinea was one of twenty-four flaked axes found on the 80-metre Huon Terraces. It was discovered in a layer of volcanic ash dated to about 40 000 years old, and is the earliest stone axe adapted for hafting yet found in the world. (By courtesy of L. Groube)

the deceased had ochre on his hair and body, as recorded ethnographically by such explorers as Baudin and Peron. The cranium, mandible, a femur, fibula, tibia, some vertebrae and other fragmentary remains were found. The individual proved to be a man aged between about 25 and 35 years. The cranium is fully rounded, the face moderate in size and flat rather than prognathous, and there is no pronounced development of a brow ridge. Thorne concludes:

> *The King Island skeleton is morphologically gracile and shows none of the cranial features that distinguish the Kow Swamp people from the Keilor or other early Holocene gracile Australian human remains ... In many ways this individual mirrors the cranial morphology of Keilor and thus expands the southerly range of the gracile group of late Pleistocene Australians. The King Island remains, with Keilor, suggest that the gracile skeletal form was the basis of the most southerly of the earliest Australians.*

Peter Brown has recently suggested that the King Island man may have been a woman, but Thorne's field measurements are confirmed by photographs with a scale, which demonstrate that the femur head is 49 millimetres in diameter, right outside the female range. The femur is also relatively short. Short, robust femurs with big heads are the classic cold-adapted limb proportions of populations from high latitudes or elevations, such as Eskimos and Sherpas. It seems that Tasmanian Aborigines too had become short and stocky by 14 000 years ago, an adaptation to conserve body heat in the Roaring Forties, where they had lived since some 35 000 years ago.[13]

These remains provide the oldest evidence of the physical form of the early Tasmanians, their custom of secondary disposal of the dead and use of ochre probably in connection with burial rites.

COOBOOL CREEK

A collection of 126 crania collected (by G. M. Black) in 1950 from the surface at Coobool Crossing on the Wakool River between Swan Hill and Deniliquin in the Murray River Valley were studied by Brown.[14] (The Murray Black collection has now been handed back to Aborigines of the region, and has been reburied.) No stratigraphic information was available, but bone from one skull, Coobool Creek 65, gave a uranium thorium date of 14 300 ± 1000 BP (LLO-416). Comparison with other Murray Valley prehistoric populations clearly links the Coobool Creek skulls with Kow Swamp, but no others. Brown concluded from this comparison that the evidence of the form and thickness of the cranium and tooth size suggests a single homogenous Pleistocene population, but Thorne stresses that Coobool Creek was an undated surface site, which 'may result from burials spanning the last 20 000 years' rather than being a homogeneous terminal Pleistocene population.[15] On the basis of the Coobool Creek findings and various comparisons of the so-called robust and gracile groups, Brown, Habgood and others have questioned the two populations theory, but this is still supported, with some modifications, by Thorne and Webb, as outlined in the next chapter.

CHAPTER FIVE

The Origin of the First Australians

WILLANDRA LAKES HOMINID 50

Some discoveries complicate the puzzle of the past; others help to clarify the picture. Fortunately, Willandra Lakes hominid 50 (plate 9), is one of the latter, at last providing a feasible ancestor for the Kow Swamp population.

Willandra Lakes hominid 50 (WLH 50) was the fiftieth set of human remains found in the Willandra region — and the most significant. In 1980 the skull and some arm, hand and foot bones were found on the surface near Lake Garnpung, which lies close to Mungo. The bones may have eroded out of the Mungo sediments, but they were not *in situ*, and it is uncertain to which sedimentary layer they belong. Thorne, whose publication of the remains is still eagerly awaited, has described WLH 50 as 'much more robust and archaic than any Australian hominid found previously'.[1]

There are two extraordinary things about WLH 50: its condition and its form. Its condition is unique: all the normal phosphate in the bone has been replaced by silicates, in the same way that things become opalised, which suggests great antiquity. And WLH 50 is massive: he is so robust, he makes Kow Swamp man look gracile! The cranium is extremely wide and approximately 210 millimetres long. The cranial vault bone averages 16 millimetres thick. Massive brow ridges form a continuous torus above the eyes, and the forehead is flat and receding. The back of the skull shows even more archaic characteristics, with substantial cranial buttressing. The neck muscle area is huge, the skull is extremely wide, the greatest width occurs very low in back view, and the difference between the width above and below the ears is much greater than in any modern people. Yet WLH 50's brain was extremely large; the estimated endocranial volume is 1540 millilitres, well above the average 1300 for modern skulls. The skull is flask-shaped, like the Kow Swamp skulls, in bird's eye view, but all the rugged features of Kow Swamp are much more pronounced in WLH 50. Unfortunately the face, jaw and teeth of WLH 50 have not survived, but enough is left of the rest of his skeleton to indicate that his body was equally massive; his elbow bone, for instance, is enormous.

The age of WLH 50 has been estimated as at least 35 000 BP, and more probably in excess of 40 000 to 50 000 years by John Head of the Radiocarbon Dating Research Unit of the Australian National University.[2] Although very little bone material survives, an electron spin resonance (ESR) date of $29\,000 \pm 5000$ BP was obtained, but this is regarded as very much a minimum age.[3] The skull contains 20 per cent of silica, indicating a hypersaline environment, like that in the Willandra Lakes region *before* 50 000 BP.

In spite of the very uncertain dating, the significance of WLH 50 is immense. Firstly, there is no way that such a robust type as WLH 50 could be descended from the gracile type of WLH 1. It is not only the size and shape of the skulls that differ, the most striking difference is in the thickness of the bone; the skull of WLH 50 is some 15–19 millimetres thick, that of WLH 1 only 2 millimetres. The contrast is as great as that between earthenware and bone china, or orange peel and eggshell. To demonstrate this, I had the memorable experience in 1982 of watching Alan Thorne in his laboratory at the Australian National University first set WLH 50 beside WLH 1 to show the striking differences, and then beside a cast of the Ngandong cranium from Java, now dated to about 100 000 years (as described below), to show the remarkable similarity. (Brown disagrees, stating that, 'In common with all of the other terminal Pleistocene crania so far recovered from Australia, WLH 50 provides little support for the notion of evolutionary continuity between the Indonesian and Australian regions'.[4])

The problem in Australia, prior to the discovery of WLH 50, was that the more massive, thick-boned and archaic-looking skulls belonged to the Kow Swamp group, which are *much* younger (by 10 000 to 20 000 years!) than the gracile Mungo group. Yet everywhere else in the world the robust, rugged, thick-boned type of physique is earlier than the gracile form. This new find, if one accepts a putative early date on the grounds of its extremely high silica content and the ESR minimum age, may be the missing link, putting Australia into step with trends in the rest of the world. The apparently archaic features of WLH 50 make him an outstanding candidate for a representative of the earliest migrants to enter Australia.

Nothing, however, seems straightforward in the world of physical anthropology, and since the last sentence was written in 1983, it has emerged that WLH 50's extraordinary thickening of the cranial vault was possibly pathological in origin, due to a genetic blood disorder.[5] This was identified by biological anthropologist Stephen Webb, who made a particular study of palaeopathology (disease in prehistoric populations) and the Willandra Lakes hominids during the 1980s.

The whole of the cranial vault of WLH 50 is exceptionally thick, ranging from 15 to 19 millimetres. Many modern Australian male skulls have thickening somewhere on the vault, but this is usually confined to one point and rarely exceeds 11 millimetres.[6] Likewise, certain Willandra hominids and other late Pleistocene Australian populations almost equal the thickness of WLH 50 at one or other point on the vault, indeed two individuals (WLH 19 and 28) actually exceed it, but their vaults are not uniformly thick like that of WLH 50. Whilst very thick cranial walls are usually associated with archaic hominids of great antiquity, the structure of the vault walls in WLH 50 is quite different from early skulls in Java or China, which all also lack both the degree and uniformity of thickening in WLH 50. The massive thickening and different cranial construction (involving the replacement of external and internal tabular bone with cancellous or diploeic tissue) of WLH 50 therefore indicates something different, which Webb convincingly argues was a pathological condition, probably some form of genetic blood disorder. Webb goes on to propose that 'this condition was brought to greater Australia as part of the genetic baggage of migrations from areas such as Indonesia, where it played an important adaptive role in helping people cope with malaria'. It might have disappeared quite early from the Australian gene pool, perhaps within a few thousand years, in view of Australia's minimal population before 30 000 BP and lack of endemic malaria. Indeed, 'the fact that WLH 50 had the condition could mean that he is amongst Australia's earliest inhabitants'.[7] The Indonesian archipelago is almost certain to have supported endemic malaria for an extremely long time, and Indonesia is the most likely place of origin of the first humans to arrive in Australia.

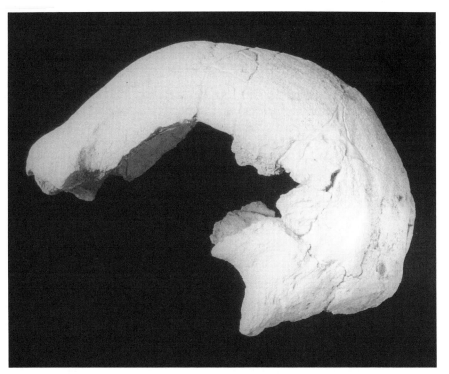

Plate 9 Willandra Lakes Hominid 50 (WLH 50). (Peter Yates, by courtesy of *The Scientific American*)

The general robusticity of WLH 50, with his large brow ridge and 'substantial cranial buttressing', is not disputed, and if his unique cranial thickening is in fact due to an adaptation to cope with malaria, the case for him as one of the first Australians is strong.

THE 135 WILLANDRA LAKES HOMINIDS

In 1989 Webb published an invaluable catalogue of the Willandra Lakes hominids. The remains of 135 individuals had been found in the region at that time, and all but five of these are described by Webb. (WLH 1, 2, 3 and 50 are being described by Thorne, and the 1986 discovery of WLH 135 is an unburnt burial in the Mungo lunette, which has been left *in situ* at Aboriginal request.) These ancient human remains are of international significance, and were a central feature of the successful nomination of the Willandra Lakes as a World Heritage Area in 1981. As stated by the Australian Heritage Commission in the nomination: 'The Willandra Lakes system stands in the same relation to the global documentation of the culture of early *Homo sapiens* as the Olduvai Gorge relates to hominid origins.'[8]

The skeletal remains described by Webb were all fragmentary, sometimes highly mineralised, surface finds, mainly collected between 1974 and 1982. Nothing has been added to the collection since then, and it has now been returned to the Willandra region to be stored in an Aboriginal Keeping Place. Whilst Aboriginal people have strong concerns about the study and care of their ancestors' remains, this collection and analysis was justified in that it preserved and put on record human remains uncovered by erosion, which otherwise would probably have been destroyed or souvenired by tourists visiting the newly established Mungo National Park. However, archaeological research in the region has now virtually ceased in accordance with current Aboriginal wishes.

This is the oldest corpus of human remains so far discovered in Australia, estimated to span the vast time period from about 15 000 to 40 000 or more years ago. Although accurate dating of surface finds is usually impossible, the vast majority of the remains were found on lunettes, and Webb is confident that, with few exceptions, all individuals in the collection predate the end of lunette formation around 15 000 BP, spanning the preceding 20 000 or so years. This conclusion is based on a small number of *in situ* finds, radiocarbon AMS dates for five samples of burnt bone from different individuals (which gave estimated ages of between 16 500 and 25 300 BP), the bones' location and condition of fragmentation and erosion, and the degree of staining, mineralisation and carbonate encrustation.

This Willandra collection, even with its fragmentary nature and time span of as much as 20 000 years, is the oldest material in the Australian fossil record, and Webb's painstaking study throws much important light on the biological origins of the continent's first inhabitants, particularly regarding the homogeneity–heterogeneity debate. His conclusions are:

> *The main results achieved ... give support for the existence of an extraordinarily gracile morphology among Pleistocene people inhabiting the area and provide evidence for biological and cultural complexity in the society. At least nine gracile individuals have been identified in the skeletal collection under review, to add to the previous two [WLH 1 and 3], and it is suggested that they represent a people of overall small body proportions. At the same time it has also been established that there were people living in the Willandra region as robust and in some cases more robust than those in other end-Pleistocene populations.*[9]

Two 'sharply contrasting morphologies' are identified — the robust, archaic-looking crania such as WLH 18, 19, 45, 50 and 69, and more delicate gracile individuals such as WLH 1, 3 and at least nine others. The gracile group incorporate distinctive features such as little or no development of brow ridges, thin cranial vaults, generally oval and fully expanded skulls, small delicately constructed mandibles, lightly built musculature and small stature. Webb stresses that all features of a cranium or skeleton must be compared, and the post-cranial bones, when present, must not be ignored.

It is, of course, necessary to differentiate between male and female skeletons when making comparisons. Gender can usually be determined from differences in the pelvic bones, the femur, or thigh bone, and from the greater size, ruggedness and muscle marking of the male skull. However, sexing of the Willandra collection was very difficult, because of its generally poor and fragmentary condition. Moreover, sexing criteria developed on Holocene skeletal collections may not be completely applicable to very different Pleistocene populations. For example, on the standard (Larnach and Freedman) suite of cranial features used by Webb and others to sex skulls, the gracile male WLH 3 would, in the absence of a pelvis, have been pronounced female.[10]

These further data on the gracility and robusticity of the Willandra hominids clearly demonstrate that WLH 1 is not unique, nor does she occupy a position at the extreme end of a single range of variation. The vault thickness of the gracile individuals is equal or less than that of modern populations, including Europeans, and strongly contrasts with the robust form. The degree of gracility of Willandra females such as WLH 11 and 68 is not matched by any female crania from the robust populations of Coobool Creek or Kow Swamp. Webb's identifications of gender, however, have been criticised by Colin Pardoe, who believes that Webb's 'robusticity and gracility are nothing more than sex-based attributes of larger male size'. Whilst agreeing that sexual dimorphism (larger size of males) seems to have led to a tendency to identify fragmentary female remains as gracile and male remains as robust, Webb did reveal a vast difference in male morphology within the series, and the differences between the gracile group of WLH 1 to 3 and the robust group of WLH 50 remain to be explained.

The distribution of robust and gracile remains, and of cremations as against inhumations, has been examined by archaeologist Peter Clark and Webb,[11] but little patterning has been found, perhaps because of the small amount of material and its random exposure. Twelve robust crania have been found around Lake Garnpung, but otherwise only one on Lake Leaghur and one on the north end of Lake Mungo. Fifteen gracile individuals lay in the same area, plus two in a locality further west on Lake Garnpung, two in the lunette on the northern side of Lake Mungo, one on its eastern side and six at its southern side. Because the vast majority of these remains are undated, it is premature to draw any conclusions, and we cannot yet tell whether the gracile and robust people were in the same place at the same time or not.

With regard to burial practices, ten individuals identified as having been cremated (found on lakes Mungo and Garnpung) display a gracile morphology, but one, an isolated find on Lake Leaghur, is definitely robust and male (WLH 28). Both men and women were cremated; of the ten gracile individuals cremated, four are females, one possibly male (the fragmentary WLH 2) and the sex of the rest is unclear. Inhumation was also practised (the gracile male, WLH 3, described in chapter 3), and Webb also identified evidence of another mortuary practice, bone-smashing without cremation. Another ritual which *may* have been practised is deliberate tooth avulsion as described in chapter 4.

AUSTRALIAN VARIABILITY

The great morphological variability among Pleistocene Australians has been convincingly demonstrated by Phillip Habgood in a major multivariate statistical analysis of both Australian and Asian skeletal material. He suggests that the morphological variation displayed by the Late Pleistocene human skeletal material developed as a result of mutation, genetic selection and drift (the accidental loss of lineages) as the first migrants moved out into a diversity of environments and climates. Habgood concludes:

> *All of the early Australian fossils fall within a morphological continuum ranging from the gracile to the more robust crania. Within this great morphological variation the crania do display an 'Australianness' which is unique to them. That is, the 'gracile' and 'robust' groups are more similar to each other, overall, than they are to any other anatomically modern* Homo sapiens *crania from around the world.*[12]

Australian Aborigines are today amongst the world's most physically varying population, and it now seems that this variability was even greater in the past.

Various theories have been proposed to explain the differing physical traits noticed by early European explorers and visitors.

In particular, a theory of three Pleistocene migrations by Oceanic Negritos, Murrayians and Carpentarians was espoused by Joseph Birdsell and Norman Tindale.[13] This three-waves-of-colonists theory provides a convenient, but incorrect, explanation for differences observed in historic times between Aborigines of the north, the Murray Valley and Tasmania. The Tasmanians are taken to have been representatives of Oceanic Negritos, largely on account of their small stature and spirally curled hair. Other remnants of the Oceanic Negritos were said to be twelve Aboriginal tribes living in the rainforests of northeastern Queensland. However, analysis of recent skeletal material from northern Queensland did not produce any evidence of a Negritic component among the rainforest Aborigines. Moreover, recent genetic studies have shown that pygmy groups are not racially distinct, but simply represent local modification in physique in relation to their neighbours.[14]

In Tasmania, skeletal remains (from King Island, West Point midden and Mount Cameron West)[15] show no differences between prehistoric Tasmanian Aborigines and contemporary mainlanders. It has also now become clear that Tasmania was populated in the Pleistocene by means of the land bridge that joined the island to the mainland. This bridge was drowned some 10 000 years ago by the post-glacial rise in sea level. The differences between Tasmanian and mainland Aborigines observed in historic times are now considered to result from genetic change in a small, isolated population. There is no evidence to support the identification of a Negrito element in Australia. Similarly, Birdsell's third type, the Carpentarians, is now thought to be the result of recent contact between Aborigines and non-Aborigines along the northern coast of Australia. There has, therefore, been a general rejection of the three-wave theory.

Physical anthropologists seem to agree on almost nothing except that Aborigines belong to *Homo sapiens*, and that there is great morphological variability in the Pleistocene population. Whilst robusticity characterises the basic contemporary Aboriginal skeletal form, the remarkable Pleistocene cranial variation still remains to be explained, as does the more 'archaic' appearance of some early Australian *Homo sapiens*.

Genetic Evidence

The search for human origins involves referral to both the fossil hominid data and genetic evidence, particularly developments in the use of DNA (deoxyribonucleic acid), the carrier of the genetic code of life. The human species shows great variation in form, but remarkably low overall genetic variation, even between geographically distant human populations.

Genetic differences between different Aboriginal groups and between Australian Aborigines and overseas peoples have been examined by a number of researchers. The genetic traits compared include blood groups, hair form and colour, and finger and palm print patterns (dermatoglyphs).

Aboriginal blood group genes were recorded and studied for many years by Roy Simmons and his colleagues of the Commonwealth Serum Laboratories. His conclusions were that Australian Aborigines are unique in certain genetic characteristics, such as the general lack of blood groups B and A$_2$, but research had been unable to provide any clues as to the biological origin of the first Australians.[16] Further research has revealed no genetic connections between Australian Aborigines and distant groups such as the Veddoid populations of India or Sri Lanka, or the Ainu of northern Japan.[17]

The problem is that most of the differences — such as hair form, blood groups and colouring — that distinguish between living human populations are not discernible on skeletons. However, over the last twenty years an exciting new approach has been used in the study of the origin of humans. This is molecular biology — the study of the molecules of life from living species. Two species descended from a common ancestor start out with identical DNA. As the generations go by, random changes accumulate. The longer two species have been separated, the greater the difference in their DNA. These differences are expressed as a percentage rate, for example haemoglobin might change 1 per cent after 6 million years. Understanding this process has led to the establishment of a 'molecular clock', which ticks off the years that elapse after two species have separated. The chronological framework is provided by the conventional dating techniques of fossils, such as radiocarbon dating or potassium argon 'calendars'. For example, it is well established that the marsupials and mammals split between 125 and 100 million years ago. One fossil date is all that is needed to set the clock. This then provides a ratio of the time elapsed since various species shared a common ancestor, because DNA accumulates mutations at a relatively slow rate, and the same molecule changes at the same rate in all species.[18] The history of our own species is encoded in the DNA in each of us. The genetic material of different human racial groups has been studied, and an evolutionary tree constructed from analysis of blood proteins and DNA in the chromosomes.

A further development has been the study of mitochondrial DNA, which is outside rather than inside the nucleus in every living cell. Mitochondrial DNA clones itself rather than recombining, is passed to the next generation only by the mother (so the genes are never subjected to shuffling and recombination), and evolves ten times faster than DNA in the nucleus. It thus provides a new and independent, fast-ticking molecular clock for the relatively recent past to reveal an individual's maternal ancestry, although there are many assumptions involved in putting absolute dates onto forks in the family tree.

The family tree based on mitochondrial DNA seems to show that the major racial grouping of humans arose perhaps 200 000 years ago with a basic three-way split into Africans, Caucasians and the Australian–Oriental lineage.[19] This theory is supported by some Australian geneticists, such as Robert Kirk, who has argued on the basis of *independent* genetic work that the divergence of the ancestral lines of Australian Aborigines, black Africans and east Asians occurred between 200 000 and 100 000 years ago.[20]

This type of analysis may eventually open a new window onto the past in the quest for the origin of the Australians, although in view of the documented variations between the rates of evolution of mitochondrial and nuclear DNA, it is difficult to place much reliance solely on genetic and molecular data. The problems of the genetic approach in trying to determine the origin of modern humans were well stated in 1992 by Thorne and Milford Wolpoff.[21] They report that Mark Stoneking, an ex-student of the late Professor Alan Wilson (the leading exponent of the molecular clock), admitted in 1992 that their conclusions were statistically flawed, and that their clock was able to date the move out of Africa only to between 50 000 and 500 000 years — not a very accurate timepiece!

REGIONAL CONTINUITY
OR RAPID REPLACEMENT?

The origin of anatomically modern humans is a major current debate among palaeoanthropologists. There are two main theories. The rapid replacement hypothesis (espoused by Chris Stringer and others) proposes a single African origin of *Homo sapiens* about 200 000 years ago, and then an outward migration and rapid replacement of existing archaic populations in Asia and the rest of the occupied world. The alternative regional continuity theory (put forward particularly by Weidenreich, Thorne and Wolpoff) suggests that modern humans evolved from already differentiated ancestral populations in a number of geographical regions.[22] Australasia (Indonesia, New Guinea and Australia) is a key area for testing the latter, since many physical anthropologists have seen a morphological link between the *Homo erectus* 'Java Man' and both prehistoric and modern Australian Aboriginal populations. If this suspected 'regional continuity' can be proved, it would show that *Homo sapiens sapiens* evolved within the region and did not migrate out of Africa.

The search for the ancestors of Pleistocene Australians suffers from the scarcity of comparable human remains in Asia. Only a handful have been found, the dating is usually uncertain, and most come from only two areas: Java or China. Some authorities, such as Peter Bellwood, consider that 'in Southeast Asia there is simply insufficient fossil evidence to allow a proper evaluation of the two theories, and it may be simplistic to regard them as all or nothing alternatives. Indeed, there are biologists who favour both a radiation of modern humans into Southeast Asia and some degree of genetic assimilation of pre-existing populations.'[23]

All the early hominids of Java are generally thought to belong to the genus *Homo erectus*. *Homo erectus* were so-called because they walked nearly or completely upright rather than semi-erect, like the apes. They made more sophisticated tools and were larger brained than their predecessors. The cranial capacity of the Sangiran *Homo erectus* from Java averages about 950 millilitres. (Modern humans' brain capacity averages 1300 millilitres, whereas the earliest humans had brains less than half this size.) Nor were Sangiran humans very tall, standing about 153 centimetres (5 feet).

Until recently, it was thought that the Sangiran hominids were about 1 million years old, but on 25 February 1994, Carl Swisher and Garniss Curtis of the Institute of Human Origins in Berkeley, California, published an article in the journal *Science* that has revolutionised the story of human evolution.[24] Two *Homo erectus* sites in Java have been shown to be as old as the oldest *Homo erectus* sites in Africa: 1.8 million years. Using state-of-the-art methods (of 40 Argon/39 Argon dating), they dated volcanic pumice associated with the skullcap of a young child at Mojokerto to 1.81 million ± 40 000 years, and some of the cranial remains at Sangiran to 1.66 million ± 40 000 years. This means that there were different populations of *Homo erectus* in two different parts of the globe — Africa and Asia — almost 2 million years ago. Did *Homo erectus* move out of Africa about 2 million years ago, much earlier than was previously thought, and some 600 000 years before the invention of the advanced Acheulean tool kit characterised by hand axes, stone cleavers and other bifacially worked stone tools? The complete absence of hand axes from Java and all other Asian *Homo erectus* sites has always puzzled archaeologists, but would be explained if the ancestors of Asian *Homo erectus* ventured out of Africa before the advent of hand axes there, about 1.4 million years ago. Another possibility is that it was an even earlier ancestor of *Homo erectus*, such as *Australopithecus* or *Homo habilis*, who moved out of Africa to Asia, but no evidence of earlier hominids has yet been found in Asia. Some physical anthropologists even question whether the Asian and African hominids are the same species, and which group gave rise to *Homo sapiens* is a similarly open question.

The youngest remains of *Homo erectus* in Java are the eleven Ngandong crania, previously known as *Homo soloensis*, Solo man, from a Late Pleistocene terrace on the Solo River. The Ngandong skulls have large broad crania with an average capacity of 1160 millilitres, and have recently been dated on bone by the uranium thorium method to about 100 000 years. Ngandong is generally classed as very early *Homo sapiens*, and regarded by those supporting the regional continuity theory as forming the central part of a continuous sequence from Javan *Homo erectus* to *Homo sapiens*.

In 1965 Macintosh made his famous comment on the Australian fossil skulls: 'the mark of Ancient Java is on all of them'.[25] He later retracted, but Thorne (in 1992) maintained that the skeletons of the first inhabitants of Australia 'show the Javan complex of features, along with further braincase expansions and other modernizations. Several dozen well-preserved fossils from the late Pleistocene and early Holocene demonstrate that the same combination of features that distinguished those Indonesian people from their contemporaries distinguishes modern Australian Aborigines from other living peoples.'[26]

The distinguishing Javan features, according to Thorne, are 'thick skull bones, with strong continuous browridges forming an almost straight bar of bone across their eye sockets and a second well-developed shelf of bone at the back of the skull for the neck muscles. Above and behind the brows, the forehead is flat and retreating. These early Indonesians [the Sangiran *Homo erectus*] also have large projecting faces with massive rounded cheekbones. Their teeth are the largest known in archaic humans from that time.' Other features are 'a rolled ridge on the lower edge of the eye sockets, a distinctive ridge on the cheekbone and a nasal floor that blends smoothly into the face'.

This 'unique morphology' was stable for at least 700 000 years in Java, Thorne claims, and is reflected in the Ngandong series of skulls, although their brain cases have evolved into the modern range. After Ngandong, unfortunately, there is a serious gap in the Southeast Asian fossil record.

The claimed morphological links between Indonesian and Australian hominids were rigorously evaluated in a recent analysis by Habgood, who concluded that 'there are a number of morphological features which, when found in combination, appear to document continuity between the early Indonesian material and some prehistoric and modern Australian crania'. He nonetheless cautions that 'the present skeletal sample from Australasia is not adequate to allow a clear distinction between the two competing explanations as to the origins of modern humans in the region'.[27]

The 'stamp of early China' has also been identified by Thorne on the 'gracile' Australian fossil group. Keilor and WLH 1 are claimed to resemble closely the Liukiang skull from southern China, the Zhoukoudian upper cave people, Niah from Borneo and Tabon from the Philippines. A recent development has been the dating of an early form of *Homo sapiens* in China — the Jinniushan skull — to the remarkably early time of 200 000 years ago.[28] The age (from ESR and uranium-series dating) is reliable, but makes it almost as old as some of the latest Chinese *Homo erectus* fossils, such as Skull V from the upper stratum at Zhoukoudian. Chen Tiemel and his colleagues from Beijing comment that, 'This raises the possibility of the coexistence of the two species in China. The morphology of the skull suggests a strong local component of evolution, consonant with the "multi-regional continuity" model of the evolution of *H. sapiens*.'

Chinese parallels, nevertheless, have been stressed less by Thorne and Wolpoff than the Javanese affinities of the robust Australian hominids. For instance, in 1980 Wolpoff wrote: 'the resemblance of some specific characteristics to the morphology common in the Solo [Ngandong] sample is so marked that it is difficult to deny an evolutionary relationship in the Australasian region, a point suggested by Weidenreich several decades ago'.[29]

POPULATING AUSTRALIA

Because the initial discoveries of human remains in Australia happened to produce individuals widely separated in time and space as well as bodily proportions, the theory of two biologically separate founding groups was formulated. Now, on the basis of a much larger, albeit still inadequate and undated sample, Webb envisages instead a continuous process of gene flow from Sunda to Sahul. The explanatory model he puts forward is that:

The natural complexities of population movement and composition from about 65,000 to 30,000 years ago set an indelible stamp on much later Australian populations. An initial population of archaic Homo sapiens *bearing a distinct robustness typical of earlier Indonesian hominid groups probably entered Sahul first and continued to move as far as its southern and, perhaps, eastern regions. The earlier these people arrived, the more archaic they are likely to have been ... Continuing trends towards gracility operating in Sunda, initiated both by migrations from the north and natural human evolutionary drift towards gracility, began to lighten the skeletal morphology of later populations there. Meanwhile founder groups from these stocks slowly moved down into Sahul in infrequent pulses, each time bringing with them a perhaps unrepresentative sample of the external morphological change, which gradually spread throughout. Sometime before 35,000 years ago migrations in the region included for the first time a proportion of people who were smaller and more gracile. It is difficult to argue whether these groups would constitute a 'second population' or just a link in the chain of human migrations ... Their subsequent mixing would have produced a descendant population over a thousand generations later at Kow Swamp and Coobool Creek, incorporating the range of variation of the two original populations ... The apparent persistence of robust features in Australia has yet to be explained, but may have resulted from a long period of time having separated the initial colonisation by robust groups and the first entry of gracile ones. Certainly the robust morphology was not swamped by the later influx, as the character of late Holocene remains testifies.*[30]

It is interesting after the heated robust–gracile debate of the last twenty years to go back to 1960 and Don Brothwell's simple statement *before* any of the Kow Swamp or Willandra hominids were discovered: 'Whichever theory one prefers, it is apparent that there is a general acceptance that the early populations of Southeast Asia included both a robust fossil type and a more slender (?later) form, the former being similar if not ancestral to the modern australoids.'[31]

It seems clear that the migrants who first landed on the Australian shore were among early, generalised representatives of modern man, *Homo sapiens*. The search for the origins of the first Australians is one of the most difficult and challenging questions for archaeologists and physical anthropologists, but as further research is carried out, and hopefully dating methods improved and new hominid discoveries made, perhaps eventually some of these issues will be conclusively resolved.

CHAPTER SIX

The Peopling of Australia

Much attention has been devoted to the question of when and how Aborigines first entered the Australian continent, but very little has been paid to what happened after that. By the time Europeans reached Australia, there were probably more than a million Aborigines in the continent, but how long did it take to build up to this number and when were the various environmental zones first occupied?[1] Three main attempts to answer these questions have been made. The first was by American anthropologist Joseph Birdsell, the second by Sandra Bowdler, and the third by David Horton (figure 6.1).

Birdsell's theory involved numerous assumptions about generation length, rate of reproduction and group size.[2] The normal size of a colonising group was taken as twenty-five persons, and it was proposed that new colonising groups hived off when a population had reached 60 per cent of an area's carrying capacity. It was assumed that when Europeans first entered Australia, the Aboriginal population was about 300 000 and that the continent was at maximum carrying capacity. However, the figure of 300 000 for the Aboriginal population of Australia at the time of European settlement is based on very slender evidence and is far too low. Nor can it be taken for granted that the continent was fully occupied during Pleistocene times; this may be a more recent phenomenon. Likewise, population density cannot be assumed to have remained unchanged from the Pleistocene, through a period of major climatic change, to modern times. It is, therefore, rather rash to use people–land ratios of modern Aboriginal groups in a model of ice age migrations.

Birdsell's model, nevertheless, may give at least a rough idea of how long it might have taken to achieve 'maximum saturation' of the Australian continent. His computer simulation gave the specific answer of '2204 years of total elapsed time'. Not only did Birdsell argue for a fairly rapid 'filling-up' of Australia, but he also saw the inland regions as being populated more quickly than the coasts. The reasoning behind this argument is that the drier inland regions could support fewer people than the well-watered coastal zones, so the land's carrying capacity would be reached sooner, and people would move on in search of a new foraging area more often.

This theory is testable from both archaeological and environmental evidence, and has been challenged on both grounds by Bowdler. She analysed the archaeological evidence and concluded that it did not support Birdsell's theory.[3] She proposed an alternative hypothesis in 1977, based on archaeological evidence, of a coastal colonisation of Australia.

Bowdler's thesis is basically that Australia was colonised by people with an economy adapted to living on tropical coasts, and that the similarities between the edible tropical plants and coastal environments of the new continent and their departed homelands would have facilitated settlement. It is argued that their marine-based technology and economy, with a heavy reliance on scale fish, shellfish and small mammals, required little change to exploit Australian coastal resources, and thus change was minimal for many thousands of years. The new settlers gradually moved around the periphery of the continent and expanded inland along major river and lake systems. It was not until much later, she suggests, that the dry heart of the continent was occupied, when people had developed techniques to hunt unfamiliar terrestrial animals such as large kangaroos and began to use grindstones to exploit grass seeds as food.

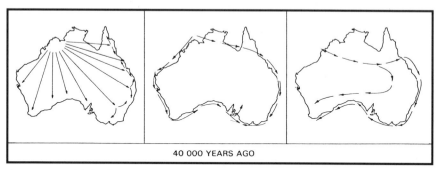

40 000 YEARS AGO

Figure 6.1 Models for the peopling of Australia. Points of entry may have been Arnhem Land and/or the Kimberley region and/or Cape York. On the left is Birdsell's radiational model; in the centre, Bowdler's coastal colonisation model; and on the right, Horton's model.

Evidence in support of this coastal, gradual and conservative colonisation, in contrast to Birdsell's rapid, radiational model, was the peripheral distribution of Pleistocene archaeological sites in Australia (see figure 2.3). Pleistocene sites tend to be either on or near the coast or lie up major river valleys and the associated lake systems such as the Willandra Lakes in the Murray–Darling basin. A few sites were several hundred kilometres inland, but Bowdler argued that they may still have been reached by following large rivers up from the coast. For example, Kenniff Cave lies on the Great Dividing Range in southern Queensland, 500 kilometres inland from the present coastline, but it is near the headwaters of the Darling River system. A trek of some 1800 kilometres would have been required to reach Kenniff by way of the Murray and the Darling, but dispersal was probably over hundreds or thousands of years.

Bowdler's theory was attractive, but in 1977 little archaeological work had been done in the centre of the continent which might support or refute it; excavation had been concentrated around the coast near the modern centres of population. When so much of Australia remained archaeologically unexplored, it was perhaps premature to try to establish the pattern of colonisation. But hypotheses derived from these models can be tested by field work. If colonisation were coastal, the earliest sites should only be found near Pleistocene coasts or major river and lake systems; sites in desert and mountain environments should be later. If, on the other hand, colonisation were radiational and continent-wide, some early sites should be found in inland areas, far from coasts, large rivers and associated lakes.

Horton's concept was that people with an adaptable, all-purpose economy moved into Australia through well-watered regions on both sides of the Great Dividing Range and penetrated all but the arid core of the continent by 25 000 years ago.[4] Then, when Australia began to dry up, Horton believed that the megafauna became extinct, and people retreated to the coastal regions, not moving back until the present climate was established about 12 000 years ago. Tindale also believed that initial migration penetrated southwards on both sides of the Dividing Range,[5] but present archaeological evidence supports neither this nor Horton's theory.

The discovery by Michael Smith in 1986 of Pleistocene occupation in the Central Desert has ended over a decade of speculation about the timing of human settlement in the core of the continent.[6] Puritjarra rock-shelter is west of Alice Springs, almost in the dead centre of Australia, and shows that the arid interior was settled extremely early. A date of about 22 000 BP for the lowest artefacts was published in 1987, but further work has now revealed that the base of the occupation dates back much further. Dating is still in progress, but Smith says the age is 'in the order of 30 000 years'.

Evidence of 'old' inland sites discovered since 1977 prompted Bowdler to re-examine her coastal colonisation theory.[7] In 1992 she wrote:

> *The process of adaptation to the new continent now seems to have been considerably more rapid than originally supposed. While it still seems probable that original colonizing routes were around the coasts and thence up the major river systems (Bowdler 1977:205; Bowdler 1990c), it is clear that non-coastal environments were successfully exploited on a regular basis quite early on. The Tasmanian evidence indicates this (Cosgrove et al. 1990), as does recent research in Western Australia. In the Kimberley, the site of Widgingarri 1 was first occupied at least 28,000 years ago, when it would have been some 50 km from the coast, and continued in occupation until the sea had reached to its maximum extent (O'Connor 1990:342).[8]*

In Cape York, Arnhem Land and the Kimberley, Pleistocene occupation has been found in rock-shelters near rivers that flow across plains to the coast. The earliest northern sites lie at least 50 kilometres from the present coast and would have been much further from the shore at times of low sea level. Soundings in the sea have revealed the existence of river valleys, through which the present rivers would have flowed across the now submerged continental shelves, along which these early people would have moved.

The first landfalls could have been made anywhere across northern Australia from the Kimberleys in the west, to Arnhem Land in the centre, to Cape York in the east. The oldest occupation yet found in the north is in Arnhem Land, but pre–30 000-year-old occupation has also been found in the Kimberleys and Cape York Peninsula (Sandy Creek Shelter near Laura — 32 000 BP — and Nurrabullgin Cave west of Cairns — 37 000 BP).

The environment on the Sahul shelf encountered by early migrants was probably similar to that of the northern third of the Australian continent today. During the last ice age, mean annual temperatures were several degrees lower than today. From about 50 000 to 30 000 years ago, the climate was cooler and moister. Then, after 30 000 BP, the climate became even colder and effective rainfall declined, leading to a period of maximum cold and aridity about 18 000 years ago. The subsequent improvement accelerated around 12 000 BP, and by 10 000 BP the climate was warm and moist. These favourable conditions gradually changed to the climate of present-day Australia by about 3000 years ago.

Increased aridity at times of lower sea level would have caused a coastward migration of the vegetation of arid inland Australia. A drop in sea level of only 80 metres would have been sufficient to turn the whole of the Arafura Sea and the Gulf of Carpentaria into land, probably covered with savanna woodland and swamps.

The resulting open woodland on the Sahul shelf would have been a suitable human habitat and facilitated movement, but newcomers would have had to adapt to the marked seasonality of climate in the north, with a long dry season in winter.

WAS THERE AN ARCHAEOLOGICALLY 'INVISIBLE' PHASE?

The question of whether there was an archaeologically 'invisible' phase is of course unanswerable, if taken literally, but it addresses the suggestion that there was a phase of 'invisible colonisation' of unknown length not yet represented in the archaeological record. Can our earliest dates be taken 'at face value' or do they represent merely the end point of a long archaeologically invisible phase, the scanty remains of which have not survived the vagaries of time?

One of the problems in the search for traces of the earliest colonists is that many of the very earliest sites now probably lie underneath the sea, drowned by the post-glacial rise in sea level. Not until the people had moved 50 or more kilometres inland, to what is now the coastline of northern Australia, would any traces of these first migrants remain. It is most unlikely, therefore, that we will find any evidence of early sea-voyaging, because of submergence of landing places and the unlikelihood of organic remains such as wood surviving for more than forty millennia. However, the move inland away from coastal swamps could have been quite rapid, and on some stretches of the Australian shore the continental shelf is not very wide, so early coastal sites would not necessarily have been later submerged.

Absence of artefacts in deposits dated to more than 60 000 years also argues against an earlier invisible phase. In the Willandra Lakes, cultural material is totally absent from the Golgol sediments, which lie underneath the artefact-bearing Mungo unit, yet the Golgol unit relates to a period when the lake contained fresh water and would have been a favourable human habitat. Similarly, sand dunes on the eastern coast from the same period are devoid of any evidence of human occupation. Moreover, in the Arnhem Land sites described below, sterile sands lie beneath the lowest artefacts.

This and other evidence has led Jim Allen, Sandra Bowdler and Rhys Jones to each independently reject the theory that there was a long invisible phase of occupation before our earliest dated sites.[9] What they disagree about is which early dates can be accepted and thus what is the time of first colonisation. Allen has opted for the more conservative 35 000 to 40 000 years (rejecting the Upper Swan site), Bowdler for 40 000 years. Jones, in contrast, has made a strong, and to me and many others convincing, case for 50 000 to 60 000 years.[10]

THE DISTRIBUTION OF PLEISTOCENE SITES

The speed of new discoveries has been astonishing. There are now more than 170 Pleistocene sites in Australia dated to more than 10 000 years. (Those referred to here are listed in the appendix.) This enables us to draw finer distinctions between

Colour plate 3 (top) Erosion at Lake Mungo, New South Wales, on the Walls of China lunette. (Australian Information Service)

Colour plate 4 (bottom) Koonalda Cave, Nullarbor Plain, South Australia. (D. J. Mulvaney)

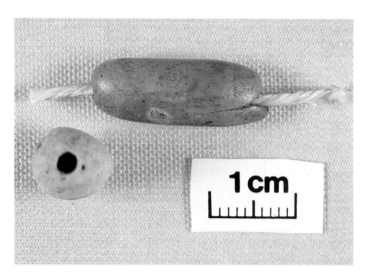

earlier and later Pleistocene sites, without putting too much reliance on precise dates. The earliest sites in Australia, giving dates around or in excess of 40 000 years, have been found in Arnhem Land (as described below), southwestern Australia (Upper Swan), western New South Wales (Mungo) and southeastern Australia (Cranebrook, near Sydney — but the Cranebrook evidence is rejected as dubious by many). These sites all fit with Bowdler's theory that the first colonisation was essentially coastal.

By about 35 000 years ago, people were occupying most major ecological zones: the tropical coasts such as the Pilbara (Mandu Mandu Creek, 34 000 BP) and Cape York Peninsula (Nurrabullgin Cave near Cairns, 37 000 BP); the arid zones such as the Nullarbor Plain (Allens Cave, with a preliminary TL date of c. 35 000 BP, and Koonalda Cave, estimated (by Head) at > 34 000 BP); the semiarid zone of the Willandra Lakes; and caves in the highlands of Tasmania such as Warreen Cave (35 000 BP) in the Maxwell River Valley.

By 30 000 years ago, the Pleistocene inhabitants were not only settled on much of the coast of Australia, at Devil's Lair in the west and Keilor in the south, but had also penetrated to the heart of Australia's desert core — to Puritjarra, by a permanent rock pool in the Cleland Hills. By 25 000 BP, there are Pleistocene sites in virtually every ecological zone.

The rest of this chapter will examine the Arnhem Land sites and dating methods involved in the claim of a 50 000 to 60 000 years antiquity. Other significant Pleistocene sites in the north and south of the continent and Tasmania will be discussed in the following chapters.

THE RADIOCARBON BOTTLENECK

Jones has argued that the reason that the oldest dates for cultural sites have stabilised to between 35 000 and 37 000 years ago since the mid-1970s is not that this is the true age of humans in Australia, but that this is close to the technical limits of the radiocarbon dating method in Australian field conditions. While the theoretical limit of radiometric carbon-14 determinations using the latest technology is 65 000 years, this is 'practically impossible to achieve' according to John Head of the Australian National University radiocarbon dating laboratory.[11] Problems are that even the best charcoal samples are only 70 per cent pure carbon, and beyond 30 000 years a very small difference in carbon-14 activity can produce a large difference in age. Head and Jones are convinced that the absolute ages of many Pleistocene sites have been underestimated due to contamination by younger carbohydrates within the soil. In other words, many of our Pleistocene sites are too young rather than too old, and 'dates older than about 25 000 years should probably be interpreted as being that value or older'.

A potential solution to this radiocarbon bottleneck was provided by the development of thermoluminescence (TL) dating of naturally deposited sands. This new method dates the time since the artefact-bearing quartz sand was *last* exposed to

Colour plate 5 (top) Bone bead from Devil's Lair, Western Australia, from a 15 000-year-old layer. (C. Dortch)

Colour plate 6 (centre) Kartan tools from South Australia: horsehoof core and pebble tools.

Colour plate 7 (bottom) Necklace made from Conus species shell beads from a 32 000-year-old layer in Mandu Mandu Creek Rock-shelter, Western Australia. (Hypothetical arrangement of the twenty-two beads by Kate Morse; photo by Douglas Elford, Western Australian Museum)

sunlight. It has been explained as follows by Bert Roberts and Nigel Spooner, who have been involved in the method's application at key early human occupation sites in Arnhem Land and the Nullarbor Plain:

> The light emitted by a mineral upon heating is called thermoluminescence (TL) while optically-stimulated luminescence (OSL) refers to the luminescence emitted by a mineral when exposed to visible (e.g. green laser) light. Luminescence dating comprises the allied techniques of TL and optical dating, both capable of providing calendar years using minerals such as quartz. The upper age limit of luminescence dating for Australian quartz is typically 200,000–300,000 years, hence enabling absolute ages to be obtained for archaeological deposits beyond the radiocarbon 'barrier' of 30,000–40,000 years...
>
> In the luminescence dating of sediments, the luminescence 'clock' is reset by sunlight and 'time zero' is the moment when the sediment is buried. However, quartz always retains a small 'residual' TL signal from the moment of burial, and determining this residual level is critical to obtaining reliable TL dates. Optical dating avoids the problem of the residual level by using only the most light-sensitive signal, which can be expected to have been fully reset at the time of burial. [The TL method dates the time since the sand was last exposed to sunlight.] Following burial, the luminescence signal increases steadily with time as a result of the energy absorbed from ionizing radiation (emanating principally from the radio-active decay of naturally-occurring isotopes in soil and rock). The luminescence signal acquired during burial is measured in the laboratory when the sediment is either heated (TL) or exposed to green laser light (OSL). The total radiation dose the sample received during burial (termed the 'palaeodose') is determined by comparing the acquired luminescence with the luminescence produced by laboratory irradiations. The sample age is then calculated as (where 1 ka = 1000 years, and Gy is a unit of radiation dose)
>
> Age (ka) = Palaeodose (gy) + Environmental dose rate (Gy per ka).[12]

Application of TL and optical dating to artefact-bearing sands at Malakunanja II, Malangangerr and Nauwalabila I rock-shelters in Arnhem Land revealed the great antiquity of human occupation in the region, suggesting human arrival 50 000 to 60 000 years ago. Comparative carbon-14 and luminescence dates were obtained from the upper levels and show a close correspondence. At Malakunanja II, calibrated carbon-14 ages of 15 000 ± 400 BP and 18 000 ± 200 BP bracket a TL date of 16 000 ± 3000 BP. At Nauwalabila I, a calibrated carbon-14 date of 23 000 ± 400 BP is in sound agreement with a preliminary optical date of 26 000 ± 5000 BP.

The lowest stone tools at Malakunanja II were stratified within sands TL-dated to between 50 000 and 60 000 BP, with culturally sterile sands below dated back to 110 000 years. When these results were first published in *Nature* in 1990, criticisms of both the dating method and the associations of the dated sand with the artefacts were made by Bowdler and Peter Hiscock, but these have been answered in detail. The researchers emphasise that 'our view that humans occupied Malakunanja II by 50,000 years ago is based on a proper statistical appreciation of the uncertainties associated with each TL age and the stratigraphic constraints placed upon these uncertainties'. This view received support in 1992 when thermoluminescence dates on Nauwalabila I gave a similar age for the first artefacts there. Optical dating of the lowest levels at Nauwalabila I has revealed 'the oldest stone artefacts are securely stratified within a basal rubble unit, bracketed between 55,000 and 60,000 years ago'.[13]

These and other early Northern Territory sites are discussed individually below, after a description of their context in Arnhem Land.

ARNHEM LAND

In Arnhem Land the present East, South and West Alligator rivers, together with the Wildman, Mary and Adelaide rivers to the west, all apparently once joined together and formed one large, deeply incised 'Arnhem Land River'. This flowed down a gently sloping valley enclosed between Cobourg Peninsula and Melville Island out onto the Arafura Plain. There it joined the 'Arafura River', which flowed south from New Guinea, then west into the Indian Ocean.

The Arnhem Land Plateau stretches 260 kilometres from north to south, and 200 kilometres from east to west. Its edges form a steep stone escarpment, rising as much as 250 metres above the alluvial plains. Large rivers flow through the escarpment in spectacular gorges. The rivers are now estuarine and full of barramundi and huge saltwater crocodiles, but estuarine conditions only came into being with the post-glacial rise in sea level about 9000 years ago.

The presence of fresh water, abundant food resources and large rock-shelters for protection against the elements made this an attractive area for prehistoric settlement. It is, therefore, not surprising that several rock-shelters have been found with occupation extending back well into the Pleistocene, when they would have lain some 350 kilometres inland.

Kakadu or Gagadju is the name of the language spoken by Aboriginal people of the coastal lowlands. Aboriginal ownership of the land known as Kakadu National Park was recognised in 1976, and in 1978 the traditional owners, the Gagadju Association, leased their land to the Australian National Parks and Wildlife Service as Stage 1 of the Kakadu National Park.

Archaeological work in the Kakadu region commenced in the 1960s. Considerable research into the prehistory of the Top End has been done over the last three decades, largely by archaeologists from the Australian National University, such as John Mulvaney, Jack Golson and Carmel Schrire (then White), who discovered the first Pleistocene sites in the 1960s, Harry Allen and Johan Kamminga in the 1970s, and a group led by Rhys Jones in the 1980s.[14] In the earth floors of rock-shelters a series of occupation deposits containing stone tools and charcoal from ancient campfires have been found.

ARTEFACTS

The handful of excavated sites in Australia had produced some remarkable discoveries long before the new evidence of their great antiquity. Two main successive stone tool traditions were identified. The more recent was distinguished by the introduction of stone spear points about 5000 years ago. This small tool tradition succeeded the earlier Australian core tool and scraper tradition. As elsewhere, this early industry was distinguished by chunky, steep-edged flakes and cores. Horsehoof cores were found in a 20 000-year-old level of Nauwalabila, and in 10 000-year-old basal levels of Ngarradj Warde Djobkeng.

The great original surprise of these Arnhem Land sites was the presence in Pleistocene levels of stone axes with grooves around their sides and a ground cutting edge. Previously ground-edge axes had only been found in Australia in contexts belonging to the last few thousand years, but since then, further specimens have been found in the basal levels of other northern sites, such as the Sandy Creek Shelter in Queensland, described in chapter 7.

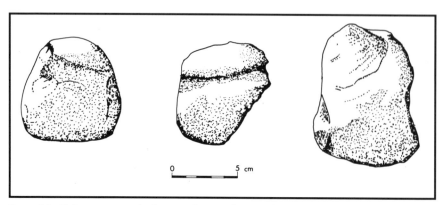

0   5 cm

Figure 6.2 Pleistocene ground-edge axes from Arnhem Land, Northern Territory. All are bifacially flaked and the cutting edge is ground to a bevel; the grooves presumably assisted the attachment of handles. Left: Axe from Malangangerr, made of hornfels, grooved on one surface (19 000–23 000 BP). Centre: Axe from Nawamoyn, made of porphyritic dolerite, grooved on one surface and one broken margin (21 500 BP). Right: Waisted axe from Nawamoyn, made of hornfels, and indented on both margins (21 500 BP). (After White 1967 and 1971)

The axes (figure 6.2) are generally smaller than more recent examples. They were manufactured by the 'pecking' technique, which involves fashioning them with a hammer or 'hammer dressing'. A remarkable feature is the groove or nick that several axes bear, apparently to facilitate hafting the axe-head to a handle. Until the discovery of these axes with their hafting grooves, it was generally thought that the concept of attaching stone tools to handles for greater leverage was a much later development, but now evidence has shown that the technique of hafting was definitely in use during the Pleistocene. Also, a ground-edge tool has a much more effective cutting edge than a flaked tool.

These ground-edge axes have provided some of the world's oldest evidence for shaping stone by hammer-dressing or pecking. So far, only in Japan does the technology of grinding stone to make a sharp, chisel-like cutting edge have a similar antiquity, although ground-edge tools do occur in what may be equally early Southeast Asian contexts. An age of about 15 000 years has been suggested for edge-grinding at Niah Cave in Sarawak, and edge-ground tools date back to between 27 000 and 30 000 years in Japan.[15] These significant technological innovations of grinding and hammer-dressing thus appear to be older in the Australasian region than in Africa, Europe or the Middle East.

Two features of the Arnhem Land ground-edge artefacts support the idea that they originated locally rather than being imported. Firstly, unlike the ground-edge tools from Asia, the Australian artefacts are hatchets rather than axes. Hatchets differ from true axes by being employed with one hand instead of two, and by having a lower mass and shorter handle. The small size and light weight of the Arnhem Land examples make it clear that they should be termed hatchets rather than axes.[16] (However, the traditional term 'axes' has been retained in this book.) Secondly, the early use of hammer-dressing on ground-edge tools is confined to northern Australia.

Some of Australia's oldest grindstones have also been found in Arnhem Land. Three grindstones were found at Malakunanja II, associated with charcoal dated to 18 000 years.[17] Two have flat to slightly concave grinding surfaces, and the face of one was impregnated with red and white ochre. The third has a circular grinding hollow about 10 centimetres in diameter on one of its faces. Similar grinding hollows were found in the lower levels of Nawamoyn and are common today in Arnhem Land rock-shelters. It is likely that, as well as grinding up ochre to make pigment for painting artefacts, rock-shelter walls or body decoration, grindstones and grinding hollows were used in the preparation of foods such as seeds and fruits.

MALANGANGERR

Charcoal at the base of the earth floor in the rock-shelter of Malangangerr — in open woodland just west of Cahill's Crossing on the East Alligator River within Kakadu National Park — was first excavated by Schrire and radiocarbon-dated to 23 000 years old (plate 10). This shelter is a deep overhang in a residual outlier of the Arnhem Land Plateau. There are a few paintings on the shelter's back wall, and shells, the remains of ancient meals, are visible in the earth floor. This shell midden deposit in the upper levels dates from about 6000 to 7000 years ago until the recent past. Below it are sandy deposits, which had charcoal in their lowest levels dated to between 23 000 and 18 000 years old. The stone tools in these lower sands were characterised

Plate 10 Malangangerr rock-shelter, Kakadu National Park, Northern Territory, contained human occupation dating back to 32 000 years.

by flaked core tools, steep-edged scrapers, utilised flakes and, most remarkably, by small ground-edge axes with grooves on their sides. Subsequent further excavation of Malangangerr by Jones and Smith yielded a sequence going back to 32 000 years, the lowest artefacts being at a depth of 2 metres.

MALAKUNANJA II

Malakunanja II, to the south of Malangangerr near Ngarradj Warde Djobkeng and Ja Ja Billabong, is a shallow rock-shelter with faded paintings on its overhanging wall. When first excavated by Kamminga, it yielded 18 000-year-old charcoal, associated with a grinding hollow, and two flattish mortars, one bearing clear traces of ochre. Further investigation in the 1980s by Jones produced some remarkably early dates,

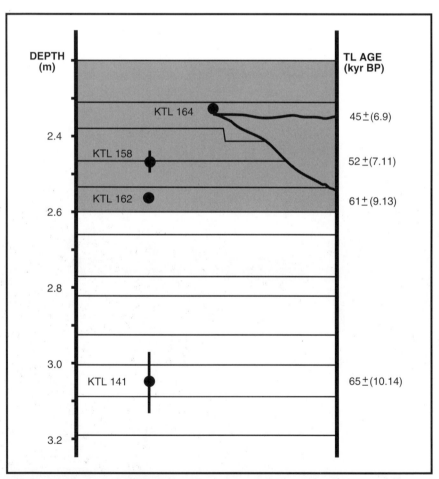

Figure 6.3 Position of thermoluminescence (TL) samples relative to the lowest occupation at Malakunanja II. Depths are metres below the surface. The vertical spread of the TL samples is indicated. Stippling shows levels with chipped stone artefacts and other occupation debris. Horizontal lines indicate boundaries of excavation units, plotted using mean start and end depths. (After Roberts, Jones and Smith 1990c)

and established Malakunanja as the oldest dated site in Australia. The layers containing the oldest human occupation were thermoluminescence (TL) dated to between 52 000 and 61 000 BP (figure 6.3). Human occupation appears to have commenced abruptly above sterile sand at a depth of 2.6 metres below present ground surface, dated to 61 000 +9000/–13 000 BP (KTL162). There was dense occupation from 2.3 to 2.5 metres depth, between 45 000 +6000/–9000 BP (KTL164) and 52 000 +7000/–11 000 BP (KTL158), with more than 1500 artefacts in this lowest occupation layer. Basal cultural material included core-scrapers, flakes and amorphous artefacts made of silcrete, quartzite and white quartz; a grindstone; pieces of dolerite and ground haematite, chlorite and mica; together with red and yellow ochre. Whilst allowing for the possibility that artefacts were trodden into soft, sandy, older sediments by the first occupants, the researchers state that a conservative estimate places initial occupation at 52 000 years. Below this was a 2-metre deep, sterile sand sheet, completely devoid of any artefacts, deposited steadily from around 110 000 years ago.

NAUWALABILA

Some of the earliest evidence for human presence so far discovered in the Top End comes from a rock-shelter in Deaf Adder Gorge in the south of Kakadu National Park. It is an area called Nauwalabila by Aborigines, and the site is now known as Nauwalabila I. (It has also been called the Lindner site after local explorer, Dave Lindner.) The rock-shelter was formed by a massive boulder which toppled off the edge of the nearby escarpment. This sloping sandstone slab shelters a level, black, sandy floor, on which lay stone tools such as spear points. The archaeological potential of the site was recognised by Rhys Jones and Betty Meehan when they were taken there by Dave Lindner in 1972, and excavations were carried out there by Kamminga in 1973 and Jones in 1981. Two elderly Aboriginal men, who remembered camping in the shelter as small boys with their families and thus depositing the topmost layer of habitation debris, took part in the latter excavation and helped to uncover the basal layers.

Stone tools were found down to a depth of almost 3 metres below present ground level, and a radiocarbon date of about 20 000 years was obtained on charcoal at a depth between 1.7 and 1.9 metres. The top 2.4 metres of deposit was fine sand which built up steadily over a period of at least 25 000 to 30 000 years. Below the sand a layer of weathered sandstone rubble some 40 centimetres thick rested on large rocks and red sand. Stone tools lay within the basal rubble — heavy weathered quartzite flakes, which, when snapped, revealed a thick chemically weathered skin on their outer surface.

Evidence of edge-grinding occurs at Nauwalabila I, where flakes of dolerite showing ground facets with striations from use-wear were found throughout the top 1.4 metres of the deposit, the lowest example of these flakes being from ground-edge axes coming from the 14 000-year-old level. Below this were pieces of volcanic rock (dolerite), which because of its hardness is the characteristic material used to make ground-edge artefacts, but these had been so heavily chemically weathered that their original form was not readily discernible. At a depth equivalent to an age of about 25 000 to 30 000 years were several extremely weathered lenticular objects of volcanic rock, which were of exactly the same shape as Schrire's Pleistocene hatchet heads, but they were too weathered for positive identification. Throughout the same

25 000- to 30 000-year-old layer were slabs of sandstone showing evidence of grinding and hard, heavy pieces of haematite (a high grade ferric iron ore) with grinding facets on their surfaces, indicating that they had been used as a source of pigment. Ochre in a wide variety of colours occurs in the lower levels of many of these Pleistocene sites, and there is some evidence that the ochre was ground up and pulverised. Small circular hollows, similar to those that are visible nowadays on flat shelves of rock in innumerable Top End rock-shelters, are clearly as old as the covering sands (i.e. more than 18 000 years) in the excavated rock-shelters of Malangangerr and Nawamoyn.

Optical (OSL) dating of the lowest levels of Nauwalabila I has shown that the earliest stone artefacts are securely stratified within a basal rubble layer bracketed between 55 000 and 60 000 years ago. As at Malakunanja II, optical dating is consistent with radiocarbon dating and with depth.

The Nauwalabila site is of particular significance for several reasons. It reveals continuous occupation throughout the height of the last glaciation, when there appears to have been a break in occupation of some other sites in the Kakadu region. The antiquity of the stone artefacts in the basal rubble makes Nauwalabila possibly the oldest human occupation site yet discovered in Australia. The site also contains vital evidence of change in the landscape.

Plate 11 The excavation of Nauwalabila rock-shelter, Kakadu National Park.
(Courtesy of R. Jones and Australian National Parks and Wildlife Service)

When hunters first inhabited the rock-shelter, the surface of the ground was 3 metres below its present level. Since that time the ground level both within the shelter and of the extensive sandsheet plain outside has risen 3 metres. Why, straight after human arrival in the valley, was there this sudden build-up of sand, with the rate of sediment accumulation increasing a thousandfold? The answer seems to lie in Aboriginal impact on the environment. When Aboriginal people reached the Top End, they used fire extensively both for cooking and as an aid in hunting and gathering, as their modern descendants still do. In the Kakadu environment, this caused massive slope instability and erosion, leading to the build-up of sediment on valley floors such as Deaf Adder Gorge. Dramatic change came to Kakadu during the last ice age not because of climatic change, but because of the one new factor in the equation, humans with their fire-sticks.

SUMMARY

This handful of excavated rock-shelters at the foot of the western Arnhem Land escarpment has given us the world's oldest ground-edge hammer-dressed axes, Australia's oldest grindstones and paint palette, and the earliest human occupation yet found in Australia. Thermoluminescence (TL) dates on artefact-bearing quartz sands in two rock-shelter deposits suggest the arrival of people in northern Australia between 50 000 and 60 000 years ago. The TL dates were obtained from sandy footslope deposits at occupation sites, which contain stone artefacts in their primary depositional setting. Comparative radiocarbon and luminescence dates obtained from the upper occupation layers of the rock-shelters Malakunanja II and Nauwalabila I show close correspondence, and the validity of the dating, supported as it is by much corroborative evidence, is now accepted by most archaeologists.

The coincidence of the timing of earliest human occupation at Nauwalabila and Malakunanja, and the complete absence of cultural remains in the sterile sands in the lowest part of the sites strengthen the case that modern humans first arrived in this region 55 000 to 60 000 years ago, or, at the most conservative guess, 50 000 years ago. In other words, the fact that these desirable, accessible pieces of prehistoric real estate were uninhabited until about 55 000 years ago means that humans did not arrive in the Kakadu region until then. This is probably the closest we will get to seeing that first footprint on an Australian beach.

CHAPTER SEVEN

Early Sites in Tropical and Arid Australia

One of the few things archaeologists seem to agree on is that the first colonists came from the north, with Arnhem Land, Cape York and the Kimberley region being the most likely entry points because of their relative accessibility from New Guinea and Island Southeast Asia. After thirty years of archaeological exploration, these three regions have all yielded Pleistocene human occupation sites as predicted, with some sites being in excess of 30 000 years old. A greater surprise were the Pleistocene sites found in extremely arid areas in the Pilbara, Central Australia and the Nullarbor Plain. A well-developed inland economy exploiting macropods and emu eggs apparently existed in the Pilbara by 25 000 BP, and in the Central Australian Ranges humans were present in the spinifex sand hills throughout the glacial maximum according to Michael Smith, who sees availability of drinking water as the governing factor.

CAPE YORK PENINSULA

At the base of Cape York Peninsula, about 100 kilometres west of Cairns, a spectacular tabletop mountain rises 400 metres above the surrounding savanna woodlands and plains. Its name is Nurrabullgin, also known as Mount Mulligan. This steep-sided mountain is 18 kilometres long and some 6 kilometres wide, with a volcanic base capped by sandstone. On its top lies Nurrabullgin Cave, a large sandstone rock-shelter with good headroom throughout and, significantly, close to deep, permanent waterholes. In this region, with little permanent ground water during the long winter dry season, permanent water sources were all-important. And in summer, the wide rock roof would have provided welcome shelter from monsoon rain and the heat of the tropical sun.

Excavations were carried out in the early 1990s by Bruno David, with the permission of the Kuku Djungan Aboriginal Corporation, who now own the land. The occupation deposit is well stratified and contains stone artefacts, bone and large quantities of charcoal, representing a number of distinct phases of habitation separated by a series of hiatuses.[1] Ochre fragments, including pieces showing striations from use, were present only in mid- and late Holocene levels. The cultural remains show considerable continuity, with the same raw materials — mainly basalt, chert and quartz — being used throughout.

The remarkable thing about the occupation at Nurrabullgin Cave is its age. An internally consistent sequence of radiocarbon dates on charcoal gave a date for the lowest occupation of greater than 37 170 BP. The oldest date came from a depth of only 30 centimetres, but David has shown that the deposition of sediments into the shelter would have been very slight, and the dates seem soundly based.

Nurrabullgin Cave presents important evidence of cultural continuity and great antiquity. It is the oldest human occupation site yet found in north Queensland, but some argue that hunters had penetrated the Atherton Tablelands region just south of Chillagoe about 38 000 years ago. This assertion is based on the long pollen sequence from Lynch's Crater, in which there is a huge increase in the amount of charcoal at the same time as the vegetation changes from rainforest to fire-adapted *Eucalyptus*. This change can only readily be explained, according to pollen analyst Peter Kershaw, by the arrival of humans with their fire-sticks.[2]

In the limestone karst formations of Chillagoe, there are many caves and rock-shelters, and Pleistocene occupation has been found in two of these. Fern Cave is a large cave with two high-domed chambers, where Bruno David found occupation at least 26 000 years old.[3] A few heavily patinated peckings on the wall adjacent to the excavation consist of a series of loosely clustered pits, a star shape and three four-pronged motifs, resembling 'tridents' or bird tracks. These have been demonstrated by David to be similar to other patinated peckings from the Chillagoe, Mitchell-Palmer, Laura and Koolburra regions, which are thought to have considerable antiquity on the basis of degree of patination and nature of superimpositions.

Another long cultural sequence at Chillagoe has been uncovered by a major, ongoing excavation by John and Mireille Campbell, and their students from James Cook University, in Walkunder Arch Cave. Occupation goes back more than 18 000 years — there are two heavily patinated geometric engravings, and the lowest level contained a horsehoof core, a waisted tool, shells and wallaby bones. Interestingly, burnt antbed or termite mound was found throughout the deposit, indicating that this was used as fuel in both Pleistocene and more recent times.[4]

Further north in the Laura region, Michael Morwood of the University of New England has recently uncovered a 32 000-year-old occupation at Sandy Creek Shelter 1.[5] Earlier, terminal Pleistocene occupation had been found by Richard Wright of Sydney University at Mushroom Rock, and Andrée Rosenfeld of the Australian National University had uncovered both occupation and patinated geometric rock engravings in excess of 13 000 years old at Early Man Shelter, described in chapter 11.[6]

Sandy Creek Shelter 1 had previously been partly excavated by Percy Trezise in 1969, yielding a deep cultural deposit, 'buried' rock engravings and many stone tools, including a ground-edge axe lying on bedrock at a depth of 3 metres. (The evidence from Sandy Creek for both petroglyphs and paintings of Pleistocene age is described in chapter 11.) Morwood's excavations in 1989–1991 of this and the adjacent Shelter 2 obtained a long and well-dated cultural sequence. The earliest evidence of occupation was a stone-knapping floor of twenty-six small artefacts of crystalline quartz, near the base of the rubble and associated with charcoal dating to 32 000 BP. There were very few artefacts above this until the first systematic use of the shelter around 18 000 years ago.

G<small>ROUND</small>-E<small>DGE</small> A<small>XES</small>

The most important artefact found at Sandy Creek was the ground-edge axe (figure 7.1). Morwood has convincingly established that the minimum age of the base of the rubble and the axe is in the order of 32 000 years. I saw the axe in 1981 when commencing my own field work in Cape York, but unfortunately it has subsequently been lost. Nevertheless, the drawing by architect Eddie Oribin and old photographs

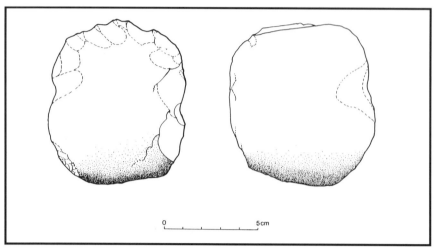

Figure 7.1   The ground-edge axe recovered by Trezise from his 1969 excavation of Sandy Creek Shelter 1. It is of pink quartzite and has a maximum length of 8.7 centimetres. It has a ground edge (the grinding is shown by stippling), and is both waisted and grooved to facilitate hafting. (Drawing by E. Oribin, after Morwood 1989, by courtesy of Trezise)

give us a good idea of its size and form. It was made from pink quartzite, 8.7 centimetres long, with a ground working edge, a slight 'waist' and a groove to aid hafting. It compares closely with the ground-edge axes from Arnhem Land (figure 6.2).

Small rock fragments with grinding marks in both the Mushroom Rock deposit and a 10 000-year-old layer at Early Man Shelter had hinted at the presence of edge-grinding in the late Pleistocene in Cape York Peninsula, but this find considerably extends the time depth of ground-edge axes both in the region and continent-wide.

Ground-edge artefacts have now been found in Pleistocene layers in a number of sites in north Queensland, the Top End of the Northern Territory and in highland New Guinea (at the sites of Kafiavana, Kiowa, Yuku and Nombe, where a complete axe was recovered from a 14 500- to 26 000-year-old layer). In the Kimberley in Western Australia, as described below, flakes showing signs of grinding were excavated from a 27 000 BP layer in Widgingarri 1 and the 18 000-year-old basal deposit of Miriwun Shelter.

Pleistocene ground-edge artefacts appear to be restricted to north of the Tropic of Cancer, and to the extreme north of the continent if we can judge by the present small sample. Later in the Holocene, ground-edge axes were the regular chopping tool over most of the mainland, but not in Tasmania. Morwood has carried out a valuable analysis of the distribution of various forms of axes in time and space (figure 7.2).[7]

It is difficult to account for the limited distribution of ground-edge axes in the Pleistocene. A case has been made that the large waisted axes in New Guinea were used for ringbarking rainforest trees, but on the mainland, the ground-edge Pleistocene axes are relatively small and light, and come from sites in *Eucalyptus* woodlands rather than rainforest. Only further research, hopefully including analysis of use-wear and any residues remaining on the working edges of these artefacts, will help to solve this puzzle of their function and restricted distribution to the north of Carpentaria.

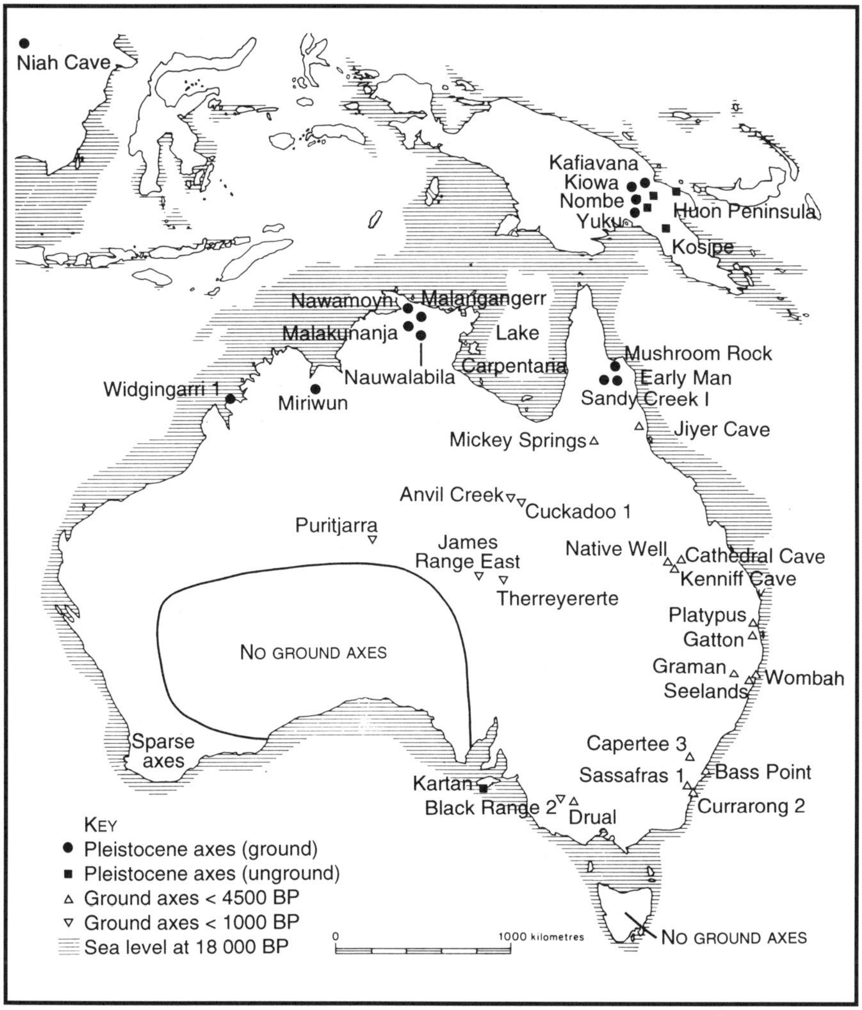

Niah Cave

Kafiavana
Kiowa
Nombe
Yuku
Huon Peninsula
Kosipe

Nawamoyn
Malangangerr
Malakunanja
Nauwalabila
Lake
Carpentaria
Widgingarri 1
Miriwun
Mushroom Rock
Early Man
Sandy Creek I
Mickey Springs
Jiyer Cave

Anvil Creek
Cuckadoo 1
Puritjarra
James
Range East
Native Well
Cathedral Cave
Kenniff Cave
Therreyererte
Platypus
Gatton
Graman
Seelands
Wombah

NO GROUND AXES

Sparse
axes
Capertee 3
Sassafras 1
Bass Point
Kartan
Black Range 2
Drual
Currarong 2

KEY
● Pleistocene axes (ground)
■ Pleistocene axes (unground)
△ Ground axes < 4500 BP
▽ Ground axes < 1000 BP
▦ Sea level at 18 000 BP

0   1000 kilometres

NO GROUND AXES

**Figure 7.2   The distribution and chronology of ground-edge axes in Greater Australia.
(After Morwood 1989)**

THE GULF OF CARPENTARIA

In northwestern Queensland on the Barkly Tableland, traces of occupation more than 17 000 years old have been found.[8] This remote area northwest of Mount Isa contains spectacular gorges, permanent rivers and waterholes with abundant fish and shellfish, and plant food such as the nuts of pandanus and cycad palms. Along 40 kilometres of river, there is only one good rock-shelter — the deep, well-protected shelter on Colless Creek.

A small excavation was carried out there by Philip Hughes and Peter Hiscock, revealing an extraordinarily rich site with an average density of 50 000 artefacts per cubic metre of deposit. The uppermost cubic metre held half a million pieces of bone. Occupation at Colless Creek certainly goes back beyond 17 550 BP — the oldest in a series of dates obtained on shell from the site.

The ancient environment was reconstructed through an analysis of sediments. Conditions in the vicinity of the shelter over the last 18 000 years were considerably drier than during the preceding phase of human occupation, which probably extended back beyond 30 000 years. The high degree of weathering of the deposit, patination on the artefacts and heavy staining on bones suggest that basal occupation is at least 30 000 BP, and perhaps much older.

During the last 18 000 years, Colless Creek Shelter and the surrounding well-watered Lawn Hills Gorge would have acted as an oasis in this arid region. The period around 17 000 years ago was a time of great aridity in other inland regions, such as the Willandra Lakes, and it may have been this climatic stress that drove people to such an 'oasis' at that time.

THE KIMBERLEY

The Kimberley region in the extreme north of Western Australia has long been thought to be one of the possible landfalls for early migrants or castaways swept southwards from Timor or the Indonesian archipelago. Such migrants would have arrived on a broad plain, but it is uncertain whether it would have been grassland, savanna woodland or mud and mangroves, with possibly an accompanying dearth of drinkable water. A few hundred kilometres inland, the migrants would have encountered the high cliffs of the edge of the Kimberley escarpment, which forms the present rugged coastline. The continental shelf is quite wide and the offshore waters shallow in the Kimberley region, so early sites may now lie beneath the sea.

The Kimberley escarpment is broken in places by plains and rivers flowing out to sea through narrow gorges or broad river valleys like the Ord. It is in the Ord Valley that two early occupation sites have been found, one of which certainly dates to the Pleistocene period. In the Miriwun rock-shelter on the Ord River, Charles Dortch of the Western Australian Museum excavated an occupation deposit in 1971 as part of a salvage program before the area was flooded by the Ord River irrigation scheme.[9] The upper levels of the site contained small tools, but in the dark brown, silty earth of the lower levels, dated between about 3000 and 18 000 years ago, was a distinctive early assemblage. Tool types included relatively thick, denticulated or notched flakes, adze flakes, a few core-scrapers and small blades, and some pebble tools. Also found were some quartzite fragments, which may be parts of grindstones or anvils.

One of the most remarkable discoveries was that two flakes recovered from below the horizon dated to 18 000 years were pieces struck from tektites. Tektites, or australites as they are called in Australia, are small glassy pebbles, up to about 2.5 centimetres in diameter, black or dark green in colour, and shaped like buttons, discs, teardrops, balls or dumb-bells. Their chemical composition is different from that of the rocks where they are found or from that of any terrestrial lava.

The origin of tektites is a puzzle. Some scientists believe that they are bits of terrestrial sedimentary rock excavated by the impact of meteorites crashing into the earth's surface, melted by the heat of impact, and congealed into glass as they are flung into the atmosphere to fall as a widely scattered shower. A more likely possibility is that they are the remains of gobs of lava fired at the earth by volcanic activity on the moon. A huge shower of tektites fell in the Australasian region 750 000 years ago. These australites are concentrated in a swathe across the southern half of Australia, particularly in Central Australia and in inland southern districts of Western Australia.

Analysis of one of the Miriwun tektites places it within the Indochinite group of tektites, the first tektite of this kind known from Australia. The seemingly remote possibility that this 18 000-year-old artefact (a very small flake) was brought from Southeast Asia cannot be entirely dismissed until finds are made in Australia of whole Indochinites (i.e. pieces showing no artificial modification) in places where there is no association with human occupation. This Miriwun tektite may be the first ice age Asian artefact found in Australia, if Indochinites are shown never to occur outside Indochina.

In the Kimberley region, there may be a long continuity of technological tradition, both in grooved ground-edge axes and in serrated flakes. Kimberley serrated spear points are renowned for their fine crafting and pleasing symmetry. They were made by pressure-flaking, a technique in which tiny flakes were pressed off by use of a bone, piece of wood or even one's teeth. Fine-grained stone was employed in their manufacture; more recently bottle glass or telephone insulators have been used. The use of these bifacially trimmed leaf-shaped points goes back at least 3000 years.

One particularly important feature of the Ord River sites is that organic material was well preserved in most of them. It shows that, throughout the 18 000 years of Miriwun's habitation, the human occupants exploited a wide range of aquatic and terrestrial fauna. Food from the surrounding land included wallabies, possums, bandicoots, lizards and rodents, and from the river and lagoons came shellfish, reptiles, catfish and goose eggs. The numerous eggshell fragments of the pied or semi-palmated goose (*Anseranas semipalmata*), which breeds only during the wet season, indicates that Miriwun was used as a wet-season camping place from late Pleistocene times until the European era.

Recent research on the west Kimberley coast and the islands of the Buccaneer Archipelago by Sue O'Connor has revealed occupation about 28 000 years ago.[10] The rock-shelters of Widgingarri 1 and 2 northeast of Derby on the Kimberley coast seem to have been inhabited from 28 000 BP, when they would have been more than 100 kilometres from the sea, until about 18 500 BP, the height of aridity at the last glacial maximum, when the sea had retreated to its maximum extent, and they were abandoned until about 7500 BP. O'Connor considers that increasing aridity rather than the retreating coastline was the prime cause of the sites' abandonment.

The fragments of baler shell (a large gastropod, *Melo* sp.) and pearl shell found in the Pleistocene layer are now interpreted by O'Connor *not* as reflecting a coastal economy, but as prized items traded from the coast. In the ethnographic present, large baler shells are valued for their usefulness as containers for water and so on, and the pearl shell is valued and traded for its aesthetic qualities. O'Connor infers that this was also the case between 30 000 and 18 000 years ago. If she is correct, this is another example of the great continuity of Australian material culture and practices.

Likewise, on a small offshore island, earliest occupation in Koolan Shelter 2 dates to a minimum age of 27 300 BP. By extrapolation, O'Connor estimated the age of first occupation as about 30 000 BP, a time of relatively higher sea level, when the sea would have been close to the shelter. The date of 27 300 BP came from the mangrove shellfish *Geloina coaxans*, which is plentiful in the site, indicating a heavy reliance on marine resources by the site's earliest as well as its most recent occupants. Koolan Shelter 2 was vacated about 24 600 BP, when conditions became more arid and the drop in sea level caused the shore to retreat some 220 kilometres, leaving the island as a peak of an inland range in the arid west Kimberley. The inhabitants seem to have followed the rising and retreating seas, reoccupying the shelter about 10 400 BP, when the rising sea had again separated Koolan Island from the mainland.

MANDU MANDU CREEK ROCK-SHELTER

On the western extremity of the Australian arid zone lies Northwest Cape, where a small excavation in Mandu Mandu Creek rock-shelter by Kate Morse of the Western Australian Museum has uncovered human occupation going back 34 000 years.[11] This sizeable limestone rock-shelter in Cape Range National Park faces west over a 1-kilometre wide coastal plain to Ningaloo Reef. The initial 1-metre square test pit yielded over 500 stone artefacts, marine mollusc shells and marine and terrestrial bone fragments. While the only faunal remains preserved in the lower, Pleistocene layer (below a date of 19 590 BP) were fish teeth and the thickest, most durable shell fragments (such as chiton valves and robust fragments of baler shell), it is clear 'that during this early phase of occupation Aboriginal people had the knowledge and skills to exploit a variety of marine foods'. The continental shelf is narrower here than anywhere else around Australia, and it seems that the sea was about 6 kilometres from the site when it was first occupied. Morse suggests that 'there may be little real difference, in the range of food types exploited, between the marine economy of the Pleistocene occupants and that practised during Holocene times'.

There is more of a contrast betweeen the Holocene and Pleistocene tool kits. The lower, Pleistocene industry is typified by large flakes and flaked pieces, mostly made on poor-quality silcrete and limestone. Flakes are significantly longer and thicker than in the younger assemblage, and there is a higher percentage of cores and amorphous flaked pieces, although small flakes also occur throughout the deposit. The most recognisable tool in the Pleistocene assemblage is a limestone horsehoof core, weighing 595 grams, in a layer about 10 centimetres below the 19 590 BP date. In Holocene times there is a significant change, marked by a preference for finer-grained materials such as silcrete, a much higher percentage of retouched pieces and the introduction of distinctive artefacts such as adzes (including one tula) in the post–2400 BP period. Morse concludes that 'the stone industry can broadly be classified as typical of the Australian core tool and scraper tradition with the addition of typical late phase tools such as adzes and a significant decrease in flake size in the Holocene layers'.

This site has provided the earliest Australian evidence for exploitation of marine resources, and the first dated evidence for Pleistocene human occupation on this vast arid stretch of the central Western Australian coast, which has long been thought to have posed a major barrier to early human settlement. Transitory visits seem to have been paid to the rock-shelter until it was more or less abandoned about 19 000 years ago, as glacial aridity increased and the shoreline retreated to about 10 kilometres from the site. It was reoccupied about 2500 BP, but extensive middens in the region have given earlier Holocene dates, including the Warroora midden dated to around 8000 years ago. On current archaeological evidence, increasing aridity about 19 000 BP is thought to have led to the abandonment of this western extremity of the Australian desert zone until the climate improved in early Holocene times.

Further work by Morse since 1988 has produced the earlier radiocarbon dates, and uncovered a unique find in Pleistocene Australia, twenty-two shell beads (colour plate 7). They are made from small marine cone shells, and are firmly associated with the baler shell which gave the date of 34 200 years. Comparison of notches on these cone shells with similarly threaded recent shell artefacts from northwestern Australia shows analogous use-wear patterns. This is an exciting addition to the 12 000- to 19 000-year-old bone beads found at Devil's Lair, the only other Pleistocene ornaments yet recovered from an archaeological site. Necklaces of shell beads were common in more recent Aboriginal Australia, and are known particularly from Tasmania, but this is another example of the incredibly long continuities discernible in Aboriginal decorative traditions.

MONTE BELLO ISLANDS

Pleistocene occupation from a time of low sea level has recently been found by Veth on the Monte Bello Islands, now located 120 kilometres off the present Pilbara coastline.[12] Three limestone caves with cultural material have been excavated on Campbell Island. The age of 27 220 BP was given by marine shell at the base of the deposit in Noala Cave, reflecting a time when it was adjacent to the Pleistocene coast. The deposit shows full use of marine resources, kangaroos and other mammals from the now submerged plains that then joined the Monte Bello and Barron Islands to the mainland.

Noala and two other adjacent caves, Morgan's and Haynes caves, all show intensive occupation around 8000 BP, with shellfish (predominantly mangrove species), fish and land mammals being exploited. Retouched, utilised stone artefacts were made from exotic materials, such as metamorphic rock, not visible on the present islands.

Between about 8000 and 7500 BP the islands became part of the mainland. Soon after 7500 BP they were apparently abandoned; by 6500 BP they were 50 kilometres offshore and uninhabited.

THE PILBARA

Surprisingly, a number of Pleistocene sites have been discovered on the Hamersley Plateau in the Pilbara. This area is part of Australia's arid zone and would have lain 500 kilometres inland and been even drier at the height of the last glacial period. The first was the Mount Newman rock-shelter Orebody XXIX (PO187), which overlooks the headwaters of the Fortescue River. Ash, charcoal and ochre were found throughout the 1-metre deposit excavated, but no bone. Eleven hearths were found, one of which was typical of fire-pits used by modern Aborigines for baking animals. Most of the 400 artefacts found were simple flaked or retouched pieces, but two diagnostic implement types were found: steep-edged scrapers and notched scrapers. Radiocarbon dates revealed that the 1-metre deep deposit is more than 20 750 years old. Eighteen kilometres to the northeast, and close to the east side of the Fortescue River, another site at Ethel Gorge (PO2055.2) gave a date on near-basal occupation of 26 300 BP.[13] These are conservative dates for initial occupation of the sites, as in neither case were the excavations taken to bedrock or culturally sterile units.

Both rock-shelters were occupied occasionally before some 20 000 years ago. Nowadays, the bed of the Fortescue River only flows after heavy rains, and normally only a few pools of water are to be found on its upper section and in the gorges of what is now the Hamersley National Park. Veth interprets the Hamersley Ranges as a 'refuge' area, but also points out that 'there is currently no unequivocal evidence for continuity of occupation during the height of the last glacial maximum from approximately 18,000 and 15,000 BP'.[14]

Another Pleistocene site has recently been identified in a coastal but arid area at Shark Bay, on Peron Peninsula — the most westerly part of the Australian continent

(450 kilometres south of Northwest Cape). This is an open site called Silver Dollar, excavated by Bowdler.[15] The lower occupational layer contained stone artefacts associated with large amounts of emu eggshell and teeth of kangaroos and wallabies, and some fragments of baler shell. Radiocarbon dating of this baler shell and emu eggshell gave an age range between 18 000 and 25 000 years old for the lower artefacts. The coast was then at least 100 kilometres from the site. There was a hiatus in use of the camp site between about 18 000 and 6000 years ago, after which marine remains became abundant.

Bowdler concluded (in 1990):[16]

I am forced by my own data to concede that well-developed inland economies might well have been in place in northwest Australia by 25,000 BP or earlier. In this case, we see exploitation of emu eggs and macropods some 100 km from the coast over a period of some 7,000 years or more. This does not disagree with my original and fundamental premise that Australia was colonised by coastally adapted people whose colonising routes were around the coasts and up the major river systems, but it certainly suggests a much earlier adaptation to peculiarly Australian interior environments than I have previously been prepared to concede.

CENTRAL AUSTRALIA

Not until 1987 did the first proof come that the arid heart was inhabited in the Pleistocene, with the discovery by Michael Smith of 22 000-year-old occupation in Puritjarra rock-shelter, almost in the dead centre of Australia.[17]

Puritjarra lies close to the only permanent water in the Cleland Hills, near the eastern boundary of the Western Desert, some 320 kilometres west of Alice Springs in the Northern Territory. It is a region of spinifex grasslands and mulga woodland broken up by the complex topography of the central ranges. Rainfall averages less than 350 millimetres a year, but the ranges have some permanent springs, waterholes, deep rock 'reservoirs' and soakages in creek beds. All the rivers in the region, such as the Finke, are intermittent, but their beds usually contain some waterholes and soakages.

Puritjarra is a huge rock-shelter, 45 metres long and about 20 metres high, in a cliff of hard red sandstone. The extensive array of rock art includes stencils, paintings and some Panaramitee-style engravings, well known at the nearby Thomas Reservoir site, as described in chapter 11. Eleven square metres of the 400 square metres of level, shaded earth floor were excavated in 1986 and 1988. Twelve radiocarbon dates were obtained on charcoal, and six thermoluminescence (TL) dates on the sediments as an independent check. The results have been startling. The very base of the lower layer has a preliminary TL date of about 30 000 years old. No details are yet available, but the internal consistency of both series of dates indicates that the site has 'good stratigraphic integrity despite the low rate of sediment accumulation', and Smith believes the earliest occupation is 'in the order of 30 000 years'.

The shelter was first occupied, albeit fleetingly, well before 22 000 years ago. The first substantial use began at about 22 000 BP — marked by charcoal, some ten pieces of red and purple high-grade ochre, sixty stone flake artefacts including 'a single large steep-edged implement', and some 200 small pieces of flaking debris. Between 22 000 and 13 000 years ago, the shelter was used only occasionally, and no more than a few artefacts were deposited each millennium. The uppermost stratigraphic layer is a loose, gritty sand containing intact cooking hearths, charcoal, flaked stone tools, many grindstones (absent from the Pleistocene layer), ochre and emu eggshell. This layer spans the last 6000 years, but also attests to a major increase in occupation of the region during the last 1000 years.

The 22 000-year-old occupation coincides with the onset of major aridity. This 'presumably reflects the beginning of the pattern of land use tethered to reliable water resources'. Between 22 000 and 13 000 BP, the period of full glacial aridity, there is evidence for repeated, if slight, usage of the shelter. The repeated use of Puritjarra, together with its location away from any natural corridor, indicates the presence of a resident local population in this 'refuge'. Smith suggests that visits may have been short affairs, without much need for the replacement or maintenance of implements (hence the low numbers of artefacts), by small, highly mobile groups resident in the main ranges to the east.

THE NULLARBOR PLAIN

Very early occupation has now been found in underground limestone caves on the Nullarbor Plain. At least two caves in the far southwest of South Australia were in use before 30 000 years ago: Koonalda Cave and Allen's Cave. Radiocarbon dates on charcoal have shown occupation at Koonalda by about 24 000 BP and at Allen's Cave (N145) by 25 000 BP.[18] Now thermoluminescence (TL) dates on lower occupation levels where charcoal did not survive have given dates in the order of 34 000 years. At Allen's Cave, an artefact lies 1 metre below a preliminary optically stimulated luminescence (OSL) date of 34 000 ± 7000 BP, and OSL dating attributes a similar antiquity to the earliest occupation at Koonalda.[19]

Koonalda Cave is a crater-like doline (limestone sinkhole) in the karst scenery of the extensive, flat, arid Nullarbor Plain (colour plate 4). The cave was a flint mine. Quarrying was done underground, at times with no natural light, and the quarried nodules were taken elsewhere to be made into tools. Hearths, charcoal and the residue of the quarrying process were found inside the cave, mainly in the first, dimly lit chamber some 100 metres down from the entrance and 76 metres below the surface of the plain. Initial pioneering exploration by Gallus was followed by major excavation by Wright. His 6-metre-deep pit produced evidence that flint miners had been visiting the cave between about 24 000 and 14 000 years ago.

The cave was thoroughly explored and found to contain a series of lakes, an invaluable source of drinking water, and, most remarkably, Pleistocene 'rock art', comprising finger markings on the walls in total darkness, some 300 metres inside the cave entrance (see chapter 11). This sinkhole had two major attractions for early humans. It was a reliable source of water on an arid plain and its walls held nodules of flint, the best raw material for stone tool manufacture available in the continent.

At Allen's Cave, some 80 kilometres west of Koonalda near Eucla, there is a culturally sterile deposit bracketed between dates of 20 200 ± 1000 BP and 11 950 ± 250 BP after the early occupation.[20] This has been taken to indicate abandonment of the site, at least between 17 500 and 15 000 years ago, a period of intense aridity. About 15 000 to 18 000 years ago, when the sea reached its lowest level of the last glaciation, the coast was some 160 kilometres further south and the Eucla–Koonalda region became treeless plains, with an estimated average annual rainfall of only 160 to 180 millimetres. Allen's Cave was virtually deserted at this time and Koonalda Cave experienced only intermittent occupation between 22 000 and 15 000 BP; no doubt the Aboriginal groups had moved south onto the wide coastal plain that emerged as a result of the fall in sea level. The sea level began to rise again about 12 000 years ago, bringing the coastline closer and thus again increasing the rainfall, water resources and mallee scrub.

COLONISATION OF THE ARID ZONE

Archaeological evidence has now established that all major geographical regions, coastal and inland, were occupied relatively early in the colonisation of Australia (that is, before 30 000 years ago). During this 'lacustral phase', when Lake Mungo and other lakes of the interior were full of fresh water, there was occupation in some extremely arid regions. Peter Veth has explained this in biogeographical terms, suggesting that there was early occupation of less marginal habitats such as 'refuges' (with reliable water), plus intermittent occupation during more climatically favourable periods of 'corridors' between 'refuges' and the extensive 'barriers' of the sandridge deserts (figure 7.3).

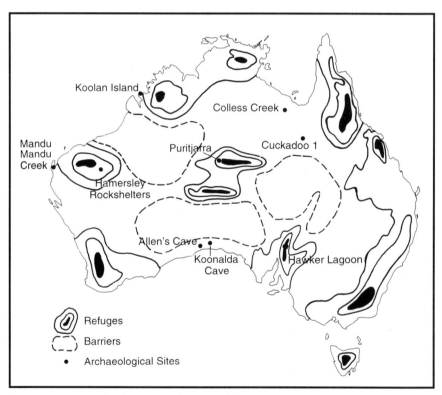

Figure 7.3 Location of 'refuges', 'corridors', dunefield 'barriers' and sites with multiple occupation events in the expanded Pleistocene arid zone. (After Veth 1989)

The onset of the full glacial climate, which was at its peak between about 18 000 and 15 000 BP, brought these hunters and gatherers the problems of intense aridity and extremely cold, frosty winters. From around 25 000 BP, it was increasingly dry and windy, with widespread drying of lakes, extensive dune-building, expansion of the arid zone and a major drop in sea level. At this stressful time, some sites in 'corridors' were vacated, according to Veth, but other sites such as Puritjarra lay in 'refuge' areas by permanent water and continued to be in use, at least occasionally.

Smith has recently seriously questioned Veth's 'barrier desert' theory, raising doubts whether the major sandridge deserts do form a biogeographic unit, whether the division into 'corridors', 'refuges' and 'barriers' can be sustained, and whether the 'barrier deserts' would indeed have represented a new challenge to humans.[21] He emphasises the strong links between Veth's 'barrier deserts' and adjacent 'refugia' and 'corridors', some of which combine dunefields with hummock grassland and unco-ordinated drainage in the same way as do sandridge deserts. Smith also points out that the evidence of Bowdler's Silver Dollar site suggests that well-developed inland economies based on macropods and emu eggs may have been in place on the arid coast of Western Australia by 25 000 BP or earlier. Throughout the late Pleistocene and early Holocene, the occupants of Puritjarra Shelter would have been dependent on the food resources of the surrounding spinifex sandhill habitat.

As the climate improved, new sites were occupied within the 'corridors', such as Cuckadoo 1 Shelter near Cloncurry in semiarid Queensland.[22] A hearth with fragments of mussel shells and charcoal, the JSN site, was dated to 13 850 + 190 BP, showing the penetration of the core of the Strzelecki dunefields by that time.[23] There was penetration of the relatively well watered Flinders Ranges at Hawker Lagoon by 15 000 BP, and two hearths associated with stone artefacts in dune cores on the Lower Cooper Creek in the central Lake Eyre Basin date to some 11 500 years.[24] The shores of Lake Frome in the arid belt became popular in the generally moister conditions between about 9500 and 4000 BP, and the widespread occupation of the Strzelecki and other dunefields came later, within the last 5000 years. Much archaeological exploration of 'barrier deserts' and adjacent dunefields (such as the Rudall River and Balgo region, Simpson Desert, Lake Eyre basin, Coongie Lakes and Cooper Basin by outstanding field workers such as Scott Cane, Michael Smith, Ron Lampert, Phillip Hughes, Peter Veth and Elizabeth Williams) has revealed many hundreds of sites belonging to the last 5000 years, but a general absence of Pleistocene cultural evidence, even in the most favourable habitats.[25]

Smith and Veth disagree on details of the timing, nature and explanation of this Holocene move into the dunefields, with Smith seeing access to potable water as the critical key, whereas Veth emphasises other factors. Nevertheless, the widespread exploitation of grass seed and the other resources of the dunefields in the mid-Holocene appears the last step in the colonisers' successful adaptation to the world's driest continent.

CHAPTER EIGHT

Early Sites in Temperate Australia

SOUTHWESTERN AUSTRALIA

It has been a surprise that extremely early human occupation has been found in both the southwest and southeast of the continent. The southwest of Western Australia boasts two sites between 40 000 and 30 000 years old, and in the southeast there are sites of similar antiquity both in the Willandra Lakes region and near Sydney, if we can credit the age of the Cranebrook artefacts discussed below. The presence of 40 000-year-old sites in the temperate southern half of Australia fits well with an earlier entry date in the north, as evidenced by the 50 000-year-old Kakadu sites. However, if, like Bowdler, one does not accept the Kakadu thermo-luminescence (TL) dates, the old problem remains of the gradient of antiquity running the wrong way, that is, from south to north.

The Upper Swan River site near Perth has the distinction of having its age of about 38 000 years old accepted by almost all leading archaeologists, even the hypersceptical Sandra Bowdler. It is an extensive, open-air camp site on an ancient floodplain bordering the upper Swan River between Perth and Walyunga. The site was found by an archaeological consultant, Bob Pearce, when he was driving past on the way to his holiday cottage. He had noticed men digging and could see that it was a clay deposit. In his own words, 'As I am interested in geology I just stopped to have a look. I spotted a couple of flakes by the roadside. It was the kind of rubble that most people would walk over and think nothing more about.'[1] What Pearce found were stone tools *in situ* in the clay at a depth of 10 to 90 centimetres. Some of the flakes were made of a distinctive chert containing fossils. This chert has only been found in Devil's Lair and other deposits older than 4600 years, and came from an offshore source that was later submerged by the rising sea. Identical fossiliferous chert has now been turned up by drilling into the sea bed offshore, and is found on a number of other Western Australian archaeological sites.

Pearce alerted the manager of Midland Brick Company, who immediately halted work in that part of their clay pit. A small excavation was carried out by Pearce, and samples of charcoal associated with the tools were sent to Sydney University radiocarbon laboratory for dating, which was generously paid for by the company. The great age of the occupation was at first not suspected, because the tools did not look particularly old and the deposit was not very deep. It was not until the first charcoal sample was processed a year later that its great antiquity was discovered. Meanwhile, the government of Western Australia had given permission for the clay pit to go ahead and the site to be destroyed. Mike Barbetti, who runs the Sydney laboratory, acted with commendable speed. Phone calls alerted the authorities in

Perth, and fortunately it emerged that the site, although released for destruction, was still intact. There was a collective sigh of relief that Australia had not inadvertently destroyed its oldest human occupation site yet discovered. It was a near miss, and a lesson for the future that permission must not be given to destroy sites, if it is suspected for any reason that they are of great antiquity, until they have been properly dated.

Further archaeological excavation of the Upper Swan site in 1981 produced many more artefacts. Further dates confirmed the age as 38 000 years or older. This is close to the limit of radiocarbon dating, but several samples were dated and gave very consistent and convincing results.[2]

About 900 artefacts have now been recovered from the site. Most are made of a deeply patinated dolerite. Stone chips (less than 15 millimetres long) account for 75 percent of the finds, and there are only thirty-seven tools showing retouch or use-wear. The small size of the tools is similar to other Western Australian Pleistocene sites such as Devil's Lair. The artefacts include small scrapers made of quartz and quartzite, and pebble fragments showing wear on their edges. The presence of chips, cores and conjoins (sets of flaked stone which can be refitted together) suggests that this was a tool-manufacturing site and that it was relatively undisturbed. The site is now in the Register of the National Estate and is under the control of the local Aboriginal community.

DEVIL'S LAIR

Devil's Lair is another of the earliest firmly dated sites in Australia, going back more than 30 000 years. This cave, in the extreme southwest, lies 20 kilometres north of Cape Leeuwin and 5 kilometres inland; it would have been not much more than 25 kilometres from the sea, even when the sea level was at its lowest. Devil's Lair is a single, dimly lit chamber with an earth floor of about 75 square metres largely covered with a layer of flowstone (a stone 'sheet' that sometimes forms on the floors of limestone caves) up to 20 centimetres thick. The name 'Devil's Lair' derives from the large quantity of remains of the Tasmanian devil found in the upper levels of the deposit.

In 1955 palaeontologist Ernest Lundelius excavated in the cave in search of a sequence of prehistoric fauna. As limestone caves provide excellent preservation conditions for bone, they are regular hunting grounds for palaeontologists, and so other collectors followed him. One collector mentioned that there were possible artefacts in the cave, and a human incisor tooth was found. A salvage excavation was organised by Dortch and Merrilees in 1970 to tidy up the disturbed material left by earlier excavators, line the pit with plastic and then back-fill it to prevent further slumping of the deposit. The presence of artefacts in the deposit was confirmed, and six more seasons of investigation of the site and surrounding region followed.[3]

The Devil's Lair deposit is extremely rich in bone: the density of animals ranges from 70 to 2040 individuals per cubic metre. Some of the faunal remains in these bone beds were the prey not of owls or predators such as the Tasmanian devil, but of humans. The case for humans as important predators rests on the unusually wide range of species present; artificial modification, including charring, of many bones; occurrence of some bones in undisturbed hearths; and the presence of items that must have been carried there by people, such as freshwater shells and even occasional marine shellfish. The people seem to have exploited most small- to medium-sized animals, including wallabies, possums, bandicoots, native rats and mice, snakes, lizards, frogs, bats and birds, including emu eggs. Apart from the absence of dingo bones and the presence of Tasmanian devil bones, the fauna represented is not very different from that of the present day.

Excavation revealed a deposit over 3 metres deep, accumulated over 37 000 years. The lowest levels that contain artefacts are dated to about 33 000 years ago, and include a dozen pieces of limestone claimed to be artefacts, four small flakes of a stone foreign to the cave, one bone artefact and several bones of extinct marsupial species such as the giant kangaroos, *Protemnodon* and *Sthenurus*. Some of the bones are fractured, and two are claimed by Dortch to be probable artefacts. If his claims are substantiated, this would be among the best evidence yet found in Australia that humans did prey on megafauna. Between about 28 000 and 6000 years ago, occupation features, such as hearths, show that repeated, if intermittent, use was made of Devil's Lair. Most of the occupation was sealed below a layer of flowstone, formed 12 000 years ago. (Sceptics such as Allen and Bowdler give 28 000 BP as the date of earliest occupation, because it is the earliest date 'which clearly derives from materials clearly associated with unquestionable cultural materials'.)[4]

The whole assemblage at Devil's Lair belongs to the early phase of Australian prehistory, although the artefacts are much smaller than those of many other Pleistocene sites. The early phase industries from both Miriwun and Devil's Lair contain small adze flakes and a variety of very small retouched tools made on flakes. It may be, therefore, that early phase tools tend to be smaller in western than eastern Australia, but much more evidence is needed before we can be sure, and regrettably few excavated tool kits have been analysed and published. The comparatively small size of the Devil's Lair tools may also result from the fracturing properties of the raw materials used: quartz and a distinctive chert. The nearest known source is 120 kilometres to the east, but it is far more likely that it came from the now-drowned continental shelf.

Only about 170 stone and 100 bone tools were recovered from the area excavated at Devil's Lair. The stone tools are made from chert, quartz and limestone. Some undoubted limestone artefacts occur, but sometimes it is difficult to decide whether pieces of limestone that resemble choppers or rough cores are indeed artefacts, since most of them have been eroded by ground water. Most of the stone artefacts are retouched flakes. Several are scrapers, perhaps intended to be hafted as adzes. Other tools have notched or toothed margins, but most lack a distinctive form.

BONE ARTEFACTS

Even more important than the stone tools at Devil's Lair are those made of bone, since bone and bone tools are preserved in so few Pleistocene sites. Those from Devil's Lair are among Australia's oldest bone tools: the earliest is estimated to be 29 500 years old. A relatively large number and variety of types were preserved. The most common were split pointed bones, 1 to 15 centimetres long. Bone points are the next most common, some made from macropod shin bones and ground to a point, probably by abrasion and whittling.

A few tiny points have been found, which may have been used to pierce holes in animal skins to be sewn together. One is only 14 millimetres long and its point has been polished by use. Another 12 000-year-old bone artefact may be a pendant or bodkin. The broad end is perforated, and the edge of the hole has been smoothed by friction on the side next to the broad end. This shows that a piece of string or sinew has been passed through the hole, and suggests that the object was used as a bodkin or suspended as an ornament.

ICE AGE ORNAMENTS

One of the most exciting finds from Devil's Lair was three 12 000- to 15 000-year-old bone beads, the first indication in Australia that Pleistocene hunter–gatherers used such ornaments. The beads were made on short sections of naturally perforated long bones, and x-ray has shown that the perforation does extend right through. Experimental work has shown how such bone beads may have been manufactured.[5] A fresh kangaroo long bone is cut deeply around its shaft with a sharp flake, then snapped in half. The process is repeated about 2 centimetres from the broken edge and snapped again. The two ends of the bead are rounded by abrading with a piece of limestone, and the narrow cavity cleaned out with a sliver of wood or bone. The Devil's Lair beads and Mandu Mandu Creek shell necklace are unique in Aboriginal culture, indicating that life in early Australia was not merely a struggle for survival, but gave time to devote to manufacturing non-utilitarian items (colour plate 5).

Other finds at Devil's Lair may also testify to the creativity and manual dexterity of its Pleistocene occupants. A perforated fragment of soft marl, definitely foreign to the locality, was found in a horizon about 14 000 years old. This may have been an ornamental pendant (figure 8.1).[6] The perforation, which may be artificial or natural, could also have served to polish the tips or shafts of wooden spears or bone points. It resembles a bird's head, and the base of the 'neck' appears to have been fractured, so it may have originally been longer.

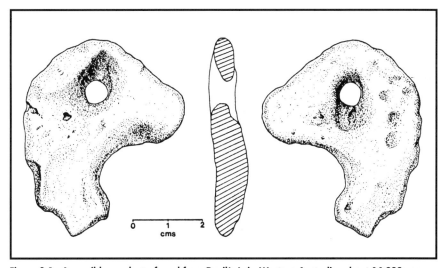

Figure 8.1 A possible pendant of marl from Devil's Lair, Western Australia, about 14 000 years old. (After Dortch 1980)

Finally, three pieces of limestone have been found, in 12 000- and 20 000-year-old horizons, which Dortch describes as 'engraved stone plaques'.[7] One flat surface of each 'plaque' is covered with faint straight lines, which could have been produced by a sharp, pointed tool of stone, bone or wood. Dortch argues that the lines must have been made by humans, but Robert Bednarik maintains they are *not* 'anthropic' marks (intentional, non-utilitarian marks made by human agency) but natural 'taphonomic' markings, caused by the process of taphonomy — the modifications experienced by materials since they become part of what is thought to form the archaeological record.[8]

THE EAST COAST

It was not until the development of radiocarbon dating in 1950 that it became possible to determine the absolute age of prehistoric sites. During the 1950s, several sites in Australia were excavated and dated, but none of these went back into the glacial period. Although it was widely argued that Aboriginal settlement of the continent must go back to times of low sea level in the ice age, there was still no firm evidence for the Pleistocene colonisation of Australia.

It was therefore a great landmark in Australian prehistory when, in 1962, the National Physical Laboratory announced a 16 000-year-old date for the lower levels of Kenniff Cave in southern Queensland. The circumstances of the announcement were characteristically Australian. John Mulvaney and his digging team were sitting round their campfire outside the cave, drinking billy tea and listening on their radio transceiver to the Royal Flying Doctor Service at Charleville. A telegram for the team from Melbourne was read out over the air, breaking the news of the Pleistocene age of the site. Mulvaney suspected a transmission error, with one zero too many, but his doubts were dispelled the next day when the age of 16 000 years was confirmed by a second telegram.

KENNIFF CAVE

Kenniff Cave lies 700 metres above sea level, near the crest of the Great Dividing Range, in a rugged region of sandstone cliffs and gorges, timbered hills and grassy plains.[9] The cave, which would have provided an excellent shelter against wet or cold, lies in a sheltered valley called Lethbridge Pocket, above Meteor Creek. It is a roomy cave with a low entrance, but it averages about 3 metres of headroom inside (plate 12). Aboriginal paintings decorate the walls. Subjects are mainly stencils of hands and feet, and items of equipment such as boomerangs, a shield and a hafted axe. Red, white, yellow and black pigments are used; the colour was blown from the mouth around the object held against the wall. The art had been recorded by a local amateur field worker and senior radio operator of the Royal Flying Doctor Base, Reg Orr, through whom Mulvaney first heard of the site. In fact, Kenniff Cave was already well known locally because of the bushranging Kenniff brothers, who stabled their horses inside and by whose name it had become known.

Excavation revealed occupation deposits going down 3.3 metres. Bone and other organic remains were not preserved, but stone artefacts were abundant. About 65 cubic metres of sand and ash were excavated, yielding more than 800 artefacts and almost 22 000 waste flakes or manufacturing debris. Kenniff Cave produced an early industry consisting entirely of scrapers and a later industry in which new, specialised small tools were added to the scraper industry.

The older industry contained retouched tools made on flakes or large cores, which are generally termed scrapers (figure 1.1). Their precise function has not been established, but it is generally thought that they were used for planing or incising wooden objects, in other words they were tools for making tools. High-backed 'core-scrapers' and 'concave or nosed scrapers' are far more numerous in the earlier than later industry, and horsehoof cores are confined to the earlier horizons.

On the basis of further radiocarbon dates, the earliest occupation of Kenniff Cave is now known to have occurred about 19 000 years ago. For 11 000 years, there was no significant change in tool size, type or manufacturing technique. Then, about 5000 years ago, the number of scrapers began to diminish and new, small, finely worked tools were added to the existing tool kit. The most striking features of all these new tools were their small size and the probability that they were all composite tools that would be hafted into a handle. In the case of the long juan knives, specimens exist in museums in which the stone knife is hafted in a handle of animal skin, fur, bark and hair twine.

The importance of the Kenniff Cave cultural sequence is threefold. Firstly, it has an unusually wide range of artefacts and contains a small but representative sample of most of the major Australian prehistoric tool types, including all the small

Plate 12 Excavation at Kenniff Cave, Queensland. The rock-shelter bears stencilled hands on its roof and contained evidence of 19 000-year-old occupation. A latex soil profile is being taken off the rear wall of the excavation pit. (Courtesy of D. J. Mulvaney)

composite tools. Secondly, occupation extended over an extremely long time, from the present back into the Pleistocene. Thirdly, and most importantly, it was the site that provided the basis for the recognition of an earlier and a later technological phase in Australian prehistory. Mulvaney's broad concept of a two-part sequence has stood the test of time, although new discoveries have inevitably led to some modification of the original hypothesis.

Once the Pleistocene barrier had been broken, the search was on, and other early sites were found. Some were chance discoveries, but others were found because archaeologists now knew where to look.

BURRILL LAKE ROCK-SHELTER

The first Pleistocene site found in southeastern Australia was the Burrill Lake Shelter, which was excavated in 1967–68.[10] This huge sandstone rock-shelter is the largest known on the south coast of New South Wales. It is now signposted and open to the public, and there is also a replica of the stratigraphy of the site in the Australian Museum in Sydney. Facing east in a narrow, thickly wooded valley, it is sheltered both from onshore winds and the prevailing southerlies. The shelter floor is only 3 metres above modern sea level and lies about 180 metres from the edge of Burrill Lake. This is a coastal estuarine lagoon, usually open to the sea through a narrow channel. The site has fresh water nearby, together with all the food resources of woodland, estuary and ocean shore.

Ron Lampert's excavation revealed that occupation began some 20 000 years ago. The discovery that humans had reached the southeast coast by that time revolutionised archaeologists' thinking about the early settlement of Australia. If people were so far south during the last glacial phase, a considerably earlier date had to be envisaged for the entry into the north of the continent. The cultural sequence at Burrill Lake had two major components: an older and a younger industry, similar but not identical to those found at Kenniff Cave. As at Kenniff, there was little technological change over 15 000 years, until about 5000 to 5500 years ago, when new small tool types were added to the tool kit.

BASS POINT

Not far north of Burrill Lake near Shellharbour is the open site of Bass Point, excavated by Bowdler.[11] The hill on which the site is located drops sharply away on the seaward side, so it would have been a camp site with a good vantage point. The offshore profile is unusually steep in the region of Bass Point and Burrill Lake, so that even at times of low sea level they would have been no more than 30 kilometres inland. It was, nevertheless, a great surprise to discover that sporadic occupation on the site went back about 17 000 years. The early stone tool industry lasted from about 17 000 to 3500 years ago. In the upper, younger levels, there is midden debris including shellfish and the bones of fish, seals, birds and land mammals. By that time the sea had risen, the hill had become a headland and people were fishing and collecting shellfish locally.

Bass Point is significant as the only open Pleistocene site yet found on the southeast coast, and one of only two Pleistocene open sites on the whole east coast, the other being Wallen Wallen Creek in southern Queensland.

WALLEN WALLEN CREEK

Discoveries of ancient camps are generally made by chance, and one lucky find of this sort was the discovery of an ancient 'transit camp'. This was used sporadically by Aborigines for over 20 000 years on the west coast of North Stradbroke Island, in Queensland, about 6 kilometres south of Dunwich.[12]

While a postgraduate student at the University of Queensland, Robert Neal found shells, animal bones, flaked stone artefacts and charcoal in a 2.5-metre deep deposit at Wallen Wallen Creek, at the foot of a high sand dune about 400 metres inland from the present coastline. Geomorphic interpretation by Errol Stock of Griffith University indicated that the site was formed at the base of a large, well-vegetated sand hill near a water source. Twenty thousand years ago sea level was some 150 metres lower, and what is now Stradbroke Island was part of the mainland, with the coast between 12 and 20 kilometres to the east. The site was then a temporary camping place on the main access route between the sea coast and the river valley and mountains to the west. As the polar ice caps began to melt about 17 000 years ago, the sea gradually rose until it stabilised at its present level some 6500 years ago, transforming what was once a high coastal dunefield into an offshore island. Other, even older prehistoric sites in the area may now lie deep beneath the waters of Moreton Bay.

In recent times, Aborigines were eating shellfish, fish and a few dugong there. The quantity of artefacts increases markedly in the upper layer, indicating a major rise in human occupation of the offshore islands of Moreton Bay during the past few thousand years; this evidence accords with that from numerous shell middens on other sand islands such as Fraser and Moreton, excavated by archaeologists such as Peter Lauer, Jay Hall and Michael Rowland.

CRANEBROOK TERRACE

Some of the potentially oldest Aboriginal artefacts yet found in Australia came from gravels beside the Nepean River, at the foot of the Blue Mountains some 50 kilometres west of Sydney. Their discoverer was a Catholic priest, Father Eugene Stockton, who became interested in the archaeology of the Blue Mountains region when at the seminary in Springwood. He first noticed a few apparent stone artefacts in the Cranebrook gravel pits in the 1960s, and obtained radiocarbon dates in excess of 31 000 years on logs buried within the gravels. However, doubts were cast on whether the stones were really artefacts or naturifacts (made by natural agencies rather than by human hand), and whether the dated wood was firmly associated with the artefacts.[13]

It was not until 1987 that further evidence was gathered and published which indicates that at least some of the stones discovered in the Cranebrook gravel pits are artefacts, fashioned more than 40 000 years ago. The artefacts were found in gravel pits on a terrace between the Nepean River and the village of Cranebrook just north of Penrith. Here a series of different sediments lie one on top of the other. The uppermost is 6 to 9 metres of orange, sandy clay dating between about 40 000 and 45 000 years old, which in places has been stripped off by river activity and replaced with younger (10 000- to 13 000-year-old) but texturally similar overburden. This gravel-free overburden lies on top of a 5- to 7-metre thick gravel layer with an undulating surface.

Stone artefacts have been found in the gravel layer, which was formed at a time when the river was much larger and more active than the present Nepean River. The absolute time of deposition of the gravels is believed to be between about 47 000 and 43 000 years ago, on the basis of eleven radiocarbon dates of huge logs within the gravels, and two thermoluminescence (TL) dates. Logs in the gravels were identified as *Casuarina*, *Eucalyptus* and *Callistemon* (bottlebrush), and pollen analysis indicated that the environment of that period was woodland and mixed grassland similar to the present day.

Seven stone artefacts have been found well within the gravel, one right beside one of the dated logs. They resemble pebble choppers, steep-edged scrapers and other scrapers and core tools, typical in form and size of the old Australian core tool and scraper tradition. They are made of a wide variety of raw material: chert, rhyolite, dacite, quartzite, ignimbrite and siliceous mudstone. One or two are weathered and may have been rolled along downstream in the river bed before being deposited, but my impression of the others was that they were remarkably fresh and undamaged. The only problem is whether their association with the dated logs is real or only apparent, and some archaeologists prefer to put this site in the 'not proven' category.

A nearby rock-shelter, Shaws Creek KII, has been excavated by Stockton, revealing occupation from 15 000 years ago to the present, and the 2-metre deep excavation has not yet reached bedrock.[14] One particularly noteworthy find associated with a radiocarbon date of 14 700 BP was a chert tool resembling an adze or chisel, apparently bearing traces of resin. If correct, this is the first firm evidence that stone tools such as adzes were fixed into a handle during the Pleistocene period.

LAKE GEORGE

At Lake George on the Southern Tablelands, some 100 kilometres inland, a completely different type of evidence has been suggested to show that humans were there more than 100 000 years ago. The evidence comes from a core drilled out of the lake sediments by Gurdip Singh.[15]

Microscopic pollen grains and charcoal particles in the upper 8.6 metres of the core — covering the past 350 000 years — have been analysed and provide the longest continuous record of vegetation and fire history in Australia. The base of the 72-metre core is estimated to represent the years between 4.2 and 7 million years ago. The sediments extend down still further, to an estimated 134 metres, which means that the formation of the Lake George basin must be reckoned to date to 20 million years ago. The sediments indicate alternating lake-full to lake-dry conditions over the past 750 000 years, reflecting the effects of changes from eight glacial to eight interglacial periods.

Pollen analysis (palynology) is used to establish the kinds of plants that grew in an area in the past. Because the pollen grains of different plants have different forms, it is possible to identify the plants from which they came. It is not easy, however, to find out how many plants are represented, since different plants produce different quantities of pollen. Yet presence and absence of particular species can be determined, together with an approximate idea of relative frequencies.

The sequence shows that in zone F there was a huge increase in the amount of charcoal in the sediment, indicating a much higher incidence of fires than before, together with a reduction in the number of fire-sensitive species and the first expansion of fire-tolerant *Eucalyptus*-dominated vegetation. This change in vegetation has continued to the present day. One key question is, what sparked it off? Singh suggested that it was humans with their fire-sticks, and that nothing except human agency can explain the sudden change to a fire-tolerant vegetation dominated by *Eucalyptus*. Aborigines used fire not only for cooking, but also as a hunting weapon, igniting the bush both to drive out game and to make fresh new grass spring up to attract browsing animals. This increase in the use of fire would account both for the change in vegetation and the great increase in charcoal remains washed or blown into the lake sediments at this period.

The other key question is, when did this change take place? The dating of the Zone F section of the core was by extrapolation, and Singh believed it was during the last interglacial period about 120 000 years ago, but this has been disputed by Richard Wright, who argues convincingly for a date of about 60 000 years ago. This is a much more feasible time, fitting well with evidence from the Kakadu sites.

In a gully (plate 13) on what would have been the lake shore during the ice age, some small amorphous quartz flakes were found by Jones in 1980, in aeolian sands

Plate 13 Fernhill Tree Gully, Lake George, New South Wales. A few stone artefacts have been found here *in situ* in Pleistocene sediments in field surveys such as this one by the Canberra Archaeological Society.

radiometrically dated by Coventry to 22 000 to 26 000 BP.[16] Further discoveries were made by Jones and Allen in 1983, in a perched sand dune site on top of Butmaroo Hill near the highest former eastern shore of the lake. They found 'stratified stone artifacts throughout the 1.5 m. of sand deposit which contained a micro-blade industry dated to 4 kyr [thousand years] in its uppermost 12–20 cm. and with its base believed on extrapolation from the six available radiocarbon dates to date back to at least 10 kyr'. This sand lay on a lag deposit of quartz and heavily metamorphosed volcanic rocks (resting on bedrock), within which was a quartz core bearing negative flake scars (signs that flakes had been deliberately detached). In the tailings of sand-mining operations around the site and on the lake floor, several large, heavily weathered artefacts of metamorphosed volcanics have been found. 'They consist of large flakes with rough lateral retouch, flaked cobbles and dome-shaped "horsehoof" cores (or core tools). There is strong presumptive evidence that these date from the terminal Pleistocene if not earlier.'

BIRRIGAI SHELTER

At the height of the last glaciation occasional hunting parties were camping on the northern fringes of the Australian Alps, according to evidence in the small montane Birrigai rock-shelter in Tidbinbilla Nature Reserve in the Australian Capital Territory, south of Canberra.[17] This granite shelter lies at 730 metres above sea level and would then have been above the tree line, but was apparently used occasionally to provide a dry roof over hunters' heads from 21 000 years ago onwards. Average annual temperature during the last glacial phase is estimated on palynological and geomorphological evidence to have been about 6 to 7 degrees Celsius lower than today. The glacial climate in the Canberra region then would have been rather like that on the top of Mount Kosciusko today — that is, snowbound in midwinter, but habitable, if rather cold and windy, in summer. Hunters probably came up in summer for hunting on what were then treeless plains, possibly carrying a high biomass of macropods, emus, plains turkeys and the like. They doubtless used Birrigai rock-shelter because of its superb weatherproof qualities. During my first season of excavation in November 1983, we had terrible cold, wet weather and it even snowed! The small 'lean-to' shelter is formed by one giant block resting on another and is open at both ends. This acts like a wind tunnel, but at the same time it was the driest place in the whole region. When we blocked off the west end of the shelter with a tarpaulin, it became a snug camping place for up to a dozen people.

The 1.5 cubic metres of earth floor excavated produced only seventy stone artefacts, but these were relatively evenly spread from top to bottom in the deposit (plate 14). All artefacts were small (77 percent are less than 2 centimetres long), and the Pleistocene ones (flakes, chips, core fragments and bipolar pieces) are almost all of quartz. Microscopic analysis by Richard Fullager of residues left on the working edges revealed, in a level dated between 16 000 and 21 000 BP, a residue of plant material, suggesting plant processing on one retouched quartz flake (Birrigai's largest tool at 5 centimetres long), and step-scarring and a residue of bone collagen on another piece of quartz, interpreted as a possible bone scraping tool.

Charcoal from a definite hearth feature gave a date of 16 000 BP. The combination of hearth stones and a depression suggests that this was a 'ground oven' used as a food preparation cooking fire, as opposed to a warming, sleeping or other type of fire. Associated with the hearth were a piece of red ochre and a quartz core

Plate 14   Birrigai shelter, Tidbinbilla Nature Reserve, Australian Capital Territory.

fragment with blood and skin collagen on the edge, suggesting butchering of animal carcasses. Another quartz bipolar tool has blood on it, not on the working edge but on the side, in the exact spot where a stonemason who mis-aimed 10 000 years ago would have hit his thumb!

The antiquity of the occupation at Birrigai has been accepted by authorities such as Rhys Jones, who visited the excavation and later described its 'stratified stone tools at the base dated securely to 21 kyr', but Bowdler and Veth are sceptical of the 21 000 BP date, evidently because of the small number of artefacts and shallow deposit.[18] However, an 18 000 BP date lends support to the earlier one, and other Pleistocene sites such as Nurrabullgin and Fern Cave have equally few artefacts and shallow deposits because of extremely low sedimentation rates. Moreover, the Birrigai evidence showing colonisation of the mountain valleys just prior to the last glacial maximum no longer seems so remarkable, when we now know that people in Tasmania were hunting wallabies within sight of glaciers right through the peak of the glacial period, as seen in the next chapter.

CHAPTER NINE

An Ice Age
Walk to Tasmania

In the Pleistocene, the most southerly part of the Australian continent was not Wilson's Promontory in Victoria, but the Southeast Cape region of Tasmania. A drop in sea level of only about 60 metres exposed the floor of what is now Bass Strait, producing a land bridge of 15 million hectares (figure 9.1). The present islands of Bass Strait would at that time have been hills overlooking a broad plain.

Since beginning field work in Tasmania early in the 1960s, Rhys Jones had always put forward the hypothesis that Tasmania was occupied by means of this land bridge at a time of lowered sea level. He had also argued that most of the Pleistocene sites would have been coastal, since during the height of the last glacial period extensive ice sheets covered the central highlands, and much of the present island of Tasmania was treeless and inhospitable. Archaeological work during the last decade has proved Jones's first prediction correct, but his second wrong. Due to his work and the work of others such as Jim Allen, Sandra Bowdler, Steve Brown, Scott Cane, Richard Cosgrove, Albert Goede, Kevin Kiernan, Harry Lourandos, Robin Sim and Jim Stockton, a great deal more is now known about Tasmanian prehistory, although many questions still remain to be answered.

CAVE BAY CAVE

On Hunter Island, 6 kilometres off what is now the northwestern tip of Tasmania, an occupational sequence embracing the past 23 000 years[1] has been found in a large sea cave at Cave Bay. Signs of both Aboriginal and European visits were found when the site was visited by Bowdler in 1973 at the suggestion of local residents. On the dusty floor there were shells and animal bones, and on the walls numerous graffiti, the oldest of which read 'Walrus 1867'.

Excavation revealed that Pleistocene occupation of Cave Bay Cave began by 22 750 BP (figure 9.2). Over the next 2000 years, half a metre of deposit built up, characterised by layers of thick ash, a few bone points and stone tools, and the smashed and burnt bones of various land animals.

Both the stone and bone tools resemble tools from mainland Pleistocene sites, yet are also forerunners of later Tasmanian forms. One bone point, 9 centimetres long and made on a macropod shin bone, was associated with charcoal dated to 18 550 BP: the others were similar, but belonged to levels of between 4000 and 6600 years ago.

The remains in the lower layers of Cave Bay Cave are best interpreted as the debris of occasional inland hunting parties. The sea at this time would have been 30 to 40 kilometres away from the cave, which would have looked out over the vast Bassian Plain. The marsupial animals in the ice age levels of the cave are, in order of frequency, the brush wallaby, barred bandicoot, tiger cat, native cat, Tasmanian

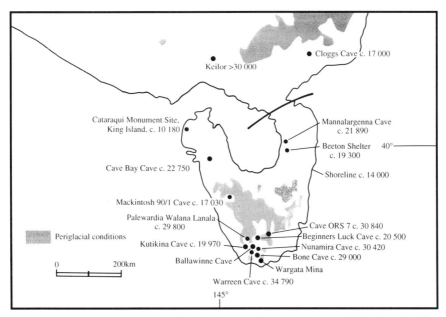

Figure 9.1 Ice age sites in Tasmania, showing the coastline at 14 000 BP, and the drowning of the land bridge at about 10 500 BP. (Based on Jones 1977; all dates are BP)

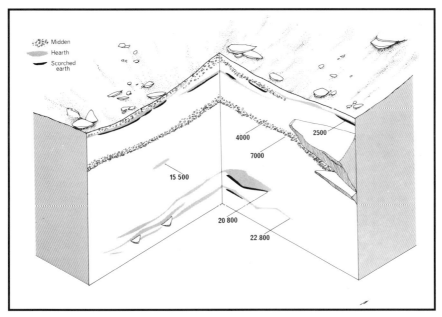

Figure 9.2 The stratigraphy of the Cave Bay Cave site, Hunter Island. The 7000 BP date for the bottom of the lower midden has now been corrected to 6600 BP. (After Bowdler 1977)

pademelon and wombat. None of these are extinct animals, but the wombat, native cat and bandicoot are not found in more recent sites and were absent from Hunter Island in historic times.

This early occupation was sporadic and fleeting, and it was followed by a phase of heavy rock-fall, which may represent the peak of the last glacial episode about 18 000 years ago. The extreme cold would have caused water to freeze in the rock cracks and crevices, and the expansion of the ice would have led to widening of the cracks and the fall of rock slabs.

From about 18 000 until 7000 years ago, when the sea reached its present level, the cave was effectively deserted. One small isolated hearth, dated to about 15 000 years ago, indicates that humans were still present then, but otherwise the main occupants of the cave were owls and carnivorous predators. Large quantities of tiny intact rodent bones are indicative of the regurgitated pellets of owls, and masses of macropod and possum bones chewed into small fragments suggest the presence of the Tasmanian devil.

Then, about 6600 years ago, when the sea was close to its present position and marine shellfish were easily obtainable, the cave again came into use. The remains in the cave suggest the new occupants had a well-developed coastal economy. The contents of this midden are similar to those from the lowest levels of Rocky Cape South, excavated by Rhys Jones and dated to around 8000 years old. At Cave Bay Cave, there was a dense shell midden — its base dated to about 6600 years ago — containing the bones of small macropods and mutton birds, the shells of rocky coast species and a few fish bones. Bone points were in layers older than 4000 years, and so were stone tools (such as quartz and quartzite flakes) and pebble tools.

Sandra Bowdler interprets this midden as representing the period when coastal people, possessing a well-developed fishing economy, had been pushed back by the rising seas to a 'Hunter Peninsula', just before the land link with Tasmania was finally severed. After this midden was deposited, the cave was not occupied for several thousand years, until Hunter Island was recolonised 2500 years ago by Tasmanian seafarers.

THE SOUTHWEST

Tasmania's southwest gave up a stone age secret on Sunday 11 January 1981, to archaeologists Rhys Jones and Don Ranson, who were carrying out a two-week survey for Aboriginal relics in the Gordon River Valley, threatened with flooding by a proposed hydroelectricity scheme.[2] The now uninhabited region is one of the world's last remaining temperate wildernesses and contains some of the densest rainforest in the world. This is some of the world's most inhospitable terrain.

When the first Europeans settled in Tasmania in the early 1880s, Aboriginal occupation was largely coastal, confined to a narrow coastal strip only a few hundred metres wide that was kept open by the use of fire. The people lived mainly off the resources of the sea, and travelled up and down the coast. One or two tracks through rainforest were also kept open by fire — for example, from Port Davey across to the south coast, a short cut across the southwest corner of Tasmania — but there was little or no occupation throughout the rest of the southwest wilderness.

As well as the notorious horizontal scrub, which is very difficult to walk through, the rivers of the southwest are extremely swift-flowing and hard to cross. They would have been a formidable obstacle to Aborigines, but provided a means for people of the twentieth-century to reach the heart of the wilderness. But only jet boats can make headway against the current, and they have to be carried around waterfalls and some rapids.

The first Aboriginal site to be discovered in the southwest rainforest was found on the bank of the Denison River 300 metres from its junction with the Gordon River (figure 9.3). In the words of Jones: 'I noticed that on a bank a great tree, a *Nothofagus*, had fallen down, taking some of the earth with it. We stopped in the little boat we were in, walked up the bank, and found stone tools. Afterwards we found more, *in situ*, buried in a clay deposit on the high river bank. This was the first evidence we have had of any prehistoric occupation of this region by man — a very interesting discovery.'[3]

When the giant *Nothofagus* beech tree had fallen, its roots had exposed a patch of clay as they were wrenched from the ground. There was found a quartz pebble core with flakes chipped from it scattered around. The flakes, which would have been

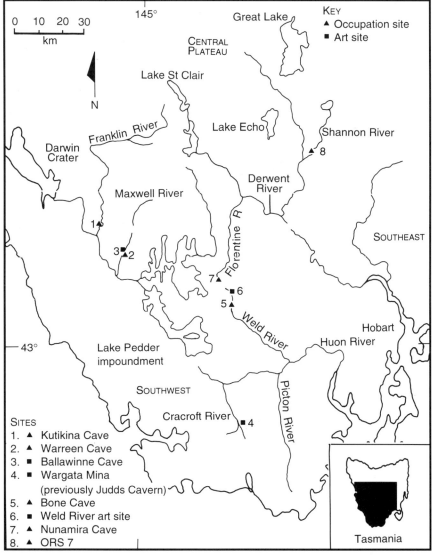

Figure 9.3 Southwest Tasmania. (Based on Cosgrove, Allen and Marshall 1990)

used as knives and scrapers, could be replaced exactly on the core, and were still as sharp as a surgeon's scalpel. Twelve tools were found, including a quartzite hammerstone. The camp site that these tools marked was originally thought to be very old, but a preliminary date on charcoal associated with the tools is 300 ± 150 BP. This means that the southwest must at least have been traversed by Aborigines in recent times.

The finding of these stone tools in dense rainforest was a million-to-one chance, but it was followed less than three weeks later by the discovery of rich Aboriginal cultural remains in a huge cave in the same primeval forest of southwest Tasmania.

KUTIKINA CAVE

The massive cave,[4] extending 170 metres into the cliff of limestone, is 35 metres back from the east bank of the Lower Franklin River and 10 kilometres from its confluence with the Gordon, at an elevation of about 40 metres above sea level. It was found in 1977 by a geomorphology student, Kevin Kiernan, and named Fraser Cave after the Prime Minister, because 'we were trying to direct the attention of politicians to the area' (colour plate 9, figure 9.4). Fraser Cave has now been given the Aboriginal name *Kutikina* (pronounced to rhyme with miner), meaning 'spirit'.

Stone flakes and animal bones were noticed on the cave floor, but the cave's discoverers did not realise their significance. Then, in February 1981, Kiernan revisited the cave on an expedition of the Tasmanian Wilderness Society and its archaeological potential was realised. Three weeks later he returned with Rhys Jones and officers of the National Parks and Wildlife Service (now the Department of Parks, Wildlife and Heritage) of Tasmania.

The cave has a floor area of about 100 square metres, covered with a 1- to 2-metre deep carpet of bone debris, tools and fireplaces. Some 250 000 animal bones and 37 000 stone flakes have been found in less than 1 cubic metre of deposit, giving an average density of 70 000 artefacts and 68 kilograms of bone per cubic metre. Jones suggested it was probably a base camp occupied by twenty to thirty people for a few weeks each year. They hunted the area for wallabies and other animals, bringing their game back to the cave to be butchered, cooked and eaten.

In places, a faint glimmer of daylight penetrates through openings in the high roof, and under each of these 'skylights' is a mass of tool manufacturing debris where an ice age craftsman sat and flaked his stone choppers and knives. A few bone points have also been found. The type of tools and sediments revealed by Jones's small test excavation of 1 cubic metre caused him to suggest a Pleistocene antiquity for occupation long before the radiocarbon dates were received. These have proved his predictions correct.

The floor of the cave was capped by a thin, white, hard layer of calcium carbonate, often called moon milk. Found immediately below this was a 30- to 40-centimetre thick occupation layer of interleaving hearths, where people had been camping. Charcoal, ash and burnt earth in shallow depressions from old fires made this a dark-coloured layer, fantastically rich in artefacts and charred animal bones. The top of this hearth layer has now been dated to 14 840 ± 930 BP.

Below the hearths was something quite different: small limestone blocks and angular fragments probably fallen from the roof. Such roof-fall would have occurred under very different climatic conditions from those of today. Stone tools and charcoal are present throughout this rubble layer and the clay below it, right down

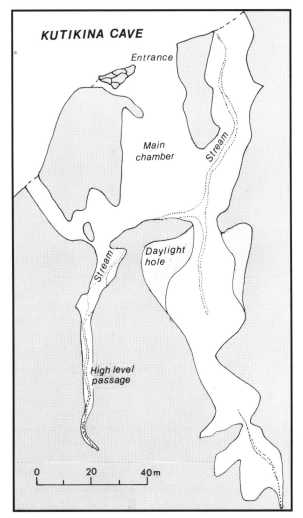

**Figure 9.4 Plan of Kutikina Cave, Franklin River.
(After R. Jones 1987)**

to bedrock. Dates from charcoal have shown that people first camped in this cave about 20 000 years ago.

The stone tools may be characterised as a regional variant of the Australian core tool and scraper tradition found in mainland Australia during the last ice age. This is typified by steep-sided, domed 'horsehoof' cores with a single striking platform and steep-edged, notched and flat scrapers. The rocks used were mainly quartzite and quartz. Most remarkably, cutting tools were made from natural glass, or Darwin glass, as it is called after the Darwin meteorite crater. Darwin glass is a true glass which was formed when a meteorite crashed into the earth. The high-energy collision melted the rocks around the collision point, forming glass. Small seams of these contorted glass 'impactites' occur around the meteorite crater, which is some 25 kilometres northwest of Kutikina Cave and was only discovered by geologists twenty years ago. The Aborigines, however, for thousands of years, selected the glass, collected it in bags, and carried it back to their cave for manufacture into sharp cutting tools.

Archaeological detective work by Loy, involving residue analysis with high-powered microscopes, has revealed some of the ways in which ice age hunters used these glass artefacts.[5] Examination of a tool's cutting edge, magnified 300 times, has revealed a residue of yellow fleshy tissue. This proved to be made up of two proteins, collagen, which is found in some bones and tissue, and haemoglobin, which gives blood its red colour. The haemoglobin was crystallised, and it was found to be from the blood of a red-necked wallaby, *Macropus rufogriseus* (also known as Bennett's wallaby). Haemoglobin crystals are like fingerprints; the shape and growth rate of the haemoglobin crystals of each animal species are unique. When the haemoglobin crystals from the tool were compared with those from a modern red-necked wallaby, they were found to be identical. This piece of Darwin glass was used as a sharp knife to cut up wallaby meat, but probably also had a multitude of uses, rather like a modern penknife.

In the lower layers between about 19 000 and 17 000 BP, 99 percent of the artefacts are quartzite, but around 17 000 BP there is a change in dominant raw material to 99 percent milky quartz. These were fashioned by the bipolar hammer and anvil technique, which is particularly associated with the manufacture of hard, intractable quartz. The greatest density of archaeological debris was in sediments deposited between 17 000 and 15 000 years ago, with more wallaby and wombat bone and the first appearance of both Darwin glass and other new tools.

Particularly surprising was the find of 160 tiny thumbnail scrapers, small round-edged scrapers roughly the size and shape of a thumbnail.[6] On average, they measure 20 by 15 millimetres, and 8 millimetres thick, but some are as small as 11 by 7 by 5 millimetres. Thumbnail scrapers are common in the Holocene small tool tradition of the mainland, but were virtually unknown in Pleistocene assemblages until these discoveries in southwest Tasmania. In spite of the superficial resemblance, detailed analysis may show significant differences between the Holocene and Pleistocene groups, and there is no evidence to suggest that the Pleistocene examples were ever hafted to a handle. The Kutikina thumbnail scrapers are all of quartz fashioned by bipolar working, but examples have now been found at other sites in chert, Darwin glass and other materials. The conclusions of functional analyses by Loy and Fullager of thumbnail scrapers from Kutikina and Nunamira Caves were that they were hand-held, for there were no signs of hafting or use-wear. The curved retouched steep edge represents backing to prevent injury to the user's hand, and residues were found on the unretouched sharp edge, which was the 'business end'.

A study was carried out by Loy and Jones comparing the residues on a sample of thumbnail scrapers from the upper assemblage with those on the working edges of the large flake scrapers of the lower industry. Jones summarised the as yet unpublished results as follows: 'Surprisingly, in both samples evidence for somewhat similar broad-range functions were found. Some 30–40% of tools from both samples had probably been used for cutting meat and other butchery functions; bone-working accounted for 20% of functions, whereas evidence for plant working of various kinds was found in about 15%. Evidence for woodworking was found on about 10% of tools in both assemblages.'[7] Jones, Loy and Fullager concluded that both the apparently specialised thumbnail scrapers and the rather amorphous flake-scrapers performed the same generalised range of functions, such as the butchering of carcasses and the working of bone, skin, wood and plant materials.

Bone points made from the shin bone (fibula) of wallabies were also found.[8] Only a few pieces of animal bone had been modified, but there were 250 000 pieces of animal bone in all, which tell us a great deal about the hunters' diet, environment and way of life. Bone is seldom preserved in archaeological sites, and even where it is, it is usually almost impossible to distinguish the prey of human hunters from bones of animals which died there of natural causes. But here the bones must be the result of human meals, for the long bones are smashed to extract the marrow, almost all the bones have been charred, and only certain body parts are present. Marrow was a very important source of essential fatty acids.[9]

These bone deposits give a unique picture of the hunting strategies of Pleistocene Tasmanians. Most (75 percent) of the bones belonged to red-necked wallabies, but wombats accounted for 12 percent, and the other 13 percent came from another fifteen species. Red-necked wallabies were then plentiful, but now occur in only very low numbers in rainforest-dominated southwest Tasmania, occupying open shrubland and sedgeland habitats, where they graze on grasslands and herbfields.

The surrounding country was completely different at the height of the last glaciation. Annual average temperatures were only about 4 degrees Celsius, that is 6 degrees Celsius below those of today, and precipitation was probably reduced by about half (to about 1500 millimetres per year). It was cold, windy and relatively dry, and icebergs would have sailed past the nearby coast. Glaciers flowed down the high mountain valleys to only about 800 metres above sea level, and the treeline was depressed by at least 230 metres. The only trees were bands of forest along the rivers in sheltered valleys. This provided red-necked wallabies with forest edges and open grassy plains similar to their modern habitat.

Like their contemporaries in the northern hemisphere, the ice age hunters of Tasmania made use of deep caves to survive the freezing temperatures. The remains found in Kutikina Cave have been compared by Jones to those from the caves of Dordogne in southern France. The stone tools are similar, the cooking methods are similar, even the hunting strategies are similar, although northern hunters concentrated on reindeer and the Tasmanians on wallabies.

ROCK ART

The presence of ochre pigment in the Kutikina Cave deposit raised the exciting possibility that these ice age Tasmanians were practising art. In January 1986, the first rock art was found in southwest Tasmania, in the Maxwell River valley which runs parallel and about 12 kilometres to the east of the Franklin, during the first archaeological survey of this rugged region (led by Ranson).[10] In all, six limestone caves which showed evidence of human occupation were discovered. One (M86/2), now called Warreen Cave, revealed a 2-metre deep cultural deposit, described below.

The most exciting find of this 1986 expedition came when Steve Brown and Roy Nichols were examining hundreds of metres of passageways and caverns beyond the daylight section of a nearby complex cave. Suddenly their torch beam lit up the outline of a human hand, stencilled in red ochre. Further examination revealed sixteen hand stencils in two groups, and a total of twenty-three have now been identified on two panels located between 15 and 25 metres inside the cave.[11] The stencils were made by grinding up iron oxide and mixing it with water and possibly animal fat into a red ochre paste, then placing the hand flat on the rock wall and spray painting it, probably by taking a mouthful of the paste and spitting it over the hand. At least five individuals were responsible for the art. Both left and right hands are equally represented. Some of the hand stencils are stunningly clear, standing out in a vivid red against the pale grey dolomite wall: others are quite indistinct. On one hand, it is evident that the middle finger is missing at the first joint; this could be due to either accidental or ritual mutilation.

In the same chamber there are small patches of red ochre on various parts of the ceiling. The chamber is in total darkness about 25 metres from the entrance, and would probably have been approached by the light of burning grass torches. Near the entrance to the passage which leads down to the hand stencil gallery, five rock protuberances are emblazoned with dramatic large streaks of blood-red ochre. These may have acted as some kind of warning marker to a special area of ritual significance. A total of sixteen ochre smears have now been identified on the cave's walls, ceilings and floors. Beyond the main entrance to the cave there is a small occupation deposit in a narrow chamber, sealed by a thin, hard, white calcareous layer, dated elsewhere to about 14 000 years old. Below this layer are tiny fragments of ochre associated with charcoal.

This find proves the ice age antiquity in Australia of hand stencils and, by implication, of rock painting. Hand stencils are associated with paintings in very many younger Australian rock art sites, but until this find neither stencils nor paintings had been found in indisputable ice age contexts in Australia, whereas in the Pleistocene cave art of Europe hand stencils often accompany paintings. This site proves once and for all that Tasmanian Aborigines practised painting in prehistoric times. Ironically, the island which has produced the first ice age stencils of Australia has a remarkable lack of more recent rock art sites, with less than twenty on record.

Figure 9.5 The hand stencil gallery in Ballawinne Cave, southwest Tasmania. (B. Prince, by courtesy of the Tasmanian Aboriginal Centre)

Significantly, the art of Ballawinne Cave (pronounced Bal-a-win-ee and meaning 'ochre'), as the Maxwell River site has now been named by Tasmanian Aborigines, is in complete darkness. This is extremely rare among Australian art sites, but more nearly parallels decorated caves of Europe such as Lascaux and Altamira. In prehistoric art, hand stencils are a worldwide motif, and this find shows that the first Tasmanians shared a common global cultural template in the marks they left behind on the walls of caves.

Once this first painted site had been found, the search was well and truly on, with archaeologists fantasising about discovering 'the frieze of the leaping wallabies'! Eighteen months later another decorated cave was found in southern Tasmania, 85 kilometres to the southeast of Ballawinne Cave. This discovery was announced by Aboriginal archaeological consultant Darrell West, geomorphologist Kevin Kiernan, and archaeologists Richard Cosgrove and Rhys Jones in the *Weekend Australian* of 17–18 October 1987.[12] The cave, Wargata Mina (pronounced War-gata Mee-na, meaning 'my blood', and formerly Judds Cavern), lies deep within the southern Tasmanian rainforests in the Cracroft Valley, bordering on the World Heritage Area of the southwest. Wargata Mina is one of the largest river caves in Australia, with passages, alcoves and caverns extending over 4.3 kilometres. One has to negotiate a way through age-old stalagmites to reach the painted alcove, some 35 metres from the entrance and at the very last glimmer of daylight penetration. The chamber is the size of a suburban house — dark, dank and bedecked with curtains of stalactites. Yet there on the wall are hand stencils, faint pale impressions of hands with red ochre sprayed around them (colour plate 11).

There are at least twenty-three stencils, very similar to those at Ballawinne Cave, and possibly dated to over 12 000 years ago. The stencils' age has been estimated through geomorphological evidence; the art is covered by a thick layer of calcium carbonate accretions, some of which extends continuously to a thick layer of flowstone on the floor and stalagmites more than a metre thick join ceiling *to* floor. Likewise, some stalactites have grown in front of the stencils, demonstrating that they post-date the art. The age of this calcium carbonate deposition has been dated in other southwest Tasmanian caves, using uranium thorium and other radiometric methods, to the humid phase at the end of the glacial period about 12 000 years ago.

Both adult and children's hands were stencilled, and there are also extensive expanses of red ochre painted or smeared onto the walls. Some of these patches are several metres across. Analysis by Loy of tiny samples of the 'pigment' from two painted panels has revealed traces of blood proteins and red blood cells from human blood.[13] These blood samples were dated using accelerator mass spectrometry to 10 730 ± 810 BP (RIDDL-1268) and 9240 ± 820 BP (RIDDL-1269). This seems to be the first time that blood has been biochemically identified as present in rock art anywhere in the world.

These cryptic signatures in blood and red ochre on the rock are a symbolic statement about identity, religion and land, reaching down across the centuries. Their similarity to early cave art in Europe and elsewhere bears witness to the evolution of humankind on a global scale and the cultural elements common in human behaviour.

EIGHT MORE EXCAVATIONS

Archaeological discoveries in Tasmania came thick and fast in the last decade. The impetus for further site survey and research came mainly from the battle for the Southern Forests between conservation interests and the forest industries, who were applying for renewal of licences for woodchip exports. The Australian National University's archaeological consultancy unit, ANUTECH, was commissioned to carry out an archaeological survey. In addition, the Southern Forests Archaeological Project was set up independently by Jim Allen and Richard Cosgrove from the Archaeology Department at La Trobe University, Melbourne.

Both these initiatives have borne great fruit. More than fifty Pleistocene sites have been found in southwest Tasmania, in an area of about 160 by 80 kilometres, or around 13 000 square kilometres. Caves have been excavated from the Franklin River in the west to the Weld River in the east, and in the north, further than Lake Mackintosh on the Pieman River. At least one Pleistocene open site has been found, the Flying Fox site on the Franklin River, dated to about 17 000 BP.[14] By 1993, more than 100 Pleistocene radiocarbon dates had been obtained on sites in the southwest. (A small selection are given for reference in the appendix.) The number of ice age art sites has risen to three and the known time of human occupation in Tasmania has been extended by more than 10 000 years.

Many of these discoveries have not yet been fully or even partially published, so the following is a summary, drawing on published articles, unpublished reports and theses such as Cosgrove's Ph.D. thesis, discussions with some of the researchers, and the oral papers presented by Jim Allen, Simon Holdaway, Brendan Marshall and Tom Richards at the Australian Archaeological Association conference in Darwin in December 1993.[15]

HUMAN REMAINS: NANWOON CAVE

The first human remains of apparent Pleistocene age have been found in Nanwoon Cave in the Upper Florentine Valley.[16] There had been previous research in the Florentine Valley by Albert Goede and Peter Murray, who had discovered Beginner's Luck Cave.[17] There it seemed that stone tools were associated with the bones of extinct fauna about 20 000 years ago, but it now appears that the megafauna dates from much earlier (about 40 000 years according to aspartic acid racemisation dates), and the artefacts and fauna are not contemporary. At Nanwoon Cave, on the other hand, there appears to be no evidence of extinct animals, but instead, numerous stone tools associated with charcoal and burnt and unburnt remains of modern animal species. On the floor of the cave part of a human skull — an occipital bone — was found. This is now in the custodianship of the Tasmanian Aboriginal Centre, but examination by physical anthropologist Steve Webb has been permitted. His conclusions are that the skull is that of a young adult, probably a woman in her late teens or early twenties. The remains are gracile in form, but unfortunately too fragmentary to compare with human skeletal remains from mainland Australia. Their age is also unknown, although circumstantial evidence makes it likely that they are probably more than 12 000 years old.

WARREEN CAVE

This large cave (M86/2, renamed Warreen, meaning 'wombat') lies on top of a limestone outcrop overlooking buttongrass and tea tree plains in the flat Maxwell River valley, east of Kutikina, at an altitude of 200 metres about sea level. It was discovered in 1986, and a preliminary test pit was dug. Further excavation by Allen in 1990 revealed the oldest occupation yet found in Tasmania, with a basal date of around 35 000 years.[18] Analysis is still in progress and full publication is awaited, but Allen and other members of the La Trobe University Research team have reported a rich assemblage of animal bones and artefacts, with a density of up to 35 000 artefacts in every 1 cubic metre. The numerous stone artefacts are still being studied by Tom Richards and others.

The beginning of occupation may even be older than the 34 790 ± 510 BP date for charcoal found at a depth of 1.7 metres, for the excavators dug to 2 metres but did not reach a sterile layer, although the quantity of cultural material was decreasing and appeared to be petering out. From 35 000 to 30 000 BP, human use was slight and sporadic. Occupation became intense between 24 000 and 22 000 BP. The earliest Darwin glass is in a 24 000 BP layer, and the earliest thumbnail scrapers (made of quartz) at 20 000 BP. The most abundant animal bones are red-necked wallaby bones, but minor prey species, such as wombat and platypus, are in greater numbers here than in Kutikina Cave. Almost all the stone artefacts are made of quartz, and 80 percent are less than 1 centimetre long, suggesting that they are waste chips from stone-working in the cave. Ochre occurs throughout the sequence, including some faceted lumps and ochre-stained limestone. More archaeological debris accumulated before the last glacial maximum than afterwards, and the site was abandoned about 16 000 years ago, when the collapse of part of the cave seems to have prevented its further use. Warreen is believed to have been originally a very large shelter, but roof collapse later reduced the interior floor area to about 15 square metres.

PALEWARDIA WALANA LANALA (ACHERON CAVE)

Approximately 9 kilometres north of Warreen Cave and 15 kilometres from Kutikina, a large limestone rock-shelter (previously ACH/84/1 = TASI-2448) faces almost due west in the small Acheron River valley at about 170 metres above sea level.[19] The floor area is about 40 square metres and the deposit is at least 140 centimetres deep. The findings regarding the long sequence excavated by Allen in 1991 have not yet been published, but it is understood to span the period from 30 000 to 13 000 BP, when the cave was abandoned.

BONE CAVE

Three highland sites with basal dates of around 30 000 years have been found further east on rivers flowing to the southeast: Bone Cave at 400 metres above sea level in the Middle Weld Valley; Nunamira Cave (previously Bluff Cave) at 400 metres, in the Florentine Valley; and Cave ORS 7 at 440 metres, on the edge of the Central Plateau in the Shannon River valley.[20]

Bone Cave is a very small, vertical limestone cave close to the Weld River. In-filling by sediments since it was first occupied has now reduced the floor area to about 9 square metres and 1 metre high. Charcoal from the base is dated to about 29 000 BP, and the uppermost cultural remains, to about 13 700 BP, after which the cave was abandoned and the deposit became sealed with a layer of moon milk. Bone points, stone artefacts and burnt bone are present in the small chamber, and Allen's 1988 excavation trench (2 metres long by 0.5 metres wide by 1.5 metres deep) revealed an extremely rich deposit, with more than 24 000 stone artefacts from 0.8 cubic metres of excavated sediment. Between 29 000 and 24 000 BP, human use seems to have been sporadic, and the most intensive human use of the cave occurred after the glacial maximum between about 16 000 and 14 000 BP. Thumbnail scrapers came in about 24 000 BP (see figure 9.6), but only one piece of Darwin glass was found, dated to 16 000 to 14 000 years ago. Bone Cave is at present the most distant site from the Darwin crater to contain the Darwin glass, and the straight-line distance of 100 kilometres between the crater and the cave may have been doubled if the most convenient route across the rugged terrain was taken.

Ian McNiven, in his analysis of the stone artefacts, has found locally available quartzite predominates as raw material, followed by chert and quartz, and very small quantities of chalcedony, silcrete and hornfels. The percentage of quartz used increases in the upper occupational levels (16 000 to 15 000 BP), accompanied by increased evidence of bipolar anvilling, the best method of fracturing the small

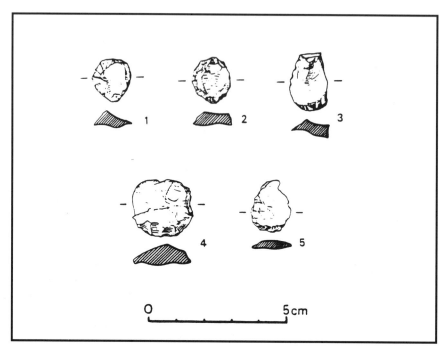

Figure 9.6 Artefacts from Bone Cave. Thumbnail scrapers made on struck flakes (with bulb of percussion present) of fine-grained chert, dated between about 13 700 and 15 300 BP. (After Allen, Cosgrove and Brown 1988)

water-rolled pebbles or crystals of hard quartz. Large flakes of quartzite or chert are common throughout the sequence, many of them being steep-edged scrapers.

The fauna is being studied by Brendan Marshall. In Bone and Nunamira caves, red-necked wallaby is preponderant throughout the sequence, with wombat as a common minor element, but there is a wider range of minor prey animals there than at Kutikina.

NUNAMIRA CAVE (BLUFF CAVE)

Nunamira Cave (meaning 'sleeping place') is a small limestone shelter now surrounded by wet sclerophyll scrub and rainforest in the flat, wide Florentine River valley, 25 kilometres north of Bone Cave.[21] It lies at 400 metres above sea level, below the Mount Field massif, which rises to 1400 metres. The shelter has a sharply sloping roof and a usable floor area of only about 15 square metres. The cultural deposit excavated by Cosgrove in 1987–88 is sealed by a layer of calcium carbonate flowstone. Although only 60 centimetres deep, the deposit spans almost 20 000 years, with a date of 11 630 ± 200 BP on charcoal only 5 centimetres below the surface and a basal date of 30 420 ± 690 BP. The site is extremely rich, with a small excavation of 1 cubic metre yielding high concentrations of charcoal, some 30 000 stone flakes and 200 000 pieces of bone. Animal remains include red-necked wallaby, pademelon, platypus, wombat, grey kangaroo, native hen and cat, bird bone and emu eggshell. The presence of emu eggshell is particularly important, as it indicates occupation in late winter to early spring, and the expansion of grassy habitats at the time. Emu eggshell is present at 28 000 BP and, in the richest bone deposit, between 16 000 and 13 000 BP. In both Nunamira and Bone Cave the ringtail possum, *Pseudocheirus peregrinus*, appears very late in the sequence, probably indicating an increase in trees in the region at the end of the glacial period, at Nunamira between approximately 12 000 and 10 000 years ago.

No bone tools but a wide variety of stone is used for tools, including chert, silcrete, crystal quartz, chalcedony, agate and hornfels. Large numbers of very small stone chips suggest on-site stone manufacturing of various local stone raw materials. Many of the finished tools are 'thumbnail scrapers', first found in layers dated between 24 000 and 21 400 BP. Five pieces of Darwin glass were also found, the lowest piece associated with a date of 27 770 BP. The Darwin meteorite crater is 75 kilometres to the west, and transport of this raw material would have necessitated a journey of over 100 kilometres along the main river valleys.

ROCK-SHELTER ORS 7

Further east at 440 metres above sea level, a large sandstone rock-shelter currently known as ORS 7 faces northeast in the deeply-cut Shannon River valley, in the catchment of the upper Derwent River.[22] An *in situ* hearth, only 60 centimetres below the surface but at the base of the occupational material, gave a date of 30 840 ± 480 BP, associated with 179 artefacts. Three cubic metres of deposit were excavated by Cosgrove in the same summer as Nunamira, and contained about 2000 artefacts, a rich site but not so rich as the caves to the west. In the lowest layer, artefacts are mainly unretouched flakes of quartzite and grey, fine-grained hornfels, together with some bones of red-necked wallaby (the major prey throughout the sequence), native cat and broad-toothed rat, and pieces of emu eggshell. Then, after 17 660 BP, there is a greater range in stone raw material used, but the site has a significantly lower artefactual density than other sites in southwest Tasmania. It was also occupied, or reoccupied, in the Holocene period, the youngest occupation dating to only about 2500 BP. There are other important differences between ORS 7 and all the other caves excavated so far in the southwest. In particular, it is the only site where no Darwin glass and no thumbnail scrapers have been found, and this is thought to be a real absence rather than the result of small sample size. Cosgrove has suggested that an eastern boundary to the transport of Darwin glass has been recorded at ORS 7.[23] It is the most southeasterly Pleistocene cave excavated to date, and lies in central rather than southwestern Tasmania.

MACKINTOSH 90/1 CAVE

In 1993 Nicola Stern and Brendan Marshall published an account of a limestone cave currently known as Mackintosh 90/1 in western Tasmania.[24] This is located in a bluff 320 metres above sea level. The cave faces east and has a floor area of some 12 square metres. The cultural sequence here is of particular significance because human occupation is confined to a 2000-year time span (represented by a 50-centimetre deep band of cultural material) immediately following the last glacial maximum, thus acting as a window into the period between 17 000 and 15 000 BP. The artefacts are mainly of quartz and resemble those in other caves of southwest Tasmania. They included thumbnail scrapers and pieces of Darwin glass; indeed, some of the thumbnail scrapers are made of Darwin glass. The Darwin crater lies about 70 kilometres to the south. Hunters seem to have targeted the red-necked wallaby and wombats almost entirely. The site does not appear to have been abruptly abandoned, but the increasing predominance of the scats (animal droppings) of marsupial carnivores, mainly the tiger cat (*Dasyurus maculatus*), suggests gradually decreasing levels of human activity.

PARMERPAR MEETHANER CAVE

An important new Tasmanian site is Parmerpar Meethaner at 350 metres in the Central Highlands, a limestone cave in the north-flowing Forth River Valley, east of Mackintosh 80/1 and Cradle Mountain and northwest of Warragarra Shelter. At Warragarra (location in figure 13.1) occupation is very sparse between 10 000 and 3000 BP, when site usage increases. Cosgrove's excavation of Parmerpar Meethaner (funded by the Tasmanian Forest Research Council) has revealed a continuous sequence from about 34 000 to 780 BP. Between 18 000 and 10 000 BP, there are thumbnail scrapers but no wallaby bones. Between 10 000 and 3000 BP, there is low density occupation, but at about 3000 BP artefact numbers increase as at Warragarra. Significantly, Parmerpar Meethaner, which lies outside the southwest, is the only known Tasmanian site with undisturbed deposit that continued to be occupied throughout the late Pleistocene to Holocene.[25]

STONE TECHNOLOGY

Analysis of the excavated assemblages is still at an early stage, but a few preliminary features are beginning to emerge. In their overview published in the journal *Antiquity* in 1990, Cosgrove, Allen and Marshall focus on 'some of the inter-assemblage similarities and differences which combine sites into a Southwestern Tasmanian Pleistocene province but which also indicate distinctions between them. While this discussion moves us towards the notion of a Southwestern stone industry, perhaps as a regional variant of the Australian core tool and scraper tradition, the distinctiveness of the faunal exploitation pattern seen in these sites is matched by the distinctiveness of the stone assemblages.'[26]

Important features are the presence of tools such as steep-edged flat and notched scrapers characteristic of the Australian core tool and scraper tradition, as originally defined at Mungo, among the 'largely amorphous stone industries in these sites'. The raw materials used reflect available local sources, quartz predominating in the western sites but being rare in the east. Elements which distinguish these southwestern assemblages from the wider core tool and scraper tradition are their richness and the presence of thumbnail scrapers, common in mainland Holocene sites but very rare in other Pleistocene ones.

Thumbnail scrapers were evidently used for butchering carcasses and for working skin, bone, wood and plant material. They are made of various materials, including Darwin glass. They have been found in small numbers in all the excavated sequences of southwest Tasmania, except in the most southeasterly site, ORS 7. Most thumbnail scrapers occur after the glacial maximum (about 18 000 BP), but they were also used before it, at least as early as 24 000 BP.

Darwin glass was in use for at least 12 000 years in the southwest. Its earliest occurrence recorded so far is 27 770 BP at Nunamira. Use seems to have increased in some sites during and immediately after the glacial maximum, perhaps because of easier access to the Darwin crater in the treeless conditions. The glass was transported 75 kilometres to Nunamira and 100 kilometres to Bone Cave, as the crow flies, so actual routes traversed might have doubled these distances. Like thumbnail scrapers, Darwin glass was absent from ORS 7. The latter is only about 10 kilometres further from the Darwin crater than Bone Cave, and much the same route would probably have been used, the line of least resistance being across the deeply dissected country followed by the modern Lyell Highway. The absence of Darwin glass from ORS 7 is therefore probably a significant cultural difference rather than simply being as a result of its location, particularly in conjunction with the other differences between it and the western sites. Not only does it lack thumbnail scrapers, but there is a distinctly lower density of artefactual remains and significant distinctions in technology, raw materials, faunal quantities and processing strategies.

The excavator of ORS 7, Cosgrove, concluded that, 'In short, site ORS 7 reflects a distinctly different archaeological signature from the Southwestern Pleistocene sites and supports the idea that the eastern border of the Southwestern geographic zone also marked a human behavioural boundary in the late Pleistocene'.[27]

BONE ARTEFACTS

Bone points have been found in small numbers in several mainland sites, such as Cloggs Cave and Devil's Lair, as well as in Cave Bay Cave and in most of the caves of the southwest. It has been suggested that these ice age bone points were used as awls or reamers for making fur cloaks. In historic times in the cold parts of southeastern Australia, similar bone points were observed in use by Aborigines for piercing holes to sew skins together with sinew thread. A recent study by Cathy Webb of bone tools from Pleistocene caves in the southwest (Warreen and Bone Cave) indicates their functions in skin-processing, and as cloak toggles, marrow extractors and possibly spear points.[28] These ice age hunters doubtless used the skins of wallabies and other animals they killed as clothing, and Webb identified use-wear caused by scraping the inner surface of skins and piercing dry skins. More surprising was the evident use of bone points (Webb's 'fine points' category with acute-angled tips) to spear furred mammals, implying that they were bone spear points hafted to a shaft. The case rests on the type of tip damage and use-wear, including possible hafting marks on the bases of two fine points, and the recovery of both tips and shafts, 'consistent with damaged spears being repaired at these sites and with tips being returned to them inside game carcases'. If this interpretation is correct, and Webb has made a strong case, this is the only type of hafted tool known in Pleistocene or Holocene Tasmania.

FOOD

The major animal exploited by the Pleistocene hunters in southwest Tasmania was the red-necked wallaby, which usually accounts for over 90 percent of identifiable pieces of bone. (The following account is based on Cosgrove, Allen and Marshall's research into palaeo-ecology, published in the journal *Antiquity* in 1990.) In spite of significant changes in the quantity of bone in some deposits, there seem to be few changes over time in the relative importance of the red-necked wallaby. This concentrated and repeated exploitation of one animal species is a remarkable feature of all the Pleistocene caves excavated in the southwest. After the red-necked wallaby, the wombat is the next most abundant human prey, followed by a few medium-sized animals, such as the native cat and the platypus.

In most of the caves, the majority of vertebrate faunal bones in all but the very earliest and latest periods of occupation seem to be 'cultural', that is, the result of human subsistence activity, from which prey of other creatures, such as owls or marsupial carnivores, can readily be distinguished.[29] At Warreen bone from owl pellets is common in the lowest layer but decreases as human habitation increases. At other sites, such as Bone, Mackintosh and Nunamira, accumulations of 'natural' bone become common in the upper layers as human occupation becomes less intensive and eventually ceases.

A striking aspect of the faunal remains is the quantity of smashed bones.[30] The marrow-bearing long bones of the limbs of red-necked wallabies have been systematically and consistently broken. They were cracked open at both ends to extract the marrow, whilst the foot bones (metatarsals) were split longitudinally. Impact marks on the margins and crests of long bones such as tibias are associated with this process, and on some there are cut marks adjacent to muscle attachments, indicating the long bones were de-fleshed during processing. The first processing of these animals evidently took place away from the caves, for not all body parts are equally represented in the deposits.

Bone marrow contains essential fatty acids, which are needed for the metabolism of protein. Wallaby meat is lean, with limited fat deposits in the kidneys, marrow, back and tail, but the males put on condition towards the end of winter, in readiness for the mating season, and even during the period of winter stress, wallaby populations living in higher rainfall areas on more fertile land stay in relatively good physical condition.

There were probably several reasons for this tight targeting of red-necked wallabies. First, although adult wallabies average only 15 kilograms in weight, they are much easier to catch than larger species, such as the grey kangaroo or the emu, because of their relatively slow pace, large groups and sedentary habits. Their average home range is only 15 to 20 hectares and they remain focused on a particular area for two to three years, shifting their centre of activity less than 30 metres, in contrast to the much larger mainland grey and red kangaroos, which have a range of about 10 square kilometres and change their centre of activity by about 1 kilometre. Secondly, they were available all year round, probably in relative abundance on grassland patches. Living red-necked wallabies have a wide altitudinal range and graze primarily in grassy woodlands. They are no longer common in the southwest, occurring only in very low numbers on open shrubland and sedgeland, but are still numerous in the Florentine and Shannon valleys, where the fertile soils support some grasslands and herbfields, on which they feed. Grasses and herbs need fertile soils and reliable drainage, and tend to grow during cold phases in a mosaic of patches on alluvial river flats or on limestone areas, which often contain caves or rock-shelters. There was therefore a happy juxtaposition for hunters of habitable caves and wallaby feeding grounds.

Red-necked wallabies would have acted as a reliable, sedentary food source of particular value at the most stressful time of the year, from late winter to early spring. In this sense, they represent a glacial mid-latitude food staple, equivalent to the plant foods of other regions. At that time of year, Pleistocene highland hunters may have had to exist largely on red-necked wallaby and the occasional emu egg. Possums, which were a staple in the Australian Alps in the Holocene, are strikingly absent from all but the youngest occupation layers in the Pleistocene caves of southwest Tasmania. This means that the environment lacked large trees, and palynological studies by Macphail, Colhoun and others have confirmed a marked increase in grass and herb pollen between 22 000 and 18 000 BP. Trees and shrubs gradually became more important after 14 000 BP, and temperate rainforest finally came to dominate the southwest after 11 000 BP, when the climate had become warm and moist. Even if Aborigines tried to keep the area open by burning, fire-sticks would have been ineffective in the face of such a major, climatically induced vegetation change.

ABANDONMENT

The reasons for the wallaby hunters abandoning the caves of the south west are still a matter of debate. Allen and Jones see the change as a 'climate-driven' response to the changing environment, and draw attention to the early abandonment of Kutikina Cave (some 14 000 years ago), by far the lowest of these cave sites at only 40 metres above sea level, and therefore the first to be affected by the encroaching rainforest. Ian Thomas has put forward a counter-argument that 'it is just as likely that more humid conditions at that time simply made cave dwelling an uncomfortable option'.[31] However, anyone who has walked in southwest Tasmania or rafted down the Franklin River, as I have, will know both that rainforest renders the region almost impenetrable on foot and that for those who do penetrate the wet and horizontal shrub, caves provide a welcome haven to shelter from the frequent rain and to sleep on relatively dry, soft ground.

Caves such as Parmerpar Meethaner in the north of the island continued in use from the Pleistocene to Holocene, as did Beeton Shelter and Mannalargenna Cave in the Furneaux Group of islands (described in chapter 13). Other sites, such as Warragarra Shelter in the northwest, were first occupied in post-glacial times. Warragarra also lies within rainforest and both archaeological and ethnographic evidence shows that the southwest was at least occasionally visited during the Holocene, especially the less rugged, more accessible and open areas like the King River valley, but occupation was only slight.

The dramatic change in the southwest was the complete abandonment of the previous intensive occupation of limestone caves by the wallaby hunters. A reliable food supply is the most important factor in human location; when this was no longer available, the hunters moved elsewhere. In the Holocene the southwestern highlands became a region of little food and dense, often impassable rainforest. Small wonder that the focus of Aboriginal occupation moved to food-rich regions elsewhere.

OVERVIEW

Tasmania is further south than any other place in the southern hemisphere inhabited during the ice age. Not only were there glaciers on its mountains, but icebergs would have come floating past the coast from the great Antarctic ice sheet only 1000 kilometres to the south. Into this freezing toe on the foot of the world moved the Aborigines, virtually as soon as the land bridge was exposed by the drop in sea level, perhaps impelled into empty space by an urge to explore. The land bridge is thought to have become available from about 37 000 to 29 000 BP, and then again right through the glacial maximum until it was finally inundated in about 10 500 BP.[32] The earliest occupation found so far (at Warreen Cave) goes back slightly beyond 35 000 BP, and at least four sites have occupation going back 30 000 years or more (Nunamira, ORS 7, Palewardia Walana Lanala and Bone Cave). There is a repeated pattern of low use of caves at the start of occupation and changes in the archaeological record, particularly over the period of glacial maximum. Interesting common features throughout the Pleistocene occupation are the repeated exploitation of one particular species, the red-necked wallaby, and the constant extraction of marrow from its bones.

Some general patterns are beginning to emerge, although fieldwork is continuing and much of the detailed analysis still remains to be done. Excavations limited to small test pits have already revealed a picture that necessitates a complete revision of earlier theories about the nature of Pleistocene society in Australia.

Pleistocene Aboriginal populations in Australia had previously been characterised, on the basis of the meagre remains at the few known sites, as low in numbers and highly nomadic. Bowdler in particular has argued that the economy of the first Australians was based on an aquatic environment of coasts, rivers and lakes, and that they were unable to exploit the highlands of the mainland and Tasmania until after about 14 000 BP, because these were marginal environments, 'cold, rugged, inaccessible and relatively poor in resources'.[33]

Human presence in the upland periglacial regions of south central Tasmania from 35 000 BP has shown that Bowdler has seriously underestimated the abilities of Pleistocene Tasmanians, who developed a successful way of life in an alpine environment and a specialised and complex economic, social and cultural system. At the glacial maximum at about 18 000 BP, annual average temperatures were about 6 degrees Celsius lower than today, glaciers extended down to only 800 metres above sea level and the treeline was depressed by at least 230 metres. Allen has equated the glacial Tasmanian climate with alpine areas above 1750 metres in the Victorian Alps today, such as Mount Hotham at 1862 metres, although probably with much shorter summers.

This was not a struggle for survival in harsh highlands but a deliberate choosing of a food-rich environment. Deep limestone caves provided shelter from wind chill and icy cold, aiding the effective exploitation of a particular sedentary and readily available prey. Conditions before and during the height of the last glaciation were periglacial or sub-Antarctic, but the dearth of trees made the river valleys far easier to traverse than when they became choked with rainforest at the end of the Pleistocene, in spite of their steep slopes and rugged topography.

The presence of emu eggshell in some of the cave deposits indicates habitation during late winter to early spring, and it is possible that the hunters used the caves primarily to ward off the winter cold. In other words, caves may have been winter base camps rather than summer hunting camps as Jones originally speculated, envisaging hunting forays from what is now Victoria. It is also possible but unlikely that the caves were used all the year round, and that the hunters were almost as sedentary as their main prey. The huge quantities of camping debris in some sites might support this suggestion, although they may equally well reflect intensive but seasonal use over a long period. For a healthy diet, their high-protein intake of wallaby meat would have needed to be balanced by other food, particularly carbohydrate from plants. It is very likely, but as yet unproven, that the tubers of the daisy yam (*Microseris scapigera*), which exists in present-day Tasmania, were used here as in the Australian Alps, as a summer vegetable food.

The hunters' prey was a small range of terrestrial faunal species, which still survive in modern Tasmania. No extinct species of megafauna have been found in the caves, but few conclusions can be drawn from its absence, since kills of very large animals are far more likely to be consumed away from the base camp. Only one definite kill site has yet been found in the whole of Australia, and that is an open site (described in chapter 12). Thus, absence of megafauna from cave sites does not necessarily mean either that the megafauna were already extinct or that they were not exploited by human hunters.

The economy of these ice age hunters in southwestern Tasmania is more highly structured than anywhere else in Australia. Cosgrove, Allen and Marshall see it as bearing little resemblance to either the Holocene economies of Tasmania or other Pleistocene economies on the mainland. In their model, 'humans moved between discrete grassland patches to hunt "ecologically tethered" animal resources. The implications of this strategy are far-reaching, suggesting for example that culling practices were employed 30,000 years ago which allowed wallaby populations to maintain themselves under the ecological constraints of changing environments and human predation for nearly 20 millennia. Such ideas challenge notions of Pleistocene [foragers'] behaviour.'[34]

The Pleistocene sites of southwest Tasmania show a higher degree of archaeological richness, complexity and variability than any other known Australian Pleistocene sites. The presence of apparently hafted bone points for spearing animals and of thumbnail scrapers distinguishes these from all other Australian Pleistocene industries. Transportation of Darwin glass more than 100 kilometres from its source implies either long-distance resource exploitation, or exchange or trading networks. At the same time, differences between the western and eastern suites of Pleistocene sites in southern Tasmania indicate local adjustments to differing local environments and resources. There are also changes in technology and economy over time; for instance, neither Darwin glass nor thumbnail scrapers are found in the lowest layers of any of the deposits, and there is possibly an increase in mobility and a change in land-use patterns during and after the glacial maximum.

Cosgrove has argued that 'the new Tasmanian data challenge the linear evolutionary view of "simple" to "complex" social structures'.[35] The intensities of site use and comparative densities of material suggesting increased usage of sites are higher by several orders of magnitude than many of the Holocene sites used by Lourandos and others to support the concept of 'intensification' and the mid-Holocene transformation from simple to complex Aboriginal society. The high number of Tasmanian Pleistocene sites in marginal climatic zones and their specialised economy, technology and culture, including pigmented art suggestive of religious activity deep within caves, demonstrate the existence of complex societies with their own distinctive archaeological signatures long before the changes of the mid-Holocene.

Allen and Cosgrove emphasise both the wide variability found within Pleistocene Tasmanian assemblages and the cultural differences between the assemblages of the two different environmental zones in southern Tasmania: the fold-structured topography now vegetated by temperate rainforest in the west and the fault-structured geology dominated by dry sclerophyll forest to the east. These environmental contrasts are mirrored in different archaeological signatures, and do not conform to the earlier widespread concept of a pan-Australian Pleistocene culture and technology, which was relatively uniform, simple and unchanging. The subsistence system revealed by the good faunal assemblages and environmental records of southwest Tasmania are considered to be 'different in character from those modelled on a European Pleistocene prototype'.[36]

In contrast, Jones sees a relatively low level of variability in Pleistocene human behaviour Australia-wide. He believes that the closest parallels for the Tasmanian ice age caves are the remains left in the caves of southern Europe by hunters of the same epoch. In spite of criticisms of such comparisons, in 1992 he wrote unrepentingly: 'At 14,000 years ago, the way of life of these palaeo-Tasmanians, in terms of subsistence, technology and social scale, must have been similar to those of their contemporaries in western Europe'.[37]

Whilst some archaeologists emphasis similarities and others differences between past societies, all agree that there are no ethnographic parallels for Tasmanian Pleistocene culture, even in Holocene Tasmania. It is a system that has been extinct for over 10 000 years. The greatest density of sites in southwest Tasmania occurred at the height of the last glacial period, and this rich Pleistocene culture is a unique human exploitation of the glacier-edge conditions of a southern ice age.

When the glaciers disappeared and their hunting grounds were replaced by rainforest, these remarkable hunters of southwest Tasmania left their caves only to find that the melting ice caps had drowned their link to the mainland. Their society, which had thrived in the highlands for 20 000 years, was now to face 10 000 years of complete isolation from the rest of the world, after their peninsular home became an island, separated from the mainland by the 250-kilometre wide, storm-racked Bass Strait. The culture, art, religion and specialised economic strategies developed by these hunters living within sight of glaciers at the height of the last glaciation are eloquent testimony to the indomitable spirit of these early humans. The ice age sites of Tasmania are of immeasurable significance both to all humankind, as part of the world's heritage, and to the several thousand people of Aboriginal descent in Tasmania.

CHAPTER TEN

Karta:
Island of the Dead

Alarge offshore island without human inhabitants, called 'island of the dead' by mainland Aborigines, separated from the Australian continent for almost 10 000 years, yet with abundant evidence of a prehistoric population. These are all the ingredients of a classic mystery story, which scholars have been trying to solve since 1802.

Kangaroo Island, about 150 kilometres long and 50 kilometres wide, lies 14.5 kilometres from the coast of South Australia, across Backstairs Passage. This strait is bedevilled by strong currents, heavy tidal swells and steep breaking seas that make crossings in canoes or small boats a hazardous undertaking. The island's first European visitors were Captain Flinders in HMS *Investigator* in March 1802, and Nicolas Baudin, who followed in the same year. Both immediately noticed the lack of fires on Kangaroo Island in contrast to the adjacent mainland, where skies were constantly smoke-filled from Aborigines burning off the vegetation. When Flinders landed, he found no humans, only extraordinarily tame kangaroos and seals.

Kangaroo Island was settled later in 1802 by European sealers, who took with them Aboriginal women abducted from Tasmania and the adjacent mainland. Official settlement followed in 1836, and much of the land was cleared for agriculture. It was not, however, until a century after the first Europeans set foot on the island that evidence of prehistoric human inhabitants was discovered. In 1903, geologist Walter Howchin found some hammer-stones at Hawk's Nest near Murray's Lagoon towards the centre of the island. In 1930, more stone tools were discovered, and Norman Tindale was invited to investigate.

It was Tindale and his associate Harold Cooper who first seriously suggested that human occupation of Australia went back into the Pleistocene. They based this opinion largely on evidence from Kangaroo Island. Tindale's field work in the early 1930s around the freshwater, land-locked Murray's Lagoon produced hammer-stones and some massive trimmed pebble implements.[1] Further work by Harold Cooper between 1934 and 1939 disclosed the existence of forty-seven camp sites throughout the island. By 1958, the number had risen to 120 sites. Cooper collected some 1400 pebble choppers and horsehoof cores, and more than 150 hammer-stones.

The large tool industry represented by these pieces was termed the 'Kartan' by Tindale, after 'Karta', the name given to the island by the mainland Ramindjeri tribe. It is characterised by the massiveness of its core tools (colour plate 6). The dominant implements are hammer-stones and pebble choppers. The latter are made by hammer-flaking one side of a large quartzite pebble, usually oval in shape, and then trimming the margin to produce a sharp edge. Many are finely made and perfectly symmetrical, suggesting that their manufacturers were superb craftspeople with a strong aesthetic sense. Large, heavy, horsehoof-shaped cores are also characteristic of this Kangaroo Island industry, but they are less numerous than the pebble choppers.

The Kartan tools were generally found in fields where ploughing had brought them to the surface from about 30 centimetres below present ground level. Others lay in the higher ridges around Murray's Lagoon, on a shoreline 5 metres above the present one, suggesting that the Kartan camp sites belong to a period when the lake was fuller than at present. Other tools were found in what is now almost impenetrable scrub country, but it seems likely that in earlier times the vegetation was sparser because of the effects of glacial climate combined with the Aboriginal use of fire.

Most of the Kartan tools are made of quartzite, which must have been carried a considerable distance to these inland camp sites. The nearest source of quartzite for the tools found at Hawk's Nest is at least 35 kilometres away on the north coast of the island. This factor could account for the lack of manufacturing debris and the few flakes in the Kartan industry.

How the former islanders, with their Kartan stone tools, first reached Kangaroo Island provided an intriguing problem for Tindale and Cooper. They both reached the conclusion that occupation must have taken place at a time of low sea level when Kangaroo Island was still joined to the mainland. This guess, for it was long before the advent of radiocarbon dating, was based on several different strands of circumstantial evidence. Firstly, there was the massive size and archaic appearance of the Kartan tools, unlike anything found off the mainland in more recent sites such as Devon Downs.[2] Moreover, their location suggested that the occupation had a considerable antiquity and derived from a time when the island's climate and environment were rather different from the present. And, if the people did not walk to Kangaroo Island, how did they get there? Backstairs Passage is notoriously rough, and at the time of European settlement none of the neighbouring mainland Aboriginal tribes had any watercraft capable of getting across it. Indeed, only frail bark canoes and rafts of reeds were used, both propelled solely by means of poles.

The absence of the dingo from Kangaroo Island and of the specialised small tools found in younger mainland sites supported the idea that the island was occupied during the Pleistocene, before the dingo was brought to Australia, and that subsequently it was cut off by the rising sea and isolated from later developments on the mainland. The development in the local fauna and flora of many subspecies also favours a considerable period of isolation.

Finally, there was an interesting myth about Kangaroo Island, widespread among Aborigines of South Australia, according to which the island is the home of the spirits of departed ancestors:

> *Ngurunderi was a great Ancestral figure of the southern tribes in South Australia, who established Tribal Laws. After death, the spirits of men follow his ancient travel paths to the island of Nar-oong-owie [Kangaroo Island] and thence to Ngurunderi's home in the sky.*
>
> *Long ago, Ngurunderi's two wives ran away from him, and he was forced to follow them. He pursued them and as he did so he crossed Lake Albert and went along the beach to Cape Jervis. When he arrived there he saw his wives wading half-way across the shallow channel which divided Nar-oong-owie from the mainland.*
>
> *He was determined to punish his wives, and angrily ordered the water to rise up and drown them. With a terrific rush the waters roared and the women were carried back towards the mainland. Although they tried frantically to swim against the tidal wave they were powerless to do so and were drowned. Their bodies turned to stone and are seen as two rocks off the coast of Cape Jervis, called the The Pages or the Two Sisters.*

Ngurunderi dived into the water and swam out towards the island. As it was a hot day he wanted shade so he made a she-oak tree which is said to be the largest in Australia. He lay down in the shade and tried to sleep but could not for as every breeze blew he heard the wailing of his drowning wives. Finding he could get no rest, he walked to the end of the island and threw his spear out into the sea. Immediately a reef of rocks appeared. He then threw away all his other weapons and departed to his home in the skies, where those who have kept the Laws he gave the tribes will some day join him.

To this day anyone who tries to sleep under a she-oak tree will hear the wailing that Ngurunderi heard beneath the giant tree on Kangaroo Island, the sacred island of the spirits of the dead.[3]

This story seems to be based on fact. Aboriginal oral history provides us with many accounts of the great climatic and geological changes that have taken place on the continent. There is a fascinating myth of the time when the earth blew up, which seems almost certainly to describe the volcanic eruption of Mount Wilson in the Blue Mountains near Sydney. Since erupting volcanoes have not been seen in the Sydney region for several thousand years, this testifies to the incredibly long persistence of oral tradition. And on the Atherton Tableland in Queensland, stories about volcanic eruptions seem to have lasted more than 10 000 years.[4] If memory of volcanoes can persist over thousands of years, there is no reason why traditions of rising seas drowning the land should not also persist. It has been estimated that Kangaroo Island was separated from the mainland about 10 000 years ago, but the drowning process continued until the sea stabilised at its present height between 5000 and 7000 years ago.

Ron Lampert, in an attempt to solve the riddle of stone tools on an island isolated for 10 000 years, surveyed the whole island in search of stratified occupation deposits that might establish the antiquity of the Kartan industry.[5] Only one cave was found that appeared promising: this was a small limestone cave beside a freshwater lagoon, 8 kilometres from the south coast. This was named the Seton site after the local landowner.[6]

Excavation in 1971 and 1973 revealed an occupation deposit 1.5 metres deep, resting on bedrock. Dating of the deposit indicated that people first visited the cave about 16 000 years ago when the site would have been some 40 kilometres from the coast. They manufactured small scrapers from flint, and their diet possibly included the now extinct giant kangaroo, *Sthenurus*, bones of which were found in association with the earliest tools. Thereafter, the hunting site was visited infrequently, until about 11 000 years ago, when a period of intensive occupation began. Small flint scrapers were manufactured at the site, quartz was flaked and some quartz flakes were retouched for use as scrapers. Two small bone points were found in the 11 000-year-old level. These were made from kangaroo shin bones, and the dull polish on their tips suggests they were used for skin-working. The Kangaroo Islanders' subsistence economy was broadly based; a wide variety of inland fauna were hunted, among which the modern grey kangaroo was of particular importance. Because of the rising sea level, Seton was by then within easy reach of the seashore and some marine shellfish formed part of the diet.

Then, abruptly, visits ceased. This abandonment of the Seton cave coincides with the time of final separation of the island from the mainland. The islanders' impending isolation would have become clear from daily and seasonal tidal fluctuations, which would gradually have produced breaks of longer and longer duration between the island and mainland.

Originally Lampert thought that Kangaroo Island was then consciously abandoned, but later he found several small sites belonging to the post-separation period. Some are coastal sites that contain small shell middens associated with flakes; shells from one of these middens gave an age of 6000 years. Other sites are inland, stratified open camp sites with small flakes and scrapers, for example Rowell's site and the Sand Quarry site, dated respectively to about 5200 and 4300 years ago.

This younger occupation is extremely sparse compared both with the earlier Kartan sites and with the very numerous Holocene shell middens of the adjacent coast of South Australia. There are two possible explanations for the presence of sites on Kangaroo Island post-dating isolation from the mainland. Either a relict population survived on the island for several thousand years before becoming extinct, or the island was reoccupied occasionally from the mainland by Aborigines with watercraft. From considering varied evidences — palaeoenvironmental, archaeological and ethnographic — the case of a relict population is favoured. The demise of such a community before European contact might be explained largely by the steady deterioration of Kangaroo Island as a human habitat during the Holocene, though demographic imbalances and short-term disasters could also have played a role.[7]

The case for a relict population, which eventually died out, is mainly based on the evidence that watercraft suitable for the crossing were not available in historic times, and that the island's stone tools show no sign of outside influence — despite significant changes and new tool types on the adjacent mainland. The extinction of the Kangaroo Island population was probably due to a variety of causes. The island could only have supported a few hundred people after separation, and such a small population is always at risk from naturally occurring imbalances in sex and age ratios, and natural disasters. There is also evidence that there was a gradual deterioration in the island's environment, which became increasingly arid between about 5000 and 2000 years ago. Analysis of pollen from a core from Lashmar's Lagoon shows a change in vegetation towards drier shrubs, and there are strong signs that regular burning of the vegetation by Aborigines ceased after 2500 years ago. Burning of the bush was such a common practice in Aboriginal Australia that cessation of burning in all likelihood indicates that the last Kangaroo Islander had either left or died. Indeed, it was the absence of smoke from burning off which made Flinders assume the island was uninhabited even before he landed.

The discovery of traces of a relict population stranded by the rising sea was not the only surprise produced by Lampert's research. In his search for the Kartan culture, he also found a non-Kartan industry on Kangaroo Island. This is exemplified at the Seton site. Others have suggested that the Seton industry of small flint scrapers might be the flake component of a Kartan industry, but Lampert has convincingly argued that Seton is not Kartan but post-Kartan, because among its 5000 pieces of flaked stone there was not one core tool and only a single piece of quartzite, the material out of which the heavy Kartan tools are made. Moreover, there is an enormous difference in implement size between the two industries: the average weight of a Seton tool was 9 grams, whereas that of a tool from a typical Kartan assemblage was 900 grams. The assemblages are too different to represent merely diverse aspects of the same culture caused by seasonal or environmental differences. Indeed, not only are they not contemporary, but there is also little or no continuity between the two cultures.

It may be that the Kartan industry was brought to Kangaroo Island when it was joined to the mainland at least 60 000 years ago. It seems likely, but not certain, that there was a subsequent rise in the sea level sufficient to inundate Backstairs Passage. If there was, this would have caused the Kangaroo Island population to leave the island, to stay and become extinct, or to stay and survive in isolation for a long period. Any of these alternatives would account for the great difference between the Kartan and Seton industries. The latter would be a much younger industry, either a descendant of the Kartan or developed on the mainland and introduced to the island during the next phase of low sea level.

There was also a total change between the Kartan and Seton industries, from the use of quartzite to flint as raw material, perhaps because of the unavailability of the source of quartzite beach pebbles, covered by the rising seas. Tools also became much smaller. At other sites, such as Cloggs Cave and Burrill Lake, there was a very gradual reduction in the size of tools, quite unlike the dramatic change seen on Kangaroo Island. Another possibility is that the Kartan industry died out, and the Seton assemblage mirrors new technological developments that had taken place on the mainland whilst the Kartan was isolated. These questions are now being further investigated by archaeologist Neale Draper.

A further discovery by Lampert has complicated the picture even further. This is the discovery on the island of twenty-four huge, flaked stone tools with notches on each margin (figure 10.1).[8] Such waisted tools have also been found in mainland

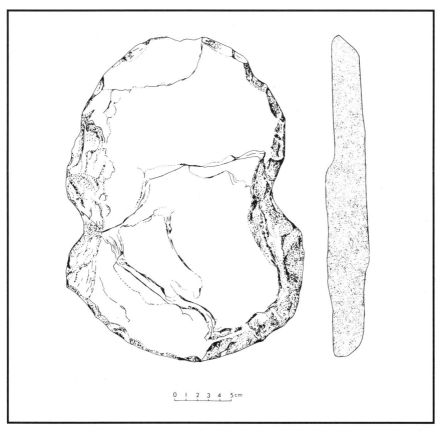

0 1 2 3 4 5cm

Figure 10.1 Waisted axe from Kangaroo Island, South Australia. This axe is exceptionally large. (After Lampert 1979)

South Australia, at Wepowie Creek in the southern Flinders Ranges, and in the Mackay district of Queensland, 6 kilometres from the present coast in sugarcane fields at the base of Mount Jukes, which rises 500 metres above sea level.[9] The eighty waisted tools from Queensland have been examined by Lampert, who has shown that they closely resemble those from Kangaroo Island.

The function of these waisted tools is unknown. Lampert has remarked on their resemblance to the sago pounders of New Guinea, and thinks they may have been used to pound some hard foodstuff. Another possibility is forest clearance, as postulated for the New Guinea waisted axes (see chapter 2). Tindale suggested they were used to kill large animals caught in pitfall traps.[10] He drew attention to the Aboriginal practice in the Queensland rainforest in recent times of using large, heavy-bladed, sometimes grooved stone axes, with very long handles of the so-called 'lawyer cane' wrapped around the axe head and bound with cane lashings, to kill animals caught in pitfall traps.

MAINLAND KARTAN SITES

Kartan tools, although named after Kangaroo Island, were made by people occupying an area of more than 100 000 square kilometres, covering South Australia and the adjacent islands which then formed part of a single landmass. Kartan sites have been found on the mainland on the Fleurieu, Yorke and Eyre peninsulas — but none has come from a stratified deposit.

One of the best-known mainland surface sites was at Hallett Cove. In 1934, Cooper discovered at Hallett Cove, about 16 kilometres south of Adelaide, crude, heavily weathered stone implements lying on a ploughed hillside above a creek overlooking the beach. In the course of his 220 visits to the site over thirty-six years, Cooper found some 400 Kartan core tools, the largest of which weighed 5.5 kilograms.[11] The site has the essential requirements of campers: a permanent water supply, well-drained ground and a commanding view. It also faces northeast, so it catches the warmth of the early morning sun.

One of the puzzling aspects of the Hallett Cove sites is that the Kartan pebble choppers, horsehoof cores and hammer-stones are all made of a poor quality siltstone found close to the camp, whereas at the foot of the cliff lie banks of fine-grained quartzite pebbles that are highly prized by more recent Aboriginal tool-makers. Why did Pleistocene tool-makers not use the better raw material? They probably could not do so, for when the sea level was low the pebble bank would have been covered by a talus slope, now washed away by the sea pounding at the foot of the cliffs. In Kartan times, the nearest pebble banks would have been a long distance away on the ice age shore.

The long-suspected ice age occupation of the lower Murray River valley has now been confirmed by the excavation of Roonka Flat near Blanchetown by Graeme Pretty (figure 10.2).[12] This has a complex history, going back 18 000 years. At that time the river flat seems to have been occasionally used as an open-air encampment by hunter–gatherers during the annual flood of the river. Charcoal (radiocarbon dated to 18 150 ± 350 BP) was found in four hearths, associated with stone cobble cooking structures and freshwater mussel shells. The Roonka site seems to have been exclusively used as a cemetery between about 7000 and 4000 years ago, and then for both burials and habitation (figure 10.2). The burials show a wide diversity of mortuary practices, and many individuals were buried with grave-goods.

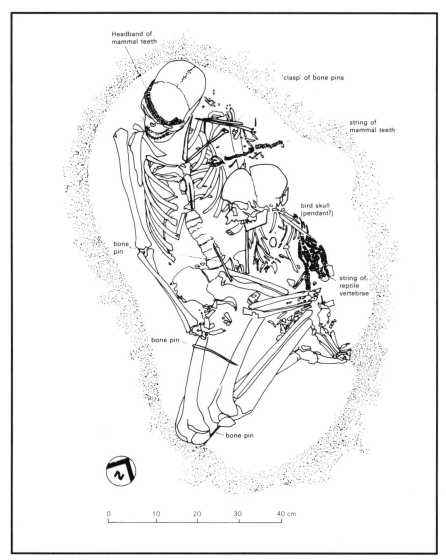

Figure 10.2 An elaborate status burial from Roonka, South Australia. In a small chamber (tomb 108) a man and small child were buried together splendidly attired 4000 years ago. A skin cloak appears to have been wrapped tightly around the man's body and fastened with bone pins. Behind his left shoulder was a dense mass of small animals' foot bones, suggesting the cloak was fixed at the shoulder with the paws of animal pelts hanging down. Bird bones found by the body probably mean the cloak was fringed with bird feathers. The child wore a bird skull pendant and a necklace of reptile vertebrae, and had ochre-stained feet. (Courtesy of the South Australian Museum and G. Pretty)

TECHNOLOGY

Comparisons of industries of the Australian core tool and scraper tradition show the Kartan to be the most archaic on two grounds: its massiveness and the high percentage of core tools to scrapers. Not only are there far more core tools in the Kartan industry, but they are also considerably larger and heavier than those of any other Australian industry. This is not due to their raw material, since Kartan tools were made of many different rock types. Finally, the waisted tools that are part of the Kartan industry suggest the possibility of great antiquity. Made of quartzite, like the Kartan core tools, the waisted tools are even more massive, weighing an average of 1837 grams, compared with 882 grams for Kartan tools. Their edges are usually sharpened by crude bifacial flaking, whereas all Kartan tools are unifacially flaked. They may have been hafted to a handle or used in a two-handed grip, a hand on each notched margin.

Classic Kartan sites are concentrated in the region of South Australia around the mouth of the Murray and on the northeast coast of Queensland. Both these regions are high ground near fresh water. They are among the few surviving remnants of Australia's continental shelf; if the earliest population were concentrated on the coast, most other sites would now be submerged. The reasons Kangaroo Island has such prolific remains of the Kartan industry are probably twofold: sufficient altitude to place it above the present sea level and a particularly favourable location, close to both the sea and to the mouth of Australia's largest river.

The emerging picture of Pleistocene technology is of a varied and efficient tool kit, including stone, bone and wooden tools, and no doubt many other items made of organic materials. This Australian core tool and scraper tradition is characterised by pebble choppers, horsehoof cores, steep-edge scrapers, notched and other types of scraper, including many small flakes and artefacts made of sharp quartz by the bipolar technique. Many of these artefacts are primarily tools to make tools; they were used for manufacturing, maintenance and food processing, evidenced by use-wear and residue analysis.

The stone tools are remarkably similar all over the continent, even when made from different raw materials, and appear to belong to a single distinctive Australoid technological tradition, readily distinguishable from the stone tool industries of Asia, Europe and Africa. Nevertheless, they encompass much variation, like thumbnail scrapers in some Tasmanian Pleistocene sites. Australia's Pleistocene artefacts have been called homogeneous by some and heterogeneous by others, depending on their particular perspective. My own view is that the Pleistocene assemblages are much more homogeneous than those of the Holocene, but also include some distinctive regional variations of the basic old Australian core tool and scraper tradition.

There is strong circumstantial evidence that the ice age inhabitants of Australia wore skin clothing. The whole tool kit used for skin-working in historic times has been found in Pleistocene sites, and some of the bone points have use-wear on their tips consistent with piercing skins. Stone tools played a very small part in traditional Aboriginal equipment: most artefacts were of wood, bone, shell or plant material. Unfortunately, after even only a thousand years in the ground, almost everything has disappeared except items made of stone. Very special conditions are needed to preserve wooden tools, in particular a constantly wet or dry environment. These conditions are found in peat bogs, such as Wyrie Swamp in South Australia.[13]

This site was discovered by accident, literally! Roger Luebbers was doing field work in the Millicent district when he fell, slipped a disc, and ended up in hospital. Whilst convalescing, the man in the next bed, Hans Van Schaik, casually mentioned there were boomerangs in a peat bog on his land. Luebbers investigated and discovered the lakeside camp of Wyrie Swamp, which was later flooded and preserved by the encroaching swamp (colour plate 8).

The stone tool kit included core tools and scrapers, with organic residues indicating processing of wood and plant foods. Associated was the missing element from all sites hitherto excavated in Australia: the wooden artefacts. Twenty-five wooden tools were recovered, complete or in fragments. Types represented were a digging stick, pointed stakes (about 40 centimetres long, possibly also for digging), a short simple spear, two barbed spears, and nine boomerangs, three of them complete. The barbed spears were a real surprise — no one had thought they went so far back in time in Australia, and they are the oldest examples found anywhere in the world. The boomerangs are clearly the returning type, because the two ends are orientated in different aerodynamic planes. The curvature and lateral twist they exhibit are the classic properties of a well-designed aerodynamic missile. The wing span is 29 to 50 centimetres and the arms join in a sharp elbow.

Australian prehistoric technology was not static. There was a gradual development towards less massive, more efficient and more varied tools: later Pleistocene industries have fewer core tools, smaller scrapers and a greater range of types. This decrease in size reflects progress towards greater efficiency in the use of raw material. It has been calculated by Rhys Jones that over a period of 25 000 years, stone tools became eight times more efficient. (These figures are based on an increase in the average length of working edge per unit weight of tool from 0.5 millimetres per gram 25 000 years ago to 4 millimetres per gram 5000 years ago.)[14]

This single glimpse of Pleistocene wooden technology reveals the characteristic equipment of traditional Aboriginal society. Then, as now, it seems women were equipped with digging sticks, men with spears and boomerangs. A strong, fire-hardened wooden spear was an efficient weapon which has been used throughout Aboriginal history. The barbed, javelin-type spear was an unexpected refinement in the Pleistocene, but would have been effective in spearing large game. When such barbed spears enter man or beast they are difficult to dislodge, and tend to cause death through loss of blood. The returning boomerangs are even more sophisticated. It is a salutary thought that 10 000 years ago, Aborigines understood the principles of torque and aerodynamic flight, something most of us cannot do today.

In summary, prehistoric technology in Australia was neither simple nor primitive. The tool kit was limited in range and highly portable, but it was adapted to cope successfully with a wide variety of environments and harsh conditions which, 30 000 years later, were to prove too much for many of the European 'explorers' and settlers.

CHAPTER ELEVEN
Pleistocene Rock Art

Graphic markings painted, drawn, stencilled, imprinted or carved on cliff, cave or rock surfaces have come to be known as 'rock art', although the use of the term 'art' may be misleading, in that art played a distinctive role in prehistoric non-literate societies such as Australian Aboriginal culture, very different from its place in the art galleries of modern life. In Europe, rock art is divided into *parietal* art, literally meaning 'art on the walls', and *mobiliary* art, which is movable or portable art, usually pieces of carved or engraved stone, bone or fired clay, but mobiliary art is almost entirely absent from prehistoric Australia.

Petroglyphs (often called 'engravings' in Australia without implying use of an engraving technique) are carvings made into a rock surface using any implement in two basic methods. These are *abrasion* (linear friction by pushing an implement over the surface, or rotating friction by drilling with an instrument under pressure) and *percussion* (applying vertical pressure by hammering). Friction produces an abraded or

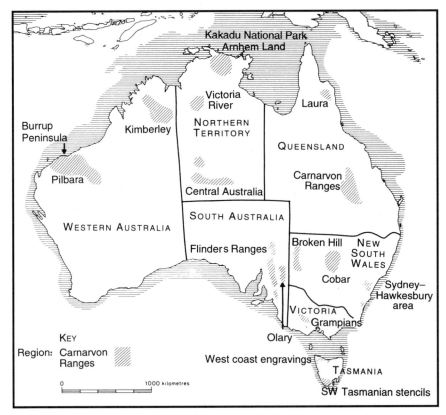

Figure 11.1 Major rock art regions in Australia.

scratched groove or a rubbed or drilled area; percussion makes small pits, which may then be linked together into a line or motif.[1] Designs are made by percussion by pounding or hammer-dressing the surface with a lump of stone (direct percussion), or by pecking by indirect percussion, using a sharp pointed tool placed in position and then hit with a hammer-stone. Indirect percussion by this hammer and chisel method gives clean edges, precise lines and some depth to a petroglyph in contrast to the shallow and more diffused outline of pounded examples.

ANTIQUITY OF PETROGLYPHS

The great age of Australian petroglyphs has long been suspected; for example in 1914 Basedow published a paper entitled 'Aboriginal rock carvings of great antiquity in South Australia'.[2] The case made by Basedow, and later by Mountford and Tindale, was based mainly on the presence of a thick sheen or varnish on the petroglyphs, the apparent depiction of the tracks of some extinct animals such as the *Diprotodon*, and the absence of dingo tracks (implying they were made before the

Plate 15 Incised markings at the Lightning Brothers site, Yiwarlarlay, Northern Territory, are believed to have been an important element in local rain-making ceremonies. (R. Edwards)

dingo reached Australia about 4000 years ago). The inaccessible location and heavily patinated condition of some of the pecked motifs was also significant. For example, at Red Gorge in the Flinders Ranges, some petroglyphs occur on the cliffs in places now impossible to reach, showing that there has been rockfall and erosion since they were first chipped out. Tumbled rocks at the bottom of the gorge often bear parts of designs, the remains of which are still in position on the cliff above. Other designs are bisected by gaping cracks that have opened up in the rock.

The first firm evidence of the antiquity of rock art came in 1929, when an engraved slab was found 3 to 4 metres below ground level in the Devon Downs rock-shelter. This limestone shelter on the lower Murray River in South Australia was the subject of the first scientific archaeological excavation in Australia.[3] Methods of absolute dating were not developed for another two decades, but when radiocarbon dating became available, samples of charcoal carefully bagged and stored twenty years before were dated. It emerged that the engraved rocks were in a 3000-year-old layer, but this is very much a minimum age since the date only indicates when the fragments fell into the occupation deposit, not when they were first carved onto the wall.

The first absolute age on Australian rock art came from Ingaladdi, west of Katherine in the Northern Territory, in 1966.[4] Around the large, permanent Ingaladdi waterhole lies a series of sandstone outcrops. Most bear rock paintings, and the back walls of some of the shelters are also engraved with animal tracks, human

Plate 16 Petroglyphs in a regional variant of the Panaramitee style in Early Man Shelter, near Laura, Queensland, with its discoverer, Captain Percy Trezise.

feet and thousands of linear, abraded grooves. These may have been produced in rain-making ceremonies; identical grooves were rubbed at Yiwarlarlay, 80 kilometres to the south, only fifty years ago. These ceremonies involved abrading grooves in the rock to bring rain (plate 15), and were associated with the myth of the Lightning Brothers, who are depicted in vivid multicoloured paintings there.

In his excavation, John Mulvaney found pieces of engraved rock below a 5000-year-old layer, resting on a 7000-year-old occupation floor. The minimum age of the petroglyphs is, therefore, between 5000 and 7000 years. They are probably much older, and bear parallel abraded grooves and a large 'bird track', common motifs in other art sites of suspected Pleistocene age.

Similar evidence was found in far north Queensland by Dr Andree Rosenfeld in Early Man Shelter.[5] Heavily weathered and patinated petroglyphs cover the back wall of the shelter in a diagonal frieze and clearly continue on below the present ground surface (plate 16). Excavation revealed the presence of petroglyphs on the rock wall below an occupation level dated to 13 000 years, which must therefore be older than this. They are pecked out on the shelter wall to form a long frieze, which rises obliquely, parallel to the ancient floor and bedding planes of the rock. The designs have been influenced by the natural contours of the rock surface; hollows have been emphasised by outlining or by filling with petroglyphs. Most common are gridded designs, simple three-pronged trident-like forms (some resembling bird tracks), circular forms and extensive maze-like patterns of lines. Natalie Franklin, who did a doctoral thesis on the Panaramitee style (described below) and made a special field study of the Early Man petroglyphs, considers them to be a regional variant of the Panaramitee style.[6]

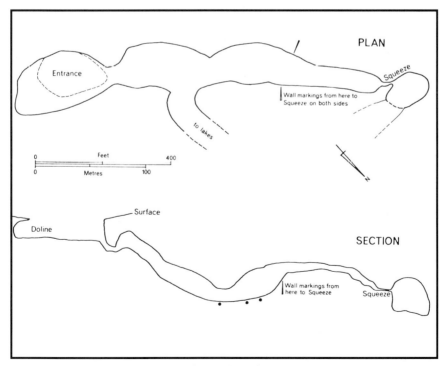

Figure 11.2 Plan of Koonalda Cave, South Australia. (After Wright 1971)

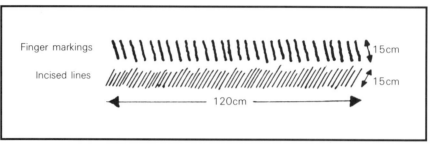

Finger markings

Incised lines

15cm

15cm

120cm

Figure 11.3 Herringbone design from Koonalda Cave, South Australia, consisting of seventy-four diagonal incised lines in a row below thirty-seven finger markings. (After Edwards and Maynard in Wright 1971)

KOONALDA CAVE

One of the most remarkable discoveries in Australia is the presence of Pleistocene 'art' deep inside Koonalda Cave far below the Nullarbor Plain in South Australia (figure 11.2).[7] In total darkness, some 300 metres inside the cave, graphic markings were found on the walls, resembling the so-called 'macaroni' or meander style of the earliest European cave art.

The wall markings vary according to the texture of the wall. In one part of the cave, now known as the art passage, the walls are exceptionally soft and friable, with a surface the colour and texture of compacted talcum powder. There the slightest touch of a finger marked the wall. In other parts firm finger pressure was used to leave an impression, and elsewhere one or more strokes of a stone or stick would have been needed to scratch fine incised lines into the harder surface (plate 17).

Some large, flat wall surfaces are completely covered with randomly crisscrossing sets of parallel finger markings. Large groups of vertical and sometimes horizontal lines occur, together with a few definite patterns, such as regularly spaced grids or lattices. There are also two sets of four concentric circles, both about 20 centimetres in diameter. One unique design is a 120-centimetre long herringbone (figure 11.3). It consists of seventy-four diagonal incised lines in a row below thirty-seven short finger markings. The fact that the number of the former is exactly twice the number of finger markings can hardly be accidental. This is, therefore, probably a deliberate design with symbolic significance.

Among these eroded markings, recent names, initials, dates and other markings made by recent visitors stand out fresh and clear. The fresh markings have small sharp ridges between the finger lines, which are smooth and compacted, whereas the old markings have less pronounced ridges and concavities. There is thus no difficulty in distinguishing between old and new.

There is strong presumptive evidence that this art is 20 000 or more years old. Charcoal from just below the surface of the passage before 'the Squeeze' gave a date of 20 000 years. The wall above was covered with incised markings, and the charcoal could have come from crude torches held by early humans to light their way along the dark passages in these deepest recesses of the cave. Futher markings are located in a cavity 15 metres below massive rock-fall, indicating considerable antiquity. Others lie above a platform high in the dome of a large chamber containing a lake. This platform can only be reached through 'the Squeeze'. Beyond the platform, on a part of the wall that cannot now be reached, are yet more markings. Clearly part of the ledge has fallen into the lake far below since they were made. There is thus strong circumstantial evidence that the markings derive from the distant past and were contemporary with other prehistoric activity in the cave, some 15 000 to 24 000 years ago.

Some controversy arose after the discovery of the wall markings as to whether they should be regarded as 'art' or not. It was claimed that they were produced by accident, the sharpening of bone points, or by scraping off limestone powder for some particular purpose, for instance symbolic signs with the character of a message or script, which directed the prehistoric miners to the presence of flint veins. None of these pragmatic explanations, however, accounts for the definite designs that occur, nor do they accord with the evidence. If produced by accident, why are most of the lines vertical, and why do no haphazard, smudged patches occur? If they derive from sharpening bone points, why was this done in total darkness? And if they were mining indicators, why are the markings restricted to one small part of the cave, whereas flint veins occur, and were mined, throughout the cave?

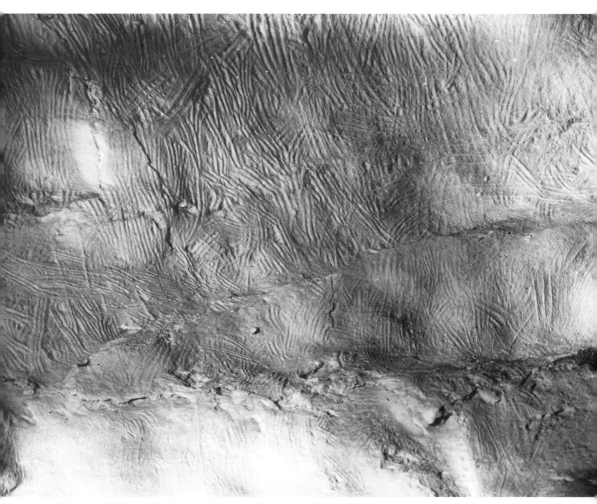

Plate 17 Wall markings in Koonalda Cave, South Australia. (R. Edwards)

There are several other possible explanations. One is that the markings mirror the instinctive human impulse to make marks on blank surfaces. This is a well-documented reaction, common to *Homo sapiens* all over the globe, which may well be the first step in the development of art in all societies. Another possibility is that the markings were produced in the course of ritual activity. In hunter–gatherer societies most art forms part of religious ritual, and this is certainly true of traditional Aboriginal society in more recent times. The ritual may have been associated also with flint-mining in this remote, dark part of the cave.

Markings similar to those at Koonalda have been found in another cave on the Nullarbor in Western Australia. This is totally untouched by vandalism and is currently being studied and protected. Among other sites with wall markings are Kintore and Cutta Cutta caves in the Northern Territory and Orchestra Shell Cave studied by Sylvia Hallam[8] in Western Australia, but the possibility that animal claws could have been used as engravers' tools complicates the problem of distinguishing between human-made and animal-made markings.

SNOWY RIVER CAVE, BUCHAN

In the wild gorge of the Snowy River, north of Buchan in eastern Victoria, a spectacular area of limestone cliffs and caves lies on the west bank. The region has

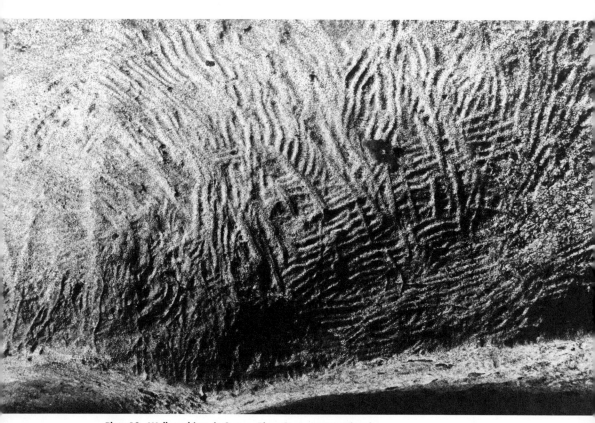

Plate 18 Wall markings in Snowy River Cave, eastern Victoria.

become known as New Guinea because of its rainforest vegetation and rugged terrain. Traces of Aboriginal occupation have been found in one cave, New Guinea 2. The cave system leads far underground, but outside the entrance is a rock-shelter overlooking a slope covered with grass-trees, which leads down to the Snowy River 100 metres away. The floor of the rock-shelter is earth interspersed with huge blocks of roof-fall. Excavations here in the 1980s by Paul Ossa of La Trobe University (unpublished) revealed stone tools and occupation going back almost 20 000 years.

A narrow entrance and steep descent lead into a large chamber with a high roof and several entrances. A permanent stream trickles across the chamber floor, but on a dry earth bank above the stream is an Aboriginal fireplace and midden heap, with shells clearly visible in the dim light filtering in from the entrance above. Aborigines evidently scrambled down into this deep cavern, but with what purpose in mind? A glance around provided an answer: the mud-covered, soft limestone walls formed a perfect canvas for prehistoric artists. Mud had been deposited on the walls by occasional flooding, leaving a smooth surface that could easily be marked with the fingers or a sharp object such as a bone or pointed stick (plate 18).

It has been suggested that the markings may have been made by the claws of animals scrambling to get out of the cave, but several features argue against this interpretation. The markings are not found indiscriminately all over the cave but tend to occur in 'panels' on the smoother sections of wall. They are not merely random markings but include some apparent patterns, such as a whole mass of diagonally crossing lines and circles. Finally, they are extremely similar to the wall markings at Koonalda Cave. As at Koonalda, some of the Snowy River Cave markings are in inaccessible positions and complete darkness. They may have been made in the course of secret ceremonies in this deep, dark cave and date from the beginnings of Aboriginal art, more than 20 000 years ago.

THE MOUNT GAMBIER CAVES

Startling new evidence has come to light in the 1980s of an ancient body of graphic markings in underground limestone caves in the Mount Gambier district of southeastern South Australia. The discovery was made by Robert Bednarik, founder of the Australian Rock Art Research Association, and local resident and speleologist Geoffrey Aslin.[9] Finger markings and petroglyphs have now been found in more than twenty-five caves in the Mount Gambier region, and three succeeding styles have been identified.

The earliest and most common style is characterised by multiple finger lines or flutings on formerly soft surface deposits together with linear markings engraved with pieces of stone in harder surfaces on the walls of caves. From the size of the finger lines it is possible to get some idea of the age of their makers, and one surprise was the high number made by juveniles. This 'finger-lines' style has now been found over a distance of 3000 kilometres along the entire south coast of Australia. Although not yet securely dated, it is probably more, possibly much more, than 20 000 years old, on the evidence from Koonalda Cave, the overgrowth of finger grooves by a more recent deposit of reprecipitated carbonate in several sites and the major tectonic changes which have occurred in many caves since the markings were made.

Superimposed on finger lines in several Mount Gambier caves are deeply carved motifs, particularly circles. These may be incised, pounded or abraded, and the circles include concentric, dissected and other forms. This style has been termed by

Plate 19 Petroglyphs covered with a gypsum oxalate crust at Sandy Creek Shelter 1, Cape York Peninsula. Detail of an engraved sloping boulder (the left side is uppermost) covered with curvilinear enclosures with grids and pits in a variant of the Panaramitee style.

Bednarik the Karake style, and is thought to be more than 10 000 years old. Like the preceding finger lines tradition, it is entirely non-figurative. The youngest style in the Mount Gambier caves is a tradition of shallow incisions executed with single strokes, believed to be less than 10 000 years old.

Several thousand of these petroglyphs have now been found in the underground limestone caves of the Mount Gambier district, five of which also contain evidence of prehistoric mining of chert to make stone tools. This is already the largest known concentration of non-figurative cave art in the world, but its relationship to the Panaramitee-style petroglyphs is still unclear.

BURIED ROCK ART

Sandy Creek Shelter 1, near Laura on Cape York Peninsula, contained not only 32 000-year-old stone tools, including a waisted ground-edge axe at the base of a 3-metre deep occupation (described in chapter 7), but also 'buried' petroglyphs.[10] A pecked panel on the rear wall of the rock-shelter was partially buried under occupation deposits. Excavation by Trezise in 1969 revealed that the panel extended 75 centimetres below ground level, and the petroglyphs comprise pecked straight and radiating lines, curves, bird tracks and pecked pits (plate 19). Further archaeological work by Morwood in 1991 recovered a sandstone fragment with pecked engraving from a layer dated to 14 400 BP. This appeared to have become detached from the frieze on the rear wall, providing a minimum age for this panel. The petroglyphs have not yet been published, but from my own site visit (in 1981) my impression is that they belong to the Panaramitee tradition (described below). Franklin agrees.[11]

Direct dating of the Sandy Creek petroglyphs may not be possible, although Alan Watchman is trying to date the oxalate minerals in the coating overlying the petroglyphs (plate 19), but great antiquity would be compatible with the high degree of patination and thick rock varnish on some petroglyphs and their close, if not direct, association with 32 000-year-old occupation. This is important independent evidence of probable great age for petroglyphs in the Panaramitee style, in view of the remarkable dates obtained recently on similar petroglyphs in South Australia.

DATING

Until recently, rock art could only be dated by circumstantial evidence, but some exciting breakthroughs have been made in the last decade. The development of the accelerator mass spectrometry (AMS) radiocarbon dating method (described in the glossary) permits the dating of tiny samples of organic matter, as little as 1 milligram. This allows some charcoal drawings or pigment containing an organic ingredient to be dated. It also means that organic matter, such as lichens incorporated in layers of rock varnish over petroglyphs, is datable. A large series of AMS dates has recently been obtained for petroglyphs in South Australia that are covered in desert varnish. This appears as a thick, blackish, shiny veneer on rock surfaces, particularly in desert regions — hence the name — but it should properly be called 'rock varnish', since it is also found in many non-desert environments. It is a chemical crust of bacterial origin, consisting primarily of manganese and iron oxides.

Plate 20 Petroglyphs such as this from Yunta Springs have been interpreted as signifying an emu leaving a nest. Cation-ration (CR) and radiocarbon (C-14) dating of a similar 'composition' at Karolta (figure 11.5) date the bird tracks (K21 and K28) and one of the cluster of dots (K27) as belonging to the 22 000 to 24 000 BP period. (R. Edwards)

ARCHAEOLOGY OF THE DREAMTIME

Plate 21 Petroglyphs at Karolta. The numbers indicate motifs selected for dating (compare figures 11.4 and 11.5). K20 (abraded grooves) CR date 16 200 ± 2500 BP; K21 (bird track) C-14 date 22 480 ± 340 BP; K22 (circle) CR date 25 500 ± 4000 BP; K23 (curved line) C-14 date 30 230 ± 770 BP (the oldest petroglyph of the twenty-four dates at Karolta). (M. Nobbs, dates from Nobbs and Dorn 1993)

PETROGLYPH NUMBER	RADIOCARBON YEARS BP	LAB. NUMBER
Panaramitee North		
PN4 Circle with spiral	5635 ± 90	AA 6549
PN5 Maze (sample 1)	3575 ± 65	AA 6913
PN5 Maze (sample 2)	3795 ± 70	AA 6903
PN6 Curved line (sample 1)	43 140 ± 3000	AA 6898
PN6 Curved line (sample 2)	> 43 100	AA 6920
Karolta 1		
K15 Curved line	12 650 ± 150	NZA 1369
K21 Bird track	22 480 ± 340	NZA 1366
K23 Curved line	30 230 ± 770	NZA 1378
K24 'Abstract' motif	12 970 ± 150	NZA 1414
K26 Curved line	31 230 ± 920	NZA 1370
K28A Hand	9125 ± 100	AA 6916
K29 Foot print	9980 ± 85	AA 6910
K30 Foot print	20 105 ± 185	AA 6548
K32 Foot print	21 195 ± 220	AA 6905
Yunta Springs		
YS1 Maze	13 950 ± 110	AA 6914
YS2 Macropod track	7365 ± 85	AA 6909
YS3 Barred shield	1510 ± 50	AA 6906
YS4 Abraded groove	6355 ± 85	AA 6551
Wharton Hill		
WH1 Drominorthid track	14 910 ± 180	NZA 1367
WH2 Foot print	18 485 ± 165	AA 6918
WH5 Oval	36 400 ± 1700	NZA 1356
WH5 Oval (split sample 1)	37 890 ± 820	NZA 2180
WH5 Oval (split sample 2)	> 42 700	AA 6907

Figure 11.4 Radiocarbon dates obtained on Olary petroglyphs. (After Nobbs and Dorn 1993)

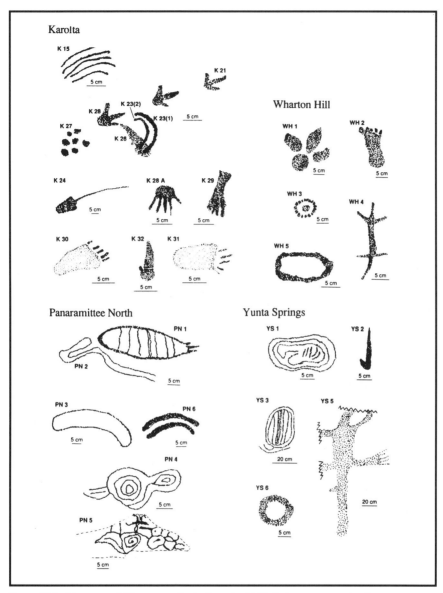

Figure 11.5 Diagrams of Olary petroglyphs from the 1990 dating program. Numbers were assigned according to the order of sampling. (After Nobbs and Dorn 1993) Radiocarbon dates for some of these motifs are given in figure 11.4, other dates (some radiocarbon (C-14) and some cation-ratio (CR)) are given in Nobbs and Dorn 1993.

Varnished petroglyphs have also been dated by the developing cation-ratio dating technique. Ron Dorn, who pioneered its use in Australia, explains that: 'Cation-ratio (CR) dating is a method that assigns relative or calibrated ages to rock varnishes. A ratio of cations (positive ions) of (potassium + calcium) to titanium decreases with age. If this CR is measured at sites with known exposure ages in a region, a calibration can be constructed called a "cation-leaching" curve. The CRs in unknown samples are then compared with this curve and a calibrated CR age is assigned.'[12]

When Ron Dorn and Margaret Nobbs first claimed great antiquity for the Olary petroglyphs on the basis of CR dates in 1988, there was a storm of controversy, but in their most recent paper (1993) they describe refinements and modifications to the method, which has now been replicated by five other groups worldwide, and has performed well when it has been subjected to blind tests, for example 'blind' comparison of CR and conventional radiocarbon dates by Loendorf on North American petroglyphs. Dorn and Nobbs have now presented a very strong case, for instead of relying on any single approach, they use three independent techniques to date the rock varnish formed over the petroglyphs and thus to assign minimum ages to them. These are: 'Carbon 14 measurements of organic matter at the varnish/weathering rind interface provides numerical ages; calibrated ages are obtained by cation-ratio dating; and sequences of layers within varnish are used to discriminate relative ages'.

In their new series of dates for Olary petroglyphs, the radiocarbon dates and stratigraphic time signals in rock varnish stand on their own, independent of any results from the experimental CR dating. And the results are internally consistent, for where one motif is engraved on top of another, the uppermost one's date is more recent, and when separate dates have been obtained on two parts of the same motif, the dates are approximately the same.

The way the process works is that:

> First a human exposes a new surface to the atmosphere [by pecking out a petroglyph]. Next, aerosolic organic matter falls into rock depressions or rock-surface organisms such as lichen, cyanobacteria, or fungi grow in rock depressions and penetrate into the rock weathering rind [cortex]. Then rock varnish growth, first in the depressions and then all over the petroglyph encapsulates the organic matter, either at the varnish/rock interface or in the underlying weathering rind. Radiocarbon dating this subvarnish organic matter, therefore, provides a minimum age for the exposure of the underlying surface [i.e. for the making of the petroglyph].[13]

Dating was done on petroglyphs on four exposed surfaces of silicified dolomitic siltstone in the Olary region, first Karolta and then Panaramitee North,[14] the type site of the style bearing its name, Wharton Hill and Yunta Springs (plates 19 and 20 and figures 11.4 and 11.5). (Only pinpricks of material are needed for the determination of varnish ages, so sampling does not damage the petroglyphs.)

The results 'suggest that petroglyphs have been made in the Olary Province for the last 40,000 radiocarbon years, making its rock art the oldest known in the world'. The two oldest petroglyphs — the oval motif (WH5) and the curved lines motif (PN6) — are 'at the limits of radiocarbon dating', but Dorn and Nobbs maintain that they are minimum ages. They believe that 'By using four different age signals, we have greater faith in our findings that the WH5 and PN6 engravings are truly ancient, probably exceeding 40,000 radiocarbon years'.

The debate on CR dating has become regrettably polarised and personalised, so that Dorn and Nobbs have been moved to state that 'we recognize that several individuals do not like CR dating, or the results obtained'. However, these Olary petroglyphs have always, or at least since Basedow's 1914 paper, been thought to be extremely old on the grounds of their incredibly thick covering of desert varnish, pecked technique and narrow range of non-figurative motifs. The CR method is at the cutting edge of dating techniques, but, speaking personally, the researchers' painstaking refinement of the technique to answer critics of their 1988 preliminary report and the vast array of generally consistent C-14 and CR dates they now have, confirm for me the 'gut feeling' I had when I first visited Karolta and Panaramitee (in 1971 with C. P. Mountford), that these petroglyphs are incredibly old. Thirty years ago a date of 40 000 years for any Australian site would have been unbelievable, but now it is far from startling, as we have several firmly dated occupation sites of that age scattered around the continent, including some claimed to be more than 50 000 years. Olary is not far west from the Willandra Lakes region, and the semiarid environments are similar. There are some fifty petroglyph sites in the Olary region, and the four dated sites lie close to the most secure water supplies in the region. Stone tool scatters are frequent, but few camp sites, young or old, have been found, perhaps mainly because there are no caves, large rock-shelters or sandy lake-shores to focus occupation.

As so often in archaeology, this new discovery means revision of our ideas about the past, and raises new questions. Did the first colonists practise rock art? Did they bring an art tradition from their original homeland? If so, is there any Asian art which could be ancestral? Or was Australian rock art an independent development? If so, when, where, how and why did it develop? Did they paint or carve rocks, or both? What is the relationship between the meander style of the caves and these ancient petroglyphs in the open air?

THE PANARAMITEE TRADITION

In the 1970s Lesley Maynard proposed a three-part sequence to explain the patterned variation she observed within Australian rock art.[15] Her evolutionary model postulated an early homogeneous continent-wide corpus of petroglyphs known as 'the Panaramitee', believed to be of Pleistocene antiquity. The Panaramitee was followed by two generalised groups of regionally diverse styles, the simple figurative and the complex figurative (figure 11.6). (See glossary for definitions of 'style'.) The Panaramitee art style is widely distributed across Australia but is best known from the arid centre, where the 'classic' track and circle tradition was identified by Edwards, Mountford and others. The Panaramitee style is characterised by thousands of small, pecked petroglyphs. Most figures are less than 10 centimetres in length, and are pecked out either in outline or as a solid, 'intagliated' form. A limited range of motifs is depicted, dominated by circles and tracks. Among the tracks, macropod, bird and human are very common. Other very frequent motifs are circles, which may be simple or complex in form, 'pits' or 'dots' (small, pecked concavities), and lines, either simple, complex, crescents, radiating or 'mazes'. Infrequently, figurative motifs also occur, such as lizards, human figures, faces or vulvas. (To avoid confusion, tracks are now treated as distinct from both non-figurative 'geometric' motifs and figurative representational art.)

Maynard's much-quoted model has stood the test of time remarkably well, but has recently been re-evaluated by Franklin using multivariate statistical analysis. Her results confirmed that 'the Panaramitee style can be distinguished as a separate entity', and that 'although there was some degree of homogeneity between engraving sites widely dispersed throughout the continent, variations were also apparent'. Such a marked degree of homogeneity between petroglyph traditions widely separated in space, despite regional differences in the numerical significance of particular motifs, is consistent with the connections one would expect to see as a result of the 'open'

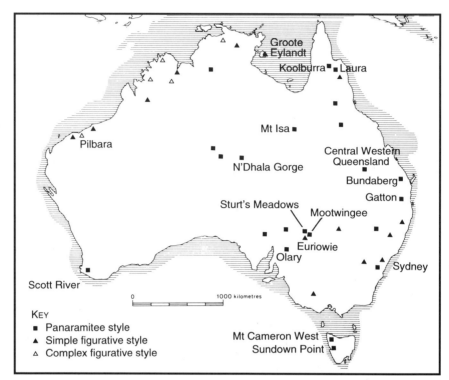

Figure 11.6 Distribution of the Panaramitee, simple figurative and complex figurative rock art styles. Named sites and regions were included in Franklin's multivariate analyses of the Panaramitee style. (After N. Franklin's 1991 revision of Maynard 1979)

social networks between small founding populations in Australia, with cross-fertilisation of ideas between widely dispersed groups of people.[16]

Maynard's sequence represented an evolutionary progression from basically non-figurative to figurative motifs, and from Panaramitee-style petroglyphs to the simple and complex figurative styles (in both paintings and petroglyphs), which comprised several distinct, regionally varied styles united by a number of common characteristics. In fact, the situation is far more complex. There is evidence (described below) of pigmented art contemporaneous with Panaramitee-style petroglyphs, and in the Olary region the occurrence of a painted Panaramitee style is a distinct possibility. (The present paintings in Olary rock-shelters cannot be dated, but it is interesting that they have even higher percentages of tracks than do the petroglyphs, and their motif range is even more restricted.) In some parts of Australia the only rock art is Panaramitee-style, notably the Olary Province and much of Central Australia; in others there is only simple figurative pigmented art, for example the Grampians. In sum, there are many varied combinations of Maynard's three styles, some contemporaneous, and little evidence for the straightforward chronological development from one to another which she suggests.

One of the surprises of the Karolta dates was their great time spread. If they are to be believed, they imply the use of the same petroglyph site over 30 000 years, to manufacture similar motifs, such as circles and lines of tracks. The dates on Panaramitee North, Yunta Springs and Wharton Hill tell a similar story. While no conclusions can be drawn from such a small sample, it may be significant that the oldest motifs have the simplest forms — rough circles and curved lines. The more complex curvilinear shapes and figurative motifs, like lizards, gave younger minimum ages, whilst tracks and circles occur throughout.

In other words, in the Panaramitee tradition there is both continuity and change, the change being in the direction of more complex and figurative pictures. Cultural continuity is particularly striking in the art of arid Central Australia. Petroglyphs were still being made there in the twentieth century, as evidenced by eyewitness accounts and by the appearance of petroglyphs of cars, trucks and European boats.[17] Aboriginal artists in Central Australia have consistently stated that there has been no change in artistic motifs and that they must be reproduced in exactly the same way as they have always been. However, they also relate that the Ancestors come to them in dreams, telling of new designs.[18]

Arid Australia is the core area of the 'classic' Panaramitee tradition, with the whole range and greatest diversity of Panaramitee motifs. In recent Central Australian artistic systems, there are basically two forms of artistic expression: figurative art, which is predominantly secular, and geometric art, of a predominantly sacred character. The figurative art mainly occurs in rock paintings such as those at Uluru, whereas geometric art is mainly manifested as engravings on sacred objects such as churinga and 'poundings on the rock surface' (witnessed by Mountford), body painting, ground paintings using ochres, feathers and blood, and the recent dot paintings in acrylics (not all necessarily sacred).[19]

This geometric art has a very small range of designs, employed in innumerable different arrangements. Munn's classic study of the Walbiri artistic system revealed that motifs 'cover highly general categories, each of which includes a variety of different classes of phenomena'.[20] For example, the circle can be used to specify a waterhole, fire, fruits, the base of a tree, a cave, etc. In recent paintings women also use it to denote a billy-can. Likewise a straight line can denote a straight path, a spear, a kangaroo's tail, a backbone, the trunk of a tree, etc. Much of the art forms maps of tribal territory and illustrations of the myths relating to the passage of Ancestral Beings across the country. The various 'geometric' elements of the Walbiri art system — circles, lines, tracks, crescents — are combined to represent these myths in a plan or bird's eye view. A circle often refers to a particular named site, and connecting lines the paths taken from one place to another. The use of concentric circles usually relates to the presence of an Ancestral Being.

In this system the number of classes of meaning can be increased without increasing the number of motifs in the repertoire. If the Panaramitee artistic system was similar or ancestral to such living cultural traditions as those of contemporary Central Australia, its use of a very narrow range of motifs over such a long time period would be readily understandable.

CLELAND HILLS FACES

Remarkable, heavily weathered, pecked motifs resembling human faces were found in the Cleland Hills, 320 kilometres west of Alice Springs.[21] The art has not been dated, but its heavily weathered condition suggests great age. Not far away is Puritjarra occupation site, dated to more than 22 000 years. Similar 'faces' have been found in equally weathered rock engravings in the Pilbara.

The sixteen Cleland Hills 'faces' are small — 10 to 20 centimetres wide and 30 centimetres long — and tend to be heart-shaped with eyes, nose and mouth

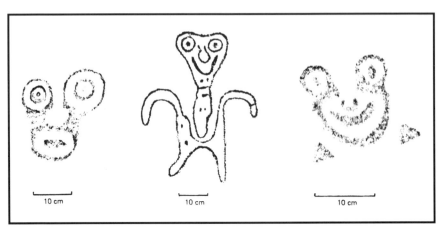

Figure 11.7   Cleland Hills faces, Northern Territory. These weathered engravings were pecked out of sandstone on cliffs around the rockhole of Thomas Reservoir. Left: Disembodied face with a distinct impression of sadness. Centre: Happy face with a curious body. Right: Face with a happy expression. There are two small triangles below the face and two long lines below, perhaps indicating a body. (After Dix 1977; drawings based on photographs by R. Edwards 1968)

(figure 11.7). One has a body with two legs and rather strange, wing-like arms. These 'faces' form only a small proportion of the designs at the Cleland Hills site. Of 387 motifs, 50 percent are tracks and 33 percent circles.

Tasmanian Petroglyphs

There are only seven petroglyph sites in Tasmania, all on the northwest coast. The most extensive is Mount Cameron West (plate 22). The site has been extensively recorded and excavations carried out there by Jones (unpublished).[22] The petroglyphs lie on two outcrops on a long beach exposed to the full force of the westerlies. An undercut cliff face provided an overhang under which prehistoric hunters camped, and the cliff face and large rock slabs that fell from it were decorated by early artists. The designs are non-figurative, geometric forms. The motifs include plain circles, concentric circles, overlapping and barred circles, crosses, rows of holes, trellis-like designs, and animal tracks. The petroglyphs were made by pecking a line of holes into the soft rock and then abrading the ridges between them to make deeply incised lines. Excavation of the site produced a few large, pointed tools of hard rock, such as basalt and quartzite, which may well have been the sculptors' chisels.

The shelter was occupied from about 1350 to 850 BP, when the midden spilled over and covered some of the carved blocks in front of the camp site. The minimum, but *not* the maximum, age for the art is therefore 1350 BP.

The largest and most complex art site yet found in Tasmania, Mount Cameron West is also widely recognised as one of the most outstanding artistic achievements of any hunter–gatherer society. It is conceived on a grand scale, and the designs are so deeply incised that they have a sculptural quality.

Several other art sites have been found, such as Sundown Point and Green's Creek[23] on the west coast, which have as wide a range of designs as Mount Cameron West. The main motif everywhere is the circle, which varies from a few centimetres in diameter to more than 1 metre across at Mount Cameron West. The sites all lie close to the present high water mark and are associated with Holocene shell middens. Rosenfeld considers the Tasmanian petroglyphs so generalised and simple in form that their independent 'invention' is likely in the Holocene, but Franklin regards them as a regional variant of the Panaramitee style.[24] Support for the latter view is that similar Panaramitee-style motifs of circles and lines occur in the recent artistic system of Tasmania in designs painted on bark, and in cicatrice designs, as put on record by Stephen Brown.[25] Thus Panaramitee-style motifs may have survived but in an impoverished form because of the long post-glacial isolation of a small population, whose material technology had become the simplest in the world by the eighteenth century.

The earlier west coast petroglyph sites may now lie under the sea, as may many Pleistocene occupation sites. In other words, the few simple petroglyphs of circles, pits and lines which survive in Tasmania may be but the last vestiges of the far more complex and extensive culture of the first Aborigines to venture into this extreme climatic place, more than 30 000 years ago.

Plate 22   Mount Cameron West petroglyphs, Tasmania. (R. Edwards)

There is every reason to believe that the art of painting has an antiquity similar to that of engraving in Australia, and in Tasmania Pleistocene pigmented art has been found, as described in chapter 9. Accelerator mass spectrometry (AMS) dating of extremely small carbon samples now allows direct determination of the age of organic remains in pigment. Three painting sites on the mainland have now yielded AMS radiocarbon dates on organic matter preserved within the pigment. In Laurie Creek shelter in the Northern Territory human blood protein was detected as a constituent of red pigment on the wall of the rock-shelter, with an age of 20 320 +3100/–2300 BP (RIDDL-1270).[26] This is the first time that prehistoric art pigment in Australia has been directly dated, and indeed it is the first time in the world that any direct dates of Pleistocene antiquity for rock paintings have been obtained.

A similar age, of 24 600 BP, was obtained in 1992 by Alan Watchman for paintings on the rear wall of Sandy Creek Shelter 2 in North Queensland. Layers of red ochre were sandwiched between mineral coatings, and these were dated to 24 600 years.[27] There are those who are sceptical, but another Pleistocene date (plus an anomalous Holocene date) has been obtained on a charcoal drawing in a shelter south of Sydney by Officer, although there, two parts of the same motif gave widely differing AMS dates, probably due to inadequate pretreatment of the samples.[28]

Pieces of ochre, some showing clear striations from use, occur in most Pleistocene sites in Australia, including the lowest levels in Nauwalabila and Malakunanja II, first occupied before 50 000 BP.[29] The first colonists of Australia almost certainly brought painting with them as part of their 'cultural baggage'. Commonsense tells us that it is much easier to paint than to carve on walls, so we would expect painting to be as early or earlier than rock carving, although the disappearance of almost all the early pigmented art but the preservation of ancient petroglyphs has given the opposite impression. Indeed, in the Kakadu region, where the rock is extremely hard, there are very few, in fact almost no, petroglyphs, but claims for early pigmented art.

Arnhem Land contains the most complex and prolific rock art not only in Australia but the world. There are thousands of painted rock-shelters. The paintings are generally naturalistic, documenting the local environment, lifestyle and material culture.[30] A study of the art has been carried out over many years by Chaloupka of the Northern Territory Museum in Darwin, who has recorded and analysed more than a thousand galleries. On the basis of superimposition, changes in style, and the motifs apparently portrayed in the paintings, Chaloupka has proposed a sequence of four styles. The four styles are called pre-estuarine, estuarine, freshwater and contact. According to Chaloupka, the earliest art predates the post-glacial rise in sea level and development of estuarine conditions 7000 to 9000 years ago. His case is based on the apparent depiction of extinct animals, such as the thylacine, in the early art and the predominance of land animals among the motifs, whereas the later estuarine style is dominated by fish and crocodiles, often portrayed in the polychrome x-ray style, in which the spine or intestinal organs are shown. The estuarine period was succeeded by a time when the salt plains became freshwater swamps, covered with lotus flowers and surrounded by graceful paperbark trees. This freshwater phase is reflected in the appearance of goose wing fans in the rock paintings. The final period is that mirroring contact with Macassans from Indonesia, who fished in the area, and European settlers. Boats and ships, horses and guns were then painted, and there was much sorcery painting, until rock painting in Arnhem Land virtually came to an end with the death of the last main rock painter in 1972.

In the earliest style, the animals portrayed resemble kangaroos and wallabies, emus, echidnas, and the Tasmanian tiger, or thylacine. The thylacine is locally extinct, but more than a dozen representations of striped animals have now been found (plate 23). The overall shape and physical features of these have been compared with other striped animals and the dingo.[31] It was concluded that thylacine designs can be clearly differentiated from those of dingoes, the striped numbats, kangaroos or wallabies. The characteristics of thylacines are well known from photographs, film, and museum specimens (and a major search continues in Tasmania to try to find living survivors). Other extinct creatures that Chaloupka has tentatively identified in the early paintings are the long-beaked echidna, *Zaglossus*, and the marsupial tapir, *Palorchestes*. Both appear to have been extinct in Australia for at least 18 000 years, but *Zaglossus* still exists in New Guinea.

Not only do animals resembling these locally extinct species appear in early-style art, but the other creatures portrayed seem to be land-based animals of the inland

Plate 23 Painting of thylacine (Tasmanian tiger) at Ubirr, Kakadu National Park, Northern Territory. Water has washed away the back of the figure.

plains. The animals apparently most frequently depicted are kangaroos, wallabies, emus, echidnas, bandicoots, rock possums and thylacines. The few fish that occur are all freshwater species, in contrast to the many barramundi, saltwater crocodiles and other estuarine species of the succeeding period.

One fascinating aspect of the paintings of humans in the dynamic style is their evidence of personal adornment in the form of armlets, neck ornaments and head-dresses decorated with tassels and feathers (figures 11.8, 11.9). There even seems to be a stencil of a tooth necklace, reminiscent of that found in the Nitchie burial. Another remarkable feature of this style is the portrayal of zoomorphs — human figures with animal heads, some of which may represent flying foxes.

In addition to large, naturalistic representations of single animals and zoomorphs, there are many small, superbly drawn scenes of people and animals in narrative compositions from everyday life, such as dances and kangaroo hunts. As many as sixty figures appear in one painting. The scenes are full of expressive movements, which is why Chaloupka has named this the dynamic style. Previously, it was known as Mimi art, because Aborigines had no direct knowledge of the paintings but described them as being the work of Mimi spirit people who live in the rocks. This is not surprising because the early Mimi, or dynamic, style is totally different in style and technique from the much younger and more familiar x-ray style.

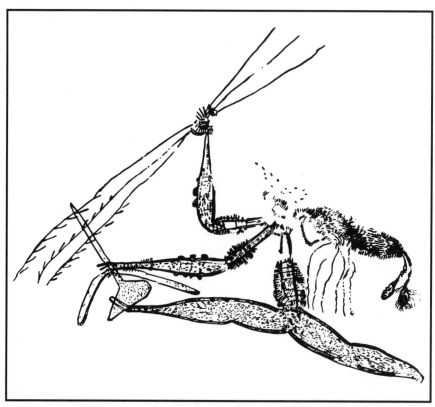

Figure 11.8 Male figure in the dynamic style, Arnhem Land, Northern Territory. This hunter from Kolondjorluk Site 2, Deaf Adder Creek, wears a long, tasselled ceremonial head-dress and holds barbed spears, a boomerang and a hafted stone axe. (After Brandl 1973, by courtesy of the Australian Institute of Aboriginal Studies)

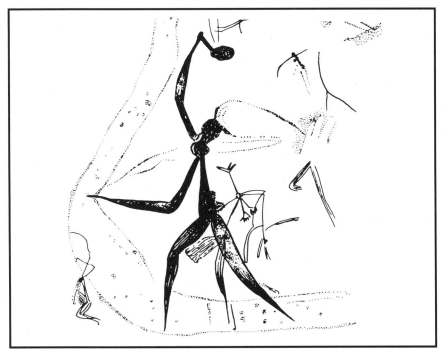

Figure 11.9 Dynamic style figures from Deaf Adder Creek, Arnhem Land, of a hunter holding a hafted stone axe, and a 'kangaroo man' with boomerangs painted over a dotted snake, according to Aboriginal informants. (After Brandl 1973, courtesy of Australian Institute of Aboriginal Studies)

In the Kimberley to the west, the so-called 'Bradshaw' figures are similar to the early Mimi style (plate 24). They are depicted in red ochre, or at least only red pigment still survives, and average only 25 to 30 centimetres in height. Both Mimi and Bradshaw figures wear similar elongated head-dresses, pubic skirts, armlets and tassels and use the same type of barbed spear and boomerang. Barbed spears were not part of Aboriginal culture in the Kimberley for the last 3000 years; spears there seem to have been unbarbed but tipped with a pressure-flaked stone spear point. These paintings are not of importance to present-day Kimberley Aborigines, who say they cannot interpret the meaning of the scenes because they were the work of a bird, which painted spirits that are invisible to humans.[32] The Bradshaw figures are very faint and weathered in comparison with the spectacular later Wandjina spirit paintings (plate 25), and they are probably of a similar or greater antiquity than the dynamic style in Arnhem Land.

Several changes took place in the development of this Arnhem Land rock art, some reflecting environmental change. The end of the Pleistocene period saw development of the yam figures, in which both human beings and animals were given the outward form of a yam (figure 11.10). This is the first known example of the portrayal of any edible plant in Australian rock art. The introduction of the yam style may indicate that yams (*Dioscorea* species) were becoming an important food source at the end of the Pleistocene period when rainfall increased. Chaloupka also points out that the encroaching sea may have led to the myth of the Rainbow Serpent, which makes its first appearance in the rock art of the yam style. The Rainbow Serpent is generally associated in northern Australia with myths concerning

rain and floods, which could reflect the rising post-glacial sea, which has been estimated to have swallowed up several hundred metres of land each decade. If Chaloupka is correct, the change from pre-estuarine conditions and the appearance of the Rainbow Serpent belong to the years between 9000 and 7000 years ago, which would make the Rainbow Serpent myth the longest continuing religious belief documented in the world.

The early phase of Arnhem Land prehistory came to an end when the sea reached its present level and the environment became estuarine. Elements in the more recent art are the x-ray style and polychrome paintings using a wide range of colourful pigments (see colour plate 12). The hunters for the first time carried spear-throwers. This is an important clue to the time of development of the spear-thrower, which appears to have been independently invented within Australia. Spears are now multi-pronged or stone-tipped, and boomerangs gradually disappeared from their equipment. Boomerangs are now not used in Arnhem Land except as musical 'clap-sticks', imported from the desert people to the south.

In this naturalistic rock art the animals are portrayed with such realism and accuracy that it is possible to identify the particular species depicted. In this respect Australian rock art is similar to the cave art of Europe. And in both the European and Australian early cave art, zoomorphic figures occur, such as humans with bird or animal heads.

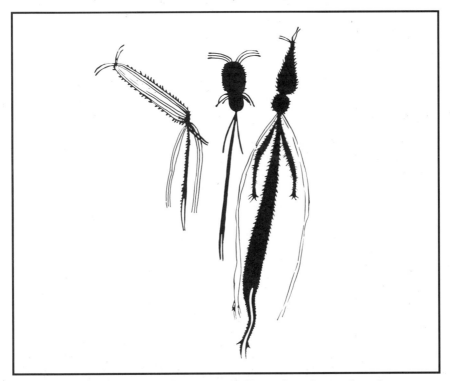

Figure 11.10 Anthropomorphic yam figures, Deaf Adder Creek, Arnhem Land, Northern Territory. The figures are painted in red; the tallest figure is 1 metre high. (After Brandl 1973, by courtesy of the Australian Institute of Aboriginal Studies)

Plate 24 (left) Bradshaw dancing figures, the Kimberley, Western Australia. (G. Walsh)

SUMMARY

The development of rock art is an integral part of Australia's prehistory. Whilst it is still very difficult to establish a chronological framework in spite of the new dating techniques, it is essential that this aspect of the human story is not ignored. Rock art is now an academic discipline in its own right, thanks to the outstanding work of leading specialists and their students, such as Andrée Rosenfeld of the Australian National University, who is involved in a special study of the Panaramitee style, Michael Morwood of the University of New England, who has focused on the archaeology of art in Queensland, and John Clegg of the University of Sydney, whose detailed study of the Panaramitee-style petroglyphs of one site, Sturt's Meadows near Broken Hill, is a model of the rigorous archaeological approach to art analysis. The subject has become so vast that it is beyond the scope of this book to do more

Plate 25   Wandjina art site, the Kimberley, Western Australia. (G. Walsh)

than give a brief overview of a few art sites which play a vital part in the story of prehistoric Australia, but the reader is referred to the preface for a discussion of further reading.

There are inevitably many uncertainties in trying to identify tangible evidence of the awakening of early human intellect, and far more questions than answers. What we now know is that art was part of the culture of the earliest Australians, for pieces of utilised pigment or 'crayons' occur right down to the base of most Pleistocene occupation sites, notably in the 50 000-year-old levels of the Kakadu rock-shelters of Nauwalabila and Malakunanja II. Certainly, hands were being stencilled and ochre mixed with blood and applied to rock walls in Tasmanian caves during the last glaciation, and three rock painting sites (Laurie Creek, Sandy Creek 2 and Gnatalia Creek shelters) have given radiocarbon dates on organic material within pigment of between 24 000 and 29 000 years, although some problems with this dating of ancient pigment remain to be resolved.

The great antiquity of petroglyphs has long been suspected through circumstantial evidence, so the absolute dates of around 40 000 years given by AMS dating of Panaramitee petroglyphs are not unexpected. It seems that art was part of the 'cultural baggage' of Australia's first settlers. The early art takes various forms, tentative finger meanders and geometric motifs incised on the soft walls of underground caves such as Koonalda and the Mount Gambier caves in South Australia, and the continent-wide Panaramitee style, dominated by geometric motifs, particularly circles, but also including many tracks and human footprints. Contemporary Aborigines of Central Australia, who still paint and engrave tracks, have explained these as depicting the earth's view of the creatures who walk on its surface. This symbolic art is a continuous, significant part of Aboriginal culture, but there were also numerous additions and changes, in the direction of more figurative art, particularly figures engraved or painted in silhouette. The relatively homogeneous, continent-wide Panaramitee tradition can be seen, through transitional sites such as the Mootwingee petroglyphs, developing into the incredibly rich and diverse figurative art of recent times, such as the x-ray paintings of Arnhem Land, the Kimberley Wandjina or the huge, figurative rock engravings of the Sydney sandstone.

CHAPTER TWELVE

Extinction of the Megafauna

There are many Aboriginal legends about giant mythical beings of the Dreamtime, and some of these stories handed down from generation to generation may well enshrine memories of the now extinct megafauna (large creatures) that once roamed Australia more than 15 000 years ago. One such story tells of the hunting of huge kangaroos with fire and weapons in western New South Wales.

Long ago, many people were camped at the confluence of the Lachlan and Murrumbidgee Rivers. The day was very hot and a haze rose from the windless plain so that the horizon danced, and mirages distorted the landscape. Everyone lay motionless, resting in the heat. Suddenly, a tribe of giant Kangaroos were seen away in the distance and the headman leapt to his feet with a galvanizing cry. The camp became a scene of wild excitement and fear. Children were quickly seized and everyone dispersed into the bush. In those times, however, the men had no weapons and were defenceless against the enemy. The Kangaroos relentlessly advanced on them through the bush and without mercy crushed their victims with their powerful arms. When the animals were finished, few of the tribe remained. The headman, however, lived, and in desperation he called the remaining band together to discuss methods of defence. At that meeting the men devised the weapons of spears, shields, clubs and boomerangs, some of which are still used today in many parts of Australia. Many young women had lost their children as they fled, and needing a device in which to carry their babies they made the ingenious bark cradle.

But Wirroowaa, the cleverest of the men, thought of enlisting the help of the Great Spirit. To do this, however, he needed to paint his chest with sacred designs in white clay which had to be collected from the banks of the river bed where the giant Kangaroos were camped.

Fearlessly he set out across the plain for the river bed. He turned over a hollow log with his foot and found a big, brown-banded goanna, his beady eyes blinking and his wide yellow jaws apart. Quickly killing the goanna, Wirroowaa slit the belly open with a stone tool and extracted the body fat. This he smeared all over his skin until it glistened in the hot sun; then he rolled in the dust until he was as brown as the earth, and then picked up a branch of leaves to hold before him. This was the first time a man had used the technique of camouflage. Completely disguised, he quietly crept on towards the Kangaroo camp and without being observed stole the sacred clay.

Behind him a small breeze had come up, and the nearer he got to the river bed the stronger the breeze became. Two sticks which first were gently rubbing together soon became warm, then red hot, and suddenly a spark flew from the smoking twigs into a patch of dry grass. A fire was made. Wirroowaa quickly smeared his body with the clay, making sacred designs which would bring the presence of the Great Spirit to him.

The wind gradually grew in volume and spread over the grassy plain. The little breeze became a gale. The Great Spirit came and told Wirroowaa to keep to the dry patches of ground. Some of the people had already been caught in the fire, but others picking up their babies in the bark cradles, rushed to the treeless area. The giant Kangaroos appeared on the horizon but were driven back immediately by the fire. The danger from them was over for a while.

But the leader, the headman, was dying and Wirroowaa painted him with the sacred clay so that the power of the Great Spirit would be with him. Then the old man spoke. He said that one day the giant Kangaroos would be overcome. Each man must carry spears and clubs, and bark must be stripped from trees to make shelters for each family, so that the sun would not weaken the people as it had in the past. Shields were also to be used in defence.[1]

Since 1830 it has been known that megafauna once existed in Australia. In that year Sir Thomas Mitchell, Surveyor-General of New South Wales, found in the Wellington Caves west of Sydney a tooth of *Diprotodon optatum*, the largest marsupial known to have lived. Indeed, one of Mitchell's party tied a rope to a projection in order to lower himself into the cave, only to find that the projection was the bone of a giant marsupial. At that time much of the Australian continent was unknown to Europeans, and early explorers such as Ludwig Leichhardt quite expected to come across live *Diprotodon* in their travels. However, it emerged that the megafauna were all extinct.

The demise of Pleistocene megafauna must not be confused with earlier extinctions like that of the dinosaurs, who met their end as much as 65 million years earlier. Down the ages many creatures have become extinct, but extinction is part of evolution and extinct animals were usually replaced by new ones. Then at the end of the Pleistocene the extinction rate accelerated. An extraordinary number of large vertebrate animals suddenly disappeared, relatively simultaneously (in terms of geological time), over much of the globe in a 'last revolution in the history of life'. There was extinction without replacement. Extinction means permanent irreversible disappearance of a taxonomic lineage, either a genus or individual species; in other words, 'extinction is for ever'.

These late Pleistocene extinctions have long fascinated archaeologists because of the possibility that they were caused, totally or partially, by prehistoric people. The last 100 000 years witnessed both massive global extinction of many genera and species of large mammals and the first global spread of *Homo sapiens*, who colonised two entire continents for the first time, Australia and America. Were human invasion of a new landmass and megafaunal extinctions just a coincidence? Or was the arrival of humans who were hunters the primary cause?

A theory of 'overkill' by hunters as the worldwide agent of destruction of megafauna has been proposed, notably by Paul Martin, a geosciences professor at the University of Arizona with a lifelong interest in the puzzle of Pleistocene extinctions, and the editor of and a major contributor to two key books on megafaunal extinction.[2] 'Overkill' is taken to mean human destruction of native fauna either by gradual attrition over many thousands of years or suddenly, in as little as a few hundred years or less. Sudden megafaunal 'extinction following initial colonization of a land mass inhabited by animals especially vulnerable to the new human predator represents, in effect, a prehistoric faunal "blitzkrieg", in Martin's term. Blitzkrieg or overkill models do not mean that the hunters killed every last individual of a species, but that their predation caused the faunal population to drop below the critical minimum population size for survival.

ARCHAEOLOGY OF THE DREAMTIME

SPECIES	DISTRIBUTION	DIET	HABITAT
Diprotodon optatum	all	browse/graze	desert/forest
Diprotodon minor	east	browse/graze	desert/forest
Zygomaturus trilobus	south/east	browse/graze	forest
Palorchestes azael	east	browse/graze	forest
Euwenia grata	north	browse/graze	forest
Nototherium mitchelli	north	browse	forest
Euryzygoma dunense	north	browse/graze	forest
Phascolonus gigas	all	graze	desert/forest
Ramsayia magna	east	graze	forest
Procoptodon goliah	east	graze	desert/savanna
Palorchestes parvus	east	graze	forest
Protemnodon anak	east	browse	forest
Protemnodon roechus	south/east	browse	forest
Protemnodon brehus	east	browse	forest
Macropus pearsoni	north	graze	savannah
Macropus ferragus	north/east	graze	savannah
Procoptodon rapha	east	graze	forest
Procoptodon pusio	east	graze	forest
Procoptodon texasensis	east	graze	forest
Simosthenurus pales	east	browse	forest
Sthenurus tindalei	centre	browse	desert
Sthenurus atlas	east	browse	forest
Simosthenurus orientalis	east	browse	forest
Phascolomys medius	east	graze	forest
Lasiorhinus angustioens	east	graze	forest
Troposodon minor	east	browse	forest
Sthenurus oreas	east	browse	forest
Simosthenurus occidentalis	south	browse	forest
Simosthenurus brownei	south	browse	forest
Propleopus oscillans	east	omnivore	all
Simosthenurus maddocki	east	browse	forest
Sthenurus andersoni	east	browse	forest
Thylacoleo carnifex	all	carnivore	all
Vombatus hacketti	west	graze	forest
Macropus thor	east	browse/graze	forest
Macropus piltonensis	east	browse/graze	forest
Zaglossus hacketti	west	insectivore	forest
Macropus rama	east	browse/graze	forest
Simosthenurus gilli	south	browse	forest
Warendja wakefieldi	south	graze	forest
Zaglossus ramsayi	south/east	insectivore	forest

Table 12.1 List of mammalian species that became extinct in Australia at the end of the Pleistocene, along with estimates of distribution, postulated diet and habitat. Compass points give a general idea of distribution only, for example east means eastern third of Australia. The tropical north and centre have few fossil localities, and thus may be under-represented in these estimates. Forest is here used as short-hand for any wooded habitat except rainforest; more precision is unwarranted as the extinct species are so poorly known. (Flannery 1990)

Figure 12.1 All Australian mammal species exceeding 10 kilograms in weight, as they were at the time of the Aboriginal occupation of Australia. They are organised according to body size (the largest at the top left, smallest at lower right). The extinct Pleistocene fauna are shaded in black, species that became extinct in historic times are shaded with a cross hatch, and those that have lost 90 percent or more of their range are hatched.

1. *Diprotodon optatum.* 2. *Diprotodon minor.* 3. *Zygomaturus trilobus.* 4. *Palorchestes azael.*
5. *Euwenia grata.* 6. *Nototherium mitchelli.* 7. *Euryzygoma dunense.* 8. *Phascolonus gigas.*
9. *Ramsayia magna.* 10. *Procoptodon goliah.* 11. *Palorchestes parvus.* 12. *Protemnodon anak.*
13. *Protemnodon roechus.* 14. *Protemnodon brehus.* 15. *Macropus pearsoni.* 16. *Macropus ferragus.* 17. *Procoptodon rapha.* 18. *Procoptodon pusio.* 19. *Procoptodon texasensis.*
20. *Simosthenurus pales.* 21. *Sthenurus tindalei.* 22. *Sthenurus atlas.* 23. *Simosthenurus orientalis.* 24. *Phascolomys medius.* 25. *Lasiorhinus angustioens.* 26. *Troposodon minor.*
27. *Macropus rufus.* 28. *Simosthenurus oreas.* 29. *Simosthenurus occidentalis.*
30. *Simosthenurus brownei.* 31. *Macropus giganteus.* 32. *Macropus fuliginosus.* 33. *Propleopus oscillans.* 34. *Simosthenurus maddocki.* 35. *Sthenurus andersoni.* 36. *Thylacoleo carnifex.*
37. *Macropus antilopinus.* 38. *Macropus robustus.* 39. *Macropus bernardus.* 40. *Thylacinus cynocephalus.* 41. *Lasiorhinus kreffti.* 42. *Vombatus ursinus.* 43. *Vombatus hacketti.*
44. *Lasiorhinus latifrons.* 45. *Macropus thor.* 46. *Macropus piltonensis.* 47. *Macropus agilis.*
48. *Macropus rufogriseus.* 49. *Macropus greyi.* 50. *Zaglossus hacketti.* 51. *Macropus rama.*
52. *Simosthenurus gilli.* 53. *Wallabia bicolor.* 54. *Macropus dorsalis.* 55. *Dendrolagus bennettianus.* 56. *Warendja wakefieldi.* 57. *Zaglossus ramsayi.*
(Flannery 1990, courtesy of the editors of *Archaeology in Oceania*)

The overkill theory suggests that megafaunal extinction never precedes but always follows closely the arrival of humans or their development of big-game hunting techniques. There is no doubt that on certain islands the extinction of fauna followed closely on the arrival of humans who hunted. When the first Maoris reached New Zealand about 1000 years ago, they quickly became moa-hunters and hunted these giant flightless birds to extinction within 300 to 400 years. Early archaeological sites, particularly on the South Island, show that the moa was important in both Maori diet and technology, but that it rapidly decreased in number and range of species under the onslaught of the islands' first human hunters and their fire-sticks. The fire-lighting activities of early Maoris also wrought significant destruction and change on the vegetation and increased the rate of erosion.[3]

On other islands the same story has been repeated. Madagascar witnessed the disappearance of the local fauna, the lemuroids, within a thousand years of human settlement, in about AD 1200. On the volcanic islands of Mauritius and Reunion, the swan-like, flightless bird, the dodo, was eradicated soon after the arrival of European settlers with their guns and pigs that ran wild and ate the eggs. The year 1681 saw the death of the last bird and the birth of the phrase 'dead as a dodo'.

On the continents of Africa and Eurasia the picture is not as clear-cut, for there, humans were present long before the late Pleistocene extinctions, which were also not as total as they were on islands. In Africa, about fifty animal species comprising 30 percent of Pleistocene big game disappeared some 50 000 years ago. This is seen as a result of the development of big-game hunting techniques.

In America, according to Martin, the first big-game hunters swept through the continent from Alaska to Tierra del Fuego in only 1000 years, decimating the giant beasts and triggering changes that led to the extinction of mammoths, mastodons, ground sloths, horses, camels and twenty-six other families of megafauna. These late Pleistocene extinctions were unique in their intensity, rapidity, and their selection of larger herd animals. Extinction struck only large terrestrial herbivores, their ecologically dependent carnivores, and scavengers. Small animals were not affected, nor were the giants of the sea, such as the world's largest mammals, the whales. The Pleistocene megafauna of America had survived until the arrival of humans — they disappeared 'not because they lost their food supply but because they became one'.

AUSTRALIAN MEGAFAUNA

During the late Pleistocene, the last glacial period spanning roughly the last 100 000 years, extinct animals in Australia included the super-family, Diprotodontidae, the family of carnivores, Thylacoleonidae, two genera and one species of kangaroos (*Sthenurus*, *Procoptodon* and *Protemnodon* species), several species of wombats (*Vombatus* species and *Phascolonus* species) and the large flightless bird, *Genyornis*.[4] In some other species, such as wombats, koalas and certain kangaroos, large Pleistocene ancestors have evolved into smaller 'dwarfed' forms. Most of the larger species of the family Macropodidae, the family of kangaroos and wallabies (literally meaning 'big feet'), evolved smaller-sized descendants that did not become extinct. Thus *Macropus titan* used to be classed as megafauna, but is now considered (e.g. by Flannery in his 1990 article[5]) as a large Pleistocene form of the large living grey kangaroo, *Macropus giganteus*, which is only two-thirds its size. This is important, since *Macropus titan* is a major component of late Pleistocene 'megafauna' at key sites in the megafaunal debate, such as Lancefield Swamp, described below.

America) and approximately forty-seven species (against fifty-one in America).
Precise numbers of species depend on taxonomic definitions, and Murray's 1984 list
has been revised by Flannery, whose 1990 list of mammalian species that became
extinct in Australia in the Late Pleistocene are shown in figure 12.1 and table 12.1.
Flannery's tables omit the large birds and reptiles which also formed part of
the Australian megafauna. When these are added, it emerges that in the last
100 000 years, Australia lost nineteen out of a total of twenty-two genera of terrestrial
megafauna, or 86 percent. (Martin's equivalent figures for North America are
73 percent and for South America, 79 percent.)

'Megafauna' means large animals, but how large is large? Martin used a working
definition of terrestrial megafauna exceeding 44 kilograms in adult body weight, but
in Australia this would result in including four species of large living kangaroos (the
grey, red, antilopine and wallaroo), and probably excluding the extinct carnivore
Thylacoleo and the smaller *Sthenurus* from the megafauna. Palaeoecologist David
Horton has come up with a precise, if cumbersome, definition for Australian
megafauna: 'Animals that became extinct before the Holocene and are large, either
in an absolute sense or relative to other members of some taxonomic rank, or are part
of a taxonomic category all of whose members became extinct and some of whose
members are large.'[6] In his provocative 1984 paper entitled 'Red kangaroos: last of
the Australian megafauna', Horton points out that the reasons for the survival of large
modern kangaroos such as the big red, *Macropus rufus*, which stands up to 2 metres
tall and weighs as much as 90 kilograms, are extremely relevant to understanding the
causes of the extinction of the other megafauna.

Australia's late Pleistocene fauna is not well known to palaeontologists, for much
of the evidence is sparse and fragmentary, and interpretations quoted here from
authorities such as Peter Murray and Tim Flannery are subject to constant revision as
new data emerge. The chronology of extinction is problematic, and, in spite of
Horton's meticulous (1984) distribution maps of fossil finds, the lack of systematic
survey, particularly in northern and Central Australia, means that absence of
evidence cannot be taken as evidence of absence.

The megafauna which disappeared in Australia over the last 100 000 years
numbers approximately fifty species, and includes reptiles and birds as well as
mammals. The extinct reptiles exceeded 50 kilograms in adult body weight, as did
the megafaunal bird *Genyornis*, a flightless, emu-like, herbivorous species weighing
around 100 kilograms and with a beak about 30 centimetres in length.

Among extinct reptiles, the massive lizard *Megalania prisca* was far bigger than the
world's largest living lizard, the Komodo dragon of Indonesia. It grew to 7 metres
long and had sharp teeth and claws like the largest living Australian lizard, the
perentie of Central Australia, which reaches 2.5 metres in length. It was the largest
terrestrial carnivore in Australia, and may well have given rise to some of the
Aboriginal legends of monsters such as the bunyip and yowie. An enormous snake,
Wonambi narracourtensis, weighing up to 50 kilograms, and 5 metres long, inhabited
southern Australia. Its size and numerous small teeth indicate that it could have
taken mammals weighing as much as 10 kilograms as prey.

Two large crocodiles also survived into the Pleistocene, one enormous riverine
species, *Pallimnarchus pollens*, and *Quinkana fortirostrum*, a crocodile of medium size
(weighing a mere 200 kilograms!), which had teeth resembling those of carnivorous
dinosaurs, and which was possibly entirely terrestrial, according to Molnar.[7] The
petroglyph (figure 12.2) from the Panaramitee North site in the Olary region (now in

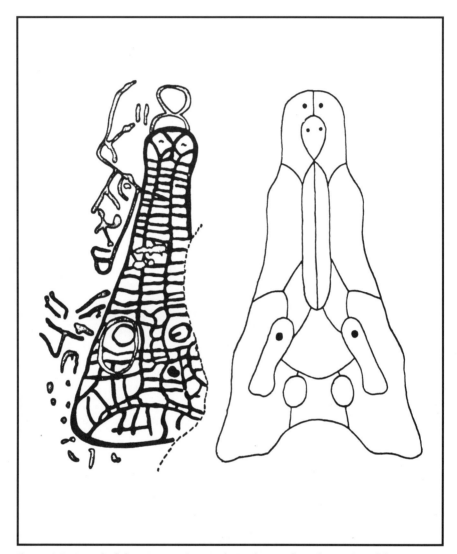

Figure 12.2 Petroglyph from Panaramitee North, South Australia. Left: Drawing of the petroglyph. Right: Sketch of a crocodile's head. (After Mountford and Edwards 1962)

the South Australian Museum) strongly resembling a crocodile's head or skull has always been an enigma, so far from any rivers or the sea, but in view of the 40 000-year-old dates now obtained on that site and the thick layer of desert varnish on the petroglyph, I am going to be so bold as to suggest that it may derive from a time when terrestrial crocodiles and humans actually co-existed in South Australia.

Around forty-one species of large mammals became extinct during the late Pleistocene (table 12.1). The most enormous was *Diprotodon*, a browser of wombat-like build and rhinoceros size, weighing an estimated 2000 kilograms (plate 26). A smaller, cow-sized relative was *Zygomaturus trilobus*, weighing in at about 1 tonne (1000 kilograms). Most of the extinct macropods were probably browsers, but those occupying treeless plains such as *Procoptodon* (estimated weight, 300 kilograms) in the Willandra Lakes region and *Protemnodon* (estimated weight, 40 kilograms) in the

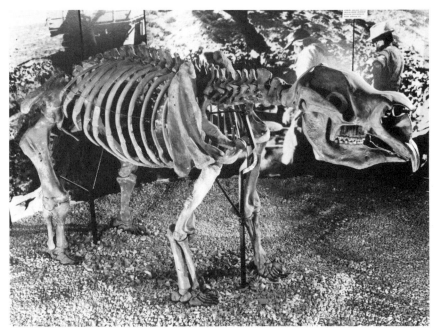

Plate 26 *Diprotodon* skeleton found at Lake Callabonna, South Australia. The head is about 1 metre long and an adult would have weighed about 2 tonnes. Its teeth make it clear that it was a plant-eater, adapted for both browsing and grazing. (B. Macdonald, by courtesy of the South Australian Museum, Adelaide)

Lancefield area were also adapted for grazing. In most marsupial families there was at least one large form that became extinct. The stumpy giant wombat, *Phascolonus gigas*, was twice as large as modern wombats and weighed about 500 kilograms.

One remarkable feature of Australian megafauna is the relative lack of carnivores, limited to just three species: the leopard-sized *Thylacoleo carnifex*, known as the marsupial 'lion' or 'giant killer possum'; the carnivorous giant lizard *Megalania*; and the Tasmanian 'tiger', *Thylacinus*, the size of a large dog. Only the thylacine could have functioned as a 'cursorial predator'. Because the large herbivores of Australia did not co-evolve with fleet predators like the hyaenas, canids and felids of Africa, they did not have to become effective long-distance runners, and most of the extinct ones seem to have been rather lumbering beasts. Even the extinct kangaroos are thought to have been much less fleet of foot than their living successors.[8]

The thylacine (figure 12.3) became extinct on the Australian mainland very much later than other megafauna, but still survives, we hope, in Tasmania, where it was alive in historic times, although one has not been captured or photographed for the last fifty years. Sightings have been reported but not substantiated both in Tasmania and on the mainland. The youngest thylacine bones found on the mainland are about 3300 years old, from Murra-el-Elevyn Cave on the Nullarbor Plain. Another cave on the Nullarbor, Thylacine Hole, contained an incredibly well preserved thylacine skeleton 4600 years old.[9] The area's extreme aridity had preserved the carcass so well that the tongue and one eyeball were still recognisable. The Tasmanian devil, *Sarcophilus*, appears to have become extinct on the mainland only a few hundred years ago, so both the thylacine and devil are excluded from this discussion of Australian extinctions.

Figure 12.3 The Tasmanian 'tiger', *Thylacinus cynocephalus,* **the largest marsupial flesh-eater.**
(Courtesy Bay Picture Library)

CAUSES OF EXTINCTION

One of the main problems in obtaining reliable dates on megafauna has been the
difficulty of dating bone, so palaeontologists have had to rely on stratigraphic
association using more reliable, datable materials, such as charcoal and shell. Bone
samples tend to have lost much of their collagen after 20 or 30 millennia, and bone is
particularly susceptible to contamination, especially by younger calcium carbonate
carried downwards by ground water. Bone dates therefore tend to be too young; this
has been demonstrated by comparing dates derived from charcoal, shell and bone in
the same archaeological layer. Analysis of the fluorine content of bones can be used
to tell whether bones found together are broadly contemporary or not, but fluorine
analysis does not give absolute ages.

In spite of all these problems, within the last decade the general chronological
framework of late Pleistocene extinctions has been established, although there is still
controversy over some individual sites. The main concern here is the part hunters
may have played in Pleistocene extinctions. The most reliable dates associated with
extinct fauna during the time span of known human occupation in Australia are set
out in table 12.2.

The most recent phase of extinction involved the disappearance from mainland
Australia of two medium-sized, flesh-eating predators, the Tasmanian devil and the
thylacine. The reason for at least the thylacine's demise seems to have been the
arrival of a more efficient predator: the dingo. No dingo bones have been found in
Pleistocene faunal deposits, and the oldest firmly dated ones go back only some 3000 years,
at Fromm's Landing rock-shelter in South Australia, and Wombah midden, New
South Wales.[10] It is now generally thought that the dingo was brought by
hunter–gatherers to Australia around 4000 years ago, and certainly after 10 500 years
ago, when the post-glacial melt-water finally severed Tasmania from the mainland.
This would explain the dingo's absence from Tasmania and older mainland sites, but

Table 12.2 Some occurrences of extinct fauna in Australia since 40 000 BP.

DATING CODE	DATE BP	FAUNA	SITE
	> 37 000	Thylacoleo Zaglossus Zygomaturus Sthenurus	* Mammoth Cave, WA
SUA-585–6 SUA-546	32 800 ± 830 (average of three dates)	Sthenurus Protemnodon Zygomaturus	* Devil's Lair, WA
ANU-65	31 600 ± 1300	Diprotodon Thylacoleo Macropus titan	Arundel Terrace, Keilor, Vic. (in 'D' clay)
Beta-44376 Beta-44374	30 280 ± 450 to 19 270 ± 320	Diprotodon Sthenurus Protemnodon Genyornis	*** Cuddie Springs, NSW
SUA-538 SUA-685	26 600 ± 650 25 200 ± 800	Macropus titan Diprotodon Protemnodon Genyornis Sthenurus	Lancefield, Vic.
L.J.-204 GaK-335	26 300 ± 1500 to 18 800 ± 800	Diprotodon Procoptodon Protemnodon Phascolonus Thylacoleo Macropus titan Sthenurus	** Lake Menindee Lunette, NSW
ANU-1220	22 980 ± 2000	Sthenurus	Cloggs Cave, E Vic.
	c. 19 000	Zygomaturus Diprotodon Protemnodon	* Rocky River, Kangaroo Is., SA
GaK-7081	20 650 ± 1790	Macropus titan	Beginners' Luck, Tas.
T.I.-1-11018	19 800 ± 390	Diprotodon Sthenurus	* Spring Creek, SW Vic.†
	< 20 000	Sthenurus Macropus titan	Titan's Shelter, Tas.
SUA-915	19 300 ± 500	Diprotodon Macropus titan Protemnodon Procoptodon Sthenurus	Lime Springs, NSW
ANU-1221	16 100 ± 100	Sthenurus	* Seton, Kangaroo Is., SA
GaK–693	3280 ± 90	Thylacinus	Murra-el-Elevyn, Nullarbor, Australia WA

  * Indicates sites where the fauna may be associated with human activity.
  ** Indicates sites where the fauna seems to be associated with human activity.
  *** Indicates sites where the fauna is associated with human occupation.
  † A humanly engraved Diprotodon tooth found at Spring Creek may be younger than 19 800 BP
     (Vanderwal and Fullager 1989).

its presence in younger sites and historic times on the mainland. It would also account for the extinction of such predators as the thylacine on the mainland but their survival in Tasmania, where they were free from competition with the dingo.

Moving back in time, there is now plenty of evidence that megafauna and prehistoric humans overlap in time in Australia. Clearly, the megafauna did not become extinct before human arrival, as was once thought the case. The overlap of the co-existence of megafauna and humans in Australia is at least 20 000 years. There are now sufficient well-dated sites containing megafauna that, even if some of those listed in table 12.2 are rejected as not being absolutely proven, it is inarguable that some megafauna survived in some regions of Australia until around 20 000 years ago or less. (The evidence was well summarised by Peter White and Jim O'Connell in 1982, and is not at issue.[11]) What is still extremely contentious is what part, if any, humans played in megafaunal extinctions, and the rest of this chapter will take a fresh look at this. It is an extremely complex question, which warrants a whole book rather than a brief discussion, because we are dealing with extinction of a wide variety of megafauna in a great variety of environments across a whole continent over an extremely long time period. In this situation the explanation is likely to be multi-causal rather than uni-causal, for many factors may have had a role, but here we will examine only the arguments for possible human causation. This has been most strongly propounded by Duncan Merrilees in his classic paper, 'Man the destroyer', and by Jones, who (at least in 1968) saw humans as 'the decisive factor'.[12]

SPECIES STABILITY AND CLIMATIC CHANGE

There was a sudden extinction at the end of the Pleistocene of species which had been stable for the 2 million years of the Quaternary period, for example *Diprotodon*, short-faced macropods such as *Sthenurus* and *Procoptodon*, and the carnivorous phalanger *Thylacoleo*. Even if the extinctions took place over 20 or 30 millennia, this is still a sudden event in the geological time scale. The cause could not have been a global climate change or a sudden extra-terrestrial catastrophe like asteroid impact, for late Pleistocene extinctions occurred at different times and at different intensities in different landmasses. Moreover, the species that died out had survived major climatic changes throughout the ice age; stresses just as severe as the last glacial maximum had been recurring events in Australia during the Pleistocene. The distribution of megafaunal species across Greater Australia shows they were tolerant of diverse habitats, as are some modern species, like the grey kangaroo. For example, *Diprotodon* inhabited environments as varied as New Guinea, the arid Lake Eyre basin and Tasmania. Nor were the megafauna's ecological niches filled by other species.

Environmental determinists such as Horton still invoke climatic change as the main cause of megafaunal extinctions. In 1990 he wrote:

> For the record I don't believe the megafauna all went extinct at one time in response to a single climatic event. I do believe that most extinctions began to occur around 25,000 BP (at least 15,000 years after human arrival) in response to major climatic fluctuations and may well have continued into the Holocene. I also believe that the majority occurred in the late, rather than the earlier, Pleistocene because the climatic changes at that time were greater, if only marginally, than those earlier ones. A marginal difference can be a decisive difference in a continent as much on the edge (in all kinds of ways) as Australia.[13]

This climatic extinction model seems to me to have two weaknesses — its heavy reliance on one site, Lancefield Swamp, and its non-recognition of the fact that the main period of extinction in Australia *preceded* the main late Pleistocene climatic change. Horton's admirable excavation of Lancefield Swamp led him to formulate what I have called 'the last waterhole' hypothesis. In his words:

> *The megafaunal species that became extinct relied on the availability of water much more heavily than the species that have survived. The combination of these two biological attributes was the cause of the extinctions, and it also resulted in their being concentrated in time. The concentric arrangement of habitats in Australia creates a threshold effect. The arid area of central Australia expanded and contracted throughout the Pleistocene without crossing the threshold because woodland areas with adequate water supplies always remained, and few extinctions were caused. The threshold was crossed between 26,000 and 15,000 yr B.P. when the arid area expanded further than usual and water resources in the woodland areas were severely reduced. In some cases populations were trapped around drying-up water supplies, in others food supplies were eaten out even though the water remained. Smaller species with less water dependence could travel far enough to find food.*[14]

The one characteristic that the megafauna had in common was their large size, which made them especially vulnerable to drought. Horton has elegantly demonstrated that large animals at Lancefield Swamp became inexorably tied to the one waterhole, until they died of hunger or thirst or became the prey of carnivores or human hunters. One flaw has recently developed in this argument: 90 percent of the animals that died there were *Macropus titan*, a kangaroo species which is now considered to be just a large Pleistocene ancestor of the modern grey kangaroo.[15]

A much more serious problem with the climatic extinction model is that it ignores the substantial body of evidence for earlier megafaunal extinctions in other parts of Australia, such as the southwest of Western Australia[16] and western New South Wales, where megafaunal extinctions correlate with Bowler's lacustral phase, when lakes were full of fresh water.

At most sites in the Darling River region, there is almost no overlap between megafauna and human occupation. For example, in the lunette at Lake Victoria, a now dry lake near the Murray River in the far southwest of New South Wales, more than 177 occurrences of extinct species, sixty-seven human skeletons and numerous middens have been found, but not one of the extinct animals found was associated with cultural material.[17]

At Lake Mungo and the other Willandra Lakes, megafauna is conspicuous by its rarity. Only a few remains of one species, *Procoptodon*, have been found as yet. These came from the southern shore of Lake Garnpung in sediments that also contain middens dated to about 31 000 BP, and from the northern shore of Lake Mungo, from within the Mungo sediments, dated between 25 000 and 19 000 years ago. At one of the Garnpung sites the *Procoptodon* remains were associated with artefacts and some of the bone was burnt. At Mungo, however, the fauna found in the human occupation sites are all modern species. The scarcity of megafauna at Mungo has been cited as evidence that the huge Pleistocene species had become extinct before 30 000 years ago as a result of overkill by human hunters.[18]

The large, eroded lunette at Lake Tandou on the lower Darling River has provided a long sequence at eleven soundly dated sites, showing that most of the extinct species had disappeared from the region prior to 27 000 BP.[19] Jeannette Hope's meticulous work has convincingly demonstrated that there is an unarguable rarity of fossil fauna in the upper (Bootingee) stratigraphic unit, dating to less than 27 000 BP, which cannot be explained by invoking poor preservation of bone, as has been suggested at Mungo. There was 'minimal overlap' between the megafaunal fossils in the older units and the abundant cultural material in the younger. The fossil record at Tandou suggests that the main phase of Pleistocene extinctions in western New South Wales had already occurred by the time of the major climatic shift of 25 000 years ago, although some megafauna, notably *Procoptodon*, may have survived until later. Hope concluded: 'These new data do not support the hypothesis that the extinctions were primarily due to the extreme arid conditions between 17,000 and 15,000 years, or indeed, to aridity over the longer period between 25,000 and 15,000 years ... In fact both the disappearance of megafauna and the size reduction in *Sarcophilus* [Tasmanian devil] seem to have occurred during the Mungo lacustral period [50 000 to 25 000 BP] which has been characterised as a period of high lake levels and regionally high watertables.'[20]

The only major change that took place in the region before or at the time of the extinctions was the arrival of humans with their fire-sticks, so this evidence supports human agency as a cause of the death of the megafauna.

In Western Australia several limestone caves in the southwest contain megafauna. Evidence of what seems to be deliberate breaking, cutting and burning of megafaunal bones comes from Mammoth Cave. The bones are older than 37 000 years, and until 1993 this was the best evidence that Aborigines preyed upon the large extinct animals.[21] The situation in other caves, such as Devil's Lair, is less clear, and Merrilees cautiously concluded regarding southwestern Australia in 1984:

> *The crucial question — what happened to the taxa now totally extinct — cannot be answered yet. It does seem that some process or processes bore more heavily on the larger than on the smaller mammals, and that man was present during the operation of these processes. While it is possible that the processes were geologically instantaneous (spread over one or a few thousand years), the evidence taken at face value is for some longer period, say tens of thousands of years. It is unlikely that any major climatic swing is responsible for the extinction processes, for they seem to antedate the last major swing, and nothing indicates that they represent the next to last. Therefore, it is tempting to suggest that some human activity underlies these extinctions, whether habitat modification by fire (Hallam 1975), selective hunting or indiscriminately wasteful methods of hunting, or some other activity as yet undiscerned.*[22]

One type of habitat alteration by use of fire that might have had a profound effect on megafauna is the destruction of particular fire-sensitive plant species that formed their food supply, since many of the large animals that became extinct in Australia were browsers. Others argue that if fire were used in the Pleistocene in a similar fashion to that observed ethnographically, it probably contributed to increases in the number and diversity of local animal communities. Traditionally, small areas are burnt at intervals to clear the way for easier travel, as a hunting aid, and to promote the growth of new grass on which macropods can feed. This regular, light, mosaic pattern of burning creates a varied array of habitats and conserves the modern macropod species, providing good grazing but also the shelter of unburnt areas, and lessening the occurrence of the disastrous blanket burns that often devastate parts of Australia nowadays. In 1990 Flannery contributed yet another theory, the 'aftershock hypothesis', suggesting that Pleistocene extinctions led to a build-up of fuel in the Australian landscape, which led to the occurrence of huge fires. Aborigines responded with 'fire-stick farming', reducing the danger of mass burning.[23] This aroused a storm of criticism, but far too little is known of the habits of megafaunal species to test any of these theories, so all that can be said with any certainty is that although Aboriginal use of fire certainly modified the environment, firing is unlikely to have been the sole or even a major cause of megafaunal extinction.

KILL SITES?

While the weight of circumstantial evidence favours human hunters as the decisive factor, certain archaeologists remain firmly opposed to any human role in megafaunal extinctions. Horton 'found no need for the hypothesis that human activity is involved in the extinctions'. Nor did Bowdler mince her words in commenting on Flannery's model: 'We are left with that dreadful old chestnut, the Blitzkrieg model, and that terrible old argument that there is no actual evidence for it [predation on large mammals] because the sites are or will be hard to find. Furthermore, the North American and New Zealand situations are trotted out for comparison, but without pointing out that there are in those countries KILL SITES.'[24]

Several possible sites have been put forward over the years as kill sites. In 1955 it was a site in a sand dune bordering extinct Lake Menindee in the Darling River basin in western New South Wales.[25] Bones of both extinct and modern species, fireplaces dating to between 18 000 and 26 000 years, and about 300 tools were found, including bone points, a few large 'Kartan-type' stone tools, horsehoof cores, adzes, and specialised, small Holocene tools, such as stone points. This mixing of young and old tool types and megafauna indicated deflation of the sand dune, causing items of different ages to lie together on an eroded surface. Thus Menindee is a possible but unproven kill site, but further work should now be done there and residue analysis carried out on the artefacts.

In recent years Richard Wright of Sydney University has claimed coexistence of humans and megafauna at three spring-fed swamps on the Liverpool Plains, south of Gunnedah in northeastern New South Wales. These are Lime Springs, Trinkey and Tambar Springs.[26] At Lime Springs, the only site about which findings have been published, albeit very briefly, there is a clear association between stone tools and the megafaunal bone (*Diprotodon, Procoptodon, Macropus titan* and smaller animals), which endures through a stratigraphic succession, and is dated between about 19 000 and 6000 BP. About one-quarter of the bone is burnt, and the quantity of burnt bone increases when the number of stone artefacts increases. The lowest artefacts are small, amorphous flakes of chert and quartzite, succeeded by large flakes, horsehoof cores and other implements of 'Kartan' type.

This sounds good, doesn't it? Except for the claimed 6000-year-old date on *Diprotodon*, which, if correct, would mean *really* rewriting the textbooks. And the claim of a Holocene Kartan industry, which elsewhere is Pleistocene — I think the problem here is terminological, and the name Kartan should be strictly confined to the industries of Kangaroo Island and the adjacent mainland or to other artefact assemblages that are virtually identical, rather than just vaguely similar. (One can compare industries by sophisticated multivariate statistical computer analyses or the pragmatic approach of mixing them all up on a table (after writing tiny identification numbers on them) and seeing if the two assemblages can be separated again.)

In the 1989 edition of this book I was rash enough to accept the validity of the coexistence of megafauna and humans at Lime Springs at a date of less than

19 300 BP, although I reserved judgment on the claimed but unpublished 6000 BP date. I have never accepted a Holocene date for megafauna in any of the Liverpool Plains sites, and I now wish to retract my 1989 acceptance of the claim that these sites demonstrate human predation on fauna. My planned site visit unfortunately had to be cancelled for personal reasons, but I began to have grave misgivings when I saw the bone remains in Horton's laboratory in Canberra. They were tiny! None seemed larger than my thumbnail. These remains are minute fragments of tooth enamel, which could easily have washed or blown into the swamp. A much more likely explanation seems to me, and many others, to be that Aborigines camped by the springs on a ground surface bearing fragments of Pleistocene megafaunal bone, these became burnt by their campfires, and later were washed or blown into the deposit.

My doubts were confirmed by a 1987 paper by Fethney, Roman and Wright, which describes the results of uranium series dating (see glossary) of excavated tooth fragments of megafauna and still-living species. The dates were 'an attempt to test unexpected Holocene radiocarbon dates for archaeological deposits containing tooth fragments of *Diprotodon* (and other megafauna). All proved 2 to 4 times older than radiocarbon ages for the deposits. This apparently excess age included dates on control species [*Lagorchestes* sp. = hare wallaby] still extant and found associated with the megafauna.'[27] The actual dates ranged from 23 000 $\pm$ 1000 BP (TR-107) to 47 000 $\pm$ 3000 BP (LS-N/2) for *Diprotodon* tooth enamel, and 42 000 +4000/–3000 BP (LS-N/2A) to 52 000 +5000/–6000 for hare wallaby enamel. There were anomalies: dates on the same *Diprotodon* tooth ranged from 23 000 BP on the enamel to 35 000 $\pm$ 2000 BP (TR-107) on the dentine. Fethney, Roman and Wright therefore dismiss the dentine date as problematic and the enamel ones as apparently contaminated, and state that 'uranium series dating has not resolved the archaeological question of a recent age for megafauna', something of an understatement!

Whilst contamination of samples is an acceptable and much-used explanation for dates that do not fit one's expectations, I was distinctly surprised to see Wright (in his comment on Flannery's 1990 paper) refer to these dates as supporting 'evidence for Holocene megafauna': 'We took two sets of tooth enamel, from *Diprotodon* sp. and *Lagorchestes* sp. (surely nobody would quarrel with hare wallaby being associated with artifacts in Holocene deposits dating to 6kyr). When we look at the uranium and thorium isotope profiles in this enamel (Fethney et al. 1987), we cannot distinguish between the profiles. This analysis sits uncomfortably with Flannery's notion of redeposition of *Diprotodon*.'[28] It also sits more than a little uncomfortably with ages ranging from 23 000 to 47 000 BP (not mentioned here) for this fauna which Wright is claiming as Holocene. It seems to me that Wright cannot have it both ways.

In fact, what the uranium thorium dates are telling us, I think, is that the excavated remains of *Diprotodon* and hare wallaby are not both Holocene but are both Pleistocene, with one, a wallaby the size of a hare, surviving to the present day, because it is minifauna rather than megafauna. Reading, in my new spirit of scepticism, the publications on what has become known as the 'Tambar Springs project', there are many other clues that the megafaunal remains are redeposited; for example, 'we cannot differentiate the state of preservation of extant and extinct species', and 'pieces of bone are more frequent towards the margin of the swamp'.[29]

I have gone into detail about this because Wright's confidence in his interpretation seems unshakeable (personal communication, November 1993), and he predicted in his 1990 comment that 'within five years I shall have megafaunal bone from the Holocene, extracted amino acids and obtained a Holocene radiocarbon date on those acids'. If unequivocal proof of Holocene megafauna has not been produced by then, perhaps a public retraction, published in a widely read journal, would be appropriate, so that this vision of *Diprotodon* lumbering around the Liverpool Plains only 6000 years ago can be stopped before it becomes any further quoted and accepted as fact, both nationally and internationally.

BLOOD ON THE STONE

The good news is that after all these unproven or problematic candidates for kill sites, at last we have the proof. The site is the shallow ephemeral lake of Cuddie Springs in semiarid northwestern New South Wales.[30] It has long been known as a source of fossil bone, but ecological investigations since 1990 by Judith Furby, John Dodson and Ian Prosser from the School of Geography at the University of New South Wales and Richard Fullager and Robert Jones of the Australian Museum have revealed that the site also contains cultural material. It was the subject of Furby's Honours thesis at the University of New South Wales, and two fairly detailed accounts were published in 1993, so I will only summarise here the most significant findings that impinge on the megafaunal debate. The research report states:

> *Cuddie Springs contains several distinct concentrations of megafaunal bone, in addition to a scatter of bone through all the sediments examined. Most of the deposit is beyond radiocarbon dating but an upper portion of sediment has been dated between 19,000 and 30,000 BP. Artefacts and increased charcoal appear about 30,000 BP and then have a continuous presence. The artefact assemblage includes grindstones with starch residues, ochre, a probable cylcon and artefacts with reworked edges containing blood and hair. These combine to provide evidence of plant and animal processing and cultural practices at 30,000 BP. The bones and artefacts were deposited when Cuddie Springs was a shallow freshwater lake surrounded by a relatively arid shrubland, the lake then became ephemeral and the environment more arid as the glacial maximum approached.[31]*

The key points about Cuddie Springs are that megafaunal bones and artefacts occur together in a secure stratigraphic sequence, well dated by a consistent series of radiocarbon dates on charcoal (figure 12.3). Stone tools are found above, below and between megafaunal bones, which are sufficiently large and well preserved to show up in photographs (plate 27). The youngest megafauna is associated with a date of about 19 300 years and extends back to a depth of 3 metres (beyond the limit of radiocarbon dating). The association of megafaunal bones with cultural material is confined to the central layer of the site, dated between about 19 000 and 30 000 BP. Charcoal adjacent to the lowest artefact in the sequence gave a date of 29 570 ± 280 BP, regarded as a minimum age, 'given the lack of evidence for rapid deposition, proximity to the limit of radiocarbon dating, and rudimentary pre-treatment of charcoal'.[32] The first appearance of artefacts in the sequence, in a layer dated to at least 30 000 BP, coincides with an increase in charcoal and is unequivocally associated with megafauna, such as *Diprotodon* and *Genyornis* (plate 27).

> *The well-preserved pollen, charcoal and the number of intact small bones seem to preclude the possibility that the materials have been naturally transported to the lake, especially given the very low gradients of the surrounding country. Many artefacts have well preserved residues and usewear suggesting minimal disturbance . . . Although the artefacts and bones appear to be in situ, the nature of the*

association of megafauna and humans requires further investigation. Two possible scenarios under investigation are that the large species became trapped in marshy conditions and either died naturally or were scavenged and butchered by humans.[33]

Since those words were written in mid 1992, further analysis has taken place. The blood and hair on the edges of some stone tools has been analysed by Loy, who has made positive identification of the blood of *Macropus titan* and *Diprotodon*. This was done by extracting DNA from bones of extinct species and then matching their 'fingerprint' with that of the blood residues on the artefacts. This is as yet unpublished but incontrovertible proof that Aborigines were at least scavenging the carcasses of dead megafauna, or possibly butchering trapped animals, or hunting them and transporting some bones back to their camp. The presence of hearths indicates cooking, and Dodson considers it was a camp site.

Ochre was in Unit 5, dated between about 30 000 and 19 000 BP, together with many stone tools, mainly flakes, cores and scrapers, made predominantly of silcrete, but also quartzite, quartz, feldspar porphyry, conglomerate and chert. The preferred raw material changed over time, with the use of quartzite decreasing and the use of chert increasing. Stone artefacts ranged in weight from 0.02 grams to 300 grams. Preliminary analysis of use-wear and residues indicates woodworking and other plant processing. Tool types included horsehoof cores and tula adzes.

A number of flat grindstone fragments were recovered from Units 3, 4, and 5. A preliminary microscopic study of the largest, which was in Unit 5 associated with the date of 28 310 BP, revealed a 'clear association of plant tissue and starch grains on the polished surface. Starch grains could have been derived from a number of plant

Plate 27 An *in situ* association of artefacts with megafaunal bone at Cuddie Springs, New South Wales. An artefact (a silcrete core) associated with charcoal dated to about 29 570 BP lies below a *Genyornis newtoni* tarsus-metatarsus and above a *Diprotodon optatum* mandible. It has use-wear and blood residues on its worked surfaces. The blood has been identified by Loy as *Diprotodon* blood. Several other silcrete flakes were found in the immediate vicinity of the megafaunal bones. (By courtesy of J. Dodson and J. Furby)

Figure 12.4 The stratigraphy of the Cuddie Springs megafauna site. (Based on information supplied by J. H. Furby and J. Dodson 1993)

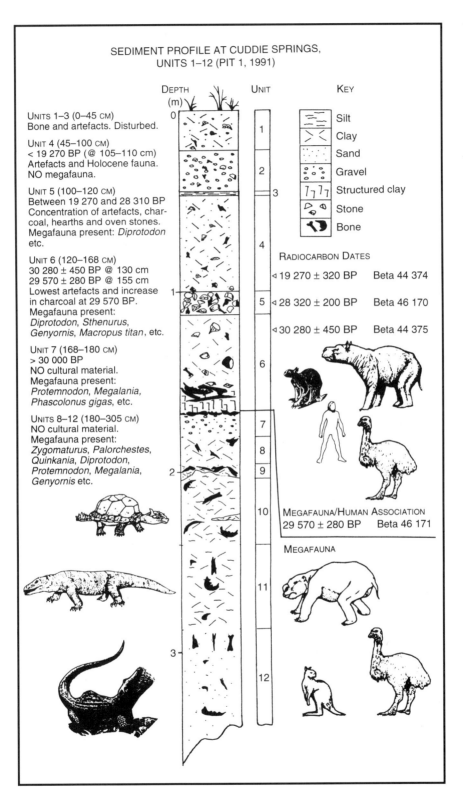

SEDIMENT PROFILE AT CUDDIE SPRINGS,
UNITS 1–12 (PIT 1, 1991)

DEPTH (m)

UNIT

KEY

UNITS 1–3 (0–45 CM)
Bone and artefacts. Disturbed.

UNIT 4 (45–100 CM)
< 19 270 BP (@ 105–110 cm)
Artefacts and Holocene fauna.
NO megafauna.

UNIT 5 (100–120 CM)
Between 19 270 and 28 310 BP
Concentration of artefacts, char-
coal, hearths and oven stones.
Megafauna present: *Diprotodon*
etc.

UNIT 6 (120–168 CM)
30 280 ± 450 BP @ 130 cm
29 570 ± 280 BP @ 155 cm
Lowest artefacts and increase
in charcoal at 29 570 BP.
Megafauna present:
*Diprotodon, Sthenurus,
Genyornis, Macropus titan*, etc.

UNIT 7 (168–180 CM)
> 30 000 BP
NO cultural material.
Megafauna present:
*Protemnodon, Megalania,
Phascolonus gigas*, etc.

UNITS 8–12 (180–305 CM)
NO cultural material.
Megafauna present:
*Zygomaturus, Palorchestes,
Quinkania, Diprotodon,
Protemnodon, Megalania,
Genyornis* etc.

KEY

Silt
Clay
Sand
Gravel
Structured clay
Stone
Bone

RADIOCARBON DATES

◁ 19 270 ± 320 BP   Beta 44 374

◁ 28 320 ± 200 BP   Beta 46 170

◁ 30 280 ± 450 BP   Beta 44 375

MEGAFAUNA/HUMAN ASSOCIATION
29 570 ± 280 BP   Beta 46 171

MEGAFAUNA

sources including grass seeds, *Acacia* [wattle] seeds and the pounding of tubers such as those of the bulrush, *Typha*, pollen of which showed up in the palynological sequence for this period. However the polish is most likely to be from processing siliceous material and is similar to the polish on Holocene seedgrinders.[34] Further studies are being undertaken to try to establish which particular plants were being processed, since there is much uncertainty at present concerning the antiquity of the grinding of grass seeds on millstones, which was such a feature of later Aboriginal exploitation of the arid zone. Meanwhile, these grindstones, with use-polish and siliceous starchy residues in a 28 000-year-old context, provide Australia's oldest direct evidence for Aboriginal processing of plant foods.

One of the most significant finds at Cuddie Springs was a weathered cylindrical stone, a cylcon.[35] It had been ground to a cone at one end and was broken at the other. Cylcons are thought to be sacred stones used in rituals, and have a restricted geographical distribution in Australia, being found on surface sites virtually confined to western New South Wales. Never before has a cylcon been found in a datable context, and their Pleistocene antiquity was completely unexpected but again shows the astounding time-depth and continuity of Aboriginal religion and culture.

The environmental data from Cuddie Springs will be invaluable in refining our understanding of climatic change in the late Pleistocene. The pollen record shows a decreasing tree, shrub and grass cover but a rise in saltbush (Chenopodiaceae) in the growing aridity as the glacial maximum approached. This evidence agrees with an environmental record from 30 000 to 10 000 BP from Ulungra Springs, 180 kilometres southeast, suggesting an expansion of the arid core of the continent by at least 150 kilometres during the latter part of the last glacial period.[36] Cuddie Springs lay within the arid zone. It was an ephemeral, freshwater lake by which people camped as early as 30 000 years ago, carrying out their rituals, manufacturing wooden and stone tools, grinding up seeds into food and having at least an occasional meal from the megafauna.

AN EXTINCTION SCENARIO

Humans first arrived in Australia sometime before 50 000 years ago, gradually spreading around the continent and using fire in hunting. The giant marsupials would have been relatively slow-moving prey, vulnerable to hunters. They would also have been naïve, that is they would have had no fear of humans, a situation comparable to the Galapagos Islands today. It may be significant that in the areas where some of the earliest occupation has been found, such as western New South Wales and the Perth region, the megafauna apparently disappeared earliest.

Those huge browsers that survived the initial impact of human hunters finally seem to have met their end during the Great Dry at the end of the Pleistocene. The one thing they all had in common was large size and a gigantic thirst, so as the lakes and waterholes dried up, one by one, they became doomed to extinction. Some, like the red kangaroo, managed to adapt; others evolved smaller forms; the rest died out. The period from about 25 000 to 15 000 years ago was a time of stress: stress from diminishing water supplies, from changes in vegetation and climate, and from the ever-present hunters with their spears and fire-sticks. Wooded areas near the coast probably acted as refuge areas, which would account for the megafauna's apparent survival there longer than in the arid inland. It seems that, directly or indirectly, Aboriginal occupation of the continent had as great an impact on Australian fauna in the Pleistocene as European settlement was to have in recent times.

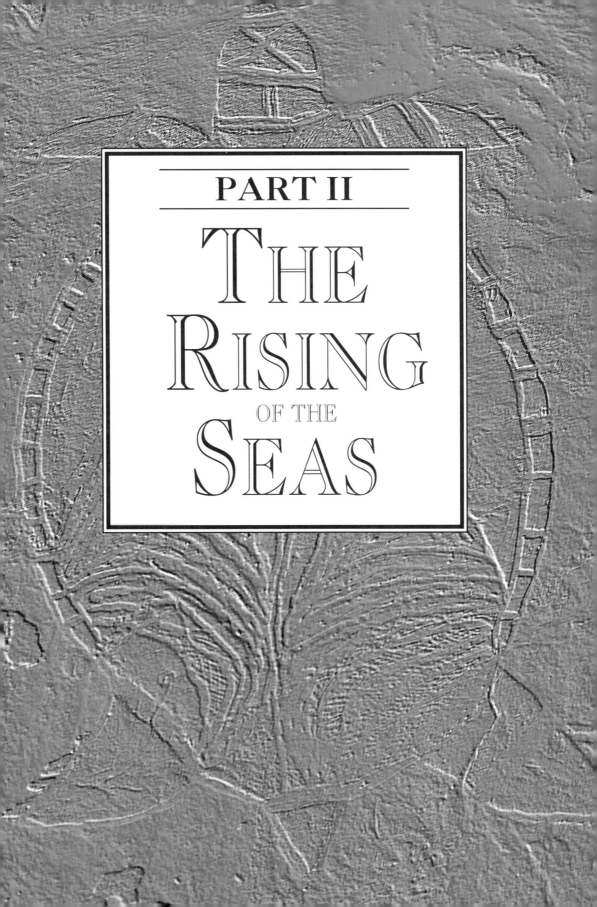

PART II

THE RISING

OF THE

SEAS

CHAPTER THIRTEEN

Tasmania: 10 000 Years of Isolation

No other surviving human society has ever been isolated for so long or so completely as were Tasmanian Aborigines over the last 10 500 years (figure 13.1). (The land bridge was gradually inundated between 12 000 and 10 500 BP, according to world expert on sea levels, John Chappell, and Blom's estimate of 8000 BP quoted in earlier editions of this book has proved incorrect.[1]) The storm-wracked waters surging through Bass Strait ensured that there was no contact with the mainland 250 kilometres away, and none of the new developments there, such as stone spear points, penetrated Tasmania. Nor did the dingo reach the island. Dingoes were found all over mainland Australia, so they must have reached southeast Australia *after* Bass Strait formed.

To archaeologists, the most interesting question is what effect 10 000 years of isolation had on the culture of these Aborigines, stranded on an island of 67 870 square kilometres — about the same size as Sri Lanka or Ireland. The Tasmanian Aboriginal population was estimated by Jones, on ethnographic evidence, to number between 3000 and 5000 at the time of European contact, but Colin Pardoe considers this a serious underestimate on biological grounds. A much higher population must have existed at least at the time of Tasmania's separation from the mainland to account for the lack of biological divergence due to genetic drift, which would be expected if a population of only about 5000 had been totally isolated for 10 000 years.[2] An alternative possibility is that the population multiplied through natural increase from the time of initial colonisation about 35 000 years ago, and was quite large at the time of separation, but that it declined in more recent times to the relatively low numbers recorded at the time of European contact. The evidence from ice age sites (described in chapter 9) suggests that, at the time the island was cut off, the Tasmanians' tool kit was similar to that of those on the mainland. A more comprehensive picture of early Holocene Tasmanian technology and diet is provided by Warragarra Shelter in the Central Highlands and, notably, by fauna-rich Rocky Cape caves, excavated by Jones.[3]

ROCKY CAPE

On the rugged headland of Rocky Cape, on the northwest coast, are two old sea caves cut into the face of great quartzite cliffs. Aboriginal shell middens in the caves were known since the end of the last century, but the first scientific excavation was not carried out until 1965. The work revealed the importance of Rocky Cape, and the area was declared a National Park in 1967.

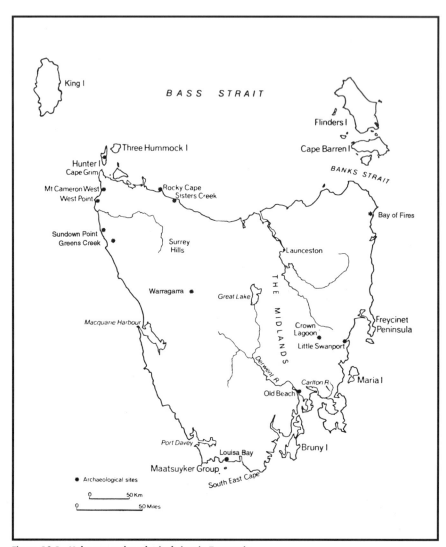

Figure 13.1 Holocene archaeological sites in Tasmania.

Holes dug into the sites earlier by amateur collectors made the excavators' task difficult, but some undisturbed parts of the deposits were found, from which the cultural sequence could be established. The huge shell midden in the South Cave was 3.5 metres deep, representing about 4000 years of occupation, from 8000 to about 3800 years ago. By then, the cave had become so full of food refuse that the midden heap almost reached the roof.

Inside the cave, a small inner chamber had already been sealed off by 6800 BP by midden accumulation outside its mouth (plate 28). The archaeologists found these cramped living quarters just as they had been left.[4] Piles of big abalone shells were dumped around the walls, but in the centre the floor had been swept clear for comfortable sitting around the fireplace. Here, five small ashy hearths, placed close to the rock wall for maximum heat reflection, were found. Food refuse included bones of seals, fish, a few birds and small mammals, shells of rocky coastal species, bracken fern stems, a lily tuber and split sections of the pith of the grass-tree. Faeces found in the rubbish dump were at first thought to be human, but analysis showed them to belong to Tasmanian devils, which no doubt scavenged there when the cave was unoccupied. Stone scrapers and a stone mortar, with pestle neatly placed on top, had been left behind by the last occupants for their next visit — a visit that never took place.

When the main chamber as well as the inner chamber became choked with refuse, the occupants seem to have decided that, rather than clearing it out, they would move to another cave about 300 metres to the north. This North Cave had been used intermittently since 5500 years ago, and its use continued until AD 1500.

Rocky Cape South and North caves together contain over 6 metres of midden, spanning 8000 years. This is the longest and most complete record of the technology and diet of coastal hunter–gatherers in Tasmania.

Plate 28 Inner chamber of Rocky Cape South Cave, Tasmania. The small piles of abalone shells against the walls have lain undisturbed since the cave's inhabitants vacated the inner chamber 6800 years ago. (W. Ambrose, by courtesy R. Jones)

STONE AND BONE TOOLS

Flaked stone tools, found in all levels, included scrapers, unretouched flakes and large choppers (figure 13.2).[5] The tasks for which these tools were used have been established with a reasonable degree of certainty from analysis of their shape, microscopic traces of use-wear along their working edges, and observations recorded in historic times of Tasmanian Aborigines using stone tools. Tasmanians used stone tools overwhelmingly for cutting purposes and for manufacturing wooden tools, especially spears. Sometimes shells performed the same tasks. Large scrapers and choppers were utilised for general chopping and hammering, and to chop toe-holds in trees when climbing the trunks to catch possums. Holes were also chopped in the bark of the cider gum tree *Eucalyptus gunnii*, to tap its sweet, semi-intoxicating sap, the nearest thing to an alcoholic drink available in prehistoric Australia.

These Tasmanian stone tools were all hand-held; the concept of hafting stone tools was apparently unknown on the island, although hafting was employed in northern Australia in the Pleistocene. It seems likely now (from evidence in the ice age caves of western Tasmania) that *bone* points were hafted onto shafts for spearing game. Blood residues on Pleistocene bone points indicate wallaby hunting, and

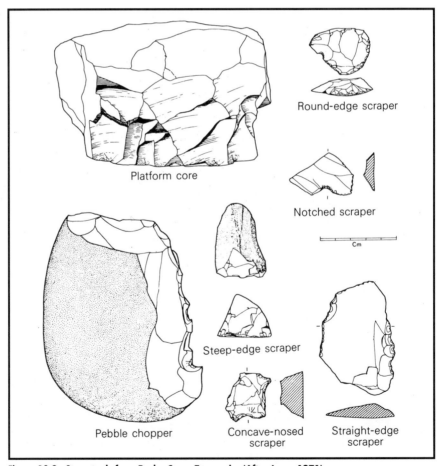

Round-edge scraper

Platform core

Notched scraper

Cm

Steep-edge scraper

Pebble chopper

Concave-nosed
scraper

Straight-edge
scraper

Figure 13.2   Stone tools from Rocky Cape, Tasmania. (After Jones 1971)

bone-tipped spears may also have been used for spearing large fish during the early occupation of Rocky Cape.

There was continuity in technological tradition in Tasmania from ice age to historic times; the same tool types and manufacturing techniques continued throughout. But within this general continuity there was also change. Two major changes were a steady decrease in the size of stone tools, and the increased use of better raw materials, such as chert, spongolite and siliceous breccia, brought from quarries like the Rebecca Creek spongolite quarry as far as 100 kilometres away on the west coast.[6] These changes are linked: the better flaking qualities of the new raw materials made it worthwhile to carry them over long distances, but this also meant that more efficient and economical use was made of the exotic stone than had been of the local veins of hard quartzite and beach pebbles of shale and argillite used in the earliest period of habitation. At first, stone tool manufacturing was done in the caves, but when the exotic raw materials began to be used, stone tools were fashioned, or at least roughed out, at the quarries and transported ready-made.

Bone tools were also at Rocky Cape. Seven thousand years ago, people there were using a considerable number and variety of bone artefacts: large, round-tipped points or awls made from macropod shin bones, small, sharp, needle-like 'fine points' (without an eye), broad spatulae, and an assortment of split slivers of bone fashioned to a point at one end.

A remarkable change took place over the next 4000 years: bone tools dropped out of use. By 4000 years ago, roughly only one bone tool was being used for every fifteen stone ones, and by 3500 years ago they had disappeared from the Tasmanian tool kit altogether. This has been confirmed by evidence from several other sites in both the northwest and east of the island. Moreover, no bone tools were observed in use by any of the Europeans who recorded Tasmanian culture, including George Augustus Robinson, who recorded virtually every detail of the years he spent between 1830 and 1836 travelling on his mission to gather up the Aborigines still out in the bush.[7]

It has been suggested that bone tools dropped out of the equipment of Tasmanian Aborigines because they stopped making skin cloaks. In the colder regions of the mainland in historic times, bone awls or skewers were used to pierce holes in skins for 'sewing' together possum or kangaroo skins into cloaks or rugs, which were often also fastened with a bone pin or 'toggle' on the shoulder. Yet, when Europeans arrived in Tasmania, they found no bone tools and no warm possum skin rugs, but only skimpy cloaks of wallaby skin fastened with tied pieces of skin. It might be argued that possum skin cloaks were unnecessary once the glacial cold diminished, but, if so, why were Aborigines in southeastern Australia still snugly wrapped in voluminous possum skin in the nineteenth century? Tasmania lies further south, in the Roaring Forties, and can be cold even in summertime. Other artefacts and technical skills may also have been lost or abandoned over the long period of isolation. Mainland Australian Pleistocene culture included boomerangs, barbed wooden spears, and the techniques of hafting handles to stone tools and grinding the edges of axes, but none of these items existed in the Tasmania of AD 1800.

A recent study of use-wear on bone tools by Cathy Webb of La Trobe University has thrown valuable light on their functions.[8] Webb isolated distinctive use-wear patterns on bone tools by direct experiment in order to suggest functions for archaeological examples in Australia. Her analysis of bone artefacts from two Pleistocene Tasmanian sites (described in chapter 9) identified their use as being for

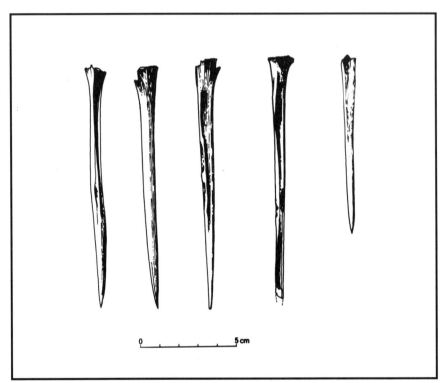

Figure 13.3 Bone tools from Cave Bay Cave, Tasmania, similar to those from Rocky Cape. The large tools are points and spatulas from the Holocene period; the small, sharp 'fine point' is from an 18 000-year-old level. (After Bowdler 1974)

skin-working and as bone spear points to hunt furred mammals, presumably the red-necked wallaby which was the Pleistocene hunters' main prey in most sites. Pleistocene bone spear points were a real surprise since no hafted spear points, of bone or stone, have been found or recorded in Holocene Tasmania.

DIET

Even more surprising is the incontrovertible evidence that after eating fish for many thousands of years, the Tasmanians dropped fish from their diet about 3500 years ago. Early explorers were amazed that the Tasmanians did not eat scale fish and did not even seem to regard it as human food. (Some of those who have eaten leatherjackets or wrasses tend to agree!) Certainly the Tasmanians had no nets or fish-hooks, so it seemed logical to some scholars, steeped in Darwinian evolutionary theory, that these most isolated representatives of the human race should be unable to catch fish, one of the basic foods of humans.

This concept was not seriously challenged until fish bones were found in the middens of Rocky Cape. Yet fish bones were not at the top, but at the base, of the deposit. The Tasmanians had once eaten fish but later gave up this source of food.[9]

In Rocky Cape South Cave there were 3196 fish bones in the lower half of the midden, dated to between 3800 and 8000 years ago, and only one fish bone in the younger, upper half. (The latter was a small vertebra, which could easily have been brought inside by a seal or cormorant.) The fish remains from the Rocky Cape sites, including the inner cave, have recently been analysed in great detail by palaeo-ichthyologist (prehistoric fish remains specialist) Sarah Colley.[10] She identified thirty-one different types of fish from rocky reefs, bays and estuaries. The data suggest that all the rocky reef species were caught by a simple baited box trap, and the others, by tidal traps made of boulders, such as the one on Sisters Beach, 6 kilometres to the east.

The average weight of the prehistoric fish was calculated by Jones from bone size as half a kilogram. He estimated that they provided about 10 percent of the total caloric intake in the diet in the fish-eating period, but such estimates are notoriously unreliable, because of differential preservation of food remains in archaeological sites. Shellfish were eaten throughout the whole occupation, the main species collected being warreners and some abalone. Other important foods were fur seals, some southern elephant seals, and small quantities of wallabies, birds (especially cormorants), bandicoots and other land mammals.

Jones envisaged a group of a few families camping there for five to ten days each year. This may well have been in winter, for winter was the time of stress in Tasmania, at least in historic times, when people fanned out in small groups along the coastline and relied heavily on the readily available shellfish.

The cessation of fish-eating was confirmed by other sites, such as Blackman's Cave on Sisters Creek, another sea cliff cave 8 kilometres east of Rocky Cape. The midden there, accumulated between about 6000 and 4000 years ago, contained fish and material similar to the lower part of the Rocky Cape sequence, with the interesting addition of crab claws, and many more small mammals, such as possums, rat kangaroos, bandicoots and rats.

Two sites, one on the west coast and one on the east coast, are examples of the later, non-fish phase: West Point midden and Little Swanport midden.

WEST POINT MIDDEN

Sixty kilometres west of Rocky Cape is the massive midden of West Point, one of the largest and richest occupation sites ever excavated in Australia.[11] It looks like a grass-covered hill and commands an extensive view seawards out over the reefs, bays and islets, as well as the swamps and tea-tree scrub behind the site. Formed on an old sand dune resting on a pebble bank, the midden rises 6 metres above the surrounding country and measures about 90 metres long by 40 metres wide. On its surface were seven or eight circular depressions, about 4 metres across and 0.5 metres deep. It seems certain that these were the foundations of dome-shaped huts, which were in use in historic times in Tasmania (figure 13.4). These huts were constructed from a framework of pliable branches, such as tea-tree stems, thatched with bark, grass or turf, and lined inside with skins, bark or feathers.

When Robinson was travelling along the western coast in the 1830s, he saw many such huts, often grouped into villages, close to a source of fresh water and a good foraging area. West Point is such a site; it was situated next to what was evidently an elephant seal breeding ground. Now elephant seals do not breed closer to Australia than Macquarie Island, 2000 kilometres to the south, but between 1300 and 1800 years ago, young seal calves were being killed at West Point, indicating that there was probably a seal colony next to the village, which was occupied in summer when the young seals were being weaned.

Seals were the major component of the diet at West Point, together with abalone and other shellfish, birds, wallabies, small marsupials and lizards. Among 20 000 bones from 75 cubic metres of deposit, there were only three fish vertebrae, which could easily have been transported there accidentally. Fish swim nowadays in the waters off West Point and are readily speared or trapped, but the prehistoric inhabitants clearly did not eat fish. However, they did eat seal, which would have provided a much richer source of energy than fish.

Figure 13.4 Tasmanian huts. Left: A simple bark windbreak. Right: Framework of a round, dome-shaped, thatched hut of the type used on the west coast. (By courtesy of the Tasmanian Museum and Art Gallery)

Rhys Jones estimated that a band of forty people could have camped there for three or four months every year for the 500 years or more that the site was occupied. If a family occupied each of the hut sites, this would give the village a population of about forty.

The way of life of these people was semi-sedentary; they probably spent about a quarter of each year in their village. Men would have clubbed young seals to death, while women would have dived for shellfish. The women were excellent swimmers and could stay under water for a long time, as observed by Robinson, the French explorer Labillardiere and others. They dived down, pried the shells off the rocks with small wooden wedges and put them into rush baskets suspended from their necks. Crayfish were also obtained by diving, sometimes in 4 metres of rough water; the fish were grabbed from under rocks and thrown up onto shore. Long, thin fronds of giant kelp were sometimes used as an underwater 'rope' to get down to such depths, for this type of 'seaweed' grows on the sea bed and sends out fronds of up to 60 metres in length. Women also used to swim between 1 and 2 kilometres across open sea straits to reach offshore islands, such as the Doughboys (rocky stacks about a kilometre offshore) and Trefoil, where muttonbirds nested. The muttonbird nests in burrows, making its nestlings easy prey for human predators. It is also an energy-rich food because of the high fat and oil content of the flesh.

No male activities needed much swimming skill, and some men could not swim at all. The reason for this may be that women, with their higher percentage of subcutaneous fat, were better adapted to withstanding the cold water in these latitudes. To protect themselves from the cold, both men and women used to rub their bodies with seal or muttonbird fat mixed with red ochre. In eastern Tasmania, shellfish were not so important in the diet, and a woman told Robinson that whereas the women in the west prided themselves on their ability to dive for shellfish, those from the eastern and inland regions could climb trees for possums. In mainland Australia it was men who cut toe-holds into trees to hunt possums, and it seems that in Tasmania women made an unusually large contribution to the diet. In many ways they were the force that kept Tasmanian Aboriginal society going. Women not only produced most of the food, but, when travelling, they carried spears and game, all equipment, babies and toddlers. They also mined ochre. And on one occasion, during an unexpected storm, Robinson witnessed the men sitting down whilst the women built huts over them!

The West Point people manufactured thousands of stone tools. More than 30 000 stone artefacts were found in West Point midden, most of them steep-edged scrapers, probably used for making digging sticks, spears and clubs. They closely resemble the industry of the upper part of the Rocky Cape sequence, and bone tools are similarly absent.

Plate 29 Little Swanport midden, Tasmania.

HUMAN REMAINS

The first prehistoric human remains to be found in Tasmania were excavated from the midden at West Point. Several human teeth were found, including one molar with severe erosion of the roots due to periodontal disease. Then three small cremation pits were discovered, two in the middle and one at the base of the midden, dating to 1800 years ago. The pits were filled with burnt and broken human bones. It seems the bodies were cremated, then the bones systematically broken, collected together with the charcoal and deposited in little pits, which were about 45 centimetres wide and were dug some 30 centimetres down into the sand or sandy midden.

In one pit were the foot bones of several wallabies and the talons of a large hawk. In another was a necklace of thirty-two shells, each pierced with a small circular hole. These were no doubt personal belongings of the dead. This is fascinating evidence that the shell necklaces worn by Tasmanians in the eighteenth century and the Tasmanians' practice of cremation go back at least 1800 years. Since cremation was practised at Lake Mungo 25 000 years ago, it is likely that it also formed part of the beliefs and customs that the first Tasmanians transported across the land bridge into what was to become their island home.

The human remains at West Point are fragmentary, but show great similarities to modern mainland Australian Aborigines.[12] In 1973, a reasonably intact burial in a sand dune near the Mount Cameron West engraving site was exposed by a gale.[13] A woman's skull was set in an upright position facing northeast, with two long bones crossed in front. In an arc on the western side were a series of carbonised remnants that appeared to be the remains of poles, set in the sand in the form of a wooden 'wigwam', like the structures observed as erected over burial pits on Maria Island, off the east coast of Tasmania, by the explorer François Peron. Carbon from the 'poles' and flecks associated with the skull were dated to 4260 ± 360 BP. The skull proved to be that of a woman, which shows that status burials were not reserved for males. She seemed to have been partially cremated and the bones smashed after death. Her teeth showed no decay, but there was chronic periodontal disease and molar wear. Her skull, whilst displaying typically Tasmanian features, falls within the range of mainland Aborigines, supporting the concept of the kinship of Tasmanian and mainland Australians.

LITTLE SWANPORT MIDDEN

In historic times, most of the Tasmanian Aborigines lived in the eastern half of the island. The terrain is still rugged but mostly composed of savanna grasslands, open sclerophyll forests, lakes and moorlands, and the coastline is indented by many sheltered bays and estuaries. Such a different environment from that of the northwest led to expectations that the east might have had a distinctive culture and economy, but these were dispelled by excavations on the central eastern coast.[14]

Several middens were excavated by Harry Lourandos, and no fish bones were found in any of them, except at the very base of the Little Swanport site. This is a huge midden, the existence of which was reported as long ago as 1891. It is the largest of a series of middens lying on the shores and islands of a sheltered tidal estuary on the central eastern coast (plate 29). Two metres thick, the midden consists

of oysters and mussels collected from the nearby muddy banks of the estuary.
Crayfish remains were also found throughout the deposit, but there were very few
bones or artefacts. The Little Swanport site was, therefore, a specialised fishing camp
rather than a home base camp, but fishing activities were confined to shellfish. There
were no fish bones at all in the upper part of the midden, but in the lowest zone,
dated to between 4750 and 3550 years ago, were the remains of at least thirteen fish
of the leatherjacket, or Aluteridae, family. These small, fast-moving fish still dart
around the estuary today, but, as in western Tasmania, it seems that they were
dropped from the diet about 3500 years ago.

SOUTHWEST TASMANIA

In the far southwest of Tasmania, the Louisa Bay area has been investigated by Ron
Vanderwal.[15] There, in a series of cave and open midden sites going back about
3000 years, shellfish predominate, and fish bones and bone tools are absent, except
for one bone point made from a wallaby shin bone, which was found in the lowest
level of an undated layer of shells in a sand dune.

South of Louisa Bay lies the Maatsuyker Island group, across a strait that takes
the full force of the frequent southerly gales and is dangerous even for modern craft.
Yet Aborigines in their frail, paperbark vessels braved these dangers to hunt seal on
Maatsuyker. Maatsuyker is 15 kilometres from the mainland, although it is likely that
the neighbouring De Witt Island, which lies between the mainland and Maatsuyker,
was used as a staging place. This would then involve two voyages of 10 and
7 kilometres. Middens and seals have been found on Maatsuyker but none on
De Witt, so a direct voyage may have been made. Given the wind and current
directions, embarkation was probably from west of Louisa Bay, making a voyage of
20 kilometres. And there are sufficient remains of prehistoric camps on Maatsuyker
to show that such visits to hunt seals and nesting muttonbirds were reasonably
commonplace in summer.

These voyages to the Maatsuyker Island group mark the most southerly
penetration by hunter–gatherers in Australia.

REASONS FOR ECONOMIC CHANGE

Tasmanian traditional material culture, by historic times, apparently included about
two dozen items: wooden spears with fire-hardened tips, throwing clubs, the
women's club–chisel–digging stick, wooden wedges or spatulae, baskets woven from
grass or rushes, possum skin pouch bags, water buckets made from kelp (figure
13.5), fire-sticks, kangaroo skin cloaks, shell necklaces, canoe-rafts, huts and a few
stone tools.

The evidence for the religious life of the Tasmanians is likewise limited, which
may or may not indicate a limited religious life. Compared with the richness of
religious life on the mainland, it was apparently largely confined to burial ceremonies
and dances depicting mythical and historical themes. But by the time Robinson
made his record of Aboriginal life, the population had been decimated and large
ceremonial gatherings would hardly have been possible. Tasmanian material

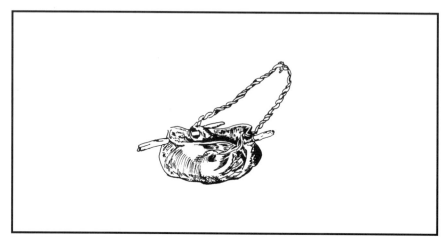

Figure 13.5 Tasmanian water container made from bull kelp. The kelp is folded onto two wooden skewers, making a flexible water bag. (After Peron and Freycinet 1807–1816)

equipment was reduced to the minimum necessary for survival, yet the Tasmanians may not have been a 'doomed' society, as some archaeologists have suggested. And their discontinuation of fishing need not have been a maladaptation, a deliberate but mistaken cultural decision to put a taboo on fishing. There may be much simpler, more plausible economic reasons why Tasmanians stopped eating fish.

Hunters in high, cold latitudes need foods rich in fat, yielding high energy. Thus, for the Tasmanians, seals and sea birds were better than fish or shellfish. Indeed, 'Had the Tasmanians the service of a consultant nutritionist, they would probably have been advised to give up fishing and concentrate their energies on more profitable foods. There is evidence in the post 3000 BP archaeological record that this is just what they did.'[16]

Robin Sim, who is doing her Ph.D. at the Australian National University on prehistoric occupation in the Furneaux Island group in Bass Strait, has shown from a whole series of middens that there was a change between about 3500 and 3000 BP in the *type* of shellfish being collected. In middens older than about 4000 years, the shellfish remains were mainly warreners and limpets, with lesser numbers of periwinkles, a few mussel shells and the rare piece of abalone. All these shellfish, except abalone, can be collected by walking around the rocks or wading. Sim suggests that the mass consumption of subtidal shellfish (abalone) and crustacea (crayfish) probably began around 3500 to 3000 years ago, when people in Tasmania started to dive and swim. Before this, it seems that they were only wading and collecting shellfish obtainable from tidally exposed rocks, although there is evidence of fishing in the older middens.[17] Fishing was done with traps, as Colley showed at Rocky Cape; it did not involve more than wading.

'So, why did bone tools drop out at the same time as fishing?', was my next question to Sim. (I had long ago investigated ethnographic records to see if bone tools of the Rocky Cape type were used to catch fish, but could find no mention of such a function.) 'Oh, that's easy', she replied. 'Tom Loy has found residues of fish blood on some bone points from Rocky Cape; they were used to spear and gut them!' In 1985 Loy gave a seminar to Australian Museum staff entitled 'Bloody stones: residue analysis of prehistoric artefacts. Methods, applications to Australian materials, and implications for Museum curation', in which he described how 'a suite of bone tools from the Rocky Cape Cave in Tasmania were identified as implements for spearing and gutting fish on the basis of their residues'.[18] I have seen no mention of this case study anywhere, but thanks to Loy's pioneering work and Ron Lampert's efficiency in reporting the seminar in the Museum's newsletter, another archaeological puzzle has at last been solved.

In contrast to the 'doomed people theory', there is a strong case for believing that the Tasmanian population was branching out in new directions during the last 3000 years. The interesting idea has been put forward that Tasmanian watercraft were only invented about 3000 to 3500 years ago, in the west of the island, where they were needed most. It has long been taken for granted that Pleistocene Tasmanians had watercraft, but there is no reason why they should have. Tasmanian watercraft are unlike any craft on the mainland (figure 13.6). They were made from three bundles of paperbark *(Melaleuca)* or stringybark *(Eucalyptus obliqua)*. Each bundle was bound with a network of bark or grass string, forming a sausage-shaped craft, tied at both ends, with a slightly hollow centre and upcurving bow and stern. The central bundle provided most of the buoyancy, and the side ones acted as stabilisers. The boat was propelled by a long pole or by swimmers pushing it along; paddles were unknown. These canoe-rafts could hold six or seven people but they were generally not taken more than 15 kilometres off the coast.[19] The problem was that, when saturated, the bark had a density similar to water, so after a few hours the craft lost its rigidity, became waterlogged, and sank or had to be dried out on a beach before being re-used.

There is no evidence that watercraft were used in Tasmania before about 4000 years ago, when Hunter Island was revisited after being vacated when it was first severed from the mainland. One strong point in favour of this notion is that it accounts for the absence of watercraft in northeastern Tasmania. With far fewer rivers, bays and offshore islands, there was no real need for boats there, so it is not surprising that the invention of a group living on the opposite side of the island was not adopted. Further field work is needed to test this theory, but it is supported by some cultural developments in the same period.

Figure 13.6 Tasmanian watercraft. (By courtesy of Tasmanian Museum and Art Gallery)

It is possible that petroglyphs at Mount Cameron West, Sundown Point, Greens Creek and a few other sites near high water mark on the west coast are not a relic of ice age art, but were carved only about 2000 years ago. The style is ancient, and Franklin sees them as part of the Panaramitee tradition, whereas Rosenfeld believes them to be independently 'invented' in the Holocene.[20] On the other side of the island, at the Bay of Fires, is a stone arrangement which was constructed less than 700 years ago.[21] Robinson, during his 'friendly mission' in 1830, came across similar arrangements on the west coast.

The Bay of Fires stone arrangement is located on a ridge overlooking a pebble beach. About 56 metres long, it consists of a single line of ninety-three flat stones, in places resembling a garden path. The stones are set into an underlying midden so that their top surfaces are flush with the ground surface. A small test excavation in the midden revealed that another stone alignment lay stratified below. The sequence of events seems to have been that a linear stone arrangement was built on the surface of a sand dune. Then, about 750 years ago, people camped by the line of stones. Shell material and discarded quartz tools accumulated around and over the original arrangement, and a new ceremonial structure was built. A further stone arrangement was subsequently found by archaeologist Scott Cane, 115 metres to the north. It has forty-three stones and extends for 6 metres in a north–south direction. On the pebble beaches nearby are many curious birdnest-shaped pits, some with low walls around them, and stone cairns, made from many rocks piled high together. Construction of these features must have taken much time and effort, but no one knows whether they are historic sealers' hides, stone 'borrow pits' or prehistoric features.

BASS STRAIT ISLANDS

What happened on the Bass Strait islands has long fascinated archaeologists. Did populations become stranded on some of the larger islands? Why were stone tools found on Flinders Island but no living inhabitants? These questions have been investigated by Jones, Bowdler and most recently by Sim, on whose excellent work the following account is based.[22]

Rising seas, caused by a global rise in air and seawater temperatures and the melting of ice in the polar ice caps, resulted in the flooding of the Bassian Plain, the land-bridge between Tasmania and the Australian mainland, about 10 500 years ago, when the sea reached a level of about 60 metres lower than at present and drowned the remnant land-bridge. The sea kept on rising until it reached its present level around 6500 years ago. The Bassian Plain of the earliest land-bridge period consisted of vast open grasslands, according to pollen studies. Dated archaeological sites from this land-bridge period have been found on King and Hunter Islands at the western end of Bass Strait, and at Mannalargenna Cave on Prime Seal Island and Beeton Shelter on Badger Island (10 kilometres from Flinders or Cape Barren Island) in the Furneaux region in the east.

The end of occupation at Beeton Shelter dates to a little less than 9000 years ago, when the sea would have been around 40 metres below today's level, and Badger Island was a hill on a large peninsula jutting out from northeastern Tasmania into what was gradually becoming Bass Strait (figure 13.7). The rising sea brought shellfish closer to the rock-shelter, and the shellfish remains in the uppermost layer make Beeton Shelter the oldest midden in Tasmania. Sim believes that Badger Island was abandoned before the final breach from the rest of Tasmania and the island formation stage, about 9000 years ago. (It is impossible to put precise dates on when each hill and plateau would have become an island as there are many uncertainties and estimates involved. For example, sedimentation occurs as the sea rises and many metres of shelf sediments have now accumulated in the straits between the islands. Chappell's sea level curve (1993) is based on current bathymetric depths plus 10 metres of sediments, but this is an estimate and others suggest there may have been 20 or even 30 metres of sediment.[23])

The limestone shelters of both Mannalargenna and Beeton were evidently abandoned at the end of the 'peninsula phase', when the sea came close; the Mannalargenna Cave deposit is dated between 7960 and 20 560 BP, and Beeton Shelter is between 8700 and more than 21 890 BP based on shell from the base of the cultural sequence. The Beeton site contained shellfish (mainly warreners and limpets), fish bones and emu eggshells, most of them burnt, which could mean that the eggs were being cooked or the shells were discarded in hot ashes. Emu eggshell was also in the Mannalargenna deposit, and it seems that emu were common when the Bass Strait region was a land-bridge. There were also remains at Beeton of wombat, eastern grey or Forester kangaroo, pademelon, snake and bandicoot.

Figure 13.7 Bass Strait, showing bathymetric depths to bedrock plus an estimated 10 metres of shelf deposits. (After R. Sim 1994 based on J. Chappell 1990)

The several hundred stone tools were mostly small (less than 3 centimetres long) and made of quartz. Some types typical of Tasmanian Pleistocene industries were thumbnail or small, rounded scrapers and steep-edged tools, probably used for woodworking or scraping skins. A very rare find, unknown elsewhere in Australia, in both Beeton and Mannalargenna was a number of tools made of a fine-grained fossil shell (a large cockle (bivalve) which is now extinct), so hard that it could be flaked like stone.

Sim concluded that, contrary to her expectations, there was 'no evidence of people living on or visiting any of the outer Furneaux Islands in the period more recent than 6,500 years ago when the sea reached its present level (causing the larger northeast Tasmanian peninsula to be flooded and the Furneaux Islands to form). However, radiocarbon dating has shown that Aboriginal shell middens were left on Flinders Island by people on the island between about 6,500 and 4,000 years ago.'[24] The absence of similar 'island phase' sites on the smaller islands offshore from Flinders supports the view that the people who left the midden evidence on Flinders Island did *not* possess watercraft and were permanently living on the island. If they had been using watercraft, then one would expect that other sites (particularly shell middens) more recent than 6500 years old would have been found on other Furneaux Islands. It seems that on Flinders Island a small population were stranded at about 8000 BP and eventually died out about 4000 years ago due to their complete isolation from other populations. The evidence on King Island, however, suggests that people lived there between 10 000 and 15 000 years ago, and that it was abandoned at about 7500 BP, when it was cut off from the mainland. Middens dated between 2000 and 1000 BP, which contain spongolite artefacts from northwestern Tasmania, show that later it may have been a refuge for castaways by way of Hunter and possibly Albatross Islands, involving open sea crossings of 60 kilometres or more.[25]

CONCLUSION

After surviving more than 35 000 years on their remote island, Tasmanian Aborigines had their land gradually taken from them by European settlers. They fought a strong guerilla war against the invaders, and, although most fell to European bullets or to disease, a few survived. While dispossessed and decimated, they did not die out. Trucanini was not 'the last Tasmanian'. In 1994 there were some 7000 Tasmanian Aborigines.

Not only have present-day Tasmanian Aborigines been denied their identity, but prehistoric Tasmanian culture has also been consistently misjudged and undervalued, in part because it has been assessed from Robinson's journals written in the 1830s, which record only the remnants of a culture of a people decimated after three decades of fighting for survival. It has been said that Tasmanian Aborigines lacked the rich ritual life of the mainlanders and did not hold large ceremonial gatherings, but by the 1830s only about 300 tribal Aborigines survived in all Tasmania, and they were fully occupied with a guerilla war.[26]

Another myth that should be laid to rest is that Tasmanian Aborigines did not know how to make fire. The only evidence for this is that Robinson never observed anyone making fire because fire-sticks were always carried. An argument based on flimsy negative evidence is always suspect, and it seems unlikely that the

Tasmanians could have made some of the water crossings that they did, such as those to Hunter, King and Maatsuyker Islands, and kept fires alight on hearths in the boats during the whole voyage. And there is no lack of charcoal in middens on the islands.

These most southerly representatives of the human race have an impressive prehistory indeed.

CHAPTER FOURTEEN

Rising Seas and Change

The end of the ice age was a period of dramatic change. Rising temperatures dried up the lakes of inland Australia, while rising seas drowned vast areas around the coasts. Not surprisingly, many Aboriginal myths reflect these events. The evaporation of inland lakes and the formation of huge salt pans are commemorated in oral traditions that tell of the time when all the waters of the earth were fresh but then became salty. The story of 'The Salt Lakes of Kiti' tells how greed turned rich fertile plains into a desert of salt lakes.

> Gumuduk was a tall, thin, medicine man, who belonged to the hills country. He owned a magical bone of such power that he could use it to make the rain fall in season, the trees bear much fruit, the animals increase, and the fish multiply. Because of such good fortune the hills people always had plenty of food.
>
> However, the tribe that lived on the fertile plain below the Kiti range captured the medicine man and his bone, convinced that they, too, would in future have more food.
>
> But instead of bringing them prosperity, the theft resulted in a calamity which totally destroyed their country. For the medicine man escaped and was so angry over the indignity he had suffered that, plunging his magical bone into the ground, Gumuduk decreed that wherever he walked in the country of his enemies salt water would rise in his footsteps.
>
> Those waters not only contaminated the rivers and lagoons, but completely inundated the tribal lands. And when these waters dried up, the whole area was changed to an inhospitable desert of salt lakes, useless to both the creatures and the Aborigines.[1]

The drowning of the coastal plains must have had a profound impact on those who lived there, particularly as they had no means of knowing that the seas would ever stop rising. As the world's ice melted and the oceans rose, not only were hills on the continental shelf transformed into islands, but immense areas were also submerged. About one-seventh of the land mass of Greater Australia — 2.5 million square kilometres — was inundated by the rising glacial melt-water. And around the shore of Southeast Asia, an area the size of the Indian subcontinent went under. Over 10 000 to 15 000 years, the average rise was between 1 and 3 centimetres a year, but the sea's advance was erratic. Sometimes it rose quickly, sometimes it stood still, and occasionally it even retreated. When the sea was rising most quickly, it could, within

Colour plate 8 (top)   Barbed spear from Wyrie Swamp, South Australia, approximately 10 000 years old. (R. Luebbers)

Colour plate 9 (bottom)   Kutikina Cave (previously Fraser Cave), Tasmania. Wallaby hunters inhabited this limestone cave between 20 000 and 15 000 years ago. (By courtesy of R. Jones)

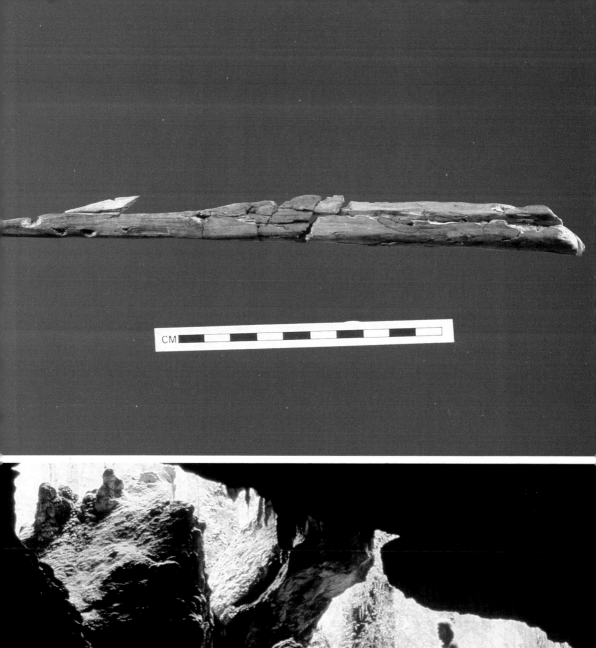

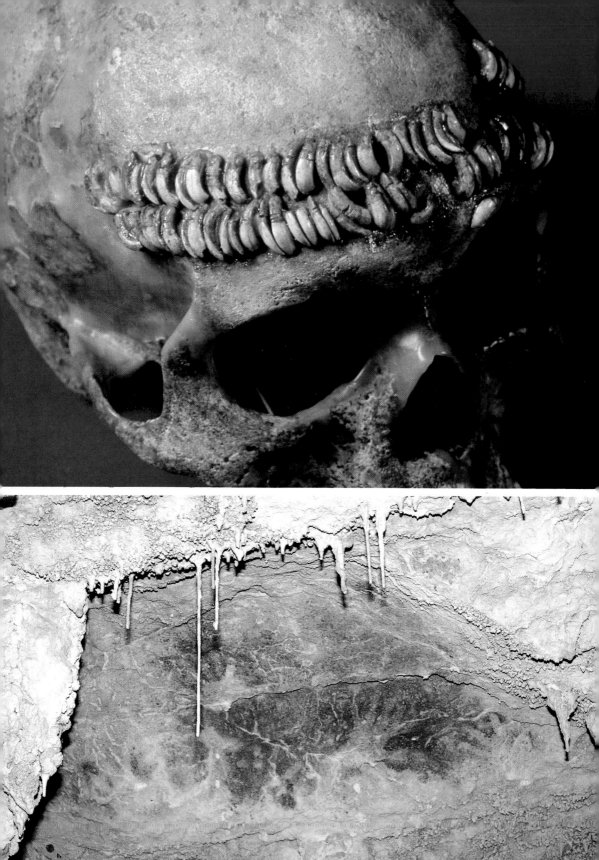

one generation, have drowned a strip of land over 100 kilometres wide, which would greatly reduce a coastal tribe's territory.

All over the world the event seems to be commemorated in legends about a great flood, and in Australia the stories are so detailed and specific that there can be no doubt that they recall events thousands of years ago. Various explanations are given for the separation of offshore islands from the mainland. From Mornington Island come stories of the seagull woman, Garnguur, who pulled her raft backwards and forwards across what was then a peninsula to form the channels that now separate the island from the mainland. Elcho Island was similarly severed from the mainland when the Djankawu brother tripped and accidentally pushed his stick into the sand there, causing the sea to rush in. The narrow seas between Milingimbi in the Crocodile Islands and the mainland were made by the Creation Shark. And the separation of Kangaroo Island from South Australia, which occurred about 10 000 years ago, is remembered in the legend of Ngurunderi drowning his wives as they fled across the land on foot.[2]

The drowning of great expanses of the mainland is related in a number of stories from both northern and southern Australia. A time when Port Phillip Bay (near Melbourne) was dry land and excellent hunting ground is recalled in a legend of the Kulin people,[3] and in South Australia a story about a great flood inundating Spencer Gulf is told.[4] The rising of the seas was indeed one of the major events in the prehistory of Australia. Coastal people became islanders, or were forced back from the coast as their tribal territory was inundated.

THE GREAT BARRIER REEF ISLANDS

Archaeological work on Queensland islands has been concentrated largely on those close to the mainland and under threat from sand-mining, tourism or other development. This research is but a drop in the ocean of the prehistory of offshore islands, for in the Barrier Reef there are over 1200 islands, and it seems all the larger ones were inhabited by Aborigines at the time of European settlement. The earliest sites yet known are Nara Inlet Shelter 1 on Hook Island and Border Island Shelter 1 in the Whitsundays, where Bryce Barker of the University of Queensland found 8150- and 7200-year-old occupation respectively.[5] These sites were not used before the sea began to rise, for the rock-shelters were then on mountain tops as part of a mainland range. It seems that over the generations, humans followed the coastline as the sea level rose. Some time between 8150 and 6000 BP, the coastal mountain ranges became islands. The Nara Inlet and Border Island rock-shelters were first occupied when the sea came into close proximity to them.

Barker's archaeological evidence demonstrates continuous use of marine resources throughout the Holocene, effectively spanning the last phases of the marine transgression, involving a dramatic rise in sea level of more than 20 metres. There was constant occupation with little change until 2500 BP, when major technological and economic changes took place. A new technology including bone points and turtle

Colour plate 10 (top) Burial from tomb 108 Roonka, South Australia. A double-stranded band of notched wallaby teeth encircled the forehead of this man buried at Roonka on the Murray River over 4000 years ago. (By courtesy of the South Australian Museum and G. Pretty)

Colour plate 11 (bottom) Stalactites have almost covered these traces of ice age hand stencils in Wargata Mina Cave, Southern Forests, Tasmania. (S. Brown)

shell artefacts was developed, specially adapted to the procurement of large marine creatures such as dugong, turtle and whale. There was an increase in the rate of deposition of cultural material and more sites in the region were occupied for the first time. Barker argues that (a) the greater intensity of site use, (b) the occupation of new sites, (c) the technological change related to greater marine specialisation, and (d) the introduction of a unique art style as shown in the archaeological record, are linked to social and demographic factors. These resulted in a change from a largely open and less formally structured social network to a more closed system. This model for change is supported by linguistic differences from mainland peoples and historical records which treat the island people as a distinct entity. After 2500 BP the resource base is entirely marine (apart from plant foods) and the island people are best characterised as maritime fisher–gatherers.

On North Keppel Island the open site of Mazie Bay, excavated by Michael Rowland, was occupied for about 5000 years, probably since shortly after the island was cut off from the mainland by the rising sea.[6] The Keppel Islands now lie 13 kilometres from the mainland, but the journey to the island could be made in two legs: 4.5 kilometres to Pelican Island and then 8.5 kilometres to South Keppel. The islanders were rather isolated because of this distance from the mainland, and the effects of isolation can be seen in their language, physical appearance and material culture. Their language was unintelligible to the mainlanders, and they spoke so quickly that mainland Aborigines said they 'yabbered like crows'.

Keppel Islanders' material culture was also different from that of the mainland. They had no boomerangs, shields or ground-edge axes, and only one type of club, but they possessed other items apparently absent from the adjacent coast, such as necklaces made of shell and 'bits of red toadstool', fish-hooks (made of coconut or turtle shell) and stone drills for manufacturing the hooks. For transport, they had one-piece bark canoes, not the three-piece ones of the mainland, but their usual means of transport were what have been termed 'swimming logs' (figure 14.1). At the time of the visit of W. E. Roth, then Protector of Aborigines in Queensland, to the Keppel Islands in 1897, these logs were the only form of water transport. They were hand-propelled and were paddled from island to island and even on occasion to the mainland.[7] This co-operative use of logs as watercraft seems to be unique to the Keppel Islands; elsewhere, logs were used by only one person at a time, and they were straddled as floats, particularly in waters infested by crocodiles or sharks.

It seems the Keppel Islanders were more or less isolated for 5000 years. A small population of about eighty-five people exploited their limited territory of 20 square kilometres, including about 38 kilometres of coastline: there would have been about two people to each kilometre of coast, a similar population density to that found among other coastal groups, such as the Bentinck Islanders or the Anbara of Arnhem Land. Over the centuries the language and physical characteristics of Keppel Island people changed as a result of evolution in a small, isolated community. Their material culture became almost as simple and limited in range as that of the Tasmanians.

The survival of prehistoric people stranded on islands has been studied by Jones, who has come to the conclusion that 'totally isolated populations of between 1000 and 4000 people are perfectly viable over extremely lengthy periods, but . . . ones of under about 350 or 400 are vulnerable in the long run. In hunter–gatherer conditions, the limiting viable population may be somewhere in the range of 400 to 600 depending on local circumstances and the vagaries of chance.'[8]

It may be significant that this estimated minimum viable population of about 500 is also the average size of a so-called 'tribe' in Australia.[9] The term 'tribe', which

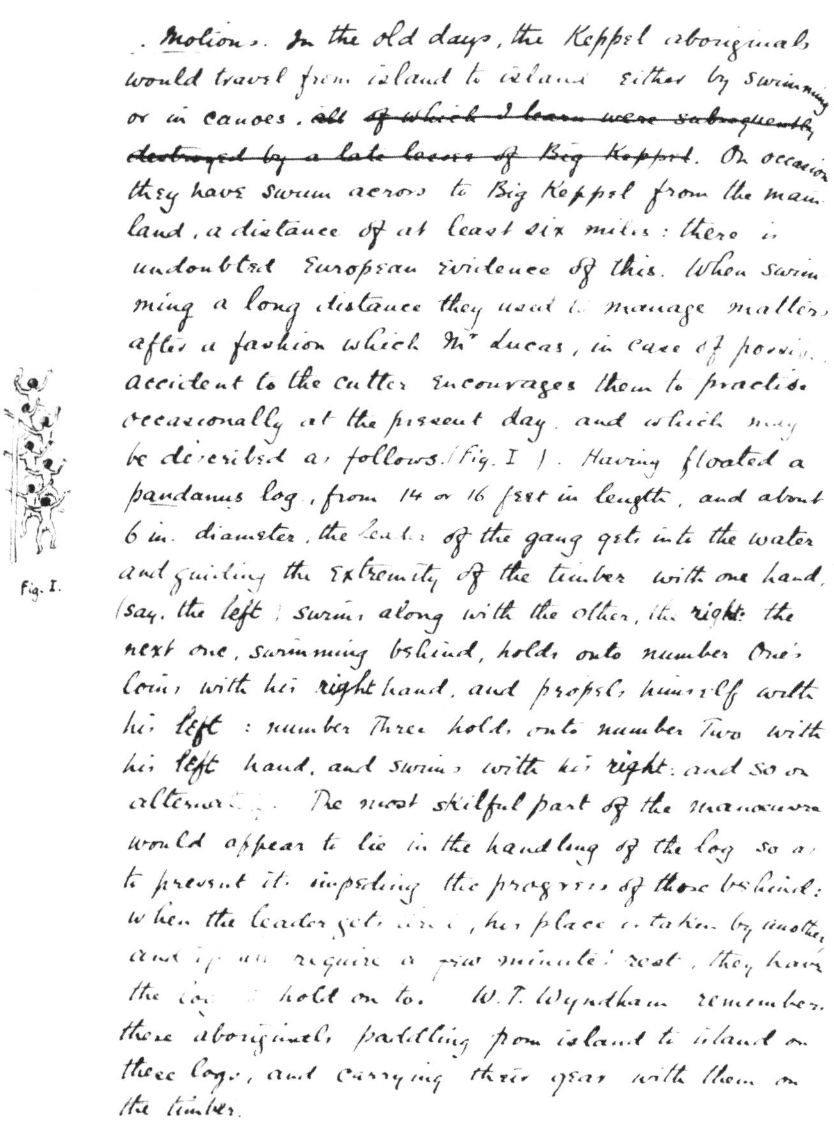

. *Motion*. In the old days, the Keppel aboriginals would travel from island to island either by swimming or in canoes, ~~all of which I learn were subsequently destroyed by a late lessee of Big Keppel~~. On occasion they have swum across to Big Keppel from the main land, a distance of at least six miles: there is undoubted European evidence of this. When swimming a long distance they used to manage matters, after a fashion which Mr Lucas, in case of possible accident to the cutter encourages them to practise occasionally at the present day, and which may be described as follows (Fig. I). Having floated a pandanus log, from 14 or 16 feet in length, and about 6 in. diameter, the leader of the gang gets into the water and guiding the extremity of the timber with one hand, (say, the left) swims along with the other, the right: the next one, swimming behind, holds onto number One's loins with his right hand, and propels himself with his left: number Three holds onto number Two with his left hand, and swims with his right: and so on alternately. The most skilful part of the manoeuvre would appear to lie in the handling of the log so as to prevent it impeding the progress of those behind: when the leader gets tired, his place is taken by another, and if all require a few minutes' rest, they have the log to hold on to. W. T. Wyndham remembers these aboriginals paddling from island to island on these logs, and carrying their gear with them on the timber.

Fig. I.

Figure 14.1 A page from W. E. Roth's manuscript report on *The Aborigines of the Rockhampton and Surrounding Coast Districts*, 1898. (By courtesy of the Queensland State Archives and the Premier's Department)

was adopted from nineteenth-century Europe, has often been used to describe the organisation of Aboriginal hunter–gatherer societies in Australia. In using this term, it is commonly implied that the tribe constitutes a cultural, linguistic and geographical unit. Several anthropologists, such as Berndt and Peterson, are critical of this concept of 'the tribe', believing that this term inaccurately portrays the social, political and linguistic complexities of Aboriginal hunter–gatherer society.[10] These workers consider the 'band' to be the most appropriate term to describe the basic social and economic unit of Aboriginal society. It is described as a small-scale population, comprising between two to six extended family units, who together occupied and exploited a specific range.

The band was by no means a social or cultural isolate but, rather, interacted with other bands in a variety of ways. Typically these interactions involved visits, marriage, ceremonies and trade. As a result of these interactions, clusters of bands were formed, wherein there was a sense of collective identity, often expressed in terms of common and distinctive language.

THE MAINLAND

Less catastrophic than being trapped on offshore islands, but still traumatic, was the effect of rising seas on the mainlanders. The land submerged by the encroaching ocean was equivalent to the loss of the whole of the present state of Western Australia. On the gently sloping coastal plains of northern Australia, the sea at times ate up 5 kilometres of land in one year. Even in southern Australia, in the Great Australian Bight, the coastal strip was consumed at a rate of about 1 kilometre every fifteen years.

The loss of territory would have been much less severe on the east coast of Australia, where the continental shelf slopes down fairly steeply. Over 15 000 years, a strip of only about 20 kilometres wide was submerged along the south coast of New South Wales. In recent times the territories of Aboriginal tribes on this coast extended inland a considerable distance. Most encompass the drainage basin of one river and stretch from the shoreline up to the top of the coastal escarpment, at least 30 kilometres inland. There is no way of knowing how far back in time this territorial organisation goes, but it may well be quite ancient. If so, it would mean that the coastal tribes were pushed back by the rising sea into their own hinterland, rather than into the territory of other groups. This would have been a much less traumatic event than that experienced in the Gulf of Carpentaria.

It is thought that the sea rose fairly rapidly until about 7000 years ago, and then more slowly until the present level was reached about 5000 years ago. This means that the coast of New South Wales has been much as it is today for the last 5000 to 7000 years, but before that a fairly steep coastal slope stretched down to the shore. Under these early conditions there would have been only a narrow tidal zone, with the sea deepening rapidly offshore. The amount of food people could have obtained from the deep water of such a shoreline would have been substantially less than in later times, when the sea level had stabilised.

The rising of the seas drowned large tracts of land, but at the same time stabilisation of the sea level extended estuaries and tidal reefs, the zones of the shore most productive of fish and shellfish that were accessible to Aborigines. Lagoons formed at the mouths of rivers held back by sandy barriers, which previously had been swept away by the constantly rising sea. And the drowning of river valleys led to the development of many food-rich small bays and inlets, such as those in the higher reaches of Sydney Harbour.

Thousands of Aboriginal middens have been found on the southeastern coast of Australia. These refuse dumps consist mainly of shell, but they also contain other remains of food, such as bird, animal and fish bones, together with broken, lost or discarded tools. Unfortunately, plant remains are rarely preserved, so it is difficult to interpret the total diet from the midden remains.

The most favoured camp site was a foredune close to a rock platform on the north side of a headland. Such a site offered easy access to shellfish, a landing place for canoes, proximity to drinking water, shelter from the prevailing winds, and soft sand for a bed. In addition, fish in the lagoons could be caught with multi-pronged spears or with shell fish-hooks and line made from twisted strands of inner bark from trees or other vegetable fibre.

A comparison of the occupation sites along the coast with those further inland indicates that the shoreline was much more densely occupied than the hinterland. Whether this was always the case is more difficult to determine. Almost all the sites known along the south coast of New South Wales were first occupied within the last 5000 years, but an equal number of older sites on earlier shorelines may now lie submerged under the ocean.

Several archaeologists, notably Harry Lourandos and John Beaton, have argued that in certain parts of Australia, distinct changes in social and economic behaviour took place during the Holocene, and that these changes were linked to a growth in population levels.[11]

Other workers, such as David Frankel and Caroline Bird, remain critical of certain aspects of this argument, which has become known as the 'intensification model'.[12] While critics acknowledge that some changes in settlement patterns can be identified within the archaeological record, they do not view these as being part of an interrelated sequence of Holocene changes.

THE EARLY POST-GLACIAL SCENE

The end of the Pleistocene was a time of change. Some areas became less attractive human habitats; others acquired better food resources and a more tolerable climate. And in some regions the effect of the drastic loss of land to the rising sea was to push occupation into less favourable zones, which had been previously uninhabited or visited only occasionally. There is now evidence that virtually the whole of Australia was occupied by Pleistocene hunters by about 30 000 years ago. In a few regions, such as the northern tablelands of New South Wales, the heart of the Snowy Mountains and the centre of the arid mallee region of northwestern Victoria, not a single Pleistocene site has been found among the dozens of younger ones known, but this may well be due to a lack of much archaeological work in the area or poor site visibility rather than a genuine absence of sites.

These regions are all poor in food resources compared with the coast and the large inland rivers. Thus if they were inhabited during early times, short seasonal hunting visits are more likely than year-round occupation. The suggestion that the abundance of young sites but lack of older ones in these areas is simply due to a higher loss rate of early sites may be valid for the coast, where earlier sites are now under the sea, but it does not hold for inland regions. Stone tools have the same lasting qualities, whether 5000 or 30 000 years old; erosion applies to young and old sites alike; and there is generally little depth of soil above bedrock in which older tools could lie hidden.

The evidence suggests a comparatively small early population, spread thinly around the continent and concentrated in the places where food was most abundant: the coast and large inland lakes and rivers. The most inhospitable parts of mainland Australia in the Pleistocene were the Snowy Mountains and the desert core of the continent. We now know that people were camping at least occasionally on the fringes of the Snowy Mountains, in treeless country at 730 metres above sea level, at Birrigai Shelter in the Australian Capital Territory at 21 000 BP, and in the region north of Uluru (Ayers Rock), at Puritjarra, around 30 000 years ago.[13]

Some mountain regions, like the Blue Mountains near Sydney, had a comparatively mild climate, and they were inhabited at least seasonally in glacial or early post-glacial times. The large, well-protected rock-shelters of Walls Cave near Blackheath and Lyre Bird Dell at Leura (respectively 910 metres and 915 metres above sea level) were inhabited about 12 000 years ago, when the local environment was probably rather drier than it is today.[14] Even today, both sites provide excellent shelter from the elements. The King's Table Shelter, 800 metres above sea level, was definitely occupied about 14 000 years ago (the earlier occupation claimed by Stockton is possible but generally considered unproven). Another 12 000-year-old site in a valley on the northern side of the Blue Mountains is Noola rock-shelter.[15] Occupation in the same area at the Capertee shelters goes back 7500 years.[16]

The distribution of cultural material shows us the human response to the changing environment. Areas such as the Willandra Lakes were largely abandoned in favour of large rivers like the Darling and Murray, and in these regions, eroded dunes bordering the old lakes are littered with ancient core tools and chunky scrapers, but there is hardly a trace of the succeeding small-tool tradition. Elsewhere, as on the coast, the opposite is true. As well as adapting to change by altering their settlement pattern and staple foods, these prehistoric people either invented or adopted new tools and technology, leading to still more change and development.

CHAPTER FIFTEEN

Arrival of the Dingo

Some time after 6000 years ago, the dingo appears in Australia and new small tools are added to the existing tool kit. Dingoes were certainly introduced from Asia, probably deliberately but possibly as castaways, and dingo bones first appear in faunal deposits between about 3500 and 4000 BP. The origin of the new small tools is more debatable. The concept of the 'Australian small tool tradition' was first developed in the 1960s by Richard Gould, Ron Lampert and Ian Glover, in seeking an appropriate name for the 'microlithic' industry of Puntutjarpa,[1] and was eventually used to describe those tools considered small enough to require hafting. Included within the small tool tradition are backed blades, points, tulas and burren adzes. These tool types vary considerably, both in terms of geographic location and the timing of their appearance. It is generally agreed that these small tools were added to the existing Australian tool kit some time between about 6000 and 4000 BP, but there is much debate about the exact chronology, distribution and origin of each type. They may have been independently invented in Australia or may have derived from diffusion of ideas and possibly migration of people from outside. Why were the dingo and distinctive, new small tools suddenly added to all Australian industries except those on Tasmania and other distant offshore islands, and why are different new tools found in different parts of the continent (figure 15.1)? Was Australia completely isolated from Asia after the rising of the seas, or did new people migrate to or visit the island continent, adding fresh elements to Aboriginal culture?

Stone tools, the historical documents from which prehistory is written, will be discussed first. The outstanding feature of the new small tools is the symmetry and delicate trimming of tiny, slender blades made from fine-grained stone.

POINTS

Stone points are generally presumed to have been hafted onto the tip of a spear as projectile points. They occur with trimming on one or both faces (unifacial or bifacial) but one variety does not predate the other, since at some sites, such as Yarar in the Northern Territory, they are in use simultaneously.

The evidence from the Yarar rock-shelter showed that unifacial and bifacial points were of similar dimensions, averaging 3.5 centimetres in length.[2] The function of both would seem to have been as spear points. Among the broken points there were far more butts than tips, indicating that spears with the tips broken off were rehafted in the shelter, where the broken butt was discarded. They are small enough to have been arrow tips, such as those found so widely in North America, Asia and other parts

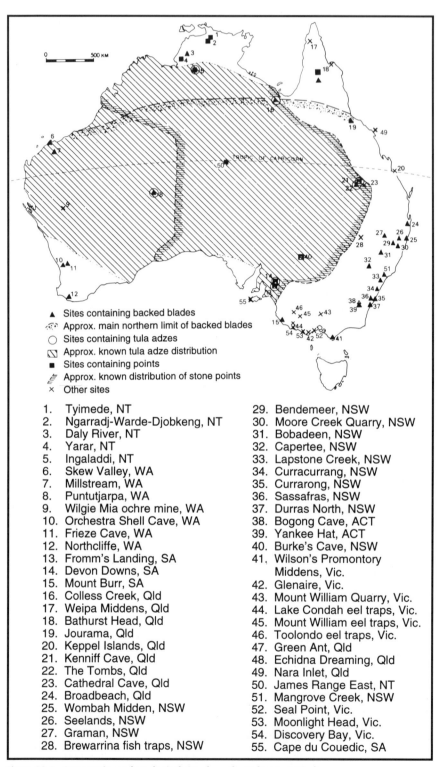

▲ Sites containing backed blades
🦋 Approx. main northern limit of backed blades
○ Sites containing tula adzes
◣ Approx. known tula adze distribution
■ Sites containing points
🪶 Approx. known distribution of stone points
✕ Other sites

1. Tyimede, NT
2. Ngarradj-Warde-Djobkeng, NT
3. Daly River, NT
4. Yarar, NT
5. Ingaladdi, NT
6. Skew Valley, WA
7. Millstream, WA
8. Puntutjarpa, WA
9. Wilgie Mia ochre mine, WA
10. Orchestra Shell Cave, WA
11. Frieze Cave, WA
12. Northcliffe, WA
13. Fromm's Landing, SA
14. Devon Downs, SA
15. Mount Burr, SA
16. Colless Creek, Qld
17. Weipa Middens, Qld
18. Bathurst Head, Qld
19. Jourama, Qld
20. Keppel Islands, Qld
21. Kenniff Cave, Qld
22. The Tombs, Qld
23. Cathedral Cave, Qld
24. Broadbeach, Qld
25. Wombah Midden, NSW
26. Seelands, NSW
27. Graman, NSW
28. Brewarrina fish traps, NSW

29. Bendemeer, NSW
30. Moore Creek Quarry, NSW
31. Bobadeen, NSW
32. Capertee, NSW
33. Lapstone Creek, NSW
34. Curracurrang, NSW
35. Currarong, NSW
36. Sassafras, NSW
37. Durras North, NSW
38. Bogong Cave, ACT
39. Yankee Hat, ACT
40. Burke's Cave, NSW
41. Wilson's Promontory
    Middens, Vic.
42. Glenaire, Vic.
43. Mount William Quarry, Vic.
44. Lake Condah eel traps, Vic.
45. Mount William eel traps, Vic.
46. Toolondo eel traps, Vic.
47. Green Ant, Qld
48. Echidna Dreaming, Qld
49. Nara Inlet, Qld
50. James Range East, NT
51. Mangrove Creek, NSW
52. Seal Point, Vic.
53. Moonlight Head, Vic.
54. Discovery Bay, Vic.
55. Cape du Couedic, SA

Figure 15.1 Some major archaeological sites from the Holocene period.

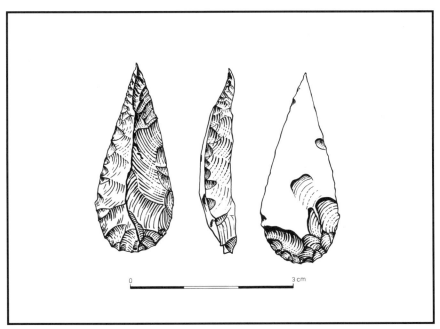

Figure 15.2 Stone projectile pirri point from Roonka, South Australia. This chert point was found in a grave. (By courtesy of the South Australian Museum)

of the world, but there is no evidence that the bow and arrow ever reached Australia. It was certainly not visible in Australia in the eighteenth century when Captain Cook arrived, whereas stone-tipped spears were still in use then in northwestern Australia. The bifacial points of the Kimberleys range from less than 3 centimetres to over 10 centimetres long; they are all spear points, and museum examples exist of 3-centimetre-long stone points hafted onto a spear handle, with only 2 centimetres projecting out of the gum hafting. Such tiny spear points would be less likely to shatter on impact than the longer variety.

Symmetrical, pressure-flaked bifacial points with serrated edges belong particularly to the Kimberleys and Arnhem Land, and many are works of art. They were traded long distances, suggesting they were regarded more as status and ritual objects than as utilitarian spear points. Indeed, in historic times some magnificent specimens have been made from glass and porcelain, the porcelain coming from insulators on the overland telegraph line — which soon lacked many of its insulators. Such finely made Kimberley stone points were used 1000 kilometres away to circumcise boys in the desert. Other symmetrical points, such as the unifacially trimmed 'pirri' typical of South Australia, were confined to prehistoric times, and Aborigines, when consulted about their function, had no knowledge of what they were and deemed them to have been made in the Dreamtime (figure 15.2).

Points occur in a broad vertical band across the centre of the continent, but are absent from the western coast and rare on the eastern. In contrast, from the west to the east of the continent, south of the tropical monsoon belt (apart from a few isolated finds in Cape York and the Top End of the Northern Territory), there is a concentration of a different, distinctive new tool type: backed blades. Dortch's claims of backed blades at Miriwun in the Kimberley were rejected by Peter White after inspection as 'probably varieties of abruptly trimmed points'.[3]

BACKED BLADES

Backed blades are tiny blades, or 'flakelets', which have one edge blunted by steep retouch to form a back, resembling a miniature pen knife (figure 15.3). Many different forms have been distinguished on the basis of small variations in shape, but they are usually divided into just two main varieties: Bondi points and geometric microliths. Bondi points are named after Bondi Beach, where they were first discovered in 1899; they are slender, asymmetrical backed blades, tapering to a point, more than twice as long as they are wide. Geometric microliths are broader and are made in a wide range of geometric shapes, such as triangles, trapezoids and half-circles.

Both varieties of backed blade are usually 'microlithic', which means 'small stone' and refers to a tool of less than 3 centimetres in the longest dimension. They also appear to have similar functions. Their major function, it has been suggested, was as spear barbs, mounted in rows on the sides of the shafts of 'death spears'.[4] In historic times death spears were used in fighting and hunting and were lethal weapons that caused great loss of blood. When they penetrated the victim's body, often they could not be extracted except by being pushed right through (figure 15.4).

A few death spears survive in museums, and they have as many as forty stone barbs, generally set with gum into grooves on the sides of the shaft. The barbs are made of sharp, unbacked quartz flakes, without secondary working. Archaeological evidence (from sites such as Sassafras and Currarong) suggests that about 2000 years ago, backed blades gradually disappeared, while the use of quartz flakes increased. It seems probable that earlier versions of death spears were barbed with backed blades. This interpretation is supported by the huge number of backed blades found, which is consistent with their use in rows rather than as individual tools, and by two discoveries by Isabel McBryde.[5] In excavations at Graman, she found backed blades that still retained traces of hafting gum on the thick, blunted back. And at Seelands,

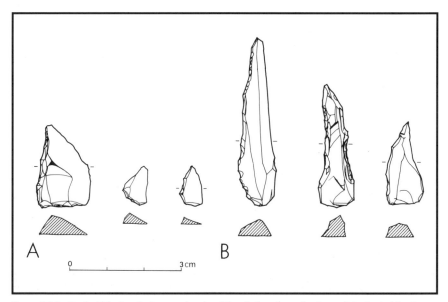

Figure 15.3 Backed blades. A: Geometric microliths of chert from the Australian Capital Territory. B: Bondi points of chert from Sassafras (on left), and the Australian Capital Territory.

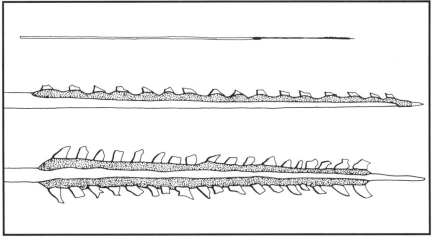

Figure 15.4   Death spears barbed with quartz flakes set in gum. Top: From the Rex Nan Kivell Collection, National Library, Canberra. Bottom: From North Queensland.

two-thirds of the excavated geometric microliths had one end broken off, a type of breakage consistent with their use as spear barbs.

Death spears were used right across the south of the continent in historic times, the same region in which backed blades are found in huge quantities, although the distributions of death spears and backed blades elsewhere in Australia do not exactly coincide. In the south of Australia, backed blades are very common.[6] The excavation of Curracurrang rock-shelter, south of Sydney, produced over 1000, and in the days before legislation made private collecting of Aboriginal artefacts illegal, one collector, Frank Dickson, found 7000 in an area of 2 to 3 square kilometres of sand dunes at Kurnell on Botany Bay, and another collected 20 000 from a small area near Lake Torrens in South Australia.

Points and backed blades were often hafted to form composite tools. The term 'composite' here refers to the fixing of small stone flakes and blades into a handle, generally by means of a groove, hafting gum or twine. Thus the small tool tradition is characterised by the introduction of composite tools, which are added to the existing tool kit. The use of hand-held tools continues; there is technological evolution, not revolution.

ADZE FLAKES

Some existing tools became much more widely used at this time. In particular, the use of adze flakes increases. These may be an Australian invention. Small, flaked stone adzes or adze flakes are woodworking 'chisels' (figure 15.5) and are not to be confused with the large ground and polished adzes found in Asia and the Pacific, which were never part of the Australian tool kit.

Adze flakes have continued in use to the present day in the Western Desert, where Aborigines use these chisel tips set in spinifex gum on the end of a stout handle or a spear-thrower, to shape hardwoods like mulga into shields, dishes and the like.[7] There are two sorts of adze flake: the 'tula', on which retouch and use-wear occur on the edge opposite the striking platform (the distal end), and the 'burren

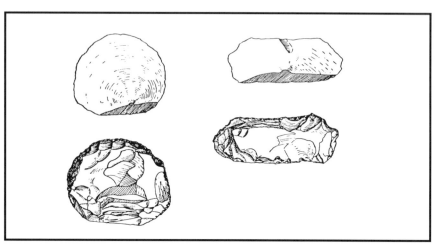

Figure 15.5 Adze stones. Left: Inner (above) and outer surface of a tula adze of ribbon stone from Antony Lagoon, Northern Territory (4.2 x 3.5 centimetres). Right: Inner (above) and outer surface of a worn-out tula adze of quartzite from Mulka, South Australia (5 x 2 centimetres). (After S. R. Mitchell 1949)

adze', on which use occurs on the lateral edges. 'Tula' is the word used by Wongkonguru Aborigines of the Lake Eyre region of South Australia for this type of adze. The two forms of tula adze (figure 15.5) were originally thought to be two different tools, but then it was discovered that the smaller, step-flaked one was the worked-out 'slug' of the original tool, which gradually became smaller and smaller with constant resharpening. Where stone is in short supply, tools are resharpened again and again until they become too small to use and are discarded.

Adze flakes appear in late Pleistocene horizons at two sites in Western Australia: at Puntutjarpa, about 10 000 years ago, and in a 12 000-year-old layer of Devil's Lair (one specimen). However, these are not the classic tula adzes, nor are they worn-out adze 'slugs'. In fact, they resemble small, steep-edged scrapers. So there is as yet no good evidence for a Pleistocene antiquity for the distinctive woodworking adzes characteristic of the drier parts of Australia over the last few thousand years.

The typical tool of Aboriginal desert people, the tula adze is largely confined to arid Central Australia, but some found in southeast Queensland, for example at Caloola with bifacial points, are interpreted by McNiven as resulting from diffusion (information flow) from inland regions. The burren adze is more widely distributed, occurring on Cape York and the east coast. The adze flake was probably an Australian invention, to solve the problem of working the tough timbers of the desert.

TOOL DISTRIBUTION AND CHRONOLOGY

After considerable homogeneity in technology in Pleistocene Australia, there is a bewildering diversity over the last 5000 years. New tools appear and others that were rare before suddenly become common. Thus ground-edge axes are found all over mainland Australia (but not Tasmania) during the last few thousand years, superseding pebble tools and horsehoof cores as the main chopping tool. Finely trimmed thumbnail scrapers occur in some Pleistocene industries but become much more widespread in the small tool phase.

There is great regional cultural diversity, but apart from the association of the tula adze with desert regions, it is impossible to equate different tools with different environments and to explain the absence of a tool from an area on the grounds of environment. If particular tools were developed to cope with particular environments, why are backed blades so numerous on the coast of New South Wales but not on the Queensland coast? And why are they also found in great quantities in the arid salt desert of South Australia but not in the Tanami Desert of Central Australia? And why are stone points so abundant in the Kimberleys and Arnhem Land, but not in the similar tropical environment of Cape York?

It is equally difficult to equate the use of these tools with cultural or linguistic groups, and their distribution bears no apparent relation to known major culture areas. Culture areas are regional groupings of interacting Aboriginal societies possessing broadly similar languages, social organisation and customs, material culture and art styles, ways of life and environment (figure 15.6). There is a general correlation between culture areas and major drainage basins, which has been explained by Peterson on the grounds that a drainage basin is unified by its river system and bounded by its watershed; the water supply determines plant cover and hence available food and Aboriginal population density.[8]

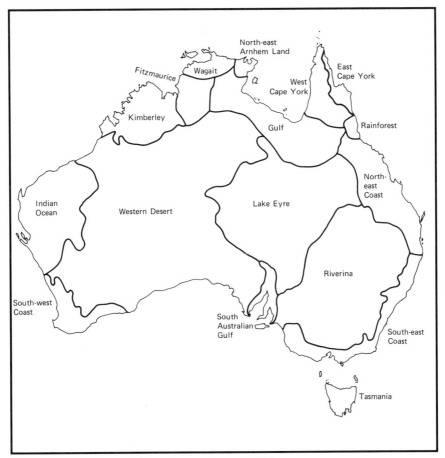

Figure 15.6 Major known culture areas. (N. Peterson 1976)

It has been widely believed that there were one or more migrations of newcomers into Australia, 4000 to 5000 years ago, who brought new tools together with the dingo, which first appeared on the continent at about the same time. Much of the speculation over the last two decades about such migrations has been based on very little evidence, and much of it has been found to be wrong. Since 1975, the dates of three key events have been revised: the time of the first appearance in Australia of backed blades, of points, and of the dingo. It is time to take a fresh look at the whole question of the origins of these new elements that appeared in Australia after the rising of the sea.

Until recently it was thought that the dingo was in Australia by 7500 years ago, the point industry by 7000, and backed blades by 6000, but it has now emerged that all these dates are too high. The dingo's arrival was dated from the presence of a few fragments of bone in the lower levels of the Mount Burr rock-shelter in South Australia, sandwiched between layers dated to about 7500 to 8500 years ago. Later re-excavation of the site indicated that, in the jumble of rocks and cracks in the deposit, a few pieces of bone could well have fallen into an earlier level. Moreover, there were only a few fragments of dingo bone in the lower level, in contrast to an abundance of it in the higher, younger levels.

Klim Gollan, who did his Ph.D. on the dingo, has examined and rejected the Mount Burr evidence.[9] The earliest dates then for the dingo in Australia cluster between 3500 and 3000 BP, and Gollan considers its absence from Devil's Lair significant, where the whole deposit predates 5000 BP. Dingo bones are associated with backed blades and unifacial pebble tools in Wombah midden on the north coast of New South Wales at 3230 BP, and dingo remains in Madura Cave on the Nullarbor Plain in Western Australia date to 3450 BP. A date of 3170 BP has been obtained for dingo at Fromm's Landing on the Murray River, again associated with backed blades. It is not known how long it took the dingo to spread across the continent, but Gollan estimates a maximum lag time of 500 years from its first entry in the north, which he therefore puts at probably not before 4000 BP. (The dingo's spread may in fact have been much quicker, since the fox, once introduced into Victoria, took only sixty years to reach the Kimberley coast on the other side of the continent.)

The chronology of point technology has been the subject of recent debate. Bowdler and O'Connor argued in 1991 that recent evidence from the West Kimberley indicated an emergence of the small tool tradition there at around 4500 BP, while in the East Kimberley it occurred rather later, with dates in the order of 3500 BP.[10] (In the Victoria River district between the Kimberley and Arnhem Land my own research work has suggested they appear around 3000 BP.) Bowdler and O'Connor concluded that 'data from the Kimberley suggest that the Australian Stone Tool Tradition in this part of Northern Australia dates to no earlier than 4500 BP, and that its inception is probably associated with the introduction of the dingo. This seems to us to be in agreement with data from elsewhere in Northern Australia, and indeed Australia generally. The only piece of evidence apparently to the contrary is that from Nauwalabila I in Kakadu National Park. We believe that this evidence is not only aberrant, but also that it could be subject to reinterpretation, which would bring it into line with the evidence presented here.' However, whilst the 7000 BP dates for the first occurrence of points in Arnhem Land have now been re-evaluated, they are still in the order of 5000 years, and that from Nauwalabila I is almost 6000 BP.

In several Arnhem Land sites excavated by Scrire, there was a clear change in the sequence from a core tool and scraper industry in the lower sand to an upper shell midden containing remains of estuarine animal species and points. At first the change in industry was equated with the change in environment: the appearance of points at sites like Nawamoyn and Malangangerr was originally correlated with the base of the midden dated to 6500 to 7000 years. Further analysis of the data[11] has revealed that the first points do not appear until halfway up the middens, some 4000 to 5000 years ago. This agrees with their appearance in the Tyimede 2 site at about 5000 BP, and points appear in a variety of other sites, from Queensland to South Australia, between 5000 and 4000 years ago. However, at one Kakadu site, Nauwalabila I, the first point is in spit 27, dated to 5860 ± 90 BP (ANU-3180).[12] This is only 5 centimetres below charcoal from spit 24, which gave a date of 4040 ± 100 BP (ANU-3178), and Bowdler and O'Connor have argued that there was downward displacement of artefacts through treadage and scuffage, as has been found at some other sandy sites.[13] The excavators, Rhys Jones and Ian Johnson, on the contrary, maintain that 'no deep site has been excavated with such precision', that there has been no loss of stratigraphic integrity, and that the appearance of the first point in the sequence is accompanied by other associated technological changes. This stand-off has been resolved by an elegant analysis by Hiscock, who has shown that the distribution of points at Nauwalabila I reflects sampling factors, and that small sample size affects the likelihood of spits containing rare artefact types such as points. Only 1 square metre was excavated. Points are a very rare artefact form, with no points being found in spits with fewer than 500 artefacts, whether above, below or between spits which do contain points. The probability of points being present relates directly to sample size, and it is possible that points may have been in use well before their appearance in spit 27, in view of the small assemblage sizes at those levels. In other words, the lowest point gives only a minimum age for the introduction of that implement type, if it can be ascertained whether or not vertical displacement has occurred. One cannot make any assumptions that absence of points in the lower levels of a small test excavation indicates a real absence of that implement type. This caution applies to Widgingarri and other sites on which Bowdler's argument is based and, equally, to trying to estimate the timing of the initial occurrence of backed blades.

Backed blades are thought to appear in Australia about 5000 years ago, but there are similar uncertainties. More than 168 radiocarbon dates are available for occupation levels containing backed blades. Dates earlier than 5000 years have been claimed for six of these backed blade industries, but close examination shows that none of the dates is absolutely reliable, although the evidence is being re-evaluated by Peter Hiscock and Val Attenbrow.[14]

The earliest reasonably reliable dates for backed blades in eastern Australia came from Burrill Lake, *after* 5320 BP, and at Graman Shelter I, at 5450 BP. Backed blades are found at a similar period in Western Australia, where at the Northcliffe open site, a few were found 1 to 3 centimetres *above* a horizon dated to 6780 BP.[15] But most Northcliffe backed blades are in a zone dating to about 3500 BP. Thus backed blades were certainly in use there by 4000 years ago and possibly earlier.

Independent invention of backed blades in southeastern Australia has been proposed on the grounds that the largest numbers and oldest dates come from there, and the dates tend to be younger further from Sydney, suggesting that they diffused from eastern New South Wales. However, the concentration of backed blades in the southeast may simply reflect the greater number of sites excavated there. Almost

70 percent of backed blade dates come from New South Wales, although that State represents less than one-seventh of the area of Australia over which they are distributed. Another factor that argues against local invention of backed blades in southeastern Australia is the lack of any prototypes from which these new tool types might have developed. Instead, they are suddenly added to the flakes and core tools of the earlier industry. The nearest things to prototypes for backed blades in Australia are the small tools found in some late Pleistocene sites, such as Miriwun in Western Australia.

New items do appear in Australia relatively suddenly more than 4000 years ago, for which there are no obvious local prototypes. One of these new elements was the dingo, which must have come from overseas, and when we turn to Asia, we find not only the possible original homelands of the dingo but also possible prototypes for backed blades and points.

ORIGIN OF THE DINGO

After studying the dingo for several years, Professor Macintosh of Sydney University concluded that 'its ancestry and affinities remain enigmatic'. Later, a study by Gollan suggested that the dingo resembles the Indian dog much more closely than any from Southeast Asia.[16]

The Indian pariah dog looks like a brother, or at least a cousin, of the dingo. In fact, the closest affinities to the dingo Gollan found were the skeletons of prehistoric dogs from India, such as those from Burzahom in Kashmir, and in particular the domesticated dogs from the Indus civilisation city of Harappa, dating from 3500 to 4000 years ago.

In 1985, Dr Laurie Corbett of the CSIRO Division of Wildlife and Ecology published eight years of research on more than one hundred canid skulls from Asia. His verdict was that the Australian dingo, far from being unique, is virtually indistinguishable from the wild dogs found throughout South and Southeast Asia, which are all descended from the Indian wolf (*Canis lupus pallipes*).[17]

When the dingo was brought to Australia, it was domesticated or semidomesticated; Gollan believes that 'About 4 thousand years ago a founder population of domestic dogs was introduced into Australia. These dogs were the genetic base for the subsequent feral population of Dingoes.' The major role of dingoes seems to have been the use of their pups as pets by adults, as a release for the affection and nurturing behaviour that would normally be lavished on children. In an environment that could not support a large human population, and where babies who could not be fed had to be killed, a woman who had recently lost a child or who was barren or beyond the age of child-bearing would carry a dingo pup wrapped around her waist. At night the dogs also served as a blanket, and a very cold night in outback Australia is still called a 'five dog night'. In Central Australia, on cold desert nights, when the temperature often drops below freezing point, Aborigines depended greatly on their dogs for warmth.[18]

Dingoes also have an important place in ritual and mythology, and several coastal middens, such as Kioloa and Murramarang in New South Wales and Mallacoota in

Colour plate 12   Fly River turtle painting, Little Nourlangie Rock, Northern Territory.
This colourful x-ray style painting depicts the Fly River turtle, until recently thought to be extinct in Arnhem Land.

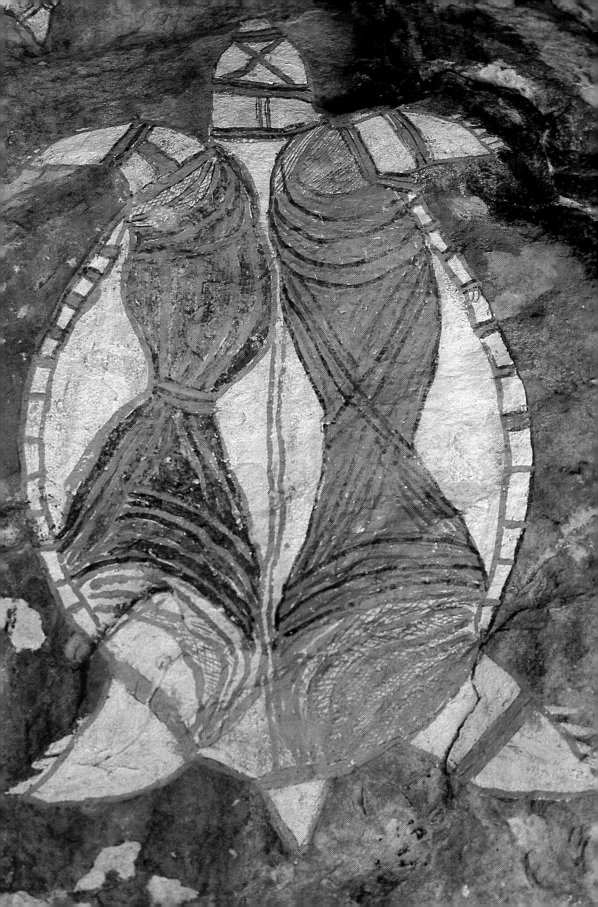

Victoria, contain burials of dingoes, evidence of the value and status of at least some. Dingoes were habitually taken as pups from the wild, to which they would eventually return. They did not create the dog overpopulation problem that modern Aboriginal camps have suffered since the acquisition of European hunting dogs, for these latter dogs never return to the wild and the dog population continues to increase.[19]

The effect of the importation of the dingo was profound. It can scarcely be coincidence that the other main carnivores, the thylacine and the Tasmanian devil, became extinct on the mainland after the dingo's arrival there, but survived in Tasmania, which the dingo never reached. The thylacine would have been no match for the dingo, which has been known to kill even German shepherd dogs in pre-mating fights. They would also have been competing for the same prey, and this may well have been the main cause of the extinctions.

INVISIBLE ARRIVALS:
LANGUAGE AND TECHNOLOGY

It has been suggested that the distribution of Aboriginal languages in Australia can best be explained by an influx of new people 4000 to 10 000 years ago, speaking a language termed by linguists 'proto-Australian', from which modern Aboriginal languages are descended. However, there is no sure way of telling whether proto-Australian was brought to Australia with the dingo about 4000 years ago or was spoken at Lake Mungo 40 000 years earlier.

There were about 250 distinct Aboriginal languages, using the criterion that two forms of speech that are mutually intelligible should be considered dialects of one language.[20] Sadly, more than half these languages are no longer spoken, and only about twenty are still being learned by children. Almost all belonged to the same language family — Australian — in the same way that most of the languages of Europe and western Asia belong to the Indo-European family. Thus two languages could be as different from each other as Russian and English and still belong to the same language family. Within an Aboriginal language there would often be several different dialects, which could be understood by other speakers of the language, usually the contiguous neighbouring groups. This situation compares with Scandinavia, where Danish, Swedish and Norwegian are mutually intelligible dialects of one Scandinavian language.

All but two or three Aboriginal languages have now been shown to be descended from one ancestral stock: proto-Australian. Australian languages have been classified in a variety of different ways, but it is agreed that the languages of southern Australia are very similar, whereas there is much more diversity in the extreme north. The languages of nine-tenths of the continent have been grouped together and termed Pama-Nyungan, after the words for 'man' at the northeastern and southwestern ends of the linguistic region.

Colour plate 13 (top) Moths at Mount Gingera, Australian Capital Territory. As many as 14 000 moths aestivate on 1 square metre of rock wall, each one resting on the moth in front of it. (By courtesy of I. Common)

Colour plate 14 (bottom) Fish traps at Brewarrina, New South Wales. These stone traps were constructed so that when high water levels receded, fish were unable to escape from the areas bounded by stones. (National Parks and Wildlife Service of NSW)

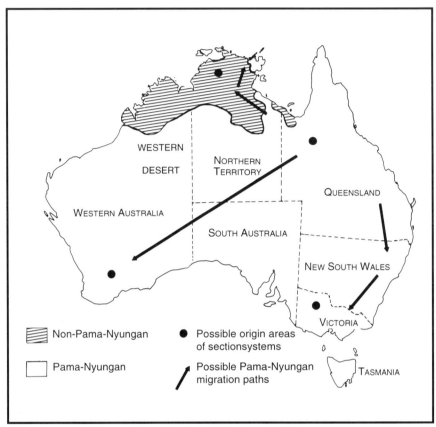

Figure 15.7 Language map of Australia. (After P. McConvell 1990)

Similarities between languages are assessed by comparing grammar, vocabulary and the sounds used. For example, although grammatically very different, the non-Pama-Nyungan languages of Arnhem Land and the Kimberley region are genetically related to Pama-Nyungan, with which they share similar verbs and sound systems. Both derive from one ancestral language (proto-Australian), but non-Pama-Nyungan languages have developed in a different direction and undergone more radical changes. Only two languages show no links with other Australian languages: those of the Djingili of the Barkly Tableland and the Tiwi of Bathurst and Melville Islands. Tasmanian languages are inadequately recorded, but there is no evidence that Tasmanian was not a language of the Australian family.

Languages outside Australia have been examined by a number of linguists, but little has emerged suggesting possible links with Australia. In Papua New Guinea there are several dozen language families, with a total of 800 or 900 languages (about 20 percent of all the languages in the world), but none of these languages appears to be genetically related to the Australian languages.

The only suggested links with Australia that deserve to be taken seriously are the Dravidian languages of southern India. Similarities between Australian and Dravidian languages were noticed as far back as 1856 by Bishop Caldwell. There are remarkable superficial similarities, especially in the sound system, but a thorough study suggests no genetic connections.

In fact, it is probably impossible ever to demonstrate a genetic connection between Australian and any other language family, since languages change at such a rate that after 3000 to 4000 years of separation, genetic links are no longer visible. For example, over only the last 2000 years the original language of France, Gaulish, was replaced so completely by Vulgar Latin, the language of the invading Roman army and the ancestor of modern French, that the existence of Gaulish would be unknown were it not for the records — written in Latin — of the conquest of Gaul.

In summary, almost all the 250 modern Aboriginal languages are genetically related and are descended from a single ancestor, called proto-Australian. There is no way of telling whether proto-Australian was spoken by the earliest Australians or introduced by later migrants, but it was probably spoken over a much longer time than proto–Indo-European. Thus, although proto-Australian could have been introduced with the dingo about 4000 years ago, it is more likely that it was the language of the original Pleistocene colonists, and that the great diversity of modern Aboriginal languages developed as the colonists spread over the continent. If so, the development of Aboriginal languages would mirror that of tool types, as there is considerable uniformity over the continent in early times but great diversity later. And some of the differences noted in the languages of Arnhem Land and the Kimberley region may reflect influences on these tropical Australians from their Asian neighbours. No evidence exists of any connection between proto-Australian and any sister language in Asia, but the time involved means that languages that were originally similar could by now have changed out of all recognition.

One other item possibly brought into eastern Australia at the same time as the small tool tradition was the knowledge of the technology for converting poisonous cycad nuts into edible food. The exploitation of this 'dangerous harvest' is described in chapter 16, but the know-how involved is so specialised that the cycad's apparently sudden appearance in Queensland about 4500 years ago has been ascribed to an outside origin rather than to Australian invention. However, evidence from southwestern Australia shows that Aborigines there had mastered leaching techniques for the same cycad, *Macrozamia*, by 13 200 years ago. In a continent as large as Australia, it is possible that plant-processing technology such as this could have been independently introduced into different regions at different times, either by independent invention or diffusion of ideas.

CONCLUSION

The dingo was imported into Australia some time between about 4000 and 3500 years ago, most probably about 4000 years ago. The most likely provenance is South or Southeast Asia. Domesticated or semidomesticated dogs could well have been taken by traders in their canoes, for as long as 8000 years ago there was a well-developed trading network in the Southeast Asian region. The presence of microliths in the Andaman Islands in the Bay of Bengal, 270 kilometres from the nearest land, implies that a marine network had developed also in the Indian Ocean. Thus contact between the Indian subcontinent and Australia could have been by way of a series of islands, such as the Andamans and Java.

The appearance of the dog and of specialised small tools in Australia but the absence of Neolithic elements, such as pottery and food production, suggest that the main migrations were in pre-Neolithic times, from a society of hunter–gatherers rather than cultivators. The different distribution of backed blade and point industries in Australia can be neatly explained by two main migration routes: one through Australia's north in the region of Arnhem Land by people using stone projectile points, and the other via the northwest coast by people using backed blades. The latter would be a natural landfall for people coming from the Indian Ocean, so the Indian subcontinent may have been the original homeland of both Australian backed blades and the dingo. The point industries could derive from the same source, or could have filtered down from Japan and northeast Asia, where projectile points were widespread in late Pleistocene times.

Those who believe in an independent Australian origin for the specialised new tools have suggested that the small tools of Sulawesi and Java might be the result of migration from Australia, rather than the other way round. While migrations are not necessarily just a one-way phenomenon, the idea of such exports from prehistoric Australia seems rather far-fetched in view of the extremely limited range of Aboriginal watercraft in historic times. Pacific voyagers, in contrast, had large outrigger sailing canoes and reached Tonga and Samoa by 5000 years ago.

The wide and apparently rapid spread of backed blades across Australia may be best understood, according to Peter White and Jim O'Connell, as a 'stylistic phenomenon analogous to Solutrean points in the French Palaeolithic or Clovis and Folsom points in northern America. The extraordinarily rapid spread of the new tools throughout Australia and their local variations in size, shape, raw materials and numbers are all compatible with this idea; so too is the fact that both major classes [points and backed blades] occurred over almost the entire range of Australian environments, though not throughout any major environmental zone . . . Some factor other than pure economy is necessary to explain this.'[21]

One factor not mentioned by White and O'Connell is that both backed blades and points are parts of composite weapons of warfare, that is, death spears and stone-tipped spears. New weapons tend to spread faster than other artefacts, and it is probably no coincidence that the spear-thrower, or woomera, seems also to have made its first appearance in Australia about the same time as the new small tools. Indeed, Roger Luebbers has suggested that the development of the new stone tools may have been directly related to the adoption of the spear-thrower, since points and backed blades would have made better spear tips and barbs than simple flakes.[22] The spear-thrower, which increased the distance a spear could be thrown to more than 100 metres, was probably invented independently within Australia, and its distribution and chronology merit further investigation.

It is also probably no coincidence that these new weapons appear at the time the sea had risen to drown huge tracts of land. About 2.5 million square kilometres of continental shelf around Australia were lost to the hunters, but the effects on the Sunda shelf were particularly dramatic. Here, a peninsula the size of India was suddenly turned into the world's largest archipelago. The tremendous loss of territory, particularly if it happened fairly rapidly, may well have been what triggered migration and conflict, bringing new technology, new tools and new ideas to Australia, and at least two dingoes. There is no evidence for a great influx of new people, and the new elements were added to the traditional Australian way of life, changing but not radically transforming it.

CHAPTER SIXTEEN

Harvesters, Engineers and Fire-Stick Farmers

Traditional Aboriginal society was much more dynamic than is usually believed. Considerable change did occur, and over the last few thousand years, the pace of development and innovation quickened. It is only within the last 5000 years that the highlands of eastern Australia have been occupied with any density. Before that, there is evidence of only slight habitation in some of the highlands, such as the Blue Mountains and the Carnarvon Ranges of southern central Queensland. The intensification of occupation in the last 5000 years saw the beginning of the small tool tradition, the adoption of new food management techniques, an apparent increase in population and an expansion into areas relatively poor in food resources.

The focus of this chapter is the Great Dividing Range, a chain of low mountains in eastern Australia running from north of the Tropic of Capricorn south to Victoria. Nowhere in this range do Aborigines still lead a hunter–gatherer way of life, so archaeological evidence and nineteenth-century historical records are our only sources of information about traditional society. These records are uneven and usually reflect a time when Aboriginal life had already been drastically disrupted by European settlement. Smallpox had decimated the Aboriginal population; measles, influenza, syphilis and alcohol had taken their toll; hunting grounds had been usurped, game wiped out, waterholes poisoned, tribes massacred. In these regions, where traditional life was shattered so early, archaeological evidence becomes an all-important means of gaining an insight into the traditional ways of life, settlement pattern and prehistory of the original inhabitants.

POISON

The most specialised and sophisticated of all the economic systems was the exploitation of *Macrozamia* nuts and other cycads, which has been studied by John Beaton in Queensland.[1] *Macrozamia* is a species of cycad, a strange, palm- or fern-like plant whose history goes back more than 200 million years. It produces unique, pineapple-like reproductive structures called 'stroboli'. These are large and brightly coloured, but extremely poisonous, as a number of explorers have discovered to their cost. They are also toxic to herds of livestock, causing what is described by stockriders in the outback as 'the zamia staggers'. Moreover, it has been discovered that cycads contain one of the most powerful cancer-causing substances in the world. 'There is no such thing as people who eat cycads and who are only just learning about how to prepare them.'

Removing the poison from cycad kernels was a lengthy, complicated procedure. Slightly different methods were used in different regions. One technique was to cut open the kernels and leach out the poison with water. Later, when the kernels were free of toxin, they were ground into a starchy, flour-like substance and baked into 'cycad bread'. Another approach was fermentation, in which the dissected kernels were placed in large containers or pits for several months. The material is safe to eat when the kernels have either frothed or grown mouldy.

The food value of cycads is exceptionally high: about 43 percent is carbohydrate, 5 percent protein. Many species produce huge quantities of kernels, yielding more food per hectare than many cultivated crops. Aborigines also increased the size of the stands of cycads by a careful use of fire to clear competing vegetation. Indeed, such cycad stands are ecological artefacts. Regular burning could also increase kernel production by seven or eight times and make them all ripen at the same time. They could be used to support large gatherings of people on ceremonial occasions.

Cycads were certainly used in Arnhem Land to provide an adequate food supply for ceremonies, when hundreds of people were gathered in a camp for weeks or months at a time. Similarly, the main use of *Macrozamia* nuts in the Carnarvon Ranges was as a 'communion food', supporting large gatherings for ceremonial or ritual purposes. Whether a staple or communion food, cycads are a highly nutritious, productive, predictable and easily harvested food, once the way to process them is known. And the whole process is not as time-consuming as one might think. The collecting and processing of cycad bread among the Anbara of Arnhem Land yielded about 1 kilogram, containing 1300 calories, per hour of work. This meant that one woman could feed herself adequately on just two hours work per day.

The exploitation of the cycad *Macrozamia* appears in southern central Queensland to be associated with the introduction of new small tools and the first intensive prehistoric settlement of this rugged region. Dozens of rock-shelters have now been excavated in the Carnarvon Ranges by Beaton and Morwood, revealing intensive use of the region during the last 4000 years, but two 10 000-year-old rock-shelter deposits, Native Well I and II, have also been found.[2] In the rainforests of North Queensland, Nicola Horsfall has found toxic nuts used at 4000 BP in Jiyer Cave.[3]

The technology is claimed to have arrived in Queensland 4500 years ago, in nearly the same form in which it is applied today. The main support for external origin of cycad use is the considerable know-how required to process the poisonous nuts, but in Cheetup Shelter near Esperance, Moya Smith found that *Macrozamia* nuts were apparently being detoxified in grass-tree–lined pits in the late Pleistocene.[4] The technology may therefore have been developed independently in different regions.

Intensive occupation associated with *Macrozamia* nuts has been discovered in the Blue Mountains, in sites such as Noola and Capertee III.[5] As in the Carnarvon Ranges, earlier occupation did exist but it was slight, and possibly intermittent, whereas there was a widespread intensification in use of the Blue Mountains region 3000 to 4000 years ago, associated with the small tool tradition.[6]

Other parts of the Great Dividing Range were far less rich in food than the Carnarvon Ranges or Blue Mountains. For example, the northern tablelands of New South Wales, around Armidale, are a particularly cold and windy environment, and only one occupation site has been found at an elevation of over 1000 metres, in spite of intensive archaeological work in the area by McBryde and others.[7] However, certain other types of site are relatively common in this bleak region: ceremonial sites and art sites. There are over a dozen bora grounds and stone arrangements and a handful of art sites. This high country may have been of religious importance, associated with the belief in a sky god — Daramulan or Baiami — which was widespread in eastern Australia. Elevated, remote sites were preferred for ceremonies, particularly ceremonies such as initiation of the young men, from which women and children were excluded. Whilst carrying out the rituals, the men could have existed on kangaroos (caught with long, fixed hunting nets made of *Kurrajong* bark) and on the region's one abundant plant food, the daisy yam, or mirr'n-yong *(Microseris scapigera)*. These have large, yellow daisy-like flowers and fat, sweet, milky tubers, which were dug up and roasted. They have a coconut-like flavour but tend to be fibrous. Common throughout New South Wales and Victoria, the daisy yam was a major Aboriginal food. So extensive was the digging for these tubers that sometimes an area was left looking like a ploughed field, as Governor Hunter observed on the banks of the Hawkesbury River near Sydney in 1793. And, like *Macrozamia*, the range of the daisy yam could be extended by careful firing.[8]

MOTHS

The daisy yam was also an important food in the southeastern highlands, but here an outstanding resource enabled large gatherings to be held: the bogong moth *(Agrotis infusa)*. Each year these small, brown moths migrate in their millions from their breeding grounds on the inland plains to spend the hot summer on the roof of Australia. On the highest peaks of the Snowy Mountains and the Victorian Alps, they aestivate — the summer equivalent of hibernate — from November to February. What made them an outstanding food for Aborigines was their habit of swarming together into rock crevices, covering the wall like a carpet (colour plate 13). As many as 14 000 have been observed on 1 square metre of rock wall.[9]

The moths usually only leave their resting places to fly around at dawn or dusk, so they were easily gathered. Since each one rests on the one in front, simply scraping a stick along the bottom row makes them all fall down into a waiting container, but Aborigines also used a fine-mesh net (made from the fibre of the *Pimelea* shrub or *Kurrajong* tree) attached to two poles, which could be introduced easily into narrow crevices. The moths seem to prefer the deepest, darkest places on the windward side of high granite tors, and sometimes they were so inaccessible that they had to be smoked out.

Before moths were gathered, a fire was prepared on a nearby rock, and then the embers were swept aside to leave a stone 'hot plate', on which the moths were grilled. Two minutes of cooking sufficed. Then the moths were winnowed to remove the ashes and dust, and the abdomens were eaten. Each is only about the size of a small peanut, but full of protein, with a taste resembling that of roast chestnuts. It was a rich diet, and Aborigines are reported to have come down from the mountains sleek and fat after several weeks or even months of feasting on moths. The moths' high protein content was as valuable a source of energy to the highlanders of the mainland as were seals to the Tasmanians coping with an even colder climate.

Moth feasts were the occasion for great gatherings of different friendly tribes. They were summoned by messengers carrying message sticks to join in the feasting and festivities. An advance party went up to the peaks to check when the moths arrived, whilst the main gathering of several hundred Aborigines took place at the foot of the mountains, at places like Jindabyne and Blowering in the Tumut Valley. These seasonal congregations were the time for initiation ceremonies, corroborees, trade, marriage arrangements, and the settling of disputes, which sometimes involved pitched battles (the unsuccessful side lost its supply of moths for the season). Then, when the moths had arrived on the summits and the necessary rituals had been performed, a smoke signal created from wet bark was sent up and the parties wended their way upwards; each group apparently owned its own moth peaks.

What traces remain of this unique phenomenon in the archaeological record? The answer is regrettably few, but nevertheless enough to show that moth hunting has been going on for at least 1000 years. Only one stone tool was used in the exploitation of this food, and that was a smooth, unmodified river stone used to grind up the cooked moths into a paste to carry them down to the valley. Such stones have been found in high-level camp sites at places such as Perisher Valley. They also occur as isolated finds high in the alpine zone, far above any natural source of river stones. The only logical explanation for anyone to carry river stones up mountains seemed to be that they were used as moth pestles, but to prove this was more difficult. The stones were examined under ultraviolet light to see if they bore any traces of organic remains, which would fluoresce. They did fluoresce, particularly on the working ends. Grinding up moths with a stone of the same kind produced fluorescence in exactly the same way as the specimens from the archaeological sites. Further evidence came from a cave that is a moth aestivation site, which also provided shelter for moth hunters. This Bogong Cave contained a similar moth pestle in an occupation deposit, and charcoal from that layer gave a date of 1000 BP.

Moth hunting is thus a specialised economic activity with an antiquity of at least 1000 years. When did it begin? The moth migrations are generally considered to be a means of escaping the oven-like heat of the breeding grounds in summer. This climatic pattern could have been established at any time after the end of the ice age, and is likely to have occurred more than 7000 years ago, during the post-glacial climatic optimum period when temperatures were higher than today.

At the northern and southern extremities of the Snowy Mountains, people were venturing on at least seasonal foraging trips in the Pleistocene, leaving slight traces of their passing around Lake George, at Birrigai and at Cloggs Cave in the Buchan Valley. But on present evidence the highlands proper seem to have been uninhabited until the small tool phase. If there was any earlier occupation, it was certainly non-intensive, and probably only seasonal.

Ceremonial gatherings were a vital part of highland life. The moth hunters could have simply exploited the moths in their own territory, but instead they trekked from more than 100 kilometres away to meet. Large gatherings need large amounts of food, and the normal highland resources, such as roasted bracken roots, daisy yams and possums, might have been inadequate without the moths. Moths are relatively abundant, reliable and easily collected; they are the easiest food to survive on if 'living off the land' in summer in the mountains, and can be eaten by the kilogram for breakfast, lunch and dinner with no ill-effects. This unusual resource enabled men to carry out initiation and other ceremonies in seclusion, as some of their stone arrangements and bora grounds on remote mountain peaks still silently testify.

EELS

The same coincidence of new stone tool forms and intensive exploitation of a special food resource associated with large ceremonial gatherings is found not only in the highlands of Queensland and New South Wales but also among the swamps and plains of southwestern Victoria. Here the special food was eels.

Eels were a major food source of the fast, coastward-flowing rivers in southeastern Australia. Each year the large, fat, silver eels migrate upstream in spring to their inland feeding grounds, then downstream in autumn to the sea and their breeding places far away in tropical waters. This eel *(Anguilla australis occidentalis)* is a temperate freshwater species, which grows to 1 metre or more in length and to the thickness of a man's arm.

The fertile coastal plain of southwestern Victoria is intersected by a network of small, perennial rivers, swamps and wetlands. Rainfall occurs mainly in the autumn and winter and, before European settlement, used to turn vast stretches of land into marshes each year. There were thus extensive wetlands each autumn, the main eel fishing season, and elaborate canals and traps were constructed to catch the eels during their migrations.

Archaeological work by Harry Lourandos, Peter Coutts, Jane Wesson and others in the Western District of Victoria has revealed the existence of specialised, large-scale stone structures to exploit eels as a major seasonal food. Extensive eel traps still exist at Lake Condah, Ettrick (also called the Mainsbridge Weir site), Toolondo and Mount William. The Lake Condah system was mapped and studied in detail by the Victoria Archaeological Survey during a series of archaeological summer schools from

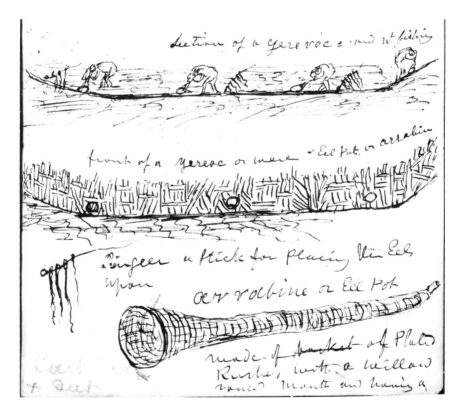

Figure 16.1 An eel pot and trap sketched by G. A. Robinson in western Victoria, 1841, showing above: the 'front of a yeroec or weir' with 'eel pot or arrabine', set into the holes in the weir; centre: 'lingeer or stick for placing eels upon'; and below: 'arrabine or eel pot made of plaited rushes'. (After Robinson 1841, by courtesy of the Mitchell Library, Sydney)

1977 to 1981, and the results published in a volume called *Aboriginal Engineers of the Western Districts, Victoria.*[10] These archaeologists found a large number of 'stone races, canals, traps and stone walls'. The races, defined as 'above ground structures for directing water', were constructed by building walls from broken blocks of the black volcanic rock that litters the Lake Condah region. The walls were up to 1 metre in height and width and often more than 50 metres long. In some places, 'canals' or 'channels dug into the ground' were dug into basalt bedrock by removing loose and broken rock, and extended up to 1 metre in depth and as much as 300 metres in length.

Traps were built across the stone races and canals; nets or eel pots were set in apertures in the stone walls, which were often constructed in a V-shape. The eel pots were made from strips of bark or plaited rushes with a willow hoop at the mouth (figure 16.1). The tapered shape allowed men standing behind the weirs to grab the eels as they emerged through the narrow end of the pot. The fishermen killed the eels by biting them on the back of the head. The same method of killing has been observed in Arnhem Land in recent times, but in this case women killed sea snakes by putting the heads in their mouths and biting.[11] When dead, the eels were threaded onto a stick to take back to camp.

The Aboriginal fishermen understood the hydrology of the lake perfectly. They designed and constructed an ingenious system for catching the maximum number of eels with minimum effort. Considerable organisation of labour would have been required initially to excavate the canals, but Coutts estimated that no more than twenty people were needed to operate the traps once they were built. The sophisticated network was so cunningly designed that it took advantage of both rising and falling water. Traps were built at different levels, and as the lake rose or fell, different traps came into operation progressively. The archaeologists at Lake Condah, after a period of heavy rain, were treated to a demonstration of how the whole system might have operated.

Even more remarkable than the complex eel harvesting at Lake Condah is the evidence of Aboriginal 'engineering' near Mount William and Toolondo. At Toolondo an elaborate system of water control — a sort of prehistoric Snowy Mountains Scheme — was developed. Artificial channels 400 metres long were dug out with digging sticks to join two swamps, 2.5 kilometres apart, in different drainage basins. They were separated by a low divide, which was cut through to allow water to flow in either direction. Eels were thus able to extend their range and increase in number, and the channels made it easy to catch them.

The system was also designed to cope with excess water during floods and to retain water in times of drought. It is estimated that over 3000 cubic metres of earth was dug out of the Toolondo complex. The water control system at Mount William was described by Robinson in 1841:

> *At the confluence of this creek with the marsh observed an immense piece of ground trenches and banks resembling the work of civilised man but which on inspection were found to be the work of the aboriginal natives — purpose consisted for catching eels — a specimen of art of the same extent I had not before seen . . . these trenches are hundreds of yards in length — I measured in one place in one continuous triple line for the distance 500 yards. The triple water course led to other ramified and extensive trenches of a more tortuous form — an area of at least 15 acres was thus traced out . . . These works must have been executed at great cost of labour . . . There must have been some thousands of yards of this trenching and banking.*[12]

Robinson's detailed diaries provide one of the few sources of information on Aboriginal life in western Victoria. He tells us that the canals were dug with digging sticks, and that the eel fishermen at Mount William were camping on a group of oven mounds nearby.

The ethnographic evidence concerning dwellings and 'villages' in the Western District comes mainly from James Dawson's 1881 account, but also from earlier records and sketches from the time of first European settlement in the late 1830s, and has been synthesised by Elizabeth Williams during her research into the archaeology of the region.[13]

Three types of dwellings were in use in southwest Victoria at contact. These were a simple windbreak, a domed hut and a beehive-shaped hut. Windbreaks were used during fine and warm weather or for short-term occupation. The more substantial domed form of hut, consisting of a framework of boughs set into a dome shape, was used during fine weather or for shelter whilst travelling. The most substantial hut was a weatherproof, beehive-shaped dwelling made of a layer of mud, sods, bark or turf plastered over a framework of boughs. In very stony country, this form was constructed using a low wall of stones as a foundation, which was then roofed with wood and bark. Substantial huts were used on a semipermanent basis, especially during colder weather. Huts generally faced east, according to Dawson. Most huts, regardless of type, had a diameter of 'ten feet' (3 metres), but larger huts of up to 'fifteen feet' (4.5 metres) in diameter were associated with a more prolonged stay or a larger family group. Caves and rock overhangs were also occupied in some instances, and earth mounds were used as camping places and as foundations for huts.

In order to take full advantage of the fishing at Lake Condah, people needed to live within a day or two's walk of the lake. This meant that some large camp sites should exist in the area, and in January 1981 a field survey was conducted by Jane Wesson and others from the Victoria Archaeological Survey to try to find some. Not only were camp sites found, but also the remains of stone 'houses' and whole 'villages' were reported.[14] Wesson identified 128 stone structures in one paddock (at Palmer's = Allambie) as hut bases, and further field work by Katrina Geering in 1985 supported her identification of these structures as cultural sites. My account of the Lake Condah houses in the 1983 edition of this book was based on the published findings of Wesson and Coutts, which I had no reason to doubt, having visited and seen for myself a few reasonably convincing examples of stone hut bases at Macarthur and Lake Condah. However, a field survey by Anne Clarke failed to relocate many of Wesson's houses and also threw doubt on the identification of others, which she considers to be natural features misinterpreted by earlier field workers.[15] At Allambie, 83 percent of the known site data base was either not relocated or not considered to be a cultural site. However, Clarke accepts that some 'stone circles' exist; they are defined as 'semi-circular, c-shaped or u-shaped stone structures' and are considered most likely to be temporary stone hut bases, windbreaks, hunting blinds or 'dinner time camps'.

At Lake Condah stone circles were the most numerous site type recorded by Clarke, the seventy-nine found comprising 49 percent of total sites. They are concentrated on the tops of the flatter lava ridges on the western side of the lake, and most occur in clusters of five or more, with the largest group containing sixteen stone circles. No artefacts were found within any of the stone circles identified in 1990, and Clarke argues that they were probably 'seasonal trapping and fishing huts, where people waited for the traps to become operational after heavy rains and where they then processed the day's catch before leaving for other larger camps'. The mounds, which are widespread in areas adjacent to the stony rises and wetlands, are considered to be more likely foci for larger aggregations of people.

Earth mounds, or mirr'n-yong heaps as they are often called, abound along the rivers and lakes of Victoria. In western Victoria, the appearance of low earth mounds in this region is dated to around 2500 BP, and excavation evidence indicates their use as camp sites. Williams has argued that these mounds may represent deliberately constructed hut foundations, and that where these mounds appear in larger groups or clusters, this is representative of a 'village' complex. She points out that 'analyses of ethnographic material indicated that, at the time of European settlement (the late 1830s), substantial settlements comprising groups of up to 30 beehive-shaped huts were common here. It appears these settlements were occupied on a sedentary or semi-sedentary basis, and were often termed "villages" by contemporary observers.'[16]

The use of the term 'village' has been condemned by other researchers, such as Clarke, Frankel and Bird, who question whether these mound clusters are in fact evidence of large-scale settlement and sedentary occupation.[17] They point out that where adjacent mounds have been dated, they may be separated in time by up to 1000 years. As such, although large numbers of mounds are found in close proximity, there is no archaeological evidence at present to suggest that they were all occupied during the same time frame. It has been further argued that many of these 'villages' observed by Robinson may represent post-contact refuge areas, and were not an integral part of the prehistoric settlement pattern.

The same arguments apply to the stone houses of Macarthur, Lake Condah and elsewhere in western Victoria. Although large numbers of these structures may be found in close proximity, there is no evidence to suggest they were all occupied at the same time. Similarly, the eel traps of Lake Condah and the water control systems of Toolondo are unquestionably complex, but may have been developed over a long period of time, without involving a particularly large investment of labour.

Whilst agreeing that the use of Eurocentric terms such as 'villages', 'canals' and 'engineering' may be inappropriate because of their implicit connotations if taken too literally, in my view, Clarke, Frankel and Bird go too far in the other direction. Even if most of the remains of huts and 'canals' are undatable, and some of them may be natural rather than cultural features, Robinson's eye-witness accounts remain. (Similarly, if the ethnographic accounts of Aborigines gathering moths in the alps (described above) had not existed, then on the basis of the fragmentary archaeological evidence that is available, many would not believe that Aborigines ever went moth hunting![18])

Eel-fishing Aborigines of western Victoria have been called 'complex hunter–gatherers' by Williams, and defined as 'groups who are sedentary or semi-sedentary; live in sizeable settlements which are often termed "villages"; construct large, durable structures, and manipulate the environment in ways that alter the availability or abundance of resources'.[19] This seems to me a reasonable interpretation of the nineteenth-century situation, but the archaeological evidence is so fragmentary that there remains much uncertainty about the scale and nature of eel-fishing and associated settlements and the degree of sedentism in earlier times.

All sites that have been excavated so far in inland parts of the Western District have proved to be less than 3500 years old, and since both stone circles and traps at Lake Condah are generally well preserved, they may well belong to the fairly recent prehistoric past. The hydraulic systems are indeed remarkable examples of resource management and stone age 'engineering', and, like the sophisticated and large-scale eel traps of Lake Condah and elsewhere, show that Aborigines ingeniously manipulated their environment, not necessarily to increase food production but to increase the regularity and reliability of food resources, making possible a less nomadic way of life and regular, large tribal gatherings. Like moths and *Macrozamia*, eels were used as a 'communion food' to feed large numbers of people gathered together for ceremonies. They were also one of the very few food items that were traded in the exchange system (see chapter 18).

At times when eels and fish were not available, there were waterfowl, emus, plains turkeys, kangaroos and plentiful vegetable foods, particularly *Convolvulus* in winter and tubers of the daisy yam in summer. The starchy rhizomes of bracken ferns may also have been an important food here, as they were on the coast at Cape Otway, where masses of pestles and mortars have been found in the Seal Point midden by Lourandos.[20] They were used for crushing up the bracken roots, which were eaten raw or roasted. Bracken is very common, spreads after bushfires, and is native to Australia; it is not a European import as has sometimes been said.

There is a close link between the holding of lengthy ceremonies and the management of food resources. As a society becomes more complex, it increases its demands on the economy; a more intensive social system is linked to more intensive food management. Intensification of food management in southwestern Victoria probably led to population increase, which in turn triggered more intensive occupation of the less favourable regions to the north: the Grampians and the arid Mallee, studied by Anne Ross. Aborigines probably expanded into the Grampians and the Mallee proper only some 3500 years ago, mainly as a result of increased population density in southwestern Victoria. There was some earlier occupation from about 12 000 to 7000 years ago on or near the Murray River, but not in the really arid areas of low sand dunes and dense mallee scrub.[21] This view is based on the belief that 'absence of evidence is evidence of absence'. Some would say that older sites are there waiting to be found, but a strong case has been made by Ross for late occupation of this harsh environment. This fits well with the pattern of occupation found in other unfavourable habitats.

Climatic change may also have played a part in changing Aboriginal settlement patterns and economy. There is some evidence of a cold, dry spell around 3500 to 3000 years ago. This may have been one factor leading to the development of artificial water management techniques for harvesting eels; to a move into the wetter Grampian Mountains at that time; and, later, to population expansion into the Mallee once wetter conditions returned to this semiarid region, about 2500 to 1500 years ago.

In another semiarid area in southern Australia — the Nullarbor Plain — human occupation seems to have been very slight until the last few thousand years. A great increase in the Aboriginal population of the region about 4000 to 6000 years ago is suggested by a twofold to threefold increase at that time in the density of artefacts in three excavated caves: Allen's, Madura and Norina.[22] This is accompanied by an apparent increase (reflected in the sites' pollen sequences) in pressure on the vegetation, both through burning and through cutting material for hut-building.

COASTAL FISHING

The middens of southeastern Australia have yielded some fascinating evidence of diversity and change in both diet and technology of coastal fishing people during the last few thousand years.

Some middens reflect specialisation, others a more generalised subsistence, such as the Currarong sites on the Beecroft Peninsula north of Jervis Bay, excavated by Lampert.[23] Here the contents of midden deposits in four small rock-shelters showed exploitation of the food resources of the open beach, rock platform, estuary, wooded gullies and headland plateau. In the midden of Currarong Shelter I were remains of (in order of decreasing frequency) bandicoots, wallabies, potoroos, dingoes (not necessarily food remains), fur seals and possums. Among the fish remains, snapper predominated, followed by bream, parrotfish and groper. Snapper is a bottom-dwelling reef fish that was probably caught from the headland using lines and shell fish-hooks, some of which were found in the site. Bream, on the other hand, is an estuarine fish that was probably caught by spearing with a multi-pronged fishing spear. These spears were armed with bone points, some of which were also present in the deposit (figure 16.2).

Further south on the New South Wales coast, the small sea cave of Durras North, which overlooks a large ocean beach, was excavated by Lampert.[24] The deposit only spanned the last 500 years and revealed a number of surprises. There were almost no stone tools. The only numerous artefacts were fish-hooks and bone points, pointed at one or both ends and made out of bird bone (figures 16.2 and 16.3). The deposit was full of bird bones, particularly of the muttonbird. These birds migrate down the coast each year and would have been caught after they collapsed exhausted at sea and were swept ashore. The muttonbird collectors also consumed fish, shellfish and *Macrozamia* nuts, and doubtless many other foods which were eaten away from the cave or have not survived in the midden. The southerly aspect of the beach at Durras makes it an ideal location for the collection of flotsam, and we can imagine these prehistoric beachcombers sitting in their cave in October and November — the best months for muttonbird casualties — looking out across the sand to the rolling surf, which might bring them their dinner.

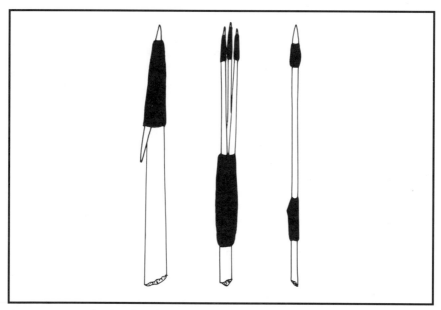

Figure 16.2 Spear heads. Left: Plain spear with single bone barb. Centre: Fishing spear with multiple bone barbs. Right: Three-piece spear shaft, detachable head and stone spear point.

Just south of Sydney, in the Royal National Park, several sandstone rock-shelters overlook the beautiful deep lagoon and sandy beach of Wattamolla Cove. This is a favourite spot for picnickers and anglers, who use metal fish-hooks, spears and scuba equipment to catch fish which Aborigines earlier caught with shell fish-hooks and vegetable lines or bone-barbed fishing spears. The public footpath to the beach runs through one of the rock-shelter sites, where Vincent Megaw excavated a shallow shell midden containing a large number of bones of reef fish, a few bones of muttonbird, seal and land mammals, together with seven bone points and eight crescentic fish-hooks.[25]

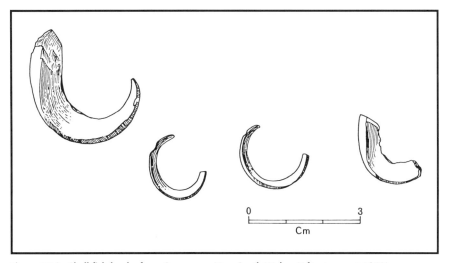

Figure 16.3   Shell fish-hooks from Currarong, New South Wales. (After Lampert 1971)

The Wattamolla sites appear to have been specialised fishing sites: the men fished with spears and the women with hook and line. This division of labour according to technique is clearly documented in the Sydney district by the earliest European arrivals, such as Captain Cook, David Collins and John Hunter.[26] Both men and women, but more particularly women, used bark canoes for fishing, which were seldom seen without the smoke of a small fire curling up from them. The fire was kindled on a bed of seaweed and clay in the centre of the canoe, and fish and shellfish caught from the craft were often cooked and eaten in them. The fires thus served for cooking and warmth, and to provide light for fishing at night. This was a frequent practice, and if we could be transported back 300 years in time, we would see Sydney Harbour and Wattamolla Lagoon sprinkled at night with dozens of fishing canoes, each with its own twinkling light.

A specialised oyster-gathering site lies on the north coast of New South Wales, on the northern bank of the mouth of the Clarence River. This is Wombah midden, which consists almost entirely of oyster shells.[27] There were no fish-hooks and only a few bone points and stone tools, including ground-edge axes and pebble tools. Historical sources indicate that large numbers of Aborigines used to congregate in summer to crop the oyster beds on the north coast. It is interesting that on these occasions, the traditional sexual division of labour broke down. Normally, gathering shellfish was women's work, but when shellfish was the main food enabling a large number of people to congregate together, both men and women did the collecting. Such seasonal abundance of particular food resources allowed large-scale social and ritual events to take place and ceremonies to be conducted in bora rings and other ceremonial grounds.

INTENSIFICATION

A remarkably consistent pattern has emerged from this overview of societies in southeastern Australia during the last few thousand years. The major happenings seem to be the adoption of small composite tools, an increase in intensity of occupation (with more sites, artefacts and people), the spread of people into harsh environments that had few or no earlier inhabitants, and the harvesting or management of special foods linked with the holding of ceremonies and the extension of social networks. Within this overall pattern there is great regional diversity. Each region had its own distinctive way of life, material culture and art style, although there was extensive social contact and exchange of ideas and goods.

An increase in the mid-Holocene in the number of sites has been well documented by Lourandos, Williams, Beaton and others, and it has been convincingly argued that this is not just a result of the better preservation and archaeological visibility of younger sites, but reflects an increase in population.[28] Stephen Sutton has made an interesting comparison (shown in figure 16.4) between the initial occupation dates of sites younger than 12 000 BP in southwestern Victoria and Tasmania.[29] He interprets this as showing that Tasmania, although totally isolated from the mainland, exhibits a very similar pattern to the mainland in its initial occupation dates for Holocene sites. He concludes that 're-assessment of the means by which we determine social complexity and changes therein from archaeological data is needed. In particular, the use of initial or basal occupation dates is called into question.' I would agree, and also point out that the sample sizes tend to be too small for valid comparisons. For example, Tasmania, according to figure 16.4, appears uninhabited before 9000 BP, which was certainly known not to be the case (even in 1981, when Stockton's data were compiled), and if one added on the Tasmanian Pleistocene sites, the picture would be very different. The interesting question which these data do raise is: what happened in the 'dark ages' of Australia? We have remarkably little evidence for the period from about 12 000 to 8000 BP all over the continent.

Others have criticised aspects of the 'intensification model' on different grounds.[30] For example, Bird and Frankel maintain that the arguments developed by Lourandos, Ross and Williams are based upon the assertion that developments in alliance networks, productivity and settlement patterns are representative of increasing social complexity and population levels. However, the chronology of these developments is far from clear and, as such, it is questionable whether these events constitute the interrelated set of Holocene changes labelled 'intensification'.

All researchers agree, I think, that there was no significant pan-continental climatic change in the mid-Holocene that could have led to these changes or 'intensification'. Some, such as Bowdler, incline to the view that a new 'cultural package' was brought into the continent along with the dingo, but there are two arguments against this view. Firstly, the changes are not simultaneous all across Australia; palaeontologists such as Jeanette Hope argue strongly against the dingo being introduced much before 4000 BP but, in spite of Bowdler's efforts, it is very

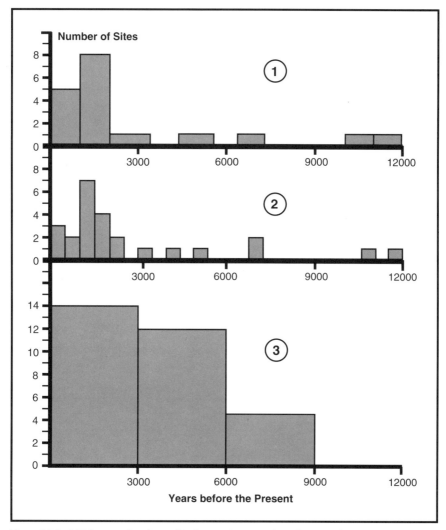

Figure 16.4 Initial occupation dates of Holocene sites. 1 and 2 refer to southwestern Victoria (data from Lourandos 1983 and Williams 1987), 3 refers to Tasmania (data after Stockton 1981). (S. Sutton 1990, figure 3)

difficult to discount all the earlier dates for points and backed blades at around 5000 BP or even earlier. Secondly, some changes also occurred in Tasmania, which all researchers agree was totally isolated from the mainland since about 10 000 years ago. In my view there is only one change that could explain all these changes in the mid-Holocene, and that is population increase. Beaton[31] has argued for a natural, incremental population increase, and whilst the details of his model are open to question, in that the rise may have been much more gentle than he has suggested, it is the most economical explanation for all the changes, such as increases in numbers of sites and artefacts, use of new food resources and food procurement techniques, expansion into marginal environments such as the highlands and deserts, greater regionalism in rock art, and adoption of new weapons — backed blades and spear points — to defend territory.

THE LAST 2000 YEARS

In southeastern Australia the small tool tradition, characterised by specialised, composite small tools, such as backed blades, survived in a remarkably consistent form for 2000 years from its beginnings about 4000 years ago. Then, from about 2000 BP, changes gradually occurred. Some items, such as backed blades, dropped out of the tool kit and there was a proportional increase in others, such as ground-edge axes. Simple flakes, often of quartz, were used, without the earlier careful preparation of their working edges. There was also a greater use of bone and shell for tool-making. In fact, some young sites contain almost no stone tools at all.

Shell fish-hooks came into use some time during this period. Whether they were independently invented in Australia or were introduced from somewhere in Melanesia to the north we do not know, but they were being used in Australia during the last 1000 years. The presence of stone 'fish-hook files' in sites cannot be taken to indicate that fish-hooks were also present but have now decayed, because there is no good evidence that these smooth, polished stones ever served as files to manufacture fish-hooks.

It may be that the development of hook- and line-fishing, and even of the multi-pronged fishing spear, was a response to population pressure, enabling greater exploitation of marine resources. The use of hook and line made available a new range of deeper-water sea fish unobtainable by spear-fishing. If line-fishing were only done by women in the prehistoric period, as in the historic period, it could also imply a new and greater role for women in coastal societies. If this is so, environmental change led to population change, which inspired technological change, which caused economic and social change.

The general characteristics of this late phase of southeastern prehistory seem to be the adoption of specialised fishing techniques, a greater use of bone and shell artefacts, a decrease in finely retouched tools and a corresponding increase in the use of untrimmed flakes. Most of these are made of quartz, the most common stone in Australia. This suggests that there were more people who were competing for the same resources and who were perhaps more restricted in their foraging area than in the earlier days of an emptier continent.

FIRE-STICK FARMERS

One of the Aborigines' most important artefacts is largely invisible to the archaeologist: fire. Much of the vegetation encountered by early white settlers in Australia was not natural but artificial; an Aboriginal artefact created by thousands of years of burning the countryside. Before the colonists started ringbarking the trees, humans had had a great impact on the Australian environment,[32] as has been shown by the research of Sylvia Hallam, Rhys Jones, Robin Clark, Peter Latz, Dick Kimber, Tim Flannery, Geoff Hope, Peter Kershaw, the late Gurdip Singh and others.

There were many reasons for the extensive burning. It was used for signalling and also to make travel easier by clearing undergrowth along the route and killing snakes lurking in the bush. Aboriginal tracks were kept open by regular firing in the heavily timbered ranges of the Blue Mountains and in the dense tea-tree scrub of western Tasmania, and fire was also used to clear a path through the tropical grasslands of Arnhem Land. Throughout the continent, burning was used as an aid to hunting; animals could be speared or clubbed as they broke cover to escape the flames.

Other uses of fire were for longer-term hunting strategies. After firing, the bush would regenerate, new grass would spring up and attract kangaroos and other herbivores, on which the hunters could prey. Likewise, fire encouraged the regrowth of eucalypt trees and of edible plant foods, such as bracken roots, young leaves and shoots. The ashes acted like manure, and sweet, new green shoots would spring up after the first hard rain following the burn.

Extensive and regular burning had the long-term effect of altering and actually extending humans' habitat. Jones has convincingly demonstrated that the sedgeland of the west coast of Tasmania is a human artefact, the result of the long use of fire, which gradually changed the original rainforest — dominated by the fire-sensitive beech, *Nothofagus* — through a phase of mixed eucalypts and rainforest to scrub and finally heath and sedgeland. Now that Aborigines are no longer burning in Tasmania, in some places rainforest is reinvading its old habitat. Likewise, in highland northern Tasmania, explorer Henry Hellyer found open grasslands among the rainforest in 1827, and he named them the Surrey and Hampshire Hills after the rolling grassy downs of England. These grasslands provided perfect pastures for sheep, but when Aborigines were no longer present to maintain them with a regular fire regime, sour grass and scrub took over, gradually obliterating the open land, so that sheep-grazing stopped around 1845, with considerable loss to the non–fire-stick farmers.

The changes brought about in Tasmania by Aboriginal use of the fire-stick had the effect of increasing the amount and diversity of food available. Tasmanian rainforest is not rich in plant and animal food, whereas the mixed heath and wet scrub and grasslands that replaced it under the Aboriginal fire regime provided an abundance of game and plant food, such as two of the carbohydrate staples of temperate Australia: bracken, a vigorous coloniser of newly burnt forest, and the grass-tree, of which the starchy pith of the trunk was eaten.

In different parts of the continent different fire regimes were used, adapted to local needs. In Arnhem Land the Anbara practise a fire-management program that maintains the existing vegetation. They spare fire-sensitive areas, such as jungle thickets, which contain many edible plants that do not readily regenerate after burning. Here, there are strong ritual prohibitions against burning: jungles are the home of spirits who, if disturbed by fire, would send smoke into the eyes of the fire-lighters and make them blind. Moreover, fire-breaks are formed around such thickets: an area of about 1 kilometre broad is carefully burnt soon after the end of the wet season. Thus when the main burning is done between June and August in the dry season, the jungle thickets are protected by a fire-break of already-burnt grasslands. The reasons given by the Anbara for burning throw an interesting light on Aboriginal attitudes to fire. Fire was seen as necessary to clean up the country, and they regarded unburnt grassland as neglected. Every part of the grasslands, savanna and eucalypt woodlands of their own territory would be burnt regularly, at least once every three or four years.

Such regular, light burning was the pattern all over Australia at the time of first European contact. The fires were of low intensity, which meant that they consumed the litter of leaves and branches on the forest floors but did not burn down the trees. Without such regular burning, forest litter accumulates at a fast rate. This litter accumulation leads to disastrous wild fires, such as that of 1 February 1967, which threatened Hobart.

It is ironic that the Australian parklands and open woodlands so admired by the early settlers should have been created by the Aborigines they regarded as ignorant nomads. Yet when Aborigines were driven off their land and the regular, light burning ceased, the old grass turned sour, scrub invaded the parkland, and the settlers' fine houses, fences and sheep became victims of occasional uncontrollable bushfires. It has taken over a century for the European settler to learn from such mistakes, and now a system of controlled, regular burning has been instituted in many National Parks. In the Kakadu National Park the burning is being done by local Aborigines.

Unlike modern conservationists, Aborigines never put out their fires. Camp fires were left burning, as were signal fires, including those lit in a sequence to indicate the direction of travel of humans or game such as kangaroos. Hunting fires were likewise left to burn themselves out, and Richard Gould reports 23 square kilometres of country being burnt in the process of catching three feral cats.[33] Indeed, Aborigines lit fires with such apparent abandon that they have been called 'peripatetic pyromaniacs'. Burning the country still continues in Central and Northern Australia, although instead of the fire-stick, lighted matches are tossed out of the back of trucks now.

In the desert regions mosaic burning was usually carried out in winter, with parts, but not the whole, of an area being burnt. Much of the desert is clothed in clumps of prickly spinifex grass, which is of little economic value apart from the black, tarry gum it produces — a strong resinous adhesive used for fixing stone adzes to handles and for other purposes. However, when large areas of spinifex are burnt, the burnt land is recolonised after rain by a variety of other desert plants more productive of food than spinifex. Gradually the country reverts to spinifex, but meanwhile, there is likely to be an increased supply of edible plants, such as the fruits of *Solanum* (wild tomatoes). These are the most important fruits of the desert people; they are up to the size of a nectarine, highly nutritious, full of vitamin C, and hang on bushes for months with excellent storage quality. Another food plant which loves to crawl up burnt trees is the 'wild banana', a vine with edible leaves, fruit and a yam-like root.

Aborigines in Arnhem Land have been observed to aim their fires in particular directions, and despite the apparently casual use of fire in the Western Desert, Gould 'never encountered an occasion when a fire actually invaded an area that was already producing wild food crops'.[34] It seems that, as well as increasing their future food supply, the Aborigines also protected their present food resources. Fire is the most versatile and important tool of hunter–gatherers. It is used for warmth, light, cooking, hunting, signalling, track-making, and, whether intentionally or not, had the effect of improving the food supplies of prehistoric Australia.

The fire-stick was one of the few artefacts that was used all over prehistoric Australia at the time of contact with Europeans. The last 1000 years had been a period of great regional diversity and complexity. There was no standard way of life but, rather, a series of remarkably different regional responses to varying environments, ranging from moth hunting to sealing, from eel trapping to cycad harvesting. There was not only diversity, but also intensification in the use of resources. The pace of change was quickening — who knows where this initiative and creativity might not have led Aboriginal society, had not those ships of doom sailed into Sydney Harbour in 1788.

CHAPTER SEVENTEEN

The Question of Agriculture

It has long been remarked that Australia remained a nation of nomadic hunter–gatherers while most people in the rest of the world, including New Guinea, became cultivators. Other traits of the Neolithic period, such as the domestication of animals and the use of pottery, likewise were never adopted in Australia. These traits never penetrated the fifth continent.

What is surprising, in view of the arrival of the dingo from the outside world, is that more new elements did not also reach Australia at that time. The pig was probably in New Guinea by 10 000 years ago, when a neck of land still linked New Guinea and Australia, and was certainly present by 6000 years ago, yet the pig was completely absent from prehistoric Australia. The pig was not native to New Guinea but must have been brought there from mainland Southeast Asia or islands such as Java or Sulawesi, where it was indigenous.

The other major element found in New Guinea at an early date but absent from Australia was agriculture. Agriculture was being practised in New Guinea by 9000 years ago. The evidence comes from the work of Jack Golson, Doug Yen and others in the Wahgi Valley, near Mount Hagen, in the Central Highlands.[1] In the late 1960s, when some tea planters drained a swamp, they discovered ancient wooden paddle-shaped spades, digging sticks and stone axes. These were associated with many water-control ditches, which were probably dug to aid the growing of taro, cultivated for its edible, starchy, tuberous root. The oldest ditch, 2 metres wide by 1 metre deep and at least 450 metres long, was radiocarbon-dated to about 9000 years old. Taro, like the pig, is not native to New Guinea, so it must also have been introduced. Other evidence in New Guinea shows that by 6000 to 5000 years ago, plant cultivation, based on both native and non-native species, forest clearance, relatively permanent village settlements, and complex water management systems had already developed.

Possible reasons put forward to explain why Australian Aborigines did not become farmers have been lack of contact with agricultural groups, cultural conservatism, hostility to newcomers, lack of suitable plants and animals to domesticate, and deliberate choice.

CONTACT WITH CULTIVATORS

At the time of the drowning of the land bridge across Torres Strait, about 6500 years ago, subsistence throughout the region was based on hunting and gathering. Although agriculture developed early in New Guinea, it only became intensive in some regions, and wild food continued, until the present day, to make a large contribution to the diet in many areas.

In lowland Papua, north of the Torres Strait, there was a blend of limited agriculture with foraging (hunting and gathering). The system in the northern Torres Strait islands was similar, but further south, in the southern Torres Strait islands and Cape York Peninsula, subsistence was based on wild plant and animal food. These differences cannot be due simply to climatic differences, since across the 1000 kilometres from Oriomo to Cooktown, the climate is relatively uniform, with a markedly seasonal rainfall. Yet across this tract there is a gradient from the horticulturalists of New Guinea, with their pottery, pigs and fenced gardens, to the nomadic hunter–gatherers of Australia, with none of those things.

The Torres Strait islands form a set of stepping stones between Papua and Cape York and thus hold the key to discovering how much contact and what sort of contact there was between prehistoric Australia and the outside world. Fortunately, a considerable amount of research on Torres Strait has been done over the last decade by David Harris, Jeremy Beckett and others.[2]

Agriculture was not practised on all the Torres Strait islands. The western islands are generally high islands, composed of old volcanic rocks, surrounded by shallow seas, reefs and sandbanks that provide a home for innumerable fish, shellfish, turtles and dugong. The land provided a variety of plant food, particularly yams and the fruits of the mangrove, the same nutritious species that was used on Cape York. In this rich environment there was normally no need to engage in the labour of gardening. But in times of stress, when there was a shortage of turtles, gardens of yams were planted as a standby. There were dingoes on the islands but no pigs, another contrast with Papua New Guinea.

North of this Prince of Wales group of islands, agriculture was more firmly established. Yams were apparently the main root crop grown, and taro, sweet potato, banana and sugar cane were also important. The crops were usually grown in plots cleared by slash and burn. The wild vegetation was cleared from an area with the aid of fire and the seeds scattered over or planted in the disturbed ground.

The eastern islands in Torres Strait, which are small and low, with rich soils but less rich marine resources than their western neighbours, practised agriculture extensively. Agriculture is an intensification of food procurement and it is very possible that it began on the Torres Strait islands because of population pressure resulting from the enormous loss of land as the Sahul shelf was flooded by post-glacial rising seas, which crowded the previously widespread population onto islands. However, this is speculation; no archaeological evidence is available to indicate how long these islands have been inhabited. Stone tools, stone arrangements, middens and fish traps have been found on the islands, but no site has yet been excavated to provide an idea of length of occupation.[3]

SHELL MOUNDS

On Cape York itself, there are indications that shellfish were an important part of the diet, at least over the last 1000 years. The existence of huge shell mounds on the west side of Cape York, at Weipa, has been known since 1901. Archaeological investigations, by Geoffrey Bailey in particular, have shown that the mounds were of human, not natural, origin. Doubts about the human origin of the Weipa mounds and other mounds, both in Australia and globally, were raised by Tim Stone in 1989, and he was still arguing in 1993 that 'natural processes of shell deposition explain the origins of the Weipa shell mounds ... The unusual shapes and heights of many of the Weipa shell deposits can be explained by the mound-building behaviour of the Orange-Footed Scrubfowl *Megapodius reinwardt*.' Other authorities disagree with Stone, and according to Roger Cribb, his hypothesis is 'strictly for the birds'![4] Excavation of sections of two of the larger mounds revealed the presence of charcoal layers, bone and stone — all distinguishing marks of midden deposits. And the shells are predominantly of a single species: cockle shell *(Anadara granosa)*.

There are about 500 shell mounds along the banks of the four rivers that flow into the bay where the modern bauxite mining town of Weipa stands. Thanks to their remoteness in the early days of European settlement, and more recently to the conservation policy of Comalco, this magnificent series is one of the few major groups of shell middens in Australia to be still almost intact (see plate 30).

The mounds generally occur in clusters. Most are only 1 to 2 metres high, but some reach a height of 9 metres, and the tallest is no less than 13 metres high. It has been calculated that the largest mound has a volume of 9400 cubic metres, and that the 500 mounds contain 200 000 tonnes of shell, or about 9000 million cockles! Radiocarbon dates from the base of the excavations show that the mounds began to accumulate about 1200 years ago. This means that at Weipa 9 million cockles were collected each year, yielding about 27 tonnes of meat: enough to feed eighteen people for the whole year. The main artefacts found were a few ground, polished bone points, of the type bound to wooden handles for use as spear barbs. Broken pieces from stingray barbs, presumably used for a similar purpose, were also present in the middens. Several wallaby incisor teeth had been artificially split to form a cutting edge, forming a toothed scraper, probably used for sharpening spear tips.

One of the puzzles about the cockle shell mounds was that more than half the cockle shells appeared to be intact and unopened. This conundrum was solved by local Aborigines, who showed that heat is traditionally used to open the shells, and the meat is removed without having to break the shell, which then closes again. (The live shells are placed in a pile on the ground and a small fire of leaves and twigs is made above them, which creates enough heat to open the valves.)

The other puzzle about the middens of Cape York and Arnhem Land is why they were so much larger and more steep-sided than the middens of the southern half of the continent. The answer would seem to be the wet season of tropical Australia, which turns low-lying land into a swamp or floodplain. Bailey revisited the Weipa mounds recently in the wet season and found a very good reason for their existence — they were the only things in the landscape above water! The tall, steep-sided mounds at Weipa are all on flattish, open ground or on isolated ridges clear of woodland, whereas on the higher ground among the trees, the mounds are lower. The reason for developing some mounds on waterlogged open ground would seem to be the desire to have dry camping places above water, to be near the cockle beds and to escape the insect pests, which at times make life in the woodlands intolerable. Shell mounds in fact make excellent living sites; they are dry, good heat insulators, comfortable to sleep on with the aid of a few sheets of bark, and they afford the chance of a sea breeze and a strategic lookout for defensive purposes.

The Weipa mounds are not unique on Cape York as originally thought, but similar huge shell middens have been studied by Beaton and Chappell on the eastern side of the cape, in the Princess Charlotte Bay–Bathurst Head area. The shell middens occur in clusters, as at Weipa, and consist mainly of cockle shells, and some are of similar dimensions. The mounds dated so far all belong to the Holocene. In the same region, dugong hunting sites, bone points, shell ornaments and many rock paintings have been found. The subjects of the colourful rock art (recorded by Tia Negerevich and

Grahame Walsh) reflect the marine environment; they are mainly sharks, porpoises, turtles, trepang, starfish, dugong and canoes. Other unusual motifs are winged insects, probably moths or butterflies.

Torres Strait has often been seen as a clear-cut frontier between the gardeners of New Guinea and the hunter–gatherers of Australia, but even this brief look at the evidence shows that there is no frontier but, rather, a complex situation, with considerable variety within a similar type of economy extending right across the Strait. Different islanders achieved different balances between wild food and cultivated food, and between a more nomadic and more sedentary type of existence, but none of them were the pig-keeping, pottery-using, gardening villagers who practised 'agriculture' in New Guinea. We know that Australian Aborigines had some contact with some of the Torres Strait islanders and with Macassan fishermen from Indonesia, but they may have seen little horticulture being carried out. So although there was contact with cultivators, there was probably not much prolonged contact.

CONSERVATISM

The argument that Aborigines were too conservative to adopt agriculture is hard to sustain in view of all the other elements in Aboriginal culture adopted from overseas. These include outrigger canoes, platform disposal of the dead, wooden sculpture, fish-hooks, complex netting techniques, and various art designs, myths and rituals.[5] The main influences in the Kimberley and Arnhem Land seem to have come from Indonesia — such as the meander-type art design found on pearl shell ornaments in the Kimberley — and the carved figures, opium-type smoking pipe and dugout canoe with sails of Arnhem Land. New Guinean influences can also be seen in Arnhem Land, for example painted grave posts, wooden gongs, painted skulls, string figures, arrow-like reed spears, and bark mourning armlets and belts.

Plate 30 Shell mound on the eastern bank of the Hey River, Weipa. (G. Bailey)

In Cape York there is undoubted Papua New Guinean influence on technology, ritual, art, mythology, language and physical characteristics.[6] The Cape York Aborigines possessed skin drums, bamboo smoking pipes, tobacco and double outrigger canoes. And in physical characteristics, New Guinean traits were marked at the north of the peninsula but declined steadily to the south. There was certainly contact and marriage with outsiders and adoption of some of their ideas and technology, although this seems to have come about through trade and raids rather than by any settlement or voyaging down the Cape York coast by islanders.

Some material items were imported, others made locally in imitation of Papuan prototypes. The Cape Yorkers had some large, double outrigger dugout canoes, up to 18long, which had originally been made in the Fly River region of Papua New Guinea and had been acquired through trade or as 'cast-offs', but most of their canoes were similar but much smaller double or single outriggers. The Aborigines were not head-hunters, so they did not participate in the extensive trade in canoes organised in Torres Strait by the head-hunters.

THE BOW AND ARROW

Something that has long puzzled cultural historians is why the bow and arrow were never used in Australia. If mainland Australia, like Tasmania, had been completely isolated from the outside world since their invention, their absence would be explicable, but this is less easily explained when other items, such as outrigger canoes, were adopted by Aborigines. The bow and arrow were in use in every inhabited continent except Australia during the post-glacial period. It has usually been assumed to be a more efficient hunting and fighting weapon than the spear, but in the case of Australia, at least, this assumption would appear to be wrong. The bow and arrow were used in Papua and in the Torres Strait islands, and they were seen by Captain Cook on small islands immediately off Cape York, but they were not used by Australian Aborigines. It seems that not only Cape York Aborigines but also the islanders regarded the mainland spears and spear-throwers as superior weapons for fighting, hunting and fishing. The main items traded by Cape York Aborigines were spears, which were eagerly sought after in the western Torres Strait islands as far north as Mabuiag. Spear-throwers were also traded to the islands and were used in spear-fishing for dugong. The two main types of spear traded were the fishing spear with four bone barbs, and the fighting spear with a bone lashed on to form both a barb and a point (see figure 16.2). Spears were probably Australia's first export goods.

A spear, particularly with its range and penetrating power increased by the extra leverage of a spear-thrower, was doubtless more effective than an arrow against the large marsupials found in Australia. Arrows were used to hunt the largest Papuan wallaby, *Macropus agilis*, in the trans–Fly River region, but much larger animals exist in Cape York and other parts of Australia, with tougher hides, against which an arrow would have little effect.

It appears that the Australian Aborigines were selective, taking what was most useful or most appealing from overseas, but rejecting other items. That they had, and have, a great capacity for change is apparent. Both in prehistoric and historic times, people successfully adapted their technology and lifestyle to the changing environment. For example, when, for the first time, Tasmanian Aborigines encountered dogs, they rapidly acquired them and turned them into effective hunting dogs. It should also be pointed out that conservatism — or at least a very slow rate of change — is the normal state of affairs in human societies. Conservatism only seems exceptional to us because we live in a period of immense change and tend automatically to equate progress with change. Thus what should surprise us about prehistoric Aboriginal society is not how little change there was but how much.

HOSTILITY

It has been suggested that new elements, such as agriculture, did not penetrate prehistoric Australia because of hostility on the part of Aborigines to newcomers. The main way that an archaeological site can tell us about relations between two peoples is when traded items are present. In any case, Aboriginal relations with the outside world varied tremendously from region to region and from time to time.

This seems to be the case with relations between Aborigines and the Indonesian fishermen, who sailed their praus from Macassar to northern Australia each year in search of trepang, also called 'bêche de mer' or 'sea slug'. The trepang industry began in AD 1720, according to Campbell MacKnight, the major authority on the Macassans. It was largely controlled by Chinese merchants resident in Macassar, who exported the dried sea slugs to China, where they were highly valued for making soup and as an aphrodisiac. Trepang fishing involved catching the animals by hand or net or by spearing, then boiling, gutting, recooking with mangrove bark to give flavour and colour, then drying and smoking. The end result, according to naturalist Alfred Wallace, looked like 'sausages which have been rolled in mud and then thrown up the chimney'.

This complex processing necessitated lengthy stays on shore and the setting-up of camps, stone fireplaces with huge, iron boiling-down cauldrons, smoke houses, and wells for drinking water. Along the coast of Arnhem Land and the Kimberleys, traces still remain of Macassan visits, the last of which took place in 1907. The remains include broken pieces of pottery and glass, and tall, green tamarind trees, sprung from the seeds of the astringent tamarind fruit brought by prau from Indonesia. The Macassan camps were situated in positions that could be readily defended, such as small islands or promontories. Historical records from Indonesia testify to hostility from Aborigines and numerous massacres of prau crews. Yet, at times, relations were friendly, and the Aborigines even travelled overseas to Macassar on praus.[7] The Arnhem-Landers adopted Macassan words as well as new items into their material culture, notably smoking pipes and small dugout sailing canoes. The Indonesian name for the canoes, 'lepa-lepa', became 'lippa-lippa' in Arnhem Land.

The trepang fishermen did not attempt permanent settlement and kept to the shore, never penenetrating far beyond the mangroves fringing the coast. Foreign intruders who did try to traverse the interior in northern Australia often did not live to tell the tale. This hostility to foreigners may well have been one reason why farmers or even their ideas did not penetrate prehistoric Australia.

ANIMALS AND PLANTS

In assessing the suitability of prehistoric Australia for agriculture, the question of the possible domestication of Australian mammals is easily answered: there were no native marsupials suitable for domestication. None of the animals that were domesticated in other countries existed in Australia in prehistoric times; there were no pigs, cows, sheep, goats or chickens in Australia then. However, other native birds, such as geese, pelicans or scrub turkeys, might have been domesticated by a people so inclined.

In northern Australia, plants are gathered which are cultivated on the other side of Torres Strait. One such food plant found at a few places along the eastern coast of Cape York in prehistoric times was the coconut palm, which probably established itself naturally following chance dispersal of coconuts across the sea as flotsam. There is no evidence that Aborigines deliberately planted or tended coconuts before the arrival of Europeans.

The yam *(Dioscorea* species) was a staple in both areas, and also present were other tubers: taro *(Colocasia* species) and 'Polynesian arrowroot' *(Tacca* species). However, it is not just the presence of a food plant that is important; its relative abundance or scarcity and its ease or otherwise of cultivation must also be considered. A large number of food plants that grow wild in Cape York, but which are domesticated in Asia, are adapted to regular rainfall and have a limited distribution in the infertile soils and seasonally dry climate of Cape York.[8] The plants that flourish in the steady rain of tropical New Guinea would need much more effort in northern Australia. The soils most favourable to agriculture in Cape York were occupied by rainforest. This could have been cleared by would-be farmers with the aid of fire, but motivation would have had to be strong to undertake such labour. Unlike the islanders, the mainland Aborigines could respond to food shortages by moving elsewhere, so the motivation to cultivate gardens was unlikely ever to be strong. The seasonally dry monsoon climate and poor soils of Cape York have been seen as the main barrier to the spread of Papuan species into Australia.[9]

The economy of one coastal group in northern Arnhem Land has been studied in depth by Betty Meehan and Rhys Jones.[10] In a year spent with the Anbara of the Gidjingali language group, they recorded every facet of the economy: what people ate, how many hours and how far they walked each day on the food quest, what artefacts were used for each activity, how often they moved camp, what refuse was left behind, and so on. This type of study, in which the researcher studies a living human society in the field to gather data that help archaeologists to understand the past, is known as 'living archaeology' or 'ethnoarchaeology'.

The important part played by Aboriginal women has been brought out by Meehan's work. In Aboriginal society there is a strong division of labour. The women generally gather plant food, shellfish and small animals, while the men hunt and fish the larger game. Women's contribution to the diet is less spectacular but more reliable, and they provide the basic regular food.

YAMS

These hunter–gatherers, on one of the world's richest coastlines, have two semi-agricultural practices. The first concern yams, one of the principal starch-yielding staples of tropical Australia. For the Anbara, the parsnip yam *Dioscorea transversa* was particularly important. When yams were dug out, the top of the tuber was left still attached to the tendril in the ground so that the yam would grow again.[11]

This same practice has been recorded from other parts of Arnhem Land and from Cape York. At Lockhart, on the eastern coast of Cape York Peninsula, the vines were marked as a sign of 'ownership'. Yams were also planted on offshore islands to extend their distribution and to ensure a 'reserve' supply. This is certainly plant tending and management, if not quite agriculture. True agriculture would have produced a higher yield per plant, but would have involved the labour of tilling the ground.

FRUIT TREES

The other semi-agricultural practice of the Anbara was the deliberate spitting out of fruit tree seeds into the debris of fish remains and shells in refuse heaps at the edge of a camp. These midden soils, with their compost of decaying organic matter and lime from shells, provided an ideal environment for tree growth, so in a few years the camp site would be well supplied with fruit trees. Indeed, there is a consistent association between old camp sites and trees with edible fruit. This meant that stands of native fruit trees can be used by archaeologists to discover prehistoric sites, in the same way that the presence of exotic trees often leads the colonial archaeologist to the ruins of a historic building.

MILLET HARVESTERS

Although prehistoric Australia was not endowed with the corn that formed the basis of agriculture in Mexico and Meso-America, or the wheat and barley of the Middle East, it does have one native cereal grain, which became the major food in parts of arid inland Australia. This was wild millet *(Panicum decompositum)*. *Panicum* and one of the main grasses utilised, the *Setaria* species, are closely related members of the same plant families, which in other parts of the world produced the domesticated common panicum *(Panicum miliaceum)* and Italian millet *(Setaria italica)*.

Cereal gathering was predominantly an adaptation to the arid lands of the dry heart of Australia, in areas that received rainfall of 300 millimetres or less. In better watered areas in the north and around the coasts, the fruits, nuts and tubers of plants provided the main vegetable food rather than seeds. The seed-collecting economy of Aborigines of the Darling Basin of western New South Wales has been studied in some detail by Harry Allen.[12]

Until the 1880s, the semiarid basin of the Darling River was inhabited by Aborigines of the Bagundji language group. The Bagundji, or 'river people', lived on both sides of the large, slow-flowing Darling River, and practised a riverine economy based mainly on aquatic foods, such as fish, shellfish, ducks and bulrush roots, and on the collection of cereals. In spring and summer food was usually plentiful, but winter was a time of stress, when the river was less productive of food. Then the people dispersed in smaller groups into the back country, where they collected wattle and flax seeds, lured emus into net traps by means of a decoy horn that imitated the cry of a female, and drove kangaroos into nets, using a team of beaters or a few men firing the grass. Pools of rainwater provided drinking water in winter, but in the scorching heat of summer these soon evaporated, and the only water available away from the river was that stored in the roots of some plants or carried in kangaroo skin bags.

In summer the main vegetable food was the seeds of the native millet, which grows only in summer and seeds between December and March. One of the main problems with gathering wild cereals is that the seeds tend to ripen at different times, making it difficult to harvest large quantities of grain at any one time. The Bagundji cleverly overcame this problem by gathering the grass when the seed was full but the grass still green. The grass was then stacked in heaps and the seeds left to dry and ripen, when they were threshed so that the seeds all fell to the ground in one place.

This harvesting of grass seed was done on a large scale. When the explorer Sir Thomas Mitchell was travelling down the Darling River in 1835, he reported that 'the grass had been pulled, to a great extent, and piled in hayricks, so that the aspect of the desert was softened into the agreeable semblance of a hayfield . . . we found the ricks, or hay-cocks, extending for miles . . . the grass was of one kind, a species of *Panicum* . . . and not a spike of it was left in the soil, over the whole of the ground . . . The grass was beautifully green beneath the heaps and full of seed.'[13] Mitchell made his observations in July, and what he saw was a method of 'in-field' storage of seeds that must have been harvested at least three months earlier.

The harvesting was done by pulling up the cereal grasses by the roots and pulling the stalks off, or just pulling the seed off into a bark dish, the usual method in Central Australia. In one area, Cooper's Creek, in southwestern Queensland, a stone knife was used for reaping. Stone knives were also used for reaping in the early days of cereal growing in the Middle East, so this is important evidence of semi-agricultural practices in inland Australia. It also shows the archaeologists what to search for at sites, for reaping grass stalks with stone knives produces a distinctive type of sheen on the edge of the tool, called 'use-polish'.

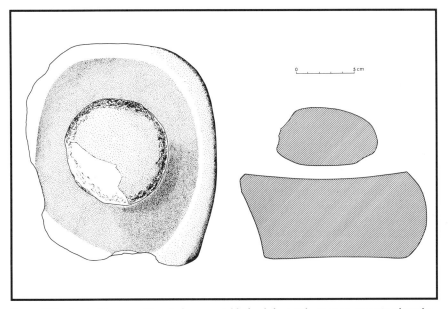

Figure 17.1 A grindstone used to grind up vegetable food, from Lake George, New South Wales.

Seed-grinding stones are distinctive, as they are larger, flatter and smoother than stones used to grind up other plant foods, such as fruits and nuts (figure 17.1). In fact, seed-grinding stones should really be called millstones, since they are used for the milling of flour. Such millstones were found in some of the Darling basin sites. And analysis of the distribution of all grindstones from New South Wales in the Australian Museum in Sydney showed a correlation between the presence of grindstones and that of wild millet.

Archaeological evidence from the Darling basin shows a strong continuity in lifestyle but also some changes, such as the adoption of the specialised small tools about 2000 years ago. Thirty thousand years ago the Mungo people lived on fish, shellfish, small mammals, reptiles, birds and emu eggs. Fifteen thousand years ago the lakes dried up and the focus of occupation shifted to the rivers, but the diet remained essentially unchanged, except for the addition of grass seeds. Seed-grinding stones are associated with middens post-dating the final drying up of the Willandra Lakes, and the same economy based on fish, shellfish, small mammals and cereals still existed in the nineteenth century.

Why did the cereal gatherers not become cereal cultivators? They had all the 'pre-adaptations' generally considered necessary: they ate a broad spectrum of wild foods, they had grindstone technology and storage facilities. The semiarid river basins and humid Western Slopes of inland New South Wales offer similar environments to those of Mexico and Mesopotamia, where agriculture did develop, although the latter two regions have more varied terrain and probably suffer less disastrous droughts and floods than inland Australia.

AFFLUENCE

It may be that hunter–gatherers in Australia were so affluent that they had no need to increase the yield of food plants or to store food. This affluence may have been achieved by the establishment of an equilibrium, in which population was kept below the level the country could support — its carrying capacity. In other words, the available food could have fed far more mouths than actually had to be fed. There would thus have been no stimulus to increase the food supply by developing agriculture, unless some environmental or population stress were experienced.

This seems to be the most plausible explanation for the absence of agriculture from prehistoric Australia. The people had no need to increase the food supply, because they kept their own population in balance with their environment. The return from their highly efficient foraging was so great that expenditure of additional effort on cultivating crops was not worthwhile.

The Bagundji were in some form of equilibrium with their food supply; their relatively low population density was due largely to the incidence of droughts. During bad seasons newborn children were killed, but there is no evidence that droughts caused deaths in the rest of the population. Thus the number of mouths to feed was regulated by bad seasons, and little effort was needed to find enough food during normal or good seasons.

STORAGE OF FOOD

Agriculture implies the production of food surpluses, which are then stored. Some storage of grass seed was practised both in the Darling basin and Central Australia. The seed was stored in skin bags or wrapped up in grass and coated with mud. In Central Australia wooden dishes might be used, and one store of seed was found in which an estimated 1000 kilograms of grain were held in seventeen huge wooden dishes, about 30 centimetres deep and 1.5 metres long.[14]

Storage of food was also practised elsewhere in Australia. The nuts of the bunya-bunya pine were sometimes buried to be eaten later, and the nuts of the cycad palm were sliced, wrapped in paperbark and placed in grass-lined trenches, which were then filled with earth. These trenches were as much as 6 metres long and formed probably the largest Aboriginal larder so far recorded in Australia.[15]

The tubers of waterlilies and yams were occasionally stored in Cape York, and in Arnhem Land yams were placed in stacks ready for the lean winter months. These yams were probably protected from animal predators by the poison they contained,

which could only be leached out of the yams by complex processing, as was the
case with cycad nuts.

Long-term preservation of many foods, however, presented serious problems. Indeed, the difficulties of food storage in the Australian environment may be of prime importance in understanding why food surpluses were not produced. The combination of high temperatures and pronounced seasonality of rainfall made food storage difficult in tropical Australia, not only for Aborigines but also for early European settlers. Early explorers, even with the benefit of salting and smoking techniques unknown to Aborigines, often found that the game they killed went bad within a few hours.

In many of the food preservation techniques used in other parts of the world boiling was an essential part of the process, but Aborigines had no way of boiling food. On the Torres Strait islands, almost within sight of the tip of Cape York, large shells were used to boil up slices of turtle meat, which were then stuck on skewers and dried in the sun. This preserved meat provided food for canoe voyages lasting several weeks. In contrast, on Cape York, shells were used as water containers but not for boiling; cooking was done in ground ovens or by broiling, grilling or roasting.

Generally, Aborigines made no attempt to store meat, fish or shellfish, but one remarkable exception has been found. Near Lake Victoria, in western New South Wales, a heap of freshwater mussels buried in a sand dune was exposed by wind erosion. Close examination of the hoard of 360 shells revealed that they had been stacked in neat layers and were still alive when buried.[16] It seems that mussels can live for weeks or even months deep in moist sand, so the hoard acted as a 'living larder', like a tank in a gourmet restaurant containing live lobsters.

While grain and other plant food is much less prone to going bad, there are still many hazards, such as damage from water, insects — especially termites — birds, diseases, locusts, dingoes and burrowing animals. Dingoes are particularly persistent. In some parts of the Australian bush, the graves of Aborigines and early settlers can be seen heaped with large stones to keep the dingoes off. Dingoes have even been observed opening food tins with their teeth and extracting the contents with their long tongues.

The other main factor operating against food storage was the traditional nomadism of Australian Aborigines. Groups might stay for several months at the same camp in a rich environment, but no groups stayed in the same place all year round. Where food was less abundant, they would move camp more often. A few items, such as heavy grindstones, might be left behind, but hunter–gatherers carried all their basic equipment along with them. And of course babies and young children also had to be carried.

Comparison of the material culture of different regions has shown that the largest range of material goods is owned by those in rich environments, where there is little nomadism. Thus the Bagundji of the Darling River had far more material possessions and more elaborate huts than Aborigines of the southeastern highlands, who had to move camp much more often.

Another type of food storage was practised, which is quite invisible in the archaeological record but was probably of considerable importance in those parts of the continent that were less rich in food and where preservation of food in the extreme heat was a real problem. This type of food storage is the concept of a 'living larder', or refuge area. In the desert and semidesert regions of Central Australia, there are a few favoured environments centred on permanent water in rock holes or in soakages in otherwise dry river beds. Such places were not used for regular foraging, but were kept as last retreats in time of drought.[17] Examples of such 'game reserves' are Partjar, in Clutterbuck Hills, Western Australia, and the Finke River at Hermannsburg Mission, west of Alice Springs. In these refuge areas, Aborigines at times increased the amount of game by moving kangaroos and other animals into them.

In the Western Desert, Aborigines possess the technology to prepare and store many of their staple plant foods, but 'it is hard to imagine what advantage these people would gain from industriously gathering, processing and storing large amounts of plant staples that are often available in a sort of de facto storage in the wild caused by natural desiccation'.[18] In particular, the quandong fruit remains available for long periods on the ground, in a sun-dried, desiccated condition, as long as the weather remains dry. This makes it an important food during drought years, and it is a highly nutritious fruit, with twice the vitamin C of an orange.

Some plant foods were stored in desert Australia, such as the fruits of the *Solanum* and the wild fig, which keep well and were packed up into balls of ochre the size of a basketball and stored in trees. There are also more quandongs growing around old Aboriginal camp sites than elsewhere; in some places, water has been diverted into small channels to water the plants. This would seem to be casual cultivation of the type also practised with fruit trees in northern Australia.

The idea of restraint in taking animal and other food is supported by the system of taboos, making certain foods forbidden fare for particular people in a tribe. Thus in the southeastern highlands and on the central Murrumbidgee River, the eating of emu flesh was forbidden until the age of manhood; as the explorer Charles Sturt commented, 'This evidently is a law of policy and necessity, for if the emus were allowed to be indiscriminately slaughtered, they would soon become extinct'.[19] Among the Walgalu tribe of the Tumut Valley it was forbidden to eat emu eggs, which must have been a conservation measure in this highland area, where emus can never have been plentiful and are now reduced to two small flocks at the northern and southern ends of the Kosciusko National Park.

The maintenance and increase of the food supply was also the subject of a great deal of ritual, involving complex and lengthy 'increase ceremonies'. These ceremonies ensure the continued fertility of both human and non-human populations by re-creating the founding drama to renew the life-force in living things. In Central Australia, about 20 percent of plants have special increase ceremonies with associated songs. Some are women's ceremonies, some men's, and some are joint. Such ceremonies serve to transmit to the next generation vital information about the location of water sources and food plants and the habits and movements of game. In a society without written records or books, information is transmitted by example and experience, and in stories, art, songs and ceremonies. This traditional life has been put on record recently by workers such as Dick Kimber, Dianne Bell, Peter Latz and Michael Smith.

THE AUSTRALIAN ECONOMIC SYSTEM

The main reason that agriculture, with its sedentary lifestyle and increased material possessions, did not develop in Australia was probably affluence. In the tropical north the abundance of wild food meant that Aborigines had no need to adopt the more laborious gardening practised on some Torres Strait islands. Once this choice had been made in the north, where there would have been knowledge of the islanders' methods of food production, intensive cultivation techniques were unlikely to spread further south in the continent.

In the centre and south of the continent there were virtually no foods that could have been domesticated except the wild millet of the Darling River and Cooper's Creek basins, which was exploited intensively but not stored on a large scale or planted. The people of these inland riverine plains were, therefore, really the only people in temperate Australia who could have become cereal farmers. Their exploitation of wild millet has been called 'incipient agriculture', and it provided about 30 percent of their diet, but they did not take the final steps of tilling the soil, planting seeds and storing the surplus food produced. No doubt the labour involved in tilling and planting outweighed the possible advantages. 'The Bagundji found, after a long period of experimentation, that by hunting and gathering a wide range of foods and by using a sophisticated array of highly specialised techniques, their labours ensured a maximum return of food.'[20]

When food was difficult to obtain, the food quest simply required more time and effort rather than new strategies. There was also little pressure on the amount of land available, in strong contrast to the Middle East and the narrow neck of Mexico. Thus when times were hard, the people could simply move more often and further afield. In the toughest environment of all, the Western Desert, journeys of 400 to 500 kilometres were common, especially during droughts. In recent times it has been recorded that the people from Tikatika moved nine times in three months, foraging over an area of almost 2600 square kilometres.[21]

Australia is the world's driest and probably most capricious continent. Sometimes there is abundance, sometimes disaster — such as the interminable drought in the 1960s which brought the last desert people to seek water at the boreholes of the white people. Conditions and rainfall are most unpredictable in the Centre, but even in the lush tropics, food sources available in profusion one year can be wiped out the next. This happened on the Arnhem Land coast, where an influx of fresh water from unusually heavy monsoon rain wiped out whole beds of one-shell species, which in the previous year had contributed 61 percent of the total weight of shellfish eaten.[22] Such shortages were infrequent but unpredictable and severe. The Anbara can cope with such losses because they have a varied, broad-based economy, and do not rely on one or two foods. In this situation it is wiser not to have all your eggs in one basket.

The typical Australian clan's economy is flexible, with a wide variety of foods being sought and advantage being taken of seasonal abundance or chance events, such as the stranding of a whale. Such a broad-based system minimises risks and overcomes shortages of any one type of food much better than can an agricultural community that relies on more restricted food sources. Aboriginal Australia was not vulnerable to famine through the failure of one crop.

The Aboriginal population was controlled by the food resources available, which in turn were related to water resources: the areas with the highest rainfall were generally richest in food. The number of mouths that could be fed was regulated by the food available at the leanest time of year. In temperate regions this was usually winter. The summer abundance of food was used not to feed more people by collecting and storing surplus food, but as a time when there was more leisure for intellectual life. In a rich environment the food quest will only occupy an hour or two each day in the good season; in the poorest environment of the Western Desert, it generally requires less than six or seven hours of work for a woman each day. Even during drought, only two or three hours of collecting by the women will provide a day's food for the whole group.[23]

Not only did Aboriginal men and women living a traditional life have more leisure than is available to the average farmer or office-worker, but they also generally ate better. The diet of those groups whose economy has been recorded in detail emerges as more balanced, varied and nutritious than that of many white people. The Anbara have an average intake of about 2400 kilocalories a day, of which 40 to 50 percent comes from the flesh of fish, shellfish, crustaceans, and about fifty species of land animals and birds. Since the recommended energy intake for adults is about 2000 kilocalories, the Anbara are feeding well. Their economy is based on the eating of meat (used in the broad sense to include the flesh of fish and shellfish also), but many plant and insect foods are also high in nutritional value. Mulga seeds contain more protein than peanut butter; yams can grow to the size of a man's head and are equivalent to sweet potatoes in food value, and one witchetty grub yields the same amount of protein as a pork chop.

The quality of life and the amount of leisure available in traditional Aboriginal communities were remarkably high. Those who are not convinced would probably have their doubts dispelled by comparing the physical and spiritual health of a group leading a traditional life, such as the Anbara, with the pitiful state of those living on tinned food and soft drinks in some government settlements.

Archaeological evidence has shown that the Australian economic system of a varied rather than specialised diet obtained by seasonal movement has great antiquity. The diet of people at Mungo 30 000 years ago is similar to that of the Bagundji in the nineteenth century, except for the addition of grass seeds. A similar, equally broad-based, diet seems to have existed 20 000 years ago at Devil's Lair and Miriwun in Western Australia. The same species of shellfish, seals, fish, birds, mammals, bracken roots and grass-tree pith were being eaten at Rocky Cape in Tasmania 8000 years ago as those on the southeastern Australian coast when Captain Cook arrived.

It seems that the basic adaptation to the Australian environment took place when the continent was first occupied, and, indeed, the environment was, to a remarkable degree, modified by its prehistoric occupants. Once the nomadic way of life had become firmly established, with its consequent need to travel lightly, it was unlikely that agriculture, pottery and a sedentary life would be adopted. The nomads scorned by early white settlers were poor in material possessions but rich in spirit, leading a secure and healthy life ideally suited to their environment. Captain Cook perceived this as long ago as 1770. Emphasising the dignity, simplicity and self-sufficiency of Aboriginal society, Cook wrote:

> *From what I have said of the Natives of New-Holland they may appear to some to be the most wretched people upon Earth, but in reality they are far more happier than we Europeans. They live in a Tranquillity which is not disturb'd by the Inequality of Condition: The Earth and sea of their own accord furnishes them with all things necessary for life, they covet not Magnificent Houses, Household-stuff &.ca, they lie in a warm and fine Climate and enjoy a very wholesome Air, so that they have very little need of Clothing and this they seem to be fully sensible of, for many to whom we gave Cloth &.ca to, left it carelessly upon the Sea beach and in the woods as a thing they had no manner of use for. In short they seem'd to set no Value upon any thing we gave them, nor would they ever part with any thing of their own for any one article we could offer them; this in my opinion argues that they think themselves provided with all the necessarys of Life and that they have no superfluities.*[24]

Plate 31 (left)   Aborigines flaking stone at Point Plomer, near Port Macquarie, New South Wales. (Dick Collection, by courtesy of the Australian Museum)

CHAPTER EIGHTEEN

The Last 1000 Years: Trade, Religion and Art

More than 50 000 Aboriginal archaeological sites have been formally recorded in Australia. The vast majority of these sites belong to the last 1000 years. From this time span, thousands of shell middens lie around the coast, dozens of camp sites and canoe trees line the banks of large rivers, while hundreds of rock-shelters contain paintings, engravings and occupation deposits. In New South Wales alone, more than 15 000 sites have been recorded, in Western Australia and Victoria some 13 000, and between about 3000 and 6000 in Queensland (> 5200), South Australia (> 3700), Tasmania (> 5500) and the Northern Territory, together with a few hundred sites in the Australian Capital Territory.

Many other archaeological sites are known to exist but have not yet been formally recorded. And thousands of natural landmarks are associated with mythology. These are sites of great significance to Aborigines, but they generally contain no material traces of Aboriginal culture. However, the life of the spirit is all-important in Aboriginal society, and these sites that lack tangible remains nevertheless usually hold as great or even greater significance for Aborigines than sites containing spectacular rock paintings.

A number of the archaeological sites from the last 1000 years provide revealing evidence of Aboriginal religious life, ceremonial exchange and trading networks. They do not, of course, provide a complete account of the rich and complex Aboriginal social and religious life, much of which is not related to material culture.

TRADE

The exchange of artefacts and other goods among prehistoric societies is usually referred to as 'trade', but 'exchange' and 'distribution' are better terms, for the far-flung Aboriginal network of exchange systems was based on social and ritual needs as well as utilitarian requirements and the laws of supply and demand. The exchange might well be rooted in systems of reciprocal gift-giving, rather than a need for raw material or a desire for exotic goods not available locally.

Not just artefacts were exchanged, but also raw materials such as ochre and spinifex gum, myths, corroborees, dances and songs. There was little or no trade in food, but a roaring trade in native tobacco. The stems and leaves of the narcotic plant pituri, which grows in southwestern Queensland and Central Australia, were dried, broken into small pieces, packed in special net bags and traded as far as 800 to 900 kilometres from their source, over a region of 500 000 square kilometres. Pituri contains nicotine and is a psychotropic plant: it has a considerable effect on the mind. It induced voluptuous dreamy sensations according to Walter Roth, and was found highly intoxicating by explorer W. J. Wills. Aborigines mixed it with alkaline wood ash, which reduced its hallucinogenic effect, and they used it as a tobacco, as a stimulant on long journeys, and for ceremonies.[1]

Pearl shell from the northwest of Western Australia travelled further perhaps than any other object.[2] The broad, gleaming, silvery-white shells of the Kimberleys, often incised with geometric patterns and perforated by a small hole, were seen worn as 'aprons' or pendants by Aborigines as far away as the Great Australian Bight, 1600 kilometres from their place of manufacture (figure 18.1). Likewise, baler shells from Cape York were chipped, ground and perforated to make oval ornaments up to 10 centimetres long. These were exchanged in many transactions between neighbouring groups, along trade routes that carried them into the deserts of Central Australia and even Western Australia, as well as down Cooper's Creek to Lake Eyre, the Flinders Ranges and, eventually, the coast of South Australia. These shells were items of enormous significance and were used in both sorcery and the most sacred rituals.

Axe stone was a more utilitarian item that was traded great distances. In southeastern Australia axes have been shown by the doyen of axe trade studies, Isabel McBryde, to have been traded 600 to 700 kilometres from their source, and some even as far as 800 kilometres (figure 18.2).[3]

Aboriginal quarry sites are not immediately obvious to the untrained eye, but on the southeastern slopes of Mount William (near Lancefield in Victoria), evidence of intensive exploitation of rock outcrops and stone-working activity is found for over a

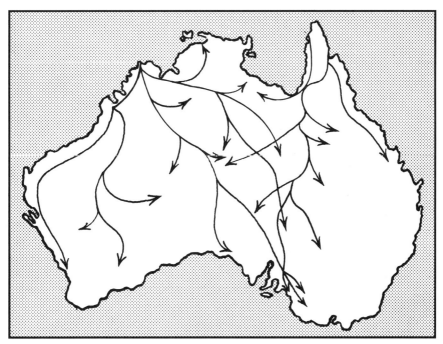

Figure 18.1 Major trade routes for pearl and baler shells. (After UNESCO 1973, based on data from D. J. Mulvaney)

kilometre along a ridge.[4] On the western side of the ridge, quarry waste and flaked stone have accumulated in heaps of up to 50 metres in length. About thirty distinct flaking floors are also visible. These are circular mounds, about 20 metres in diameter, made up of worked stone and waste flakes. On the eastern and northern sides of the ridge, over 250 circular or oval pits have been quarried to obtain stone from below the ground surface. The stone is a volcanic greenstone, which has the hardness, toughness and fine grain needed to make heavy-duty stone axes with a ground edge.

Work at the quarry would have consisted of the stone being extracted and roughly trimmed into 'blanks', pieces of a convenient size and shape for making into axes. The final trimming of the axe and the grinding of the blade would have been done elsewhere. Very few finished axes or other stone tools have been found on Mount William, and it lacks the soft rock, such as sandstone, and water needed for the grinding process. Axes were finally hafted to wooden handles by means of resin from the grass-tree or spinifex gum and sinew from kangaroo tails.

The use of the Mount William axe quarry is known through the work of early anthropologist A. W. Howitt, whose Aboriginal informant, Barak, witnessed its final operations. The last man responsible for working the outcrops was Billi-billeri, who died in 1846. Mount William was the centre of a vast exchange system. Tribes came

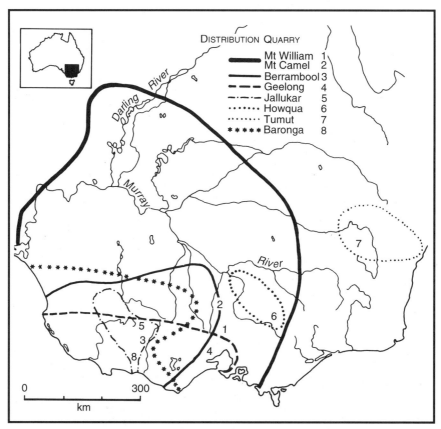

Figure 18.2 Distribution of axes from greenstone quarries in southeastern Australia.
(After I. McBryde 1984 and 1988)

from more than 100 kilometres away to conduct negotiations for the exchange of goods. It is known that axe stone was traded for reed spear shafts from the Swan Hill district on the Murray River, some 300 kilometres away to the northwest. Mount William stone was also exchanged for sandstone from St Kilda, Melbourne, 160 kilometres to the south.

The 'rate of exchange' is unknown, except that in the 1840s the donor of one possum skin rug received three axe blanks. Since it would take much longer to make a possum skin rug, which involved obtaining, preparing and sewing together as many as seventy skins, than the two hours or so of work to turn an axe blank into the finished tool, this indicates the high value placed on axe stone.

The distribution of axes has been studied in detail by Isabel McBryde and geologist Alan Watchman.[5] The distinguishing characteristics of the stone from this and other quarries were identified by microscopic examination. Then thin sections — tiny slivers of stone — were sawn from ground-edge axes in museums and private collections. The specimens were then ground down to transparent thinness and examined under the microscope. In this way the axe could be matched with quarry and distribution maps drawn up for axes from the various quarries.

This painstaking study showed that axes from Mount William were very widely dispersed: more than half the axes were carried over 100 kilometres away from their source quarry (figure 18.2). Even greater distances were covered by axes from the Moore Creek quarry near Tamworth, in New South Wales.[6] This is the largest quarry in the New England region. It is based on a greywacke deposit, which runs for about 90 metres along a saddle-back ridge. Aborigines apparently levered the stone from a trough cut into the outcrop, and the concentration of broken rock, flakes and cores indicates the prolific quarrying undertaken there.

ABORIGINAL MINERS

Ochre pigments, used regularly for cosmetics, body and artefact decoration, and cave painting, were traded widely from the main ochre quarries. Expeditions were made from western Queensland all the way to the Yarrakina red ochre mine at Parachilna, in the Flinders Ranges in South Australia, to obtain the special, sacred iridescent ochre mined there. Paint was made from ochre by crushing up lumps of the soft pigment-bearing rock into a powder and mixing it with water, or sometimes with the blood or fat of fish, emu, possum, kangaroo or goanna, or with orchid juice for a fixative.

There are several ochre mines in Australia. One near Mount Rowland in Tasmania was visited by Robinson in 1834.[7] There, Aboriginal women were the miners. They levered out the red iron ore using the hammer and chisel method, except that their hammer was simply a stone and their chisel a pointed stick. The women enthusiastically squeezed themselves down narrow crevices to get at the red ochre — one even became stuck and had to be pulled out by the legs! Everywhere there were signs of strenuous mining: heaps of stone, old workings and narrow holes. The ochre was packed into kangaroo skin bags and carried off in heavy loads by the women.

The most remarkable Aboriginal mine in Australia is that of Wilgie Mia (or Wilgamia), northwest of Cue in the Murchison district of Western Australia (plate 32). This site was almost obliterated by European quarrying, but it is now a protected area. On the northern side of a hill, Nganakurakura, an immense open cut has been excavated, between 15 and 30 metres wide and 20 metres deep. The pit opens into a cavern from which numerous small caves and galleries branch off, formed as the miners followed the seams of red and yellow ochre.

Ochre was mined at Wilgie Mia by men battering at the rock with heavy stone mauls and prying the ochre out with fire-hardened wooden wedges up to half a metre long. Pole scaffolding was erected for working at different heights. The lumps of stone were carried out to the top of the northern slope, where they were broken up to get the ochre. The ochre was then pulverised with rounded stones, dampened with water and worked into balls to be traded.

The cavity floor is stratified in places to a depth of 6 metres, and excavations have revealed stone implements and wooden wedges going back 1000 years in time.[8] The several thousand tonnes of rock that have been removed and broken up imply a considerable antiquity for the mining, which was still going on in 1939.

Red ochre was the most highly prized pigment in prehistoric Australia, and pieces from deposits created by ancestral spirits were essential for use in rituals. Long expeditions were therefore made to these sites, or sometimes the special ochre was obtained by barter. Wilgie Mia is known as 'a place of fabulous wealth' to all Aborigines in the west, and it is told how the ochre was formed by the death of a

Plate 32 Ochre mining at Wilgie Mia, Western Australia. This photograph, taken in 1910, shows traditional mining methods. (Courtesy of the Western Australian Museum)

great kangaroo, who was speared by the Spirit Being called Mondong. The kangaroo leapt in his death agony to Wilgie Mia, where the red ochre represents his blood, the yellow his liver, and the green his gall. The last leap took the kangaroo to another hill, called Little Wilgie, which marks his grave. This hill was apparently mined for ochre before Wilgie Mia, which would make it an extremely ancient mine.

Aborigines traditionally regarded the ochre mine with fear, except for the elders who were its custodians. Areas that were unsafe for the uninitiated to enter were marked by piles of stones, and no mining implements could be taken away. People leaving the site had to walk out backwards and sweep away their tracks, so that the spirit Mondong did not follow and kill them.

The ochre from Wilgie Mia was used in a huge area of Western Australia and is said to have been carried as far afield as Queensland. Not only is it an impressive example of the quarrying techniques of Aborigines, but the archaeological evidence from excavation at Wilgie Mia has also shown that the large-scale and highly organised exploitation of ochre in Australia goes back at least 1000 years and probably much further.

The major trade routes that criss-crossed the continent show that Aboriginal tribes were not isolated groups, but part of a complex social and economic network. Nearly all communities traded with their neighbours, and this exchange system served to pass on not only goods but also ideas. This is important to remember when considering the spread of new artefact types. Change could come about through the diffusion of an idea as well as of the actual artefact. It could also come about very quickly. For example, a ceremonial dance, or corroboree (the Molonga), appeared on the Great Australian Bight only twenty-five years after it was first 'exchanged' in northwestern Queensland, over 1600 kilometres to the north.[9] If the exchange had been of a stone tool, the archaeological record would seem to show the appearance of the same tool in the extreme north and south of the continent simultaneously.

RELIGION

In a country with natural wonders such as Uluru (Ayers Rock), where every major topographical feature was endowed with mythological significance, it was not part of Aboriginal culture to build monuments such as megalithic tombs or pyramids. Much of the prehistoric monumental architecture in other parts of the world is associated with religious worship, but Aboriginal religion takes a different form. Natural landmarks are the centres of religion and ceremony. The places where Aboriginal people gather for the great ceremonies are not marked by formal structures — the land is their cathedral.

In Aboriginal Australia concern for the dead is expressed not through buildings but through complex rituals, which may go on for weeks. The rituals are to safeguard the living from the spirit's anger, to avenge the deceased, and to ensure the safe return of the dead person's spirit by way of the sky, a waterhole or an offshore island, to the spirit home or totemic centre. Totemism is the religious system in which people are identified with a particular animal, plant or natural feature, which, like themselves, was endowed with life essence by creation ancestors in the Dreamtime. These totems are used to distinguish groupings in society and can be influenced by ceremonies conducted by the totems' human 'kinsmen', such as ceremonies to maintain the natural species. Some totemic increase sites are marked by arrangements not of stones, but of bones. Thus, in the Northern Territory, a striking star-shaped pile of crocodile bones was found on the floor of Sleisbeck rock-shelter, and a group of emu skulls was found at Ingaladdi.[10] These are rare examples of evidence of ceremonial life surviving in the archaeological record.

Elaborate drawings in the sand or earth were part of the ritual in many ceremonies. On the ceremonial or bora grounds of New South Wales, large, elaborate mythological figures up to 10 metres long were often moulded in earth or clay in the centre of the bora ring (plate 33). Such sand or earth sculptures were not meant to last. The most usual form of bora ground was two circles surrounded by low earth banks, linked by a connecting path, which was also marked by earth banks. One of the bora rings was a 'public place', where women and children participated in the corroborees and preliminary ceremonies. At the climax of ceremonies like these, the young men to be initiated would be led away by tribal elders to the second, secret ring for the further rituals of initiation, which might involve tooth avulsion or circumcision.

The trunks of trees surrounding the ritual site were often carved, and ceremonial grounds are on record as being surrounded by between six and 120 trees carved with massive geometric designs. Carved trees, also called dendroglyphs, have designs carved into the wood, whereas a tree from which bark has simply been removed to

Plate 33 Bora ground at Tucki Tucki, near Lismore, New South Wales, from the air. (National Parks and Wildlife Service, New South Wales)

make a container, shield, canoe or other artefact is known as a scarred tree. Carved trees were associated particularly with burial or initiation sites; initiation trees tend to have carvings only in the bark, whereas the engravings on the burial trees are in the inner sapwood or heartwood.

Carved trees have a limited distribution in Australia: they are confined to eastern and central New South Wales and southeastern Queensland, the region occupied largely by the Wiradjuri and Kamilaroi people. They are particularly vulnerable. In 1945 all the carved trees reported from New South Wales were catalogued: 131 sites were listed and contained between 700 and 1000 trees, but many of these trees have now died or disappeared in bushfires, as was found in a modern survey by David Bell.[11] Moreover, carvings on many still-living trees have been almost covered over by overgrowth of the bark.

The designs carved onto trees were usually geometric and linear patterns cut with a stone hatchet or, in the nineteenth century, with a metal axe. The motifs include circles, spirals and concentric lozenges, and diamonds. They resemble the pattern used to decorate wooden weapons and skin cloaks, patterns which were often said to indicate ownership. It may be, therefore, that the designs carved on trees beside a grave indicate the totem or kinship affiliations of the dead person.

Four carved trees still guard the grave of Yuranigh, guide to the explorer Sir Thomas Mitchell. When Yuranigh died near Molong in New South Wales in 1850, he was buried according to traditional custom, but Mitchell also had a tombstone erected over his grave, expressing his appreciation of Yuranigh's fine qualities. (This site is open to the public.)[12]

Bora grounds are also vulnerable sites, and many have disappeared under the plough or bulldozer, but a few still remain. They are almost the only Aboriginal sites to be visible on aerial photographs (plate 33).

Most Aboriginal ceremonies left no material traces behind. It took several months to carve and intricately decorate the huge grave posts used by the Tiwi of northern Australia in the final rites of the Pukimani ceremony. These were erected around the grave during the lengthy mourning ceremony, in which dancers wearing elaborate body decoration mimed events in the life of the deceased and drove the spirits away from the grave into the bush. Yet when the great collective mourning gathering was over, the magnificent poles were simply left in the ground. They were not repainted, maintained or reused, but allowed to rot away naturally.

In 1972–73 the Gidjingali of Arnhem Land organised two major Kunapipi ceremonies, which brought together 200 to 300 people. Some 400 human-weeks were invested in carrying out these ceremonies, but Rhys Jones wrote that 'visiting the great camp of *Ngaladjebama* three months after the religious climax there, all we saw was the wind, whirling red dust over midden debris, and strips of paperbark rattling against bleached poles of collapsed hut structures. The investment had been made into the intellectual and not the material sphere of life.'[13]

The only prehistoric Aboriginal religious structures that have lasted well were made of stone. Stone arrangements are very difficult to date, but they probably have been part of Aboriginal culture for a long time.[14] A wide range of types of arrangements, or alignments, of stones occur. There are circles, lines, 'corridors', single standing stones or piles of stones heaped up into a cairn (plate 34). The significance and mythology of stone arrangements is unfortunately generally unknown even to local Aborigines, for most of the sites have not been used for many decades or even for centuries. In most cases all that is known is that the stones were used to tell a mythological story and represented either certain totemic beings or enclosed areas where special events took place. The only stone arrangement so far dated is that of the Bay of Fires in northeastern Tasmania, where a new arrangement had been set on top of an earlier one covered with shell midden and charcoal, 750 years old. This gives at least a minimum antiquity for this type of prehistoric monument.

ART

Rock art sites are found in their thousands in Australia, especially in the north of the continent, and have been studied by many researchers, such as Robert Bednarik, George Chaloupka, Chris Chippindale, John Clegg, Noelene Cole, Bruno David, Bob Edwards, Natalie Franklin, Robert Gunn, Ivan Haskovec, Liz Hatte, Robert Layton, Darrell Lewis, Michel Lorblanchet, Fred McCarthy, Jo McDonald, Howard McNickle, Mike Morwood, Margaret Nobbs, Kelvin Officer, Andrée Rosenfeld, Claire Smith, Paul Tacon, Percy Trezise, Pat Vinnicombe and Grahame Walsh.[15]

Plate 34 Namadgi stone arrangement, Australian Capital Territory. It consists of a 50-metre long, single line of stones, two stone 'corridors' and a number of circles, on top of a remote granite peak.

One of the reasons prehistorians are interested in rock art is that some of it is certainly prehistoric and thus opens a window into the past. Some petroglyphs and hand stencils belong to the Pleistocene, as described in chapter 11, and some paintings may have a similar antiquity.

It was explorer George Grey who first recorded the huge Wandjina figures of Western Australia, paintings of such quality and aesthetic accomplishment that he could not believe they were the work of Aborigines. Indeed, for over a century, Aboriginal culture was held in such low esteem that simple figurative paintings were considered to be primitive, child-like daubings and anything fine or spectacular was attributed to visiting Egyptians, Hindus, Greeks, Romans, the lost tribes of Israel or visitors from outer space. It is only since the 1970s that Aboriginal art has been recognised for what it is at its best: great art of world heritage quality.

The great diversity of recent Aboriginal culture is mirrored in the very different art styles found in different parts of the continent. These differences do not stem from the different types of rock surface available as 'canvas', but appear to reflect different culture areas. Tasmanian rock art is virtually all petroglyphs, that of Victoria almost all paintings. Only two petroglyph sites have been found so far in Victoria, but some hundred painting sites have been identified, mainly in the Grampians. They are small figurative paintings and symbolic marks, such as rows of short strokes whose significance is unknown. These have been thought to be hunters' tallies of their success in the chase, but there is no evidence to support this interpretation.

The most colourful galleries in New South Wales lie in the west, in the Cobar region, where small, lively, red and white figures dance across the walls of dozens of shelters. In contrast, on the coast of New South Wales, in the Hawkesbury region, sandstone paintings are larger and include more marine subjects, but the outstanding feature of the Sydney region is the engraved art. There are thousands of outline petroglyphs, and the figures usually approximate life size. Subjects range from whales to lyre birds, from dingoes to sailing ships, from emus to what appears to be a lady in a crinoline dress. Petroglyphs are also found in western New South Wales, but these tend to be pecked rather than outlined. These are dominated by tracks and circles, like the ancient petroglyphs of southern and Central Australia.

The art of the engravers reaches its height in the Pilbara region of Western Australia. There the development of this art medium can be seen in all its richness and variety. Ancient geometric figures, concentric circles, tracks and lines have weathered back to the same dark colour as the parent rock, a process that takes many thousands, even tens of thousands, of years, suggesting great antiquity. There are realistic, linear drawings of animals, often life size, and pecked-out human and animal figures, standing out in a fresh cream colour against the brown of the background rock. Although it is impossible to date most of these petroglyphs, the fresher, lighter-coloured ones are in general younger than those almost obliterated by cracks, heavy weathering and patination.

A particularly dramatic series of apparently recent motifs occurs among the engravings at Woodstock. This younger art is full of life and movement for such a difficult medium as rock engraving, executed with stone implements. Elegant figures are shown in bold silhouette and dramatic compositions — running, dancing, fighting, love-making. The many humans include strange anthropomorphs — human-type figures. These male figures have forked hands instead of fingers, gigantic genitals, protruding muzzles and long 'antennae' waving from their heads. The Woodstock petroglyphs were not kept secret, for they are often placed on tiers high on pyramidal piles of huge boulders, where they look out, as if from the walls of a gigantic picture gallery, across the featureless sand plains. Gallery Hill contains one of the finest collections of these animated figures, which occur in sites throughout the Western Australian Museum Reserve of Abydos–Woodstock, and at numerous other sites within the Pilbara region.[16]

Not only could these sites be seen by women and children as well as by men, but some may also have been the work of women, for many are close to a waterhole and usually within a few metres of oval patches of rock worn smooth from seed grinding. Often, the upper millstone is still left on the milling floor, and debris consistent with grass seeds has been found in the cracks of some of the ground surfaces. Grinding of seeds to be mixed with water and made into dough was traditionally a woman's activity in Aboriginal Australia. There is a consistently close association between seed-grinding patches and engravings.[17] The virile Woodstock men seem likely to be women's art, in the same way that voluptuous female figures have been painted as 'love magic' by male Aboriginal artists elsewhere.

In visual splendour, the rock paintings of the Kimberley, the Northern Territory and Cape York rival those anywhere in the world. The Kimberley is famous for its huge, colourful Wandjina figures, but these replaced an equally fine earlier tradition of animated, small 'Bradshaw' figures, outstanding for their delicate drafting and bold, simple lines. Equal vigour and artistic excellence appears in the tiny Mimi figures of early Arnhem Land art. Impressionistic and dynamic, they still depict in remarkable detail lively scenes of prehistoric life.

Much better known is the later style of Arnhem Land, the elaborate x-ray rock art, in which the skeleton and internal organs of creatures are portrayed as well as the external features.[18] This tradition is continued on bark paintings. Rock art is only one aspect of Aboriginal art, which can perhaps now be more readily appreciated through bark painting. Bark paintings are easier to relate to Western art, for they have a representational form with which we immediately feel familiar. And even when decorated with what is to us an abstract pattern, this can still be assessed in terms of our own abstract art, and its technical excellence and beauty of line and colour can be admired.

The rock art of Queensland is different again. The Cape York Peninsula contains one of the most colourful and prolific bodies of rock art in the world, recorded by the pioneering endeavours of local bushman and pilot, Percy Trezise. Enormous naturalistic figures of animals, birds, plants, humans and spirit figures adorn the walls of hundreds of rock-shelters. Mythological ancestral beings are finely executed with careful decoration. Other paintings were used in magic or sorcery; one shows a pack rape, others depict men and women, upside down with distorted limbs and genitals, being struck by a spear or bitten by a snake. This use of art as an aid in death sorcery was still active in the nineteenth century, for one painting depicts a European clutching at the reins as he falls off his giant horse. However, sorcery was no match for the guns of the miners who flocked to the region during the Palmer River goldrush, and soon the rock painters were wiped out or forcibly moved away from their land.

Stencil art is found over most of Australia but is most highly developed as an art form in the Central Highlands of southern Queensland.[19] Here, most of the paintings are stencils. The motifs of hands, feet, pendants, axes, clubs, boomerangs and other artefacts are arranged in decorative patterns and stencilled with red, yellow and black pigment, which stands out vividly against the white sandstone walls. Colourful and striking as art, these stencils are also a valuable record of local material culture, although they have been subjected to innumerable graffiti and other vandalism.

Paintings decay from natural weathering and few survive more than a few hundred years unless special processes are at work, such as the natural accumulation of a siliceous film over the surface or the penetration and staining of the rock by the pigment. Traditionally, paintings were regularly retouched and repaired, or in regions such as the Kimberley, they were often whitewashed over and completely repainted. Since the disruption of Aboriginal society by European settlement, this process has largely stopped, partly because Aboriginal art is owned by individuals and no one but the traditional owners may repaint the figures.

Rock painting now seems to have ceased in Arnhem Land: the last painting was done at Nourlangie Rock (in what is now the Kakadu National Park) in 1963. This fine work depicts in colourful orange and white a group of stylised male and female spirit figures, some x-ray fish and a 'Lightning Man', who has stone axes growing from his head, arms and knees, ready to strike against the ground when angered, thereby making thunder, lightning and storms. Already the white pigment is beginning to flake off, but there are no rock painters to repaint such paintings and few scientific techniques yet available to preserve them. Aborigines traditionally believe that if paintings are not being regularly repaired or replaced by the traditional owners, they should not be artificially conserved but should be allowed to die a natural death. Non-Aborigines think differently — it seems tragic to us that this rich rock art should be vanishing.

Aboriginal art is a part of religious life and a vital accompaniment to ceremonies and rituals: it was never 'art for art's sake'. The aesthetic value has always been secondary to the religious or practical use of the decorated item. There were no professional artists in traditional Aboriginal society, although some individuals were recognised as particularly gifted.

The best and most significant art is a manifestation of spiritual beliefs. It conveys aspects of myth through symbolic representations of the great Spirit Beings, linking Aborigines to the Dreamtime. It is the tangible expression of the relevance and reality of myth and of Aboriginal unity with nature. Art is woven into the whole fabric of Aboriginal life: through art, music and dance the stories of the Dreamtime are re-enacted.

Even if the messages of Aboriginal art are not accessible, the beautiful patterns, vivid colours and elegant forms are readily appreciated. Deceptively simple, the designs are often subtle, ingenious and sophisticated. Aboriginal art has a beauty, diversity and vitality all its own.

Epilogue

Prehistoric Aboriginal society was dynamic. Neither the land nor the people were unchanging, and it is the constant human adaptation to a changing environment that provides both the challenge and fascination of Australian prehistory. Much further research in many fields remains to be done before we will know even the outline of the full story, but what we know now from the archaeological record attests to a complex and sophisticated prehistoric culture.

We will never know precisely when the first human footprint was made on an Australian beach, but it was certainly more than 40 000 and most probably at least 50 000 years ago. At that time much of the world's water was frozen into ice sheets and the level of the sea was more than 100 metres lower than it is today. This made the passage from Asia to Australia rather easier, but there was never a complete land bridge. The first humans to reach Australia must have crossed at least 70 kilometres of open sea. It may be that the craft used by the 'first boat people' were made of bamboo. Bamboo does not grow in Australia, so the first migrants might have unknowingly been blown by the northerly monsoonal winds into a trap, with no possibility of return.

Most of the earliest camp sites in Australia are now underneath the sea, for in the Pleistocene the continental shelf was dry land, so the coastline extended much further than it does today. New Guinea was linked to northern Australia by a wide plain, and it was possible to walk across what is now Bass Strait to Tasmania. The earliest occupation of the continent would have been off the present Kimberley coast or on what is now the Arafura Sea or Gulf of Carpentaria.

The oldest camp sites now known in Australia are in Arnhem Land in the Top End of the Northern Territory. These are Malakunanja II and Nauwalabila rock-shelters, which have remarkably similar cultural sequences, soundly dated by a combination of the radiocarbon and optical luminescence methods from the present back to around 53 000 years ago. Sites dating to around 40 000 years have now been found in the southeast and extreme southwest of the continent. Whilst the earliest colonisation was probably coastal, with people moving along the beaches and up the river valleys, exploiting fish, shellfish and small land animals, they seem to have moved inland fairly rapidly. By 40 000 years ago they were in the Willandra Lakes region, which is now semiarid but was then in the lacustral phase, when Lake Mungo and the other now-dry lakes were full of fresh water. By 30 000 years ago people were inhabiting the arid heart of the continent, evidenced by the Puritjarra rock-shelter west of Alice Springs, and some caves on the Nullarbor Plain. They were scattered from the highlands of New Guinea to within sight of glaciers in southwestern Tasmania; from the escarpments of tropical Arnhem Land to the arid red centre.

The first Australians were some of the earliest representatives of *Homo sapiens*. There is no evidence that *Homo erectus* ever entered Australia, and all the archaeological and physical anthropological evidence suggests that this was not the case. The most likely interpretation of the existing fossil evidence is that the earliest migrants were of large, robust build, with projecting faces and heavy brow ridges, similar to early *Homo sapiens* as represented by the Solo remains in Java. People with a different, much lighter, gracile build were living on the shores of Lake Mungo in New South Wales by 30 000 years ago, but physical anthropologists are still hotly debating whether these two morphological types represent two biologically distinct populations, or are two ends of a continuum between a light and a heavy build.

More than 150 Pleistocene sites have now been discovered in Australia. These have revealed that these early hunter–gatherers used fire, ground up ochre pigments for decoration, wore ornaments, and honoured their dead. The rite of cremation goes back 25 000 years at Lake Mungo — the earliest evidence for cremation in the world. The people used stone and bone tools and, more than 20 000 years ago, were already mining flint — the finest tool-making material in Australia — from deep within Koonalda Cave in South Australia. In northern Australia by that time, they had mastered the technique of hafting handles to stone tools and of grinding the blades of axes to fine cutting edges, remarkably early technological skills which are only rivalled by similarly early developments in Japan.

Rock art began more than 40 000 years ago; the earliest dated petroglyphs are the geometric, Panaramitee-style lines, circles and tracks from the Olary region of South Australia, dated by the radiocarbon and cation-ratio methods, and the analysis of their thick coating of desert varnish. These petroglyphs span the whole period from around 40 000 years ago to the recent past. Whilst it is surprising to find so little apparent change in subject matter and style over such a long time, there are precedents in Central Australian art for extreme conservatism, and a large series of radiocarbon dates now lend credence to the cation-ratio dates that aroused such a storm of controversy when first published in 1988. Whenever a new discovery is made which makes us 'rewrite the textbooks', there are the sceptics and hyper-sceptics who will take years to accept, or may never accept, that these 'surprise' findings may be correct. However, unless we are prepared to accept unexpected as well as expected results, the discipline of prehistory and our knowledge about the past will not progress very far.

There are now tantalising hints that the art of rock painting may be as old as, or even older than, the petroglyphs. Accelerator mass spectrometry dating of tiny samples of pigment containing organic material has yielded several Pleistocene dates, and used pieces of ochre have been found in the lowest, 50 000-year-old layers of the Nauwalabila and Malakunanja rock-shelters. Blood has been found mixed with pigment in some subterranean caves in southwestern Tasmania, suggesting early ritual use of caves. Later, the art of figurative painting developed, and the relationship between the art of the engravers and painters is one of the fascinating, unsolved questions of Australian prehistory.

Another enigma is the impact of the earliest Australians on the giant marsupials which then roamed the continent. Did they become extinct because of the extreme aridity at the end of the Pleistocene, or did they fall victim to game hunters? No doubt both played a part, but big-game hunting is indicated by the otherwise inexplicable coincidence in timing between the arrival of humans in a region, such as the Willandra Lakes or southwest Western Australia, and the speedy extinction of the megafauna in that area. And at last we do have a 'kill site' or, at the very least, a scavenging site — Cuddie Springs, in northwestern New South Wales. The blood of *Diprotodon* and other megafauna has been identified on stone butchering tools. There is a perfect match between DNA in the blood on the tools and DNA extracted from the megafaunal bones.

At the same time as they developed a rich culture, Pleistocene Australians successfully adjusted to profound environmental and climatic changes and the loss of millions of square kilometres of their land as the polar ice caps melted and the seas rose. The economic achievements of Aborigines over the last few thousand years are remarkable. Their economy supported a healthy population in some of the harshest areas of the world's driest inhabited continent, areas where, later, explorers such as Burke and Wills died of thirst and malnutrition. It is ironic that such unsuccessful explorers were hailed as heroes, whereas the Aborigines who had successfully adapted to the rigours of the desert thousands of years before were given no credit for this, and belittled because they did not develop agriculture.

Hunter–gatherers have been described as the original affluent society, and an examination of archaeological and ethnographic evidence lends support to this view. Whether gathering bogong moths or hunting seals, leaching poison out of cycads or replanting yams, Aboriginal people evolved a series of successful and varied economies. These broadly based economic systems allowed them to exploit, and to survive in, a wide range of environments where European agriculture proved to be an abysmal failure. Extensive use was made of fire as a hunting tool, modifying the Australian vegetation so profoundly that contemporary flora has been called an Aboriginal artefact.

A far cry from the usual view of Aborigines as nomadic, hungry hunters is the picture of well-fed people living in groups of well-built huts beside their eel and fish traps, traps that were cunningly engineered to ensure an abundant and reliable food supply. And these experts of stone age economics had a healthier, more nutritious diet than have many Europeans today.

Testimony to the innovations that occurred over time is provided by the evidence of many sites. In the technological sphere there is the development of barbed spears, the spear-thrower, projectile points, ground-edge tools, and special stone adzes for working the iron-hard timbers of the desert. And by 10 000 years ago, Aborigines had become skilled in the sophisticated aerodynamic principles of boomerangs. Far-flung trading networks were developed, and much time and energy was devoted to ceremonial life.

It is in the creativity of the spirit, rather than in material goods, that Aboriginal society excelled. Society was so organised that there was ample leisure time. Prehistoric Australians had more leisure to devote to matters of the mind — art, ceremonies, music, dance and myth — than did all but a few Western artists until recent times. The achievements of early Australians are constantly underestimated by those Europeans who judge a society solely by its material possessions. The real richness of Aboriginal culture is thus only now beginning to be appreciated, as anthropologists reveal the Aborigines' complex social and religious systems, and archaeologists uncover the distant past of this heritage.

The coming of white people proved almost disastrous for Aboriginal society. Yet the present renaissance of traditional culture and lifestyle and the renewing of the Dreamtime may help overcome this near-fatal impact, for the evidence of archaeology has demonstrated the extraordinary adaptability and creativity of these intellectual aristocrats of the prehistoric world.

Dates Reference List

1. Dates are radiocarbon dates unless otherwise indicated. No dates have been calibrated.

2. Full references are provided in end notes.

3. Abbreviations are as follows:

    AA = *Australian Archaeology*

    AAS = *Australian Aboriginal Studies*

    AO = *Archaeology in Oceania*

AMS = Accelerator mass spectrometer C-14 date

BGS = Below ground surface

C-14 = Radiocarbon date

char. = Charcoal

LCM = Lowest cultural material

OSL = Optically stimulated thermoluminescence date

RS = Rock-shelter or cave

PLEISTOCENE DATES

Locality	Lab. No.	Age Years BP	Type of Date	Type of Site
NORTHERN TERRITORY				
Malakunanja II (Roberts et al. *Nature* 1990)	KTL-162	61 000 +9000/ −13 000	OSL	Lowest artefacts at 260 cm BGS
Malakunanja II	KTL-158	52 000 +7000/ −11 000	OSL	Artefacts at 250 cm BGS
Malakunanja II	KTL-164	45 000 +6000/ −9000	OSL	Artefacts at 230 cm BGS
Malakunanja II	SUA-265	18 040 ± 300	C-14 (char.)	Associated with ochre and grindstone
Nauwalabila I (Roberts et al. *AA* 1993)	Ox-od K169	60 300 ± 6700	OSL	Artefacts at 285–301 cm BGS
Nauwalabila I	Ox-od K170	58 300 ± 5800	OSL	Base of rubble (auger hole)
Nauwalabila I	Ox-od K168	53 400 ± 5400	OSL	Artefacts at 228–240 cm BGS
Nauwalabila I	Ox-od K166	30 000 ± 2400	OSL	Artefacts at 170–175 cm BGS
Nauwalabila I	SUA-237	19 975 ± 265	C-14 (char.)	Lowest C-14 date
Nauwalabila I	Ox-od K172	13 500 ± 900	OSL	Artefacts at 104–110 cm BGS
Nauwalabila I	Ox-od K171	2900 ± 600	OSL	Artefacts at 1–6 cm BGS
Malangangerr (Roberts et al. *Nature* 1990)	KTL-126	32 000 +7000/ −9000	OSL	Lowest artefacts at 200 cm BGS
Malangangerr (C. White 1967, 1971)	ANU-77B GaK-629 GaK-628	22 900 ± 1000 22 700 ± 700 19 600 ± 550	C-14 (char.)	Earliest ground-edge axes
Nawamoyn (C. White 1967, 1971)	ANU-51	21 450 ± 380	C-14 (char.)	Ground-edge axes
Puritjarra (M. A. Smith *Nature* 1987)	Beta-19901	21 950 ± 270	C-14 (char.)	Artefacts below this, estimated at c. 30 000 BP

LOCALITY	LAB. NO.	AGE YEARS BP	TYPE OF DATE	TYPE OF SITE

NEW SOUTH WALES AND THE AUSTRALIAN CAPITAL TERRITORY

LOCALITY	LAB. NO.	AGE YEARS BP	TYPE OF DATE	TYPE OF SITE
Cranebrook (Nanson et al. *AO* 1987)	Alpha-908	47 000 ± 5200	TL Date	Basal gravel
	Alpha-99	43 100 ± 4700	TL Date	Upper gravel
	ANU-4016	41 700 +3000/ −2200	C-14 (wood)	Wood in basal gravel
	ANU-4017	40 500 +2150/ −1700	C-14 (wood)	Wood in basal gravel
Lake Mungo (Mulvaney excavation)	ANU-1203	c. 40 000	C-14 (shell)	Shells associated with flakes 180 cm below hearth
Lake Mungo (Mulvaney excavation)	ANU-1262	31 100 +2250/ −1750	C-14 (char.)	Hearth in Mulvaney excavation near Mungo I cremation site
Lake Mungo shell midden (Bowler 1976)	N-1665	'34 100–37 400'	C-14 (shell)	Transported unionid shells near Lake Mungo
Lake Mungo	ANU-331	32 750 ± 1250	C-14 (shell)	Shell and stone tools in Mungo unit
Lake Mungo (Barbetti *Nature* 1972)	ANU-680	30 780 ± 520	C-14 (char.)	Palaeomagnetic excursion hearth, Mungo unit
Mungo I (Bowler et al. 1970, 1972, 1976; Webb 1989)	ANU-375B	26 250 ± 1120	C-14 (char.)	Mungo I cremation site
Mungo I (= WLH 1) cremation site (Webb 1989)	ANU-618B	24 710 +1270/ −1100	C-14 (bone)	Burnt bone from WLH 1 (acid insoluble residue)
Mungo I (= WLH 1) cremation site (Webb 1989)	NZA-230	25 120 ± 1380	AMS (bone)	Burnt bone from WLH 1 (humid acid fraction)
	NZA-246	24 745 ± 2400	AMS (bone)	
Lake Outer Arumpo (McBryde)	ANU-2586	35 820 +2220/ −1740	C-14 (shell)	Top Hut 3 site, midden with shell, ash and charcoal
Lake Menindee (Tindale 1955)	LJ-204	26 300 ± 1500	C-14 (char.)	Hearths, artefacts, extinct megafauna predate hearths
	GaK-335	18 800 ± 800		
Lake Tandou (J. Hope et al. *AO* 1983)	ANU-3000	26 900 ± 590	C-14 (char.)	Earliest occupation (site TNL 15)
Lake Tandou (J. Hope et al. *AO* 1983)	ANU-2371	24 050 ± 500	C-14 (char.)	Frog kill site (site TNL 34)
Cuddie Springs (Dodson et al. *AO* 1993)	Beta-44375	30 280 ± 450	C-14 (char.)	Associated with lowest artefacts & extinct megafauna
	Beta-46171	29 570 ± 280	C-14 (char.)	
Cuddie Springs	Beta-46170	28 310 ± 200	C-14 (char.)	Associated with artefacts & extinct megafauna
Cuddie Springs (charcoal)	Beta-44374	19 270 ± 230	C-14	Large artefact assemblage; uppermost megafauna.
King's Table (Stockton & Holland *AO* 1974)	SUA-158	22 300 ± 1190	C-14 (char.)	1 flake, earliest occupation?
	SUA-194	14 534 ± 300	C-14 (char.)	Occupation: 36 flakes
Burrill Lake (Lampert 1971)	ANU-137	20 760 ± 800	C-14 (char.)	Earliest occupation
Lime Springs (Gorecki et al. *AO* 1984)	SUA-915	19 300 ± 500	C-14 (char.)	Large artefacts and megafauna
Bass Point (Bowdler 1976)	ANU-536	17 010 ± 650	C-14 (char.)	Earliest occupation
Lyre Bird Dell (Stockton & Holland *AO* 1974)	SUA-15	12 550 ± 145	C-14 (char.)	Earliest occupation
Noola (Tindale 1961)	V-35	12 550 ± 185	C-14 (char.)	Earliest occupation
Walls Cave (Stockton & Holland *AO* 1974)	GaK-3448	12 000 ± 350	C-14 (char.)	Earliest occupation
Shaws Creek RS KII (Kohen et al. *AO* 1984)	Beta-1209	12 980 ± 480	C-14 (char.)	Earliest occupation

LOCALITY	LAB. NO.	AGE YEARS BP	TYPE OF DATE	TYPE OF SITE
Birrigai RS, ACT (Flood et al. *AO* 1987)	Beta-16886	21 000 ± 220	C-14 (char.)	Lowest artefacts
	ARL-162	18 300 +1400/ −1300	C-14 (char.)	@ 70–77 cm BGS
	Beta-16654	15 930 ± 240	C-14 (char.)	Hearth @ 60–65 cm BGS
	Beta-16653	10 160 ± 160	C-14 (char.)	Artefacts @ 45–50 cm BGS

WESTERN AUSTRALIA

LOCALITY	LAB. NO.	AGE YEARS BP	TYPE OF DATE	TYPE OF SITE
Upper Swan Bridge (Pearce & Barbetti *AO* 1981)	SUA–1500	39 500 +2300/ −1800	C-14 (char.)	Open camp site. Occupation @ 88–96 cm BGS
	SUA-1665	37 100 +1600/ −1300	C-14 (char.)	Occupation @ 75–80 cm BGS
Mandu Mandu Creek RS (Morse *AO* 1988; *Antiquity* 1993; Bowdler 1992)	Wk-1513	34 200 ± 1050	C-14	Earliest occupation associated with shell necklace
	Wk-1576	30 000 ± 850	(baler shell (*Melo* sp.))	
	SUA-2354	25 200 ± 250	C-14 (carbon. nodule)	Early occupation
Devil's Lair (Dortch 1984 etc.)	SUA-585, 586 SUA-546	32 800 ± 830	C-14 (char.)	Mean pooled age of oldest occupation & extinct fauna
	SUA-539	27 700 ± 700	C-14 (char.)	Oldest indisputable artefacts
Widgingarri 1, Kimberley (O'Connor 1990)	R-11795	28 060 ± 600	C-14 (marine shell)	Basal occupation
Koolan Shelter 2, Kimberley (O'Connor *AA* 1989)	Wk-1365	27 300 ± 1100	C-14 (marine shell)	Above basal occupation
	Wk-1099	10 850 ± 160	C-14 (marine shell)	Renewal of occupation
Newman Shelter (Ethel Gorge) (Brown 1987)	SUA-1510	26 300 ± 500	C-14 (char.)	Near basal early occupation (site P2055.2)
Silver Dollar site, Shark Bay (Bowdler *AA* 1990)	ANU-7107	25 230 ± 480	C-14 (emu egg shell)	@ 60–70 cm BGS
	ANU-7458	21 700 ± 550	C-14 (emu egg shell)	@ > 70 cm BGS
	ANU-7106	19 750 ± 600	C-14 (emu egg shell)	@ 30–40 cm BGS
	ANU-7105	18 730 ± 600	C-14 (marine shell: uncorrected)	@ 30–40 cm BGS Occupation @ 25–18 000 BP
Noala Cave, Monte Bello Is. (Veth 1994)	Wk-2905	27 220 ± 640	C-14 (shell)	Basal occupation
	Wk-2912	8730 ± 80	C-14 (shell)	Uppermost occupation
Orebody XXIX RS (site PO187) (Brown 1987)	SUA-1041	20 740 ± 345	C-14 (char.)	Early near-basal occupation
Kalgan Hall, Albany (W. Ferguson)	ANU-2870	18 850 ± 370	C-14 (char.)	Earliest occupation predates this
Arumvale (Dortch & McArthur *AA* 1985)	SUA-456	18 400 ± 540	C-14 (char.)	Earliest occupation; fossil chert artefacts
Miriwun RS (Dortch *AAS* 1972)	ANU-1008	17 980 +1370/ −1170	C-14 (char.)	Artefacts, tektites, ochre, grindstone
Gum Tree Valley Top Site, Burrup Peninsula (Lorblanchet 1992)	LY-3609	18 510 ± 260	C-14 (shell (trumpet shell))	Patinated petroglyphs & stone tools
	LY-3608	1510 ± 140	C-14 (shell (*anadara*))	Last shell gathering period
Cheetup RS (M. Smith *AO* 1982)	GX-6605	13 245 ± 315	C-14 (char.)	*Macrozamia* treatment pit
Quininup Brook 4 (Ferguson *AO* 1980)	SUA-687	18 500 ± 1700	C-14 (char.)	Artefacts on open site
Puntutjarpa RS (Gould 1977)	1–5319	10 170 ± 230	C-14 (char.)	Earliest occupation

LOCALITY	LAB. NO.	AGE YEARS BP	TYPE OF DATE	TYPE OF SITE
QUEENSLAND				
Nurrabullgin RS (David *AO* 1993)	SUA-1665	37 000 +1600/ −1300	C-14 (char.)	Lowest artefacts in basal occupation
Sandy Creek RS 1, Laura (Morwood & Trezise 1989)	SUA-2870	31 900 +700/ −600	C-14 (char.)	Basal occupation & associated ground-edge axe
Fern Cave, Chillagoe (David *AO* 1991)	Beta-30403	26 010 ± 410	C-14 (land snails)	Basal occupation
Wallen Wallen Creek (Neal & Stock *Nature* 1986)	SUA-2341	20 560 ± 250	C-14 (char.)	Earliest occupation
Walkunder Arch Cave (J. Campbell *AA* 1982)	Beta-3425	19 520 ± 170	C-14 (char.)	Lowest artefacts
Kenniff Cave (Mulvaney & Joyce 1965)	ANU-345	18 800 ± 480	C-14 (char.)	Earliest occupation
Colless Creek RS (Hiscock & Hughes *AA* 1980)	ANU-2331	17 350 ± 420	C-14 (shell)	Base of upper unit, artefacts well below this date est. > 30 000 BP
Cuckadoo 1 Shelter (Davidson et al. 1993)	Beta-25058	15 270 ± 210	C-14 (char.)	Basal occupation
Early Man RS (Rosenfeld 1982)	ANU-1441	13 200 ± 170	C-14 (char.)	Early petroglyphs, occupation
Native Well I (Morwood *AO* 1981)	ANU-2034 ANU-2001	10 910 ± 140 6190 ± 100	C-14 (char.) C-14 (char.)	Earliest occupation Earliest grindstone
Native Well II (Morwood *AO* 1981)	ANU-2035	10 770 ± 140	C-14 (char.)	Earliest occupation
VICTORIA				
Keilor (Gill 1966; Gallus 1976; Pearce & Barbetti 1981)	ANU-65 ANU-1262	31 600 +1100/ −1300 31 000 +2250/ −1750	C-14 (char.) C-14 (char.)	Extinct fauna: artefacts predate this level Hearth found in 1973
Lancefield Swamp (Horton & Wright *AO* 1981)	SUA-685	26 000 ± 500	C-14 (char.)	Extinct fauna, two artefacts
Cloggs Cave (Flood 1980)	ANU-1044	17 720 ± 840	C-14 (char.)	Earliest occupation
Kow Swamp (Thorne & Macumber *Nature* 1972)	ANU-1236 ANU-869	13 000 ± 280 10 930 ± 125	C-14 (shell)) C-14 (shell)	Shells in KS5 grave Shells in grave fill
Bridgewater South Cave (Lourandos 1983, 1980)	Beta-3923	11 390 ± 310	C-14 (char.)	Earliest occupation
SOUTH AUSTRALIA				
Koonalda Cave (Wright 1971)	ANU-244 ANU-245	23 700 ± 850 21 900 ± 540	C-14 (char.) C-14 (char.)	Wall markings, flint quarry
Roonka (Pretty 1977)	ANU-406	18 150 ± 340	C-14 (char.)	Hearths
Allen's Cave (Marun 1974; Martin 1973)	ANU-1042	18 860 +2160/ −1700	C-14 (char.)	Charcoal > 1 m above earliest occupation
Seton Cave, Kangaroo Is. (Lampert 1981)	ANU-1221 ANU-925	16 100 ± 100 10 940 ± 160	C-14 (char.) C-14 (char.)	Lowest occupation Top of occupation
Hawker Lagoon (Lampert & Hughes 1988)	SUA-2131	14 770 ± 270	C-14 (char.)	Kartan tools, fireplace in pit
JSN Site, Strzelecki Desert (M. A. Smith et al. 1991)	ANU-7196 ANU-2278	14 400 ± 200 13 850 ± 190	C-14 (char.) C-14 (char.)	Earth oven (site JSN-W3) Wasson's hearth (cooking fire with shell)

LOCALITY	LAB. NO.	AGE YEARS BP	TYPE OF DATE	TYPE OF SITE
Wyrie Swamp (Luebbers *Nature* 1975)	ANU-1274	10 200 ± 150	C-14 (char.)	Wooden artefacts in peat swamp
Cooper Creek (Veth et al. 1990)	Wk-1509	11 830 ± 320	C-14 (char.)	Site CC77 hearth
	Wk-1510	11 770 ± 180	C-14 (char.)	Site CC139 hearth

TASMANIA

LOCALITY	LAB. NO.	AGE YEARS BP	TYPE OF DATE	TYPE OF SITE
Warreen Cave (= M86/2) (Allen et al. *AA* 1989)	Beta-42122 & ETH-7665	34 790 ± 510	C-14 (char.)	Near basal occupation
	Beta-26962	22 370 ± 470	C-14 (char.)	Occupation @ 90 cm BGS
	Beta-26961	18 290 ± 290	C-14 (char.)	Occupation
	Beta-42993	c. 16 000	C-14 (char.)	Youngest occupation
Cave ORS 7 (Cosgrove 1991; Bowdler 1992)	Beta-23404 & ETH-3724	30 840 ± 480	C-14 (char.)	Oldest occupation
	Beta-27078	2450 ± 70	C-14 (char.)	Youngest occupation
Nunamira Cave (= Bluff Cave) (Cosgrove *Science* 1989)	Beta-25881	30 420 ± 690	C-14 (char.)	Lowest occupation
	Beta-25877	11 630 ± 200	C-14 (char.)	Youngest occupation
Palewardia Walana Lanala (= Ach. 84/1) (Allen 1991)	Beta-44081	29 800 ± 720	C-14 (char.)	Earliest occupation
	ANU-3982	c. 13 000	C-14 (char.)	Youngest occupation
Bone Cave (Allen *AA* 1989)	Beta-29987	29 000 ± 520	C-14 (char.)	Earliest occupation
	Beta-26509	13 700 ± 860	C-14 (char.)	Youngest occupation
Kutikina Cave (= Fraser) (Kiernan et al. *Nature* 1983)	ANU-2785	19 970 ± 850	C-14 (char.)	Earliest occupation
	ANU-2781	14 480 ± 930	C-14 (char.)	Youngest occupation, cave abandoned
Beginner's Luck Cave (Murray et al. *AO* 1980)	GaK-7081	20 650 ± 1790	C-14 (char.)	Lowest artefacts
Mackintosh 90/1 (Stern & Marshall *AO* 1993)	Beta-45808	17 030 ± 430	C-14 (char.)	Lowest occupation
	Beta-46305	15 160 ± 210	C-14 (char.)	Uppermost occupation
Cave Bay Cave (Bowdler 1977)	ANU-1498	22 750 ± 420	C-14 (char.)	Earliest occupation
Mannalargenna Cave, Prime Seal Is. (S. Brown 1993; R. Sim 1994)	ANU-8999	21 890 ± 340	C-14 (char.)	Hearth @ 4 m BGS, LCM
	NZA-974	20 560 ± 290	C-14 (char.)	
	ANU-8997	17 650 ± 350	C-14 (char.)	Hearth @ 175 cm BGS
	ANU-8996	9100 ± 130	C-14 (char.)	Uppermost occupation
Beeton Shelter, Badger Is. (Sim 1994)	ANU-8752	19 300 ± 730	C-14 (char.)	Base of cultural sequence
	ANU-8130	8700 ± 125	C-14 (marine shell corrected)	Uppermost midden
Flying Fox Site (Blain et al. *AA* 1989)	ANU-3562	17 100 ± 1350	C-14 (char.)	Open site on Franklin River
Cataraqui Monument Quarry site, King Is. (Sim 1994)	ANU-7420	10 180 ± 240	C-14 (char.)	Artefacts in basal level of open site

HOLOCENE DATES

LOCALITY	LAB. NO.	AGE YEARS BP	TYPE OF DATE	TYPE OF SITE
Ngarradj-Warde-Djobkeng, NT (H. Allen & G. Barton 1989)	SUA-165	8690 ± 125	C-14 (char.)	Early occupation, no points
Walga Rock, WA (Bordes et al. *AA* 1983)	Ly-1847	9950 ± 750	C-14 (char.)	Earliest occupation
Koongine Cave, SA (Frankel *AA* 1989)	Beta-14861	9710 ± 180	C-14 (char.)	Earliest occupation
Warragarra RS, Tas. (Lourandos *AA* 1983)	Beta-4757	9760 ± 720	C-14 (char.)	Earliest occupation

LOCALITY	LAB. NO.	AGE YEARS BP	TYPE OF DATE	TYPE OF SITE
Kow Swamp 9, Vic. (Thorne 1972)	ANU-532	9 590 ± 130	C-14 (bone apatite)	Kow Swamp burial 9
The Tombs RS, Qld (Mulvaney & Joyce 1965)	NPL-64	9410 ± 100	C-14 (char.)	Earliest occupation
Haynes Cave, Monte Bello Is., WA (Veth 1994)	Wk-2911 Wk-2914	8240 ± 90 7460 ± 70	C-14 (shell) C-14 (shell)	Mangrove shells eaten Youngest occupation
Nara Inlet 1 RS, N. Qld (Barker *AO* 1991)	Beta-27835	8150 ± 80	C-14 (char.)	14 cm above base of occupation. Marine economy
Green Ant 1 RS, Qld (Flood & Horsfall 1986)	ARL-151	8660 ± 340	C-14 (char.)	Earliest occupation
Echidna Shelter, Qld (Flood & Horsfall 1986)	ARL-155	7280 ± 130	C-14 (char.)	Earliest occupation
Rocky Cape South, Tas. (Jones 1966, 1971)	GXO-266 V-89	8120 ± 165 5425 ± 135	C-14 (char.) C-14 (char.)	Earliest occupation Early occupation
Sisters Creek, Tas. (Jones 1966, 1971)	NSW-17	6050 ± 88	C-14 (char.)	Earliest occupation
Cape du Couedic, SA (Draper *AO* 1987)	CS-496 Wk-1982	7450 ± 100 5810 ± 130	C-14 (char.) C-14 (char.)	Basal occupation Hearth: uppermost occupation
Roonka Burial, SA (Pretty 1987)	ANU-1408	6910 ± 450	C-14 (char.)	Grave no. 89
Curracurrang RS, NSW (Megaw 1968)	GaK-482	7450 ± 180	C-14 (char.)	Earliest occupation
Capertee RS, NSW (McCarthy 1964)	V-18	7360 ± 125	C-14 (char.)	Earliest occupation
Seelands RS, NSW (McBryde 1974)	V-27	6445 ± 75	C-14 (char.)	Earliest occupation
Green Gully, Vic. (Mulvaney 1975)	NZ-676	6460 ± 190	C-14 (char.)	Burial
Ingaladdi 1 RS, NT (Mulvaney 1975)	ANU-60 ANU-58	6800 ± 270 4920 ± 100	C-14 (char.) C-14 (char.)	Brackets rock petroglyph fragments
Northcliffe, WA (Dortch 1975)	SUA-379	6780 ± 120	C-14 (char.)	Date 3 cm below earliest backed blades
Nauwalabila I RS, NT (Jones & Johnson 1985)	ANU-3180	5860 ± 90	C-14 (char.)	Lowest point 77–81 cm BGS
Bushrangers Cave, Qld (Hall *AA* 1986)	Beta-4852	5540 ± 100	C-14 (char.)	Base of occupation estimated at 6500–6000 BP
Jiyer Cave, Qld (N. Horsfall 1987)	Beta-13174 SUA-2240	5130 ± 140 5110 ± 100	C-14 (char.) C-14 (char.)	Earliest occupation of rainforest site
Graman (B1) RS, NSW (McBryde 1974)	GaK-806	5450 ± 100	C-14 (char.)	Earliest backed blades
Graman (A2) RS, NSW (McBryde 1974)	ANU-1353	4960 ± 200	C-14 (char.)	Backed blades established
Bobadeen, NSW (Moore 1981)	ANU-287	5150 ± 170	C-14 (char.)	Earliest backed blades
Burrill Lake, NSW (Lampert 1971)	ANU-335	5320 ± 150	C-14 (char.)	Earliest backed blades are above this
Seelands RS, NSW (McBryde 1974)	V-24	4040 ± 65	C-14 (char.)	Earliest backed blades
Leichardt RS, NT (Kamminga & Allen 1973)	SUA-244	5045 ± 125	C-14 (char.)	Earliest points are 20 cm above this
Tyimede 2 RS, NT (C. White 1967)	ANU-50	4770 ± 150	C-14 (char.)	Earliest points

LOCALITY	LAB. NO.	AGE YEARS BP	TYPE OF DATE	TYPE OF SITE
Ngarradj-Warde-Djobkeng, NT (H. Allen 1989)	SUA-225 SUA-164	3990 ± 195 3450 ± 125	C-14 (char.) C-14 (char.)	1 point was 10–15 cm below this Concentration of points
Widgingarri 2 RS, WA (O'Connor 1990; Bowdler *AAS* 1991)	Wk-1398	4660 ± 60	C-14 (marine shell corrected)	Lowest points & technological change
Fromms Landing RS, SA (Mulvaney 1960)	NZ-364 NPL-29	4850 ± 100 3170 ± 90	C-14 (shell) C-14 (char.)	Earliest points & backed blades Dingo bones
Devon Downs RS, SA (Hale & Tindale 1930; Mulvaney 1975)	L-2179	4250 ± 180	C-14 (char.)	Climax of Pirri points
Nursery Swamp 2 RS, ACT (Rosenfeld et al. *AA* 1983)	ANU-3033	3700 ± 110	C-14 (char.)	Earliest occupation; backed blades
Madura Cave, WA (Martin 1973)	ANU-807	3450 ± 95	C-14 (char.)	Dingo bones
Wombah midden, NSW (McBryde 1982)	GaK-568	3230 ± 100	C-14 (char.)	Dingo bones, backed blades
High Cliffy Shelter, WA (O'Connor 1992)	Wk-1096	2760 ± 100	C-14 (marine shell corrected)	Marine shell at base of occupation on island
Miriwun RS, WA (Dortch 1977)	SUA-142	2980 ± 95	C-14 (marine shell)	Earliest points & Kimberley backed blades
Ingaladdi 1 RS, NT (Mulvaney 1975)	ANU-58 ANU-57	4920 ± 100 2890 ± 73	C-14 (char.) C-14 (char.)	Points absent Large no. of points 23 cm above ANU-58
Currarong, NSW (Lampert 1971)	ANU-243	1970 ± 80	C-14 (char.)	Late backed blades
Curracurrang, NSW (Megaw 1968)	GaK-688 GaK-898	2865 ± 57 1930 ± 80	C-14 (char.) C-14 (char.)	Earliest backed blades Backed blades
Sassafras 1 RS, NSW (Flood 1980)	ANU-741	1690 ± 100	C-14 (char.)	Late backed blades
Sassafras 2 RS, NSW (Flood 1980)	ANU-744	2780 ± 120	C-14 (char.)	Late backed blades
King Is., Tas. (Sim 1994)	ANU-7422	1980 ± 60	C-14 (marine shell corrected)	King Is. midden
Quarantine Bay, King Is., Tas. (Sim 1994)	ANU-7058	1100 ± 70	C-14 (marine shell corrected)	King Is. midden
Mt Cameron West, Tas. (Jones 1981)	ANU-339 ANU-337	1350 ± 200 840 ± 100	C-14 (char.) C-14 (char.)	Petroglyphs predate this Top of midden covering petroglyphs
Weipa middens, N. Qld (Bailey 1977)	I-1738 SUA-149	810 ± 105 1180 ± 80	C-14 (char.) C-14 (char.)	Early stage of shell midden (Kwamter site)
Wattamolla midden, NSW (Megaw 1974)	ANU-177	840 ± 160	C-14 (char.)	Earliest shell fish hooks, backed blades
Mazie Bay, Keppel Is., Qld (Rowland *AA* 1980)	ANU-2489	1520 ± 50	C-14 (char.)	Earliest shell fish hooks
Seal Point, Vic. (Lourandos *AO* 1983)	SUA-552	1420 ± 130	C-14 (char.)	Base of midden
Bay of Fires, Tas. (Jones 1965)	ANU-2297	730 ± 100	C-14 (char.)	Stone arrangement
Durras North, NSW (Lampert *AO* 1966)	GaK-873	480 ± 80	C-14 (char.)	Bone point industry in beach cave
Glen Aire 2 RS, Vic. (Mulvaney 1962)	NZ-367	370 ± 45	C-14 (char.)	Bottom of midden; bone point industry in beach cave

Notes

CHAPTER ONE

Documents of Stone and Bone

1 H. H. Hale and N. B. Tindale, 'Notes on some human remains in the Lower Murray Valley,
South Australia'. *Records of the South Australian Museum*, vol. 4, 1930, pp. 145–218. (Describes
the excavation of Devon Downs rock-shelter and Tartanga burial site.)

2 For the history of Australian archaeology, see D. J. Mulvaney, 'Blood from stones and bones'.
Search, vol. 10, 1979, pp. 214–18; J. P. White, 'Archaeology in Australia and New Guinea'.
World Archaeology, vol. 13(2), 1981, pp. 255–63; D. Horton, *Recovering the Tracks. The Story of
Australian Archaeology*. Canberra, Aboriginal Studies Press, 1991. (Terminates with the
discovery of the Mungo remains in 1969.)

3 This definition and others in this chapter are based on B. M. Fagan, *People of the Earth. An
Introduction to World Prehistory*. Boston, Little, Brown & Co., 1980.

4 Australian stone tools are described in F. D. McCarthy, *Australian Aboriginal Stone Implements*.
Sydney, Australian Museum, 1976.

5 For Australian archaeological techniques, see G. Connah (ed.), *Australian Field Archaeology.
A Guide to Techniques*. Canberra, Aboriginal Studies Press, 1982.

6 J. M. Flood, 'Pleistocene Man at Cloggs Cave — his tool kit and environment'. *Mankind*,
vol. 9(3), 1974, pp. 175–88; J. M. Flood, *The Moth Hunters. Aboriginal Prehistory of the Australian
Alps*. Canberra, Australian Institute of Aboriginal Studies, 1980.

The First Boat People

1 J. Isaacs (ed.), *Australian Dreaming*. Sydney, Lansdowne Press, 1980, p. 5.

2 For sea levels, see J. Chappell, 'Late Pleistocene coasts and human migrations in the Austral
region', in *A Community of Culture* (eds M. Spriggs et al.). 1993, pp. 43–8; J. Chappell and
N. J. Shackleton, 'Oxygen isotopes and sea level'. *Nature*, vol. 324, 1986, pp. 137–40; J.
Chappell and B. G. Thom, 'Sea level and coasts', in *Sunda and Sahul* (eds J. Allen, J. Golson
and R. Jones). 1977, pp. 275–92; J. Chappell, 'A revised sea-level record for the last 300 000
years from Papua New Guinea'. *Search*, vol. 14(3–4), 1983, pp. 99–101. For early sites, see
R. G. Roberts, R. Jones and M. A. Smith, 'Thermoluminescence dating of a 50,000-year-old
human occupation site in northern Australia'. *Nature*, vol. 345, 10 May 1990, pp. 153–6.

3 ibid.; R. Jones, 'East of Wallace's Line: issues and problems in the colonisation of the
Australian continent', in *The Human Revolution: Behavioural and Biological Perspectives on the
Origins of Modern Humans* (eds P. Mellars and C. Stringer). 1989, pp. 743–81.

4 For a full discussion, see G. G. Simpson, 'Too many lines: the limits of the Oriental and
Australian zoogeographic regions'. *Proceedings of the American Philosophical Society*, vol. 121(2),
1977, pp. 107–20. For Asian discoveries in general, see P. Bellwood, *Man's Conquest of the
Pacific*. Sydney, Collins, 1978; P. Bellwood, *Prehistory of the Indo-Malaysian Archipelago*.
Sydney, Academic Press, 1985; R. Jones, 1989, op.cit.; P. Bellwood, 'Crossing the Wallace
Line — with style', in M. Spriggs et al., 1993, op. cit., pp. 152–63.

5 J. H. Calaby, 'Some biogeographical factors relevant to the Pleistocene movement of man in
Australia', in *The Origin of the Australians* (eds R. L. Kirk and A. G. Thorne). 1976, pp. 23–8.

6 J. Birdsell, 'The recalibration of a paradigm for the first peopling of Greater Australia',
in J. Allen, J. Golson and R. Jones, 1977, op. cit., pp. 113–67; N. G. Butlin, *Economics of the
Dreamtime. A Hypothetical History*. Cambridge University Press, 1993.

7 R. Jones, 1989, op. cit.

8 N. G. Butlin, op. cit., pp. 14–50.

9 J. Chappell, 1993, op. cit.

10 R. Jones, 'Tasmania: aquatic machines and offshore islands', in *Problems in Economic and
Social Anthropology* (eds G. de G. Sieveking et al.). 1976, pp. 235–63; 'Man as an element of a
continental fauna: the case of the sundering of the Bassian bridge', in J. Allen, J. Golson and
R. Jones, 1977, op. cit., pp. 317–86; R. Jones, 'The Tasmanian paradox', in *Stone Tools as
Cultural Markers* (ed. R. V. S. Wright). 1977, pp. 189–204.

11 N. B. Tindale, 'Some population changes among the Kaiadilt of Bentinck Island, Queensland'. *Records of the S.A. Museum*, vol. 14(2), 1962, pp. 297–336.

12 A. Thorne and R. Raymond, *Man on the Rim*. Sydney, Angus & Robertson, 1989, pp. 39–45.

13 C. E. Dortch and B. G. Muir, 'Long range sightings of bush fires as possible incentive for Pleistocene voyagers to Greater Australia'. *W.A. Naturalist*, vol. 14(7), 1980, pp. 194–8.

14 J. Golson, 'Land connections, sea barriers and the relationship of Australian and New Guinea prehistory', in *Bridge and Barrier: The Natural and Cultural History of Torres Strait* (ed. D. Walker). 1972, pp. 375–97.

15 J. Chappell, 'Geology of coral terraces on Huon Peninsula, New Guinea: a study of Quaternary tectonic movements and sea level changes'. *Bulletin of the Geological Society of America*, vol. 85, 1974, pp. 553–70.

16 L. Groube, J. Chappell, J. Muke and D. Price, 'A 40 000 year old human occupation site at Huon Peninsula, Papua New Guinea'. *Nature*, vol. 324, 1986, pp. 453–5.

17 L. Groube, 'Waisted axes of Asia, Melanesia and Australia', in *Archaeology at ANZAAS Canberra* (ed. G. K. Ward). 1986, pp. 168–77.

18 L. Groube, 'The taming of the rain forests: a model for Late Pleistocene forest exploitation in New Guinea', in *Foraging and Farming: The Evolution of Plant Exploitation* (eds D. R. Harris and G. C. Hillman). 1988, pp. 292–317. (quote at p. 299).

19 J. P. White, K. A. Crook and B. P. Ruxton, 'Kosipe: a late Pleistocene site in the Papuan highlands'. *Proceedings of the Prehistoric Society*, vol. 36, 1970, pp. 152–70.

20 G. S. Hope, 'Pollen from archaeological sites: a comparison of swamp and open archaeological site pollen spectra at Kosipe Mission, Papua New Guinea', in *Archaeometry: An Australian Perspective* (eds W. Ambrose and P. Duerden). 1982, pp. 211–19.

21 G. S. Hope, J. Golson and J. Allen, 'Palaeoecology and prehistory in Papua New Guinea'. *Journal of Human Evolution*, vol. 12, 1983, pp. 37–60.

22 M. J. Mountain, 'Preliminary report on excavations at Nombe Rockshelter, Simbu Province, Papua New Guinea'. *Indo-Pacific Prehistory Association Bulletin*, vol. 4, 1983, pp. 84–9; M. J. Mountain, 'Bones, hunting and predation in the Pleistocene of northern Sahul', in *Sahul in Review. Pleistocene Archaeology in Australia, New Guinea and Island Melanesia* (eds M. A. Smith, M. Spriggs and B. Fankhauser). Occasional Paper, Department of Prehistory, Australian National University, 1993, pp. 123–30.

23 G. S. Hope, J. Golson and J. Allen, 1983, op. cit., p. 44.

24 J. Hope and G. S. Hope, 'Palaeoenvironments for man in New Guinea', in R. L. Kirk and A. G. Thorne, 1976, op. cit., pp. 29–54.

25 P. Gorecki, M. Mabin and J. Campbell, 'Archaeology and geomorphology of the Vanimo Coast, Papua New Guinea'. *Archaeology in Oceania*, vol. 26, 1991, pp. 119–22. Pleistocene date in S. Bowdler, 'The earliest voyages: the Pleistocene colonisation of Southeast Asia and Australasia'. Paper delivered at 34th ICANAS Conference, Hong Kong, 1993 (to be published by Hong Kong University Press).

26 References are in S. Bowdler, 'Homo sapiens in Southeast Asia and the Antipodes: archaeological versus biological interpretations', in *The Evolution and Dispersal of Modern Humans in Asia* (eds T. Akasawa, K. Aoki and T. Kimura). 1992, pp. 559–89; S. Bowdler, 'Sunda and Sahul: a 30KYR culture area?', in M. A. Smith, M. Spriggs and B. Fankhauser, 1993, op. cit., pp. 60–70.

27 I. Davidson and W. Noble, 'Why the first colonisation of the Australian region is the earliest evidence of modern human behaviour'. *Archaeology in Oceania*, vol. 27, 1992, pp. 135–42.

28 J. Allen, C. Gosden, R. Jones and J. P. White, 'Pleistocene dates for human occupation of New Ireland, northern Melanesia'. *Nature*, vol. 331, 1988, pp. 707–9; J. Allen, 'Notions of the Pleistocene in Greater Australia', in M. Spriggs et al. 1993, op. cit., pp. 139–51.

29 S. Wickler and M. J. T. Spriggs, 'Pleistocene human occupation of the Solomon Islands, Melanesia'. *Antiquity*, vol. 62, 1988, pp. 703–6.

30 J. Allen, C. Gosden and J. P. White, 'Human Pleistocene adaptations in the tropical island Pacific: recent evidence from New Ireland, a Greater Australian outlier'. *Antiquity*, vol. 63, 1989, pp. 548–61; C. Gosden, 'Understanding the settlement of Pacific islands in the Pleistocene', in M. A. Smith, M. Spriggs and B. Fankhauser, 1993, op. cit., pp. 131–6.

31 C. F. Fredericksen, M. Spriggs and W. Ambrose, 'Pamwak rockshelter: a Pleistocene site on Manus Island, Papua New Guinea', in M. A. Smith, M. Spriggs and B. Fankhauser, 1993, op. cit., pp. 144–52.

32 T. H. Loy, M. Spriggs and S. Wickler, 'Direct evidence for human use of plants 28,000 years ago: starch residues on stone artefacts from the northern Solomon Islands'. *Antiquity*, vol. 66(253), 1992, pp. 898–912.

33 J. Allen, C. Gosden and J. P. White, 1989, op. cit.

CHAPTER THREE
Life and Death at Lake Mungo

1 J. M. Bowler, G. S. Hope, J. N. Jennings, G. Singh and D. Walker, 'Late Quaternary climates of Australia and New Guinea'. *Quaternary Research*, vol. 6, 1976, pp. 359–94; J. M. Bowler, 'Water and sand: climate in ancient Australia', in *Australians: A Historical Library. Australians to 1788* (eds D. J. Mulvaney and J. P. White). 1988, pp. 24–45; J. M. Bowler and R. J. Wasson, 'Glacial age environments of inland Australia', in *Late Cainozoic Palaeoclimates of the Southern Hemisphere* (ed. J. C. Vogel). 1985; J. M. Bowler in *Proceedings of the First CLIMANZ Conference, 1981* (eds J. Chappell and A. Grinrod). 1983; J. M. Bowler, 'Quaternary chronology and palaeohydrology in the evolution of mallee landscapes', in *Aeolian Landscapes in the Semi-arid Zone of South-eastern Australia* (eds R. R. Storrier and M. E. Stannard). 1980. pp. 17–36.

2 J. M. Bowler, R. Jones, H. R. Allen and A. G. Thorne, 'Pleistocene human remains from Australia: a living site and human cremation from Lake Mungo'. *World Archaeology*, vol. 2, 1970, pp. 39–60; J. M. Bowler, A. G. Thorne and H. Polach, 'Pleistocene Man in Australia: age and significance of the Mungo skeleton'. *Nature*, vol. 240, 1972, pp. 48–50; S. G. Webb, *The Willandra Lakes Hominids.* Canberra, Department of Prehistory, Research School of Pacific Studies, Australian National University, 1989 (p. 7).

3 J. M. Bowler and A. G. Thorne, 'Human remains from Lake Mungo', in R. L. Kirk and A. G. Thorne, 1976, op. cit., pp. 127–38.

4 W. Shawcross, quoted in E. Stokes, 'Skeletons in the sand'. *Geo*, vol. 3(3), 1981, pp. 27–49.

5 S. G. Webb, 1989, op. cit., p. 67.

6 ibid., p. 54–7.

7 ibid., pp. 66–7, plate 32.

8 A. H. Campbell, 'Tooth avulsion in Victorian Aboriginal skulls'. *Archaeology in Oceania*, vol. 16, 1981, pp. 116–18; A. H. Campbell and M. Prokopec, 'Antiquity of tooth avulsion in Australia'. *Artefact*, vol. 8(3–4), 1984, pp. 3–9.

9 I. Davidson and W. Noble, 1992, op. cit., Table 1.

10 Australian Heritage Commission, *Nomination of the Willandra Lakes Region for Inclusion in the World Heritage List.* Canberra, Australian Heritage Commission, 1981.

11 D. J. Mulvaney, *The Prehistory of Australia.* Ringwood, Penguin, 1975; F. W. Shawcross and M. Kaye, 'Australian archaeology: implications of current interdisciplinary research'. *Interdisciplinary Science Reviews*, vol. 5, 1980, pp. 112–28.

12 M. Barbetti, 'Evidence of a geomagnetic excursion 30 000 BP'. *Nature*, vol. 239, 1972, pp. 327–30.

13 W. T. Bell, 'Thermoluminescence dates for the Lake Mungo Aboriginal fireplaces and the implications for radiocarbon dating'. *Archaeometry*, vol. 33(1), 1991, pp. 43–50; J. Hope, 'Pleistocene archaeological sites in the central Murray–Darling basin', in M. A. Smith, M. Spriggs and B. Fankhauser, 1993, op. cit., pp. 183–96.

14 C. Webb, Use-wear on bone tools: an experimental program and three case-studies from south-east Australia, B.A. Hons thesis, Melbourne, La Trobe University, 1987.

15 P. Mellars, personal communication, Cambridge, 1992.

16 S. Bowdler, 1992, op. cit., pp. 576–7; P. Bellwood, *Man's Conquest of the Pacific. The Prehistory of Southeast Asia and Oceania.* Sydney, Collins, 1978, pp. 53–80.

17 M. Smith, 'Central Australian seed grinding implements and Pleistocene grindstones', in *Archaeology with Ethnography: An Australian Perspective* (eds B. Meehan and R. Jones). 1988, pp. 94–108. (Includes references to M. Smith's 1985 and 1986 papers.)

18 H. Allen, 'Environmental history in southwestern New South Wales during the Pleistocene', in *The World at 18,000 BP: Low Latitudes* (eds C. Gamble and O. Soffer). 1990, vol. 2, pp. 296–321; J. Balme, 'The antiquity of grinding stones in semi-arid western New South Wales'. *Australian Archaeology*, vol. 32, 1991, pp. 3–9.

19 J. Balme, 'Prehistoric fishing in the lower Darling, western New South Wales', in *Animals and Archaeology. Volume 2: Shell Middens, Fishes and Birds* (eds C. Grigson and J. Clutton-Brock). 1983, pp. 19–32; K. C. Kefous, We have a fish with ears, and wonder if it is valuable?, B.A. Hons thesis, Canberra, Australian National University, 1977.

20 H. Johnston, 'Pleistocene shell middens of the Willandra Lakes', in M. A. Smith, M. Spriggs and B. Fankhauser, 1993, op. cit., pp. 196–213.

21 T. H. Loy, 'Getting blood from a stone'. *Australian Natural History*, vol. 23(6), 1990, pp. 470–9.

22 K. Page, T. Dare-Edwards, A. Thorne, S. Webb and D. Price, 'Pleistocene human occupation site at Lake Urana, New South Wales.' *Australian Archaeology*, vol. 38, 1994, pp. 38–44.

Australoids

1 N. W. G. Macintosh, 'Recent discoveries of early Australian Man'. *Annals of the Australian College of Dental Surgeons*, vol. 1, 1967, pp. 104–26; N. W. G. Macintosh and S. L. Larnach, 'The persistence of *Homo erectus* traits in Australian Aboriginal crania'. *Archaeology and Physical Anthropology in Oceania*, vol. 7(1), 1972, pp. 1–7.

2 N. W. G. Macintosh, 'The Cohuna cranium: teeth and palate'. *Oceania*, vol. 23(2), 1952, pp. 95–105; D. Brothwell, 'Possible evidence of a cultural practice affecting head growth in some Late Pleistocene East Asian and Australian Populations'. *Journal of Archaeological Science*, vol. 2, 1975, pp. 75–7; P. Brown, 'Artificial cranial deformation: a component in the variation in Pleistocene Australian Aboriginal crania'. *Archaeology in Oceania*, vol. 16(3), 1987, pp. 156–67.

3 E. D. Gill, 'Provenance and age of the Keilor cranium — oldest known human skeletal remains in Australia'. *Current Anthropology*, vol. 7, 1966, p. 584; N. W. G. Macintosh and S. L. Larnach, 'Aboriginal affinities looked at in world context', in R. L. Kirk and A. G. Thorne, 1976, op. cit., pp. 113–26; P. Brown, 'A flawed vision: sex and robusticity on King Island'. *Australian Archaeology*, vol. 38, 1994, pp. 1–6.

4 A. Gallus, 'Excavations at Keilor'. *Artefact*, vol. 24, 1971, pp. 1–12; vol. 27, 1972, pp. 9–155; A. Gallus, 'The Middle and Early Upper Pleistocene stone industries at the Dry Creek archaeological sites near Keilor, Australia'. *Artefact*, vol. 1(2), 1976, pp. 75–108.

5 J. M. Bowler, 'Recent developments in reconstructing Late Quaternary environments in Australia', in R. L. Kirk and A. G. Thorne, 1976, op. cit., pp. 55–77.

6 A. G. Thorne and P. G. Macumber, 'Discoveries of Late Pleistocene Man at Kow Swamp, Australia'. *Nature*, vol. 238, (5363), 1972, pp. 316–19; A. G. Thorne, 'The longest link: human evolution in Southeast Asia and the settlement of Australia', in *Indonesia: Australian Perspectives* (ed. J. Fox et al.). Canberra, Australian National University, 1980, pp. 35–43.

7 N. W. G. Macintosh, 'Analysis of an Aboriginal skeleton and a pierced tooth necklace from Lake Nitchie, Australia'. *Anthropologie*, vol. 9(1), 1971, pp. 49–62.

8 P. Brown, 'Pleistocene homogeneity and Holocene size reduction: the Australian human skeletal evidence'. *Archaeology in Oceania*, vol. 22(2), 1987, pp. 41–66.

9 A. L. Freedman and M. Lofgren, 'Human skeletal remains from Cossack, Western Australia'. *Journal of Human Evolution*, vol. 8(2), 1979, pp. 283–99.

10 Quoted in P. Brown, 'Artificial cranial deformation: a component in the variation in Pleistocene Australian Aboriginal crania'. *Archaeology in Oceania*, vol. 16(3), 1987, pp. 156–67.

11 L. Freedman and M. Lofgren, 'Human skeletal remains from Lake Tandou, New South Wales'. *Archaeology in Oceania*, vol. 18(2), 1983, pp. 98–105.

12 R. Sim and A. Thorne, 'Pleistocene human remains from King Island, Southeastern Australia'. *Australian Archaeology*, vol. 31, 1990, pp. 44–51; R. Sim, 'Prehistoric sites on King Island in the Bass Strait: results of an archaeological survey'. *Australian Archaeology*, vol. 31, 1990, pp. 34–43.

13 P. Brown, 1994, op. cit.; A. Thorne and R. Sim, 'The gracile male skeleton from late Pleistocene King Island, Australia.' *Australian Archaeology*, vol. 38, 1994, pp. 8–10.

14 P. Brown, *Coobool Creek. A Morphological and Metrical Analysis of the Crania, Mandibles and Dentitions of a Prehistoric Australian Human Population*. Terra Australis 13, Canberra, Department of Prehistory, Australian National University, 1989.

15 A. Thorne and R. Sim, 1994, op. cit.

CHAPTER FIVE

The Origin of the First Australians

1 A. G. Thorne, personal communication, 1989, 1993; A. G. Thorne, 'Australian human origins — how many sources?'. *American Journal of Physical Anthropology*, vol. 63, 1984, p. 227; A. G. Thorne and M. H. Wolpoff, 'The Multiregional Evolution of Humans'. *Scientific American*, vol. 266(4), 1992, pp. 28–33.

2 J. Head, 'The reliability of radiocarbon ages of materials older than 30 000 years BP'. Paper presented at Australia Day: A Meeting on the Old and the New in Australian Archaeology, 2 March 1992, Cambridge.

3 D. A. Caddie, D. S. Hunter, P. J. Pomery and H. J. Hall, 'The ageing chemist — can electron spin resonance (ESR) help?' in *Archaeometry — Further Australian Studies* (eds W. R. Ambrose and J. M. J. Mummery), Canberra, Australian National University, 1987, pp. 167–76.

4 P. Brown, 'Human origins and antiquity in Australia', in *Encyclopedia of Physical Anthropology* (ed. F. Spencer). New York, Garland Publishing Inc., in press.

5 S. Webb, 'Cranial thickening in an Australian hominid as a possible palaeoepidemiological indicator'. *American Journal of Physical Anthropology*, vol. 82, 1990, pp. 403–12; S. G. Webb, *The Willandra Lakes Hominids*. Canberra, Department of Prehistory, Research School of Pacific Studies, Australian National University, 1989; S. Webb, *Prehistoric Stress in Australian Aborigines. A Palaeopathological Study of a Hunter–Gatherer Population*. Oxford, British Archaeological Reports, International Series No. 490, 1989.

6 T. Brown, S. K. Pinkerton and W. Lambert, 'Thickness of the cranial vault in Australian Aboriginals'. *Archaeology and Physical Anthropology in Oceania*, vol. 14, 1979, pp. 54–71.

7 S. G. Webb, 1989, op. cit.

8 Australian Heritage Commission, 1981, op. cit.

9 S. G. Webb, 1989, op. cit., p. 80.

10 ibid., p. 20; S. L. Larnach and L. Freedman, 'Sex determination of Aboriginal crania from coastal New South Wales'. *Records of the Australian Museum*, vol. 26(1), 1963, pp. 295–308; C. Pardoe, 'Competing paradigms and ancient human remains: the state of the discipline'. *Archaeology in Oceania*, vol. 26(2), 1991, pp. 79–84; C. Pardoe, 'The Pleistocene is still with us: analytical constraints and possibilities for the study of ancient human remains in archaeology', in M. A. Smith, M. Spriggs and B. Fankhauser, 1993, op. cit., pp. 81–94.

11 S. G. Webb, 1989, op. cit., pp. 78–9, figures 2, 16 and 17; P. Clark, Report on a plan of management for the Willandra Lakes region, western New South Wales. Unpublished report, Sydney, NSW National Parks & Wildlife Service, 1987.

12 P. J. Habgood, 1986, op. cit.

13 J. B. Birdsell, 1977, op. cit.

14 S. L. Larnach, 'The origin of the Australian Aboriginal'. *Archaeology and Physical Anthropology in Oceania*, vol. 9(3), 1974, pp. 206–13.

15 R. Sim and A. Thorne, 1990, op. cit.; A. G. Wallace and G. A. Doran, 'Early Man in Tasmania: new skeletal evidence', in R. L. Kirk and A. G. Thorne, 1976, op. cit., pp. 173–82.

16 R. T. Simmons, 'The biological origin of Australian Aboriginals', in R. L. Kirk and A. G. Thorne, 1976, op. cit., pp. 307–28.

17 R. L. Kirk, 'Physiological, demographic and genetic adaptation of Australian Aboriginals', in *Ecological Biogeography of Australia* (ed. A. Keast). The Hague, W. Junk, 1981, pp. 1801–15; R. L. Kirk, *Aboriginal Man Adapting*. Melbourne, OUP, 1983.

18 A. C. Wilson and R. L. Cann, 'The Recent African Genesis of Humans'. *Scientific American*, vol. 266(4), 1992, pp. 22–7; R. C. Cann, M. Stoneking and A. C. Wilson, 'Mitochondrial DNA and human evolution'. *Nature*, vol. 325, 1 January 1987, pp. 31–6.

19 A. C. Wilson and R. L. Cann, 1992, op. cit., p. 23.

20 R. L. Kirk, 'The human biology of the original Australians'. *Search*, vol. 18, 1987, pp. 220–2.

21 A. G. Thorne and M. H. Wolpoff, 'The multiregional evolution of humans'. *Scientific American*, vol. 266(4), 1992, pp. 28–33.

22 ibid.; C. B. Stringer and P. Andrews, 'Genetic and fossil evidence for the origin of modern humans'. *Science*, vol. 239, 1988, pp. 1263–8.

23 P. Bellwood, 'Southeast Asia before history', in *The Cambridge History of Southeast Asia* (ed. N. Tarling). Cambridge University Press, 1992a, pp. 58–136. (Quotation is from p. 70.)

24 For detailed information and further references on the Asian hominids see A. G. Thorne, 1980, op. cit.; T. Jacob, in R. L. Kirk and A. G. Thorne, 1976, op. cit., pp. 81–94; P. Bellwood, 1992a, op. cit.; P. Bellwood, 'Recent human evolution in East Asia and Australasia'. *Transactions of the Royal Philosophical Society London B*, vol. 337, 1992b, pp. 235–42; P. Bellwood, *Man's Conquest of the Pacific. The Prehistory of Southeast Asia and Oceania*. Sydney, Collins, 1978; P. Bellwood, *Prehistory of the Indo-Malaysian Archipelago*. Sydney, Academic Press, 1985; C. C. Swisher III, G. H. Curtis, T. Jacob, A. G. Getty, A. Suprijo, Widiasmoro, 'Age of the earliest known hominids in Java, Indonesia'. *Science*, vol. 263, 1994, pp. 118–21.

25 N. W. G. Macintosh, 'The physical aspect of man in Australia', in *Aboriginal Man in Australia* (eds R. M. and C. H. Berndt), Sydney, Angus & Robertson, 1965.

26 A. G. Thorne, 1992, op. cit., pp. 30–1.

27 P. J. Habgood, 'The origin of anatomically modern humans in Australia', in *The Human Revolution: Behavioural and Biological Perspectives on the Origins of Modern Humans* (eds P. Mellars and C. Stringer). Edinburgh University Press, 1989, pp. 245–73; P. J. Habgood, 'The origin of the Australians: a multivariate approach'. *Archaeology in Oceania*, vol. 21(2), 1986, pp. 130–7.

28 C. Tiemel, Y. Quan and W. En, 'Antiquity of *Homo sapiens* in China'. *Nature*, vol. 368, 3 March 1994, pp. 55–6.

29 M. H. Wolpoff, *Paleoanthropology*. New York, A. A. Knopf, 1980.

30 S. G. Webb, 1989, op. cit., pp. 76–7.

31 D. Brothwell, 'Upper Pleistocene human skull from Niah Caves, Sarawak'. *Sarawak Museum Journal*, vol. 9, 1960, pp. 323–49.

The Peopling of Australia

1 J. P. White and D. J. Mulvaney, 'How many people?', in *Australians to 1788*
(eds D. J. Mulvaney and J. P. White). Sydney, Fairfax, Syme and Weldon, 1987, pp. 115–17;
N. G. Butlin, *Our Original Aggression: Aboriginal Population of Southeastern Australia 1788–1850*.
Sydney, George Allen and Unwin, 1983.

2 J. B. Birdsell, 'Some population problems involving Pleistocene man'. *Cold Spring Harbor
Symposia on Quantitative Biology*, vol. 22, 1957, pp. 47–69; J. B. Birdsell, 'The recalibration of a
paradigm for the first peopling of Greater Australia', in J. Allen, J. Golson and R. Jones, 1977,
op. cit., pp. 113–67.

3 S. Bowdler, 'The coastal colonization of Australia', in J. Allen, J. Golson and R. Jones, 1977,
op. cit., pp. 205–46.

4 D. R. Horton, 'Water and woodland: the peopling of Australia'. *Australian Institute of
Aboriginal Studies Newsletter*, vol. 16, 1981, pp. 21–7; D. R. Horton, 'Seasons of repose:
environment and culture in the late Pleistocene of Australia', in *The Pleistocene Perspective*,
vol. 2, The World Archaeological Congress. London, Allen and Unwin, 1986.

5 N. B. Tindale, 'Prehistory of the Aborigines: some interesting considerations', in A. Keast,
1981, op. cit., pp. 1763–97.

6 M. A. Smith, 'Pleistocene occupation in arid Central Australia'. *Nature*, vol. 328, 1987,
pp. 710–11.

7 S. Bowdler, 'Peopling Australasia: the "Coastal Colonization" Hypothesis Re-examined',
in *The Emergence of Modern Humans* (ed. P. Mellars). Edinburgh University Press, 1990,
pp. 327–43.

8 S. Bowdler, '*Homo sapiens* in Southeast Asia and the Antipodes: archaeological versus
biological interpretations', in *The Evolution and Dispersal of Modern Humans in Asia*
(eds T. Akazawa, K. Aoki and T. Kimura). Tokyo, Hokusen-sha, 1992.

9 S. Bowdler, 'Sunda and Sahul: a 30KYR culture area?', in M. A. Smith, M. Spriggs and
B. Fankhauser, 1993, op. cit., pp. 60–70; J. Allen, 'When did humans first colonize Australia?'.
Search, vol. 20(5), 1989, pp. 149–54; R. Jones, 'A continental reconnaissance: some
observations concerning the discovery of the Pleistocene archaeology of Australia',
in M. Spriggs et al., 1993, op. cit., pp. 97–122.

10 R. G. Roberts, R. Jones and M. A. Smith, 'Thermoluminescence dating of a 50 000-year-old
human occupation site in northern Australia'. *Nature*, vol. 345 (6271), 1990a, pp. 153–56; S.
Bowdler, '50,000-year-old site in Australia — is it really that old?'. *Australian Archaeology*,
vol. 31, 1990, p. 93; R. G. Roberts, R. Jones and M. A. Smith, 'Early dates at Malakunanja II.
A reply to Bowdler'. *Australian Archaeology*, vol. 31, 1990b, pp. 94–6; S. Bowdler, 'Some sort of
dates at Malakunanja II: A reply to Roberts et al.'. *Australian Archaeology*, vol. 32, 1991,
pp. 50–1; P. Hiscock, 'How old are the artefacts in Malakunanja II?'. *Archaeology in Oceania*,
vol. 25, 1990, pp. 122–4; R. G. Roberts, R. Jones and M. A. Smith, 'Stratigraphy and statistics
at Malakunanja II: reply to Hiscock'. *Archaeology in Oceania*, vol. 25, 1990c, pp.125–9.

11 R. Jones, 1993, op. cit., pp. 113–14; J. Head, 'The reliability of radiocarbon ages of materials
older than 30 000 years BP'. Abstract of paper presented at Australia Day. A Meeting on the
Old and the New in Australian Archaeology, 2 March 1992, Cambridge; R. Jones,
'The radiocarbon bottleneck: fact or illusion?'. 1992, op.cit.; J. Head, personal
communication, 1992, R. G. Roberts, R. Jones and M. A. Smith 1990c, op. cit.;
J. Chappell, 'Radiocarbon dating uncertainties and their effects on studies of the past',
in *Archaeometry: An Australian Perspective* (eds W. Ambrose and P. Duerden). Canberra,
Australian National University Press, 1982.

12 R. G. Roberts and N. Spooner, 'Luminescence dating of early occupation sites in northern
Australia'. Abstract of paper presented at Australia Day. A Meeting on the Old and the New
in Australian Archaeology, 2 March 1992, Cambridge; R. G. Roberts, R. Jones and M. A.
Smith, 1990a and 1990c, op. cit.

13 R. G. Roberts, R. Jones and M. A. Smith, 1990a, op. cit.; R. Jones, 1992, op. cit.; R. Jones,
1993, op. cit.

14 C. White, 'Early stone axes in Arnhem Land'. *Antiquity*, vol. 41, 1967, pp. 149–52; C. White,
'Man and environment in northwest Arnhem Land', in *Aboriginal Man and Environment in
Australia* (eds D. J. Mulvaney and J. Golson). Canberra, Australian National University Press,
1971, pp. 141–57; C. Schrire, 'Ethno-archaeological models and subsistence behaviour in
Arnhem Land', in *Models in Archaeology* (ed. D. L. Clarke). London, Methuen, 1972, pp. 653–
70; C. Schrire, *The Alligator Rivers: Prehistory and Ecology in Western Arnhem Land. Terra
Australis* 7. Canberra, Department of Prehistory, Australian National University, 1982; R.
Jones (ed.), *Archaeological Research in Kakadu National Park*. Special Publication 13, Canberra,
Australian National Parks and Wildlife Service, 1985; R. Jones and I. Johnson, 'Deaf Adder

Gorge: Lindner Site, Nauwalabila I', in *Archaeological Research in Kakadu National Park*. 1985, pp.165–227; J. Kamminga and H. R. Allen, *Report of the Archaeological Survey, Alligator Rivers Environmental Fact-Finding Study*. Darwin, Australian Government, 1973.

15 Review and references are in M. J. Morwood and P. J. Trezise, 'Edge-ground axes in Pleistocene Australia: new evidence from S. E. Cape York Peninsula'. *Queensland Archaeological Research*, vol. 6, 1989, pp. 77–90. See also P. Bellwood, 1985, op. cit.

16 F. P. Dickson, *Australian Stone Hatchets*. London, Academic Press, 1981.

17 J. Kamminga and H. R. Allen, 1973, op. cit., pp. 45–52.

CHAPTER SEVEN

Early Sites in Tropical and Arid Australia

1 B. David, 'Nurrabullgin Cave: preliminary results from a pre–37,000 year old rockshelter, North Queensland'. *Archaeology in Oceania*, vol. 28(1), 1993, pp. 50–4.

2 G. Singh, A. P. Kershaw and R. L. Clark, 'Quaternary vegetation and fire history in Australia', in *Fire and the Australian Biota* (eds A. M. Gill, Groves and Noble). Canberra, Australian Academy of Science, 1981, pp. 23–54; A. P. Kershaw, 'Climatic change and Aboriginal burning in northeast Australia during the last two glacial/interglacial cycles'. *Nature*, vol. 322(6074), 1986, pp. 47–9.

3 B. David, 'Fern Cave, rock art and social formations: rock art regionalisation and demographic models in southeastern Cape York Peninsula'. *Archaeology in Oceania*, vol. 26(2), 1991, pp. 41–57.

4 J. B. Campbell, 'New radiocarbon results for North Queensland prehistory'. *Australian Archaeology*, vol. 14, 1982, pp. 62–6.

5 M. J. Morwood and P. J. Trezise, 'Edge-ground axes in Pleistocene Greater Australia: new evidence from S.E. Cape York Peninsula'. *Queensland Archaeological Research*, vol. 6, 1989, pp. 77–90.

6 R. V. S. Wright, 'Prehistory in the Cape York Peninsula', in D. J. Mulvaney and J. Golson, 1971, op. cit., pp. 133–40; A. Rosenfeld, *Early Man in North Queensland*. Canberra, Australian National University, 1982.

7 M. J. Morwood and P. J. Trezise, 1989, op. cit., pp. 80–4.

8 P. Hiscock and P. J. Hughes, 'Backed blades in northern Australia: evidence from northwest Queensland'. *Australian Archaeology*, vol. 10, 1980, pp. 86–95; P. J. Hughes, 'Colless Creek rockshelter archaeological site', in *Proceedings of the Climanz Workshop* (eds J. Bowler, J. Chappell and G. Hope). Canberra, Australian Academy of Science, 1983.

9 C. E. Dortch, 'Archaeological work in the Ord Reservoir area, east Kimberley'. *Australian Institute of Aboriginal Studies Newsletter*, vol. 3(4), 1972, pp. 13–18; C. E. Dortch, 'Early and late stone industrial phases in Western Australia', in *Stone Tools as Cultural Markers* (ed. R. V. S. Wright). Canberra, Australian Institute of Aboriginal Studies, 1977, pp. 104–32.

10 S. O'Connor, 'New radiocarbon dates from Koolan Island, west Kimberley, W.A.'. *Australian Archaeology*, vol. 28, 1989, pp. 92–104; S. Bowdler, 'The Silver Dollar site, Shark Bay: an interim report'. *Australian Aboriginal Studies*, no. 2, 1990b, pp. 60–3.

11 K. Morse, 'Mandu Mandu Creek rockshelter: Pleistocene human coastal occupation of North West Cape, Western Australia'. *Archaeology in Oceania*, vol. 23(3), 1988, pp. 81–8; K. Morse, 'Shell beads from Mandu Mandu Creek rock-shelter, Cape Range peninsula, Western Australia, dated before 30,000 BP'. *Antiquity*, vol. 67, 1993, pp. 877–83; K. Morse, 'New radiocarbon dates for North West Cape, Western Australia: a preliminary report', in M. A. Smith, M. Spriggs and B. Fankhauser, 1993, op. cit., pp. 155–63; S. Bowdler, '*Homo sapiens* in Southeast Asia and the Antipodes: archaeological versus biological interpretations', in T. Akazawa, K. Aoki and T. Kimura, 1992, op. cit., pp. 559–89.

12 P. Veth, 'Before the blast: the prehistory of the Monte Bello Islands, Northwest Australia', in *Proceedings of the Australian Archaeological Association Conference, Darwin, December 1993*. Canberra, North Australia Research Unit, Australian National University, in press.

13 S. Brown, *Towards a Prehistory of the Hamersley Plateau, North-west Australia*. Occasional Papers in Prehistory 6, Canberra, Australian National University, 1987.

14 P. Veth, 'Islands in the interior: a model for the colonization of Australia's arid zone'. *Archaeology in Oceania*, vol. 24(3), 1989, pp. 81–92.

15 S. Bowdler, 'Before Dirk Hartog: prehistoric archaeological research in Shark Bay, Western Australia'. *Australian Archaeology*, vol. 30, 1990a, pp. 46–57.

16 S. Bowdler, ibid.; 1990b, op. cit.

17 M. A. Smith, 'The case for a resident human population in the Central Australian Ranges during full glacial aridity'. *Archaeology in Oceania*, vol. 24(3), 1989, pp. 93–105; M. A. Smith, 'Pleistocene occupation in arid Australia'. *Nature*, vol. 328, 1987, pp. 710–11; M. A. Smith, personal communication, 1994.

18 H. A. Martin, 'Palynology and historical ecology of some cave excavations in the Australian Nullarbor'. *Australian Journal of Botany*, vol. 21, 1973, pp. 283–316; R. Wright (ed.), *Archaeology of the Gallus Site, Koonalda Cave*. Canberra, Australian Institute of Aboriginal Studies, 1971.

19 J. Head, R. Jones, B. Roberts, N. Spooner, personal communication, March 1992.

20 H. A. Martin, 1973, op. cit.

21 P. Veth, 1989, op. cit.; P. Veth, *Islands in the Interior: Dynamics of Prehistoric Adaptations within the Arid Zone of Australia*. Michigan, Ann Arbor, 1993; M. A. Smith, 1989, op. cit.; M. A. Smith, 'Biogeography, human ecology and prehistory in the sandridge deserts'. *Australian Archaeology*, vol. 37, 1993, pp. 35–49.

22 I. Davidson, S. A. Sutton and S. J. Gale, 'The human occupation of Cuckadoo I rockshelter, northwest central Queensland', in M. A. Smith, M. Spriggs and B. Fankhauser, 1993, op. cit., pp. 164–72.

23 R. J. Wasson, 'The Cainozoic history of the Strzlecki and Simpson dunefields (Australia), and the origin of the desert dunes'. *Zeitschrift für Geomorphologie*, vol. 45, 1983, pp. 85–115; M. A. Smith, E. Williams and R. J. Wasson, 'The archaeology of the JSN site: some implications for the dynamics of human occupation in the Strzelecki desert during the last Pleistocene'. *Records of the South Australian Museum*, vol. 25, 1991, pp. 175–92.

24 R. J. Lampert and P. J. Hughes, 'Early human occupation of the Flinders Ranges'. *Records of the South Australian Museum*, vol. 22, 1988, pp. 139–68; P. Veth, G. Hamm and R. J. Lampert, 'The archaeological significance of the lower Cooper Creek'. *Records of the South Australian Museum*, vol. 24, 1990, pp. 43–66.

25 S. O'Connor, P. Veth and N. Hubbard, 'Changing interpretations of postglacial human subsistence and demography in Sahul', in M. A. Smith, M. Spriggs and B. Fankhauser, 1993, op. cit., pp. 95–105; A. Ross et al. in *The Naive Lands. Prehistory and Environmental Change in Australia and the Southwest Pacific* (ed. J. Dodson). 1992.

CHAPTER EIGHT
Early Sites in Temperate Australia

1 *West Australian*, 2 December 1981; *Perth Daily News*, 1 December 1981.

2 R. H. Pearce and M. Barbetti, 'A 38000-year-old site at Upper Swan, W.A'. *Archaeology in Oceania*, vol. 16(3), 1981, pp. 173–8. For Kalgan Hall, which has an unbroken artefact sequence from the present to more than 18 000 BP, see W. C. Ferguson, A mid-Holocene depopulation of the Australian Southwest. Ph.D. thesis, Canberra, Australian National University, 1985.

3 C. E. Dortch, *Devil's Lair: A Study in Prehistory*. Perth, Western Australian Museum, 1984; C. E. Dortch, 'Devil's Lair, an example of prolonged cave use in southwestern Australia'. *World Archaeology*, vol. 10(3), 1979, pp. 258–79; J. Balme, D. Merrilees and J. K. Porter, 'Late Quaternary mammal remains, spanning about 30 000 years, from excavations in Devil's Lair, W.A.'. *Journal of the Royal Society of W.A.*, vol. 61, 1978, pp. 33–65; J. Balme, 'An apparent association of artifacts and extinct fauna at Devil's Lair, Western Australia'. *Artefact*, vol. 3(3), 1978, pp. 111–16; J. Balme, 'An analysis of charred bone from Devil's Lair, Western Australia'. *Archaeology in Oceania*, vol. 15, 1980, pp. 81–5.

4 S. Bowdler, 'Sunda and Sahul: A 30KYR Culture Area?', in M. A. Smith, M. Spriggs and B. Fankhauser, 1993, op. cit., pp. 60–70.

5 C. E. Dortch, 'Australia's oldest known ornaments'. *Antiquity*, vol. 53, 1979, pp. 39–43.

6 C. E. Dortch, 'A possible pendant of marl from Devil's Lair, Western Australia'. *Records of the W.A. Museum*, vol. 8(3), 1980, pp. 401–3.

7 C. E. Dortch, 'Two engraved stone plaques of late Pleistocene age from Devil's Lair, Western Australia'. *Archaeology and Physical Anthropology in Oceania*, vol. 11 (I), 1976, pp. 32–44.

8 R. Bednarik, 'The discrimination of rock markings'. *Rock Art Research*, vol. 11, 1994, pp. 23–44.

9 D. J. Mulvaney and E. B. Joyce, 'Archaeological and geomorphological investigations on Mt Moffatt Station, Queensland, Australia'. *Proceedings of the Prehistoric Society*, vol. 31, 1965, pp. 147–212.

10 R. J. Lampert, *Burrill Lake and Currarong. Terra Australis 1*. Canberra, Department of Prehistory, Australian National University, 1971; 'Coastal Aborigines of southeastern Australia', in D. J. Mulvaney and J. Golson, 1971, op. cit., pp. 14–32.

11 S. Bowdler, 'Hook, line and dillybag; an interpretation of an Australian coastal shell midden'. *Mankind*, vol. 10(4), 1976, pp. 248–58.

12 R. Neal and E. Stock, 'Pleistocene occupation in the south-east Queensland coastal region'. *Nature*, vol. 323(6089), 1986, pp. 618–21.

13 G. C. Nanson, R. W. Young and E. D. Stockton, 'Chronology and palaeoenvironment of the Cranebrook Terrace (near Sydney) containing artefacts more than 40 000 years old'. *Archaeology in Oceania*, vol. 22(2), 1987, pp. 72–8.

14 E. D. Stockton and W. N. Holland, 'Cultural sites and their environment in the Blue Mountains'. *Archaeology and Physical Anthropology in Oceania*, vol. 9(1), 1974, pp. 36–65; J. L. Kohen, E. D. Stockton and M. A. J. Williams, 'Shaws Creek KII rockshelter: a prehistoric occupation site in the Blue Mountains piedmont, eastern New South Wales'. *Archaeology in Oceania*, vol. 19, 1984, pp. 57–73.

15 G. Singh, N. D. Opdyke and J. M. Bowler, 'Late Cainozoic stratigraphy, palaeomagnetic chronology and vegetational history from Lake George, N.S.W.' *Journal of the Geological Society of Australia*, vol. 28(4), 1981, pp. 435–52; G. Singh, A. P. Kershaw and R. Clark, 'Quaternary vegetation and fire history in Australia', in *Fire and the Australian Biota* (eds A. M. Gill, Groves and W. Noble), 1981, op. cit., pp. 23–54; R. Wright, 'How old is Zone F at Lake George?'. *Archaeology in Oceania*, vol. 21, 1986, pp. 138–9.

16 R. Jones, 1989, op. cit., p. 758.

17 J. Flood, B. David, J. Magee and B. English, 'Birrigai: a Pleistocene site in the south eastern highlands'. *Archaeology in Oceania*, vol. 22, 1987, pp. 9–26.

18 R. Jones, 1989, op. cit., p. 758.

CHAPTER NINE

An Ice Age Walk to Tasmania

1 S. Bowdler, 'Hunter Hill, Hunter Island'. *Terra Australis* 8, Canberra, Prehistory Department, Australian National University, 1984.

2 *Sydney Morning Herald* and the *Age*, 21 January 1981, 19 March 1981; *Canberra Times*, 17 February 1981; *Australian*, 19 March 1981.

3 R. Jones, 'The extreme climatic place?'. *Hemisphere*, vol. 26(1), 1981, pp. 54–9.

4 K. Kiernan, R. Jones and D. Ranson, 'New evidence from Fraser Cave for glacial age man in southwest Tasmania'. *Nature*, vol. 301, 1983, pp. 28–32; R. Jones 'Tasmania's ice age hunters'. *Australian Geographic*, vol. 8, 1987, pp. 26–45.

5 R. Jones, 1987, op. cit., p. 43; T. H. Loy, personal communication, 1994; T. H. Loy, J. Kamminga and R. Jones, in preparation.

6 R. Jones, 'From Kakadu to Kutikina: the southern continent at 18,000 years ago', in *The World at 18,000 BP, Low Latitudes* (ed. C. Gamble). London, Unwin Hyman, 1990, pp. 264–95 (pp. 278–84 on Kutikina).

7 ibid., pp. 280–1; T. H. Loy, personal communication, quoted in R. F. Cosgrove, The illusion of riches: issues of scale, resolution and explanation of Pleistocene human behaviour. Ph.D. thesis, La Trobe University, 1991; R. L. K. Fullager, Use-wear and residues on stone tools: functional analysis and its application to two southeastern Australian archaeological assemblages. Ph.D. thesis, La Trobe University, 1991, p. 21.

8 Colour plate in R. Jones, 1987, op. cit., p. 84.

9 R. Cosgrove, J. Allen and B. Marshall, 'Palaeo-ecology and Pleistocene human occupation in south central Tasmania'. *Antiquity*, vol. 64, 1990, pp. 59–78.

10 S. Harris, D. Ranson and S. Brown, 'Maxwell River archaeological survey 1986'. *Australian Archaeology*, vol. 27, 1988, pp. 89–97.

11 S. Brown, 'Art and Tasmanian prehistory: evidence for changing cultural traditions in a changing environment', in *Rock Art and Prehistory* (eds P. Bahn and A. Rosenfeld). Oxford, Oxbow, 1991, pp. 96–108; A. McGowan, R. Shreeve, H. Brolsma and C. Hughes, 'Photogrammetric recording of Pleistocene cave paintings in southwest Tasmania', in M. A. Smith, M. Spriggs and B. Fankhauser, 1993, op. cit, pp. 225–32.

12 R. Jones, R. Cosgrove, J. Allen, S. Cane, K. Kiernan, S. Webb, T. Loy, D. West and E. Stadler, 'An archaeological reconnaissance of karst caves within the Southern Forests region of Tasmania, September 1987'. *Australian Archaeology*, vol. 26, 1988, pp. 1–23; R. Cosgrove and R. Jones, 'Judds Cavern: a subterranean Aboriginal painting site, southern Tasmania'. *Rock Art Research*, vol. 6(2), 1989, pp. 96–104; S. Brown, 1991, op. cit.; A. McGowan et al., 1993, op. cit.

13 T. H. Loy, 'Recent advances in blood residue analysis', in *Archaeometry: Further Australasian Studies* (eds W. R. Ambrose and J. M. Mummery). 1987, pp. 57–65; T. H. Loy, R. Jones, D. E. Nelson, B. Meehan, J. Vogel, J. Southern and R. Cosgrove, 'Accelerator radiocarbon dating of human blood proteins in pigments from late Pleistocene art sites in Australia'. *Antiquity*, vol. 64(242), 1990, pp. 110–16.

14 B. Blain et al., 'The Australian National University–Tasmanian National Parks and Wildlife Service archaeological expedition to the Franklin and Gordon Rivers, 1983: a summary of results'. *Australian Archaeology*, vol. 16, 1983, pp. 71–83.

15 R. Cosgrove, 'Thirty thousand years of human colonization in Tasmania — new Pleistocene dates'. *Science*, vol. 243, 1989, pp. 1706–8; I. McNiven, B. Marshall, J. Allen, N. Stern and R. Cosgrove, 'The Southern Forests archaeological project. an overview', in M. A. Smith, M. Spriggs and B. Fankhauser, 1993, op. cit, pp. 313–24; R. Jones, 'Hunting forebears',

in *The Flow of Culture: Tasmanian Examples* (ed. M. Roe). Canberra, Australian Academy of the Humanities, 1988, pp. 14–49; R. Jones, 1990, op. cit., pp. 275–95.

16 R. Jones et al., 1988, op. cit.

17 P. F. Murray, A. Goede and J. L. Bada, 'Pleistocene human occupation at Beginner's Luck Cave, Florentine Valley, Tasmania'. *Archaeology and Physical Anthropology in Oceania*, vol. 15(3), 1980, pp. 142–52.

18 J. Allen, B. Marshall and D. Ranson, 'A note on excavations at the Maxwell River site, M86/2, Southwest Tasmania'. *Australian Archaeology*, vol. 29, 1989, pp. 3–8.

19 J. Allen, The Southern Forests archaeological project report no. 6: excavations at ACH/84/1 (TASI 2448) 18–23 January 1991. Unpublished report to the Department of Parks, Wildlife and Heritage, Hobart, 1991.

20 J. Allen, R. Cosgrove and S. Brown, 'New archaeological data from the Southern Forest region, Tasmania: a preliminary statement'. *Australian Archaeology*, vol. 27, 1988, pp. 75–88; J. Allen, 'Excavations at Bone Cave, south central Tasmania, January–February, 1989'. *Australian Archaeology*, vol. 28, 1989, pp. 105–6.

21 R. Cosgrove, 1989, op. cit.; R. Cosgrove, 1991, op. cit.

22 ibid.

23 R. Cosgrove, 1991, op. cit., p. 356.

24 N. Stern and B. Marshall, 'Excavations at Mackintosh 90/1 in western Tasmania: a discussion of stratigraphy, chronology and site formation'. *Archaeology in Oceania*, vol. 28, 1993, pp. 8–17.

25 For Warragarra see H. Lourandos, '10,000 years in the Tasmanian highlands'. *Australian Archaeology*, vol. 16, 1983, pp. 39–47. For Parmerpar Meethaner see R. Cosgrove in *Archaeology in Oceania* (forthcoming); R. Cosgrove (pers. comm. 1994); J. Allen (pers. comm. 1993); R. Cosgrove and T. Murray, 'The management of Aboriginal archaeological resources in forested areas'. *Tasmanian Forest Rsearch Council Annual Report*, 1992–3, pp. 31–3.

26 R. Cosgrove et al., 1990, op. cit., p. 70.

27 R. Cosgrove et al., 1990, op. cit., p. 67.

28 C. Webb and J. Allen, 'A functional analysis of Pleistocene bone tools from two sites in Southwest Tasmania'. *Archaeology in Oceania*, vol. 25(2), 1990, pp. 75–8.

29 B. Marshall and R. Cosgrove, 'Tasmanian devil (*Sarcophilus harrisii*) scat-bone: signature criteria and archaeological implications'. *Archaeology in Oceania*, vol. 25, 1990, pp. 102–13.

30 I. McNiven et al., 1993, op. cit., pp. 220–2; R. Cosgrove et al., 1990, op. cit., pp. 69–73.

31 I. Thomas, 'Late Pleistocene environments and Aboriginal settlement patterns in Tasmania'. *Australian Archaeology*, vol. 36, 1993, pp. 1–11; R. Cosgrove, J. Allen and B. Marshall, 'Late Pleistocene human occupation in Tasmania'. *Australian Archaeology*, vol. 38, 1994, pp. 28–34.

32 J. H. Cann, A. P. Belperio, V. A. Gostin and C. V. Murray-Wallace, 'Sea-level history, 45 000 to 30 000 yr B.P., inferred from Benthic Foraminifera, Gulf St Vincent, South Australia'. *Quaternary Research*, vol. 29, 1988, pp. 153–75.

33 S. Bowdler, 'Hunters in the highlands: Aboriginal adaptations in the eastern Australian uplands'. *Archaeology in Oceania*, vol. 216, 1981, pp. 99–111.

34 R. Cosgrove et al., 1990, op. cit., p. 74.

35 R. Cosgrove, 1991, op. cit., p. xvi.

36 R. Cosgrove et al., 1990, op. cit., p. 59.

37 R. Jones, 'Philosophical time travellers'. *Antiquity*, vol. 66(252), 1992, pp. 744–57 (on p. 255).

CHAPTER TEN

Karta: Island of the Dead

1 N. B. Tindale and B. G. Maegraith, 'Traces of an extinct Aboriginal population on Kangaroo Island'. *Records of the S.A. Museum*, vol. 4, 1931, pp. 275–89.

2 H. M. Hale and N. B. Tindale, 'Notes on some human remains in the Lower Murray Valley, South Australia'. *Records of the S.A. Museum*, vol. 4, 1930, pp. 145–218.

3 K. L. Parker, *Australian Legendary Tales*. Bodley Head, 1978.

4 R. M. W. Dixon, *The Djirbal Language of North Queensland*. Cambridge, Cambridge University Press, 1972.

5 R. J. Lampert, *The Great Kartan Mystery. Terra Australis* 5, Canberra, Department of Prehistory, Australian National University, 1981.

6 J. H. Hope, R. J. Lampert, E. Edmonson, M. J. Smith and G. F. Van Tets. 'Late Pleistocene faunal remains from Seton rock shelter, Kangaroo Island, South Australia'. *Journal of Biogeography*, vol. 4, 1977, pp. 363–85.

7 R. J. Lampert, The Great Kartan Mystery. Ph.D. thesis, Australian National University, 1979; N. Draper, 'Context for the Kartan: a preliminary report on excavations at Cape Du Conedic rock-shelter'. *Archaeology in Oceania*, vol. 22, 1987, pp. 1–8; N. Draper, 'The history of Aboriginal land use on Kangaroo Island', in *Biological Survey of Kangaroo Island* (ed. A. C. Robinson). Adelaide, South Australian National Parks and Wildlife Service, in press.

8 R. J. Lampert, 'A preliminary report on some waisted blades found on Kangaroo Island, S.A.'. *Australian Archaeology*, vol. 2, 1975, pp. 45–8.

9 F. D. McCarthy, *Australian Aboriginal Stone Implements*. Sydney, Australian Museum, 1976.

10 N. B. Tindale, 'Aboriginal Man in Australia', in A. Keast, 1981, op. cit., pp. 1772–3.

11 H. M. Cooper, 'Large archaeological stone implements from Hallett Cove, South Australia'. *Transactions of the Royal Society of S.A.*, vol. 82, 1959, pp. 55–60.

12 G. L. Pretty, 'The cultural chronology of the Roonka Flat: a preliminary consideration', in R. V. S. Wright, 1977, op. cit., pp. 288–331.

13 R. Luebbers, 'Ancient boomerangs discovered in South Australia'. *Nature*, vol. 5486(253), 1975, p. 39; J. Dodson, 'Late Quaternary palaeoecology of Wyrie Swamp, southeastern SA'. *Quaternary Research*, vol. 8, 1977, pp. 97–114.

14 R. Jones, 'The Tasmanian paradox', in R. V. S. Wright, 1977, op. cit., pp. 189–204; B. Hayden, *Palaeolithic Reflections: Lithic Technology and Ethnographic Excavations Among Australian Aborigines*. Canberra, Australian Institute of Aboriginal Studies, 1979.

CHAPTER ELEVEN

Pleistocene Rock Art

1 L. Maynard, 'Classification and terminology in Australian rock art', in *Form in Indigenous Art* (ed. P. J. Ucko). Canberra, Australian Institute of Aboriginal Studies, 1977, pp. 387–402.

2 H. Basedow, 'Aboriginal rock carvings of great antiquity in South Australia'. *Journal of the Royal Anthropological Institute*, vol. 44, 1914, pp. 195–211.

3 H. Hale and N. B. Tindale, 1930, op. cit.

4 D. J. Mulvaney, 1975, op. cit.

5 A. Rosenfeld, *Early Man in North Queensland. Terra Australis* 6, Canberra, Prehistory Department, Australian National University, 1982.

6 N. R. Franklin, Explorations of variability in Australian prehistoric rock engravings. Ph.D. thesis, La Trobe University, 1992.

7 R. V. S. Wright, 1971, op. cit. A film was made of the site called *Flint Miners of the Nullarbor*; an earlier film entitled *Under the Nullarbor* was narrated by geomorphologist Joe Jennings and directed by Ian Dunlop, well known for his superb films about Aborigines, such as *Desert People*.

8 *S. J. Hallam, 'Roof markings in the "Orchestra Shell" Cave, Wanneroo, near Perth, Western Australia'. Mankind, vol. 8, 1971, pp. 90–103.*

9 R. G. Bednarik, 'Parietal finger markings in Europe and Australia'. *Rock Art Research*, vol. 3(1), 1986, pp. 30–61; G. C. Aslin and R. G. Bednarik, 'Karlie–Ngoinpool Cave: a preliminary report'. *Rock Art Research*, vol. 1(1), 1984, pp. 36–45; R. G. Bednarik, 'The cave petroglyphs of Australia'. *Australian Aboriginal Studies*, vol. 2, 1990, pp. 64–8.

10 M. J. Morwood and P. J. Trezise, 1989, op. cit.

11 N. R. Franklin, 1992, op. cit.

12 M. F. Nobbs and R. Dorn, 'New surface exposure ages for petroglyphs from the Olary Province, South Australia'. *Archaeology in Oceania*, vol. 28(1), 1993, pp. 18–39; M. F. Nobbs and R. I. Dorn, 'Age determinations for rock varnish formation within petroglyphs: cation-ratio dating of 24 motifs from the Olary region, South Australia'. *Rock Art Research*, vol. 5(2), 1988, pp. 108–46; R. I. Dorn, M. F. Nobbs and T. A. Cahill, 'Cation-ratio dating of rock engravings from the Olary province of arid South Australia'. *Antiquity*, vol. 62(237), 1988, pp. 681–9; D. Dragovich, 'Minimum age of some desert varnish near Broken Hill, New South Wales'. *Search*, vol. 17, 1986, pp. 149–51. For debate of CR dating, see A. Watchman, 'Doubtful dates for Karolta engravings'. *Australian Aboriginal Studies*, vol. 1, 1992, pp. 51–5; R. Dorn and M. Nobbs, 'Further support for the antiquity of South Australian rock engravings'. *Australian Aboriginal Studies*, vol. 1, 1992, pp. 56–60. For a recent overview on dating petroglyphs, see R. I. Dorn, 'Dating petroglyphs with a three tier rock varnish approach', in *New Light on Old Art* (eds D. S. Whitley and L. L. Loendorf). Los Angeles, Institute of Archaeology, University of California, Monograph 36, 1994, pp. 13–36.

13 M. F. Nobbs and R. I. Dorn, 1993, op. cit., pp. 26–7.

14 C. P. Mountford and R. Edwards, 'Rock engravings of Panaramitee Station'. *Transactions of the Royal Society of South Australia*, vol. 86, 1963, pp. 131–46.

15 L. Maynard, 1977, op. cit.; L. Maynard, 'The archaeology of Australian Aboriginal art', in *Exploring the Visual Art of Oceania* (ed. S. M. Mead). Hawaii, University Press, 1979, pp. 83–110.

16 N. Franklin, 'Explorations of the Panaramitee style', in *Rock Art and Prehistory* (eds P. Bahn and A. Rosenfeld). Oxford, Oxbow, 1991, pp. 120–35; B. David and N. Cole, 'Rock art and inter-regional interaction in northeastern Australian prehistory'. *Antiquity*, vol 64(245), 1990, pp. 788–806.

17 C. P. Mountford, 'An unrecorded method of Aboriginal rock markings'. *Records of the South Australian Museum*, vol. 11, 1955, pp. 345–51.

18 P. J. Sutton (ed.), *Dreamings — The Art of Aboriginal Australia*. Ringwood, Viking, 1988.

19 N. Franklin, 1992, op. cit.

20 N. D. Munn, *Walbiri Iconography*. Cornell University Press, 1973.

21 R. Edwards, 'Art and Aboriginal prehistory', in D. J. Mulvaney and J. Golson, 1971, op. cit., pp. 356–67; W. C. Dix, 'Facial representations in Pilbara rock engravings', in P. J. Ucko, 1977, op. cit., pp. 277–85; Australian Gallery Directors Council, *Aboriginal Australia*. Catalogue, Sydney, Australian Museum, 1981, p. 69.

22 R. Jones, 'Mount Cameron West', in Australian Heritage Commission, 1981, op. cit., pp. 786–90.

23 P. C. Sims, 'Variations in Tasmanian petroglyphs', in P. J. Ucko, 1977, op. cit., pp. 429–38; R. Cosgrove, *Tasmanian West Coast Aboriginal Rock Art Survey*. Occasional Paper no. 5, Hobart, Tasmanian National Parks and Wildlife Service, 1983; J. Stockton, *Greens Creek Aboriginal Engraving Site*. Occasional Paper no. 1, Hobart, Tasmanian National Parks and Wildlife Service, 1977.

24 A. Rosenfeld, 'Panaramitee: dead or alive?', in P. Bahn and A. Rosenfeld, 1991, op. cit., pp. 136–44; N. Franklin, 1991, op. cit.

25 S. Brown, 1991, op. cit.

26 T. H. Loy et al., 1990, op.cit.

27 A. Watchman, 'A summary of occurrences of oxalate-rich crusts in Australia'. *Rock Art Research*, vol. 7(1), 1990, pp. 44–50; A. Watchman, 'Evidence of a 25 000 year old pictograph from northern Australia'. *Geoarchaeology*, vol. 8(6), 1993, pp. 465–73. (The AMS date is 24 600 ± 220 BP (NZA–2750) on charcoal and oxalate minerals in rock surface mineral accretions covering pictographs.)

28 J. McDonald, K. Officer, T. Jull, D. Donahue, J. Head and B. Ford, 'Investigating 14C AMS: dating prehistoric rock art in the Sydney sandstone basin, Australia'. *Rock Art Research*, vol. 7(2), 1990, pp. 83–92; R. Dorn, personal communication, 1994.

29 I. Davidson and W. Noble, 1992, op. cit., give a list of ochre occurrences in Pleistocene sites.

30 R. Edwards, *Australian Aboriginal Art. The Art of the Alligator Rivers Region, Northern Territory*. Canberra, Australian Institute of Aboriginal Studies, 1979; G. Chaloupka, *From Palaeoart to Casual Paintings*. Darwin, Northern Territory Museum, 1984; G. Chaloupka, *Journey in Time*. Sydney, A. W. Reed, 1994.

31 D. J. Lewis, 'More striped designs in Arnhem Land rock paintings'. *Archaeology and Physical Anthropology in Oceania*, vol. 12(2), 1977, pp. 98–111.

32 I. M. Crawford, *The Art of the Wandjina: Aboriginal Cave Paintings in Kimberley, Western Australia*. Melbourne, Oxford University Press, 1968. (Re. Bradshaw figures, see articles by G. Walsh and D. Welch in *Rock Art Research*; G. L. Walsh, *Bradshaws. Ancient Rock Paintings of North-West Australia*. Geneva, Bradshaw Foundation, 1994.)

33 J. Clegg, 'Style and tradition at Sturt's Meadows'. *World Archaeology*, vol. 19, 1987, pp. 236–55; G. Walsh, *Australia's Greatest Rock Art*. Bathurst, Brill, Brown and Assoc., 1988; J. Clegg, 'Style of Sturts Meadows and Gap Hills', in *Rock Art Studies: The Post-Stylistic Era, or Where Do We Go from Here?* (eds M. Lorblanchet and P. Bahn). Oxford, Oxbow Books, 1993, pp. 115–26.

CHAPTER TWELVE

Extinction of the Megafauna

1 C. W. Peck, *Australian Legends*. Lothian, 1933.

2 P. S. Martin, 'Prehistoric overkill: the global model', in *Quaternary Extinctions. A Prehistoric Revolution* (eds P. S. Martin and R. G. Klein). Tucson, University of Arizona Press, 1984, pp. 354–403; P. S. Martin, 'Pleistocene overkill', in *Pleistocene Extinctions. The Search for a Cause* (eds P. S Martin and H. E. Wright). Newhaven, Yale University Press, 1967, pp. 75–120.

3 A. Anderson, 'The extinction of Moa in southern New Zealand', in P. S. Martin and R. G. Klein, 1984, op. cit., pp. 728–40.

4 P. Murray, 'Extinctions downunder: a bestiary of extinct Australian late Pleistocene monotremes and marsupials', in P. S. Martin and R. G. Klein, 1984, op. cit., pp. 600–28.

5 T. F. Flannery, 'Pleistocene faunal loss: implications of the aftershock for Australia's past'. *Archaeology in Oceania*, vol. 25(1), 1990, pp. 45–67.

6 D. R. Horton, 'Red kangaroo: last of the Australian megafauna', in P. S. Martin and R. G. Klein, 1984, op. cit., pp. 639–80; D. R. Horton, 'The great megafaunal extinction debate — 1879–1979'. *Artefact*, vol. 4, 1979, pp. 11–25; D. R. Horton, 'A review of the

extinction question: man, climate and megafauna'. *Archaeology and Physical Anthropology in Oceania*, vol. 15(2), 1980, pp. 86–97.

7 R. E. Molnar, 'Cenozoic fossil reptiles in Australia', in *The Fossil Vertebrate Record of Australasia* (eds P. V. Rich and E. M. Thompson). Melbourne, Monash University Press, 1982, pp. 227–34.

8 P. Murray, 1984, op. cit.

9 J. W. H. Lowry and D. Merrilees, 'Age of a desiccated carcass of a thylacine from Thylacine Hole, Nullarbor Region, W.A.'. *Helictite*, vol. 7, 1969, pp. 15–16.

10 D. J. Mulvaney, 1975, op. cit.; K. Gollan, 'The Australian dingo: in the shadow of man', in *Vertebrate Zoogeography and Evolution in Australasia* (eds M. Archer and G. Clayton). Perth, Hesperian Press, 1984, pp. 921–28.

11 J. P. White and J. F. O'Connell, *A Prehistory of Australia, New Guinea and Sahul*. London, Academic Press, 1982, pp. 88–95.

12 R. Jones, 1968, op. cit.; D. Merrilees, 'Man the destroyer: late Quaternary changes in the Australian marsupial fauna'. *Journal of the Royal Society of Western Australia*, vol. 51, 1968, pp. 1–24.

13 D. R. Horton, comment on T. F. Flannery, 1990, op. cit., pp. 59–60.

14 D. R. Horton, 1984, op. cit.; R. Gillespie, D. R. Horton, P. Ladd, P. G. Macumber, T. H. Rich, A. Thorne and R. V. S. Wright, 'Lancefield Swamp and the extinction of the Australian megafauna'. *Science*, vol. 200, 1978, pp. 1044–8; D. R. Horton, 'Lancefield: the problem of proof in bone analysis'. *The Artefact*, vol. 1(3), 1976, pp. 129–43; D. R. Horton and R. V. S. Wright, 'Cuts on Lancefield bones'. *Archaeology in Oceania*, vol. 16(2), 1981, pp. 78–9; P. P. Gorecki, D. R. Horton, N. Stern and R. V. S. Wright, 'Coexistence of humans and megafauna in Australia: improved stratified evidence'. *Archaeology in Oceania*, vol. 19(3), 1984, pp. 117–9.

15 T. F. Flannery, 1990, op. cit., p. 46.

16 D. Merrilees, 'Comings and goings of Late Quaternary mammals in extreme southwestern Australia', in P. S. Martin and R. G. Klein, op. cit., 1984, pp. 629–38.

17 L. G. Marshall, 'Fossil vertebrate faunas from the Lake Victoria region, southwest N.S.W.'. *Memoirs of the National Museum of Victoria*, vol. 34, 1973, pp. 151–71.

18 J. H. Hope, 'Pleistocene mammal extinctions: the problem of Mungo and Menindee, western New South Wales'. *Alcheringa*, vol. 2, 1978, pp. 65–82.

19 J. H. Hope, A. Dare-Edwards and M. L. McIntyre, 'Middens and megafauna: stratigraphy and dating of Lake Tandou Lunette, Western New South Wales'. *Archaeology in Oceania*, vol. 18, 1983, pp. 38–45.

20 J. H. Hope, 1987, op. cit., p. 52.

21 M. Archer, I. M. Crawford and D. Merrilees, 'Incisions, breakages and charring, probably man-made, in fossil bones from Mammoth Cave, Western Australia'. *Alcheringa*, vol. 4(1–2), 1980, pp. 115–31.

22 D. Merrilees, 1984, op. cit., pp. 636–7.

23 T. F. Flannery, 1990, op. cit.

24 Gorecki et al., 1984, and S. Bowdler's comment in T. F. Flannery, 1990, pp. 61–2.

25 N. B. Tindale, 'Archaeological site at Lake Menindee, New South Wales'. *Records of the S.A. Museum*, vol. 11, 1955, pp. 269–98.

26 Gorecki et al., 1984, op.cit.

27 J. Fethney, D. Roman and R. V. S. Wright, 'Uranium series dating of Diprotodon teeth from archaeological sites on the Liverpool Plains'. *Proceedings of the Fifth Australian Conference on Nuclear Techniques of Analysis*, 1987, pp. 24–6.

28 R. Wright, comment on T. F. Flannery, op. cit., 1990, p. 56.

29 R. Wright, 'New light on the extinction of the Australian megafauna'. *Proceedings of the Linnaean Society of New South Wales*, vol. 109, 1986, pp. 1–9 (the quote is from p. 5); Gorecki et al., 1984, op. cit., p. 118.

30 J. Dodson, R. Fullager, J. Furby, R. Jones and I. Prosser, 'Humans and megafauna in a late Pleistocene environment from Cuddie Springs, north western New South Wales'. *Archaeology in Oceania*, vol. 28, 1993, pp. 94–9; J. H. Furby, R. Fullager, J. R. Dodson and I. Prosser, 'The Cuddie Springs bone bed revisited, 1991,' in M. A. Smith et al., 1993, op. cit. pp. 204–10; J. H. Furby, A preliminary study of late Pleistocene megafauna, humans and environment at Cuddie Springs, northwestern New South Wales. B.Sc. Hons thesis, University of New South Wales, 1991.

31 J. Dodson et al., 1993, op. cit., p. 94.

32 ibid., p. 96.

33 ibid., p. 98.

34 Furby et al., 1993, op. cit.

35 F. D. McCarthy, *Australian Aboriginal Stone Implements*. Sydney, Australian Museum Trust, 1976.

36 J. R. Dodson and R. V. S. Wright, 'Humid to arid to subhumid vegetation shift on Pilliga Sandstone, Ulungra Springs, New South Wales'. *Quaternary Research*, vol. 32, 1989, pp. 182–92.

CHAPTER THIRTEEN
Tasmania: Ten Thousand Years of Isolation

1 J. Chappell, 'Some effects of sea level rise on riverine and coastal lowlands'. *Geological Society of Australia Symposium Proceedings*, vol. 1, 1990, pp. 37–49; J. Chappell, 1993, op. cit.

2 C. Pardoe, 'Population genetics and population size in prehistoric Tasmania'. *Australian Archaeology*, vol. 22, 1986, pp. 1–6.

3 R. Jones, 'A speculative archaeological sequence for northwest Tasmania'. *Records of the Queen Victoria Museum, Launceston*, vol. 25, 1966, pp. 1–12; R. Jones, Rocky Cape and the problem of the Tasmanians. Ph.D. thesis, Sydney University, 1971; H. Lourandos, '10,000 years in the Tasmanian Highlands'. *Australian Archaeology*, vol. 16, 1983, pp. 38–47.

4 R. Jones, in *Holier Than Thou* (ed. I. Johnson). Canberra, Prehistory Department, Australian National University, 1980, pp. 161–7.

5 R. Jones, 1977, op. cit.

6 R. Cosgrove, *The Archaeological Resources of Tasmanian Forests: Past Aboriginal Use of Forested Environments*. Occasional Paper no. 27, Hobart, Department of Parks, Wildlife and Heritage, 1990.

7 G. A. Robinson, journal edited by N. J. B. Plomley, 1966; see also L. Ryan, *The Aboriginal Tasmanians*. Brisbane, University of Queensland Press, 1968.

8 C. Webb, Use-wear on bone tools: an experimental program and three case-studies from south-east Australia. B.A. Hons thesis, Department of Archaeology, La Trobe University, Melbourne, 1987; C. Webb and J. Allen, 'A functional analysis of Pleistocene bone tools from two sites in Southwest Tasmania'. *Archaeology in Oceania*, vol. 25, 1990, pp. 75–78.

9 R. Jones, 'Why did the Tasmanians stop eating fish?', in *Explorations in Ethnoarchaeology* (ed. R. Gould), Santa Fe, University of New Mexico Press, 1978, pp. 11–47; H. Allen, 'Left out in the cold: why the Tasmanians stopped eating fish'. *Artefact*, vol. 4, 1979, pp. 1–10; D. R. Horton, 'Tasmanian adaptation'. *Mankind*, vol. 12, 1979, pp. 28–34; R. L. Vanderwal, 'Adaptive technology in South West Tasmania'. *Australian Archaeology*, vol. 8, 1978, pp. 107–27; R. Jones, 'The Tasmanian paradox', in R. V. S. Wright, 1977, op. cit., pp. 189–204.

10 S. M. Colley and R. Jones, 'New fish bone data from Rocky Cape, north west Tasmania'. *Archaeology in Oceania*, vol. 22(2), 1987, pp. 67–71. See also R. Jones, 1978, op. cit., pp. 26–7.

11 R. Jones, 1966, op. cit.

12 A. G. Thorne, 'The racial affinities and origins of the Australian Aborigines', in D. J. Mulvaney and J. Golson, 1971, op. cit., pp. 316–25.

13 A. G. Wallace and G. A. Doran, 'Early man in Tasmania', in R. L. Kirk and A. G. Thorne, 1976, op. cit., pp. 173–82.

14 H. Lourandos, 'Dispersal of activities — the east Tasmanian Aboriginal sites'. *Papers and Records of the Royal Society of Tasmania*, vol. 2, 1968, pp. 41–6; H. Lourandos, 'Stone tools, settlement, adaptation: a Tasmanian example', in R. V. S. Wright, 1977, op. cit., pp. 219–24.

15 R. L. Vanderwal and D. R. Horton, *Coastal Southwest Tasmania. Terra Australis* 9. Canberra, Department of Prehistory, Australian National University, 1984.

16 H. Allen, 1979, op. cit.

17 R. Sim, Further archaeological excavations at Beeton Shelter on Badger Island and site recording on the southerly outer islands of the Furneaux Group, Bass Strait. Unpublished report to the Tasmanian Aboriginal Land Council, the Flinders Island Aboriginal Association and the Tasmanian Aboriginal Centre, 1992, pp. 7–8.

18 R. J. Lampert, unpublished report, Australian Museum, Sydney, 1985.

19 R. Vanderwal and D. Horton, 1984, op. cit.; R. Jones, 'Tasmania: aquatic machines and offshore islands', in *Problems in Economic and Social Anthropology* (eds G. de G. Sieveking, I. H. Longworth and K. E. Wilson). London, Duckworth, 1976, pp. 235–63; R. Jones, 1971, op. cit.

20 N. Franklin, 1991, op. cit.; A. Rosenfeld, 1991, op. cit.; S. Brown, 1991, op. cit. (See references in chapter 11.)

21 J. Stockton, 'Preliminary note on an Aboriginal stone alignment and associated features'. *Proceedings of the Royal Society of Tasmania*, vol. 111, 1977, pp. 181–3; R. L. Jones, personal communication, 1989.

22 R. Sim, 1992, op. cit.; R. Sim, 'Prehistoric human occupation in the King and Furneaux Island regions, Bass Strait'. *Proceedings of the Australian Archaeological Association Conference, December 1993*. Darwin, North Australia Research Unit, Australian National University, in press.

23 J. Chappell, 1993, op. cit.; R. Sim, Prehistoric archaeological investigations on King and Flinders Islands, Bass Strait, Tasmania. MA thesis, Department of Prehistory and Anthropology, Australian National University, 1991.

24 R. Sim, Beeton Shelter Excavation. Unpublished report to the Tasmanian Environment Centre, 1992, p. 14.

25 R. Sim, The results of recent research into past Aboriginal occupation of the Furneaux group and King Island, Bass Strait. Unpublished report to the Tasmanian Aboriginal Land Council, the Flinders Island Aboriginal Association and the Tasmanian Aboriginal Centre, 1991; R. Jones, 1976, op. cit.; R. Jones, 'Man as an element of a continental fauna: the case of the sundering of the Bassian bridge', in J. Allen, J. Golson and R. Jones, 1977, op. cit., pp. 317–88.

26 L. Ryan, *The Aboriginal Tasmanians*. Brisbane, University of Queensland Press, 1981.

CHAPTER FOURTEEN
Rising Seas and Change

1 C. P. Mountford and A. Roberts, *The Dawn of Time*. Adelaide, Rigby, 1969.

2 J. Isaacs, 1980, op. cit., p. 108.

3 ibid., pp. 26, 115–16.

4 C. P. Mountford and A. Roberts, 1969, op. cit., p. 18.

5 B. C. Barker, 'Nara Inlet 1: coastal resource use and the Holocene marine transgression in the Whitsunday Islands, Central Queensland'. *Archaeology in Oceania*, vol. 26(3), 1991, pp. 102–9.

6 M. J. Rowland, 'The Keppel Islands — preliminary investigations'. *Australian Archaeology*, vol. 11, 1980, pp. 1–7.

7 W. E. Roth, *North Queensland Ethnography Bulletin*, no. 14, 1910, p. 4.

8 R. Jones, 1976, op. cit., p. 260.

9 N. B. Tindale, *Aboriginal Tribes of Australia*. Canberra, Australian National University Press, 1974.

10 N. Peterson, 'Open sites and the ethnographic approach to the archaeology of hunter–gatherers', in D. J. Mulvaney and J. Golson, 1971, op. cit., pp. 239–48; N. Peterson, 'Hunter–gatherer territoriality: the perspective from Australia'. *American Anthropologist*, vol. 77(1), 1975; N. Peterson, 'The natural and cultural areas of Aboriginal Australia: a preliminary analysis of population groupings with adaptive significance', in N. Peterson, 1976, op. cit.; N. Peterson, *Australian Territorial Organisation*. Oceania Monograph, Sydney, University of Sydney, 1986.

11 H. Lourandos, 'Intensification: a late Pleistocene–Holocene archaeological sequence from Southwestern Victoria'. *Archaeology in Oceania*, vol. 18, 1983, pp. 81–94; H. Lourandos, 'Pleistocene Australia: peopling a continent', in *The Pleistocene Old World Regional Perspectives* (ed. O. Soffer). New York, Plenum Press, 1987, pp. 147–65; H. Lourandos, 'Intensification and Australian prehistory', in *Prehistoric Hunter–Gatherers: The Emergence of Cultural Complexity* (eds T. D. Price and J. A. Brown). London, Academic Press, 1985, pp. 385–423; J. M. Beaton, 'Evidence for a coastal occupation time-lag at Princess Charlotte Bay (North Queensland) and implications for coastal colonization and population growth theories for Aboriginal Australia'. *Archaeology in Oceania*, vol. 20, 1985, pp. 1–20; A. Ross, 'Archaeological evidence for population change in the middle to late Holocene in southeastern Australia'. *Archaeology in Oceania*, vol. 20, 1985, pp. 73–80; P. J. Hughes and R. J. Lampert, 'Prehistoric population change in southern coastal New South Wales', in S. Bowdler, 1982, op. cit., pp. 16–28; M. J. Morwood, 'The archaeology of social complexity in south-east Queensland'. *Proceedings of the Prehistoric Society*, vol. 53, 1987, pp. 337–50; I. McBryde, *Aboriginal Prehistory in New England*. Sydney, Sydney University Press, 1974; J. M. Flood, 1980, op. cit.; A. Ross, 'Holocene environments and prehistoric site patterning in the Victorian Mallee'. *Archaeology in Oceania*, vol. 16(3), 1981, pp. 145–55.

12 C. F. M. Bird and D. Frankel, 'Problems in constructing a prehistoric regional sequence: Holocene south-east Australia'. *World Archaeology*, vol. 23(2), 1991, pp. 179–91; D. Frankel, 'First-order radiocarbon dating of Australian shell middens'. *Antiquity*, vol. 65(248), 1991, pp. 571–4.

13 J. Flood, B. David, J. Magee and B. English, 'Birrigai: a Pleistocene site in the south-eastern highlands'. *Archaeology in Oceania*, vol. 22, 1987, pp. 9–26; M. A. Smith, 'Pleistocene occupation in arid Central Australia'. *Nature*, vol. 328, 1987, pp. 710–11.

14 E. D. Stockton and W. Holland, 'Cultural sites and their environment in the Blue Mountains'. *Archaeology and Physical Anthropology in Oceania*, vol. 9, 1974, pp. 36–65; I. Johnson, 1980, op. cit.

15 N. B. Tindale, 'Archaeological excavation of Noola rock shelter'. *Records of the S.A. Museum*, vol. 14, 1961, pp. 193–6.

16 F. D. McCarthy, 'The archaeology of the Capertee Valley, N.S.W.'. *Records of the Australian Museum*, vol. 26, 1964, pp. 197–246.

CHAPTER FIFTEEN
Arrival of the Dingo

1 R. A.Gould, 'Puntutjarpa rockshelter and the Australian desert culture'. *Anthropology Papers of the American Museum of Natural History*, vol. 54(1) 1977; R. A. Gould, 'Puntutjarpa rockshelter. A reply to Messrs Glover and Lampert'. *Archaeology and Physical Anthropology in Oceania*, vol. 4, 1969, pp. 229–37.

2 J. M. Flood, 'A point assemblage from the Northern Territory'. *Archaeology and Physical Anthropology in Oceania*, vol. 5(1), 1970, pp. 27–52.

3 J. P. White and J. F. O'Connell, 1979, op. cit., pp. 112–15.

4 R. J. Lampert, 1971, op. cit.; J. Kamminga, 'A functional investigation of Australian microliths'. *Artefact*, vol. 5(1), 1980, pp. 1–18.

5 I. McBryde, 1974, op. cit., pp. 264–5.

6 P. Hiscock, 'Bondian technology in the Hunter Valley, New South Wales'. *Archaeology in Oceania*, vol. 28, 1993, pp. 65–76.

7 S. R. Mitchell, 'The woodworking tools of the Australian Aborigines'. *The Journal of the Royal Anthropological Institute*, vol. 89(2), 1959, pp. 191–9; I. McNiven, 'Tula adzes and bifacial points on the east coast of Australia'. *Australian Archaeology*, vol. 36, 1993, pp. 22–33.

8 N. Peterson, 1976, op. cit.

9 K. Gollan, 'The Australian dingo: in the shadow of man', in *Vertebrate Zoogeography and Evolution in Australasia* (eds M. Archer and G. Clayton). Perth, Hesperian Press, 1984, pp. 921–7.

10 S. Bowdler and S. O'Connor, 'The dating of the Australian small tool tradition, with new evidence from the Kimberley, W.A.'. *Australian Aboriginal Studies*, no. 1, 1991, pp. 53–62; S. O'Connor, 'New radiocarbon dates from Koolan Island, West Kimberley, W.A.'. *Australian Archaeology*, vol. 28, 1989, pp. 92–104.

11 J. P. White and J. F. O'Connell, 1979, op. cit., pp. 118–19; forthcoming papers on the chronology of points in *The Proceedings of the Australian Archaeological Association Conference, Darwin*, December 1993, Darwin, North Australia Research Unit, in press (PO Box 41321, Casuarina, Darwin, NT, 0811).

12 R. Jones and I. Johnson, 1985, op. cit., pp. 165–228.

13 S. Bowdler and S. O'Connor, 1991, op. cit.

14 P. Hiscock, 'Interpreting the vertical distribution of stone points within Nauwalabila I, Arnhem Land'. *The Beagle*, vol. 10(1), 1993, pp. 173–8.

15 R. H. Pearce, 'Spatial and temporal distribution of Australian backed blades'. *Mankind*, vol. 9, 1974, pp. 300–9; E. D. Stockton, 'Review of early Bondaian dates'. *Mankind*, vol. 11, 1977, pp. 48–51; C. E. Dortch, 1977, op. cit.

16 N. W. G. Macintosh, 'The origin of the dingo: an enigma', in *The Wild Canids* (ed. M. W. Fox). 1975, pp. 87–106; K. Gollan, 1984, op. cit.

17 L. K. Corbett, 'Morphological comparisons of Australian and Thai dingoes: a reappraisal of dingo status distribution and ancestry'. *Proceedings of the Ecological Society of Australia*, vol. 13, 1985, pp. 277–91.

18 R. Gould, *Living Archaeology*. New York, Cambridge University Press, 1980.

19 A. Hamilton, 'Aboriginal man's best friend?'. *Mankind*, vol. 8(4), 1972, pp. 267–95.

20 R. M. W. Dixon, *The Languages of Australia*. Melbourne, Cambridge University Press, 1980.

21 J. P. White and J. F. O'Connell, 1982, op. cit., p. 124.

22 R. A. Luebbers, Meals and menus: a study of change in prehistoric coastal settlements in South Australia. Ph.D. thesis, Australian National University, 1978.

CHAPTER SIXTEEN
Harvesters, Engineers and Fire-Stick Farmers

1 J. M. Beaton, 'Fire and water: aspects of Australian Aboriginal management of cycads'. *Archaeology in Oceania*, vol. 17(1), 1982, pp. 51–9.

2 M. J. Morwood, 'Archaeology of the central Queensland highland: the stone component'. *Archaeology in Oceania*, vol. 16(1), 1981, pp. 1–52.

3 N. Horsfall, 'Theorising about north-east Queensland prehistory'. *Queensland Archaeological Research*, vol. 1, 1984, pp. 164–72.

4 M. Smith, 'Late Pleistocene zamia exploitation in southern Western Australia'. *Archaeology in Oceania*, vol. 17(3), 1982, pp. 117–21.

5 N. B. Tindale, 1961, op. cit.; F. D. McCarthy, 1964, op. cit.

6 I. Johnson, 1979, op. cit.

7 I. McBryde, 1974, op. cit.; S. Bowdler, 1981, op. cit.

8 B. Gott, 'Murnong — *Microseris scapigera:* a study of a staple food of Victorian Aborigines'. *Australian Aboriginal Studies*, vol. 2, 1983, pp. 2–18; B. Gott, 'The uses of ethnohistory and ecology'. *Tempus*, vol. 1, 1989, pp. 197–213.

9 J. Flood, 'Moth hunters of the Southeastern Highlands', in D. J. Mulvaney and J. P. White, 1987, op. cit., pp. 274–91; J. M. Flood, *The Moth Hunters: Aboriginal Prehistory of the Australian Alps.* Canberra, Australian Institute of Aboriginal Studies, 1980; J. Flood, 'Moth hunting in the Australian Alps'. *Australian Natural History*, vol. 21 (11), 1985, pp 470–3.

10 P. J. F. Coutts, R. K. Frank and P. J. Hughes, 'Aboriginal engineers of the Western District, Victoria'. *Records of the Victorian Archaeological Survey*, vol. 7, 1978; H. Lourandos, 'Aboriginal settlement and land use in southwestern Victoria'. *Artefact*, vol. 1(4), 1976, pp. 174–9; L. Head, 'Using palaeoecology to date Aboriginal fishtraps at Lake Condah, Victoria'. *Archaeology in Oceania*, vol. 24, 1989, pp. 110–15; H. Lourandos, 'Aboriginal spatial organization and population: southwestern Victoria reconsidered'. *Archaeology and Physical Anthropology in Oceania*, vol. 12(3), 1977; H. Lourandos, 'Change or stability? Hydraulics, hunter–gatherers and population in temperate Australia'. *World Archaeology*, vol. 11(3), 1980, pp. 245–64; P. J. F. Coutts et al., 'The mound people of Western Victoria'. *Records of the Victorian Archaeological Survey*, vol. 1, 1976.

11 R. Jones, 'Hunters in the Australian coastal savanna', in *Human Ecology in Savanna Environments* (ed. D. R. Harris). 1980, pp. 128–9.

12 G. A. Robinson, Papers and journals of the Port Phillip Protectorate. Sydney, Mitchell Library, 1839–1849.

13 E. Williams, 'Complex hunter–gatherers: a view from Australia'. *Antiquity*, vol. 61, 1987, pp. 310–21; E. Williams, *Complex Hunter–Gatherers: A Late Holocene Example from Temperate Australia.* Oxford, British Archaeological Reports, International Series 423, 1988; E. Williams, 'Estimation of prehistoric populations of archaeological sites in south-western Victoria: some problems'. *Archaeology in Oceania*, vol. 20(3), 1985, pp. 73–80.

14 J. Wesson, Excavations of stone structures in the Condah area, Western Victoria. MA (preliminary) thesis, La Trobe University, 1981.

15 A. Clarke, Romancing the stones: the cultural construction of an archaeological landscape in the Western District of Victoria'. *Archaeology in Oceania*, vol. 29(1), 1994, pp. 1–15.

16 E. Williams, 1988, op. cit., p. 4.

17 A. Clarke, 1994, op. cit.; C. F. M. Bird and D. Frankel , 'Chronology and explanation in western Victoria and south-east South Australia'. *Archaeology in Oceania*, vol. 26, 1991, pp. 1–16.

18 J. Flood, 'No ethnography, no moth hunters', in *Archaeology with Ethnography* (eds B. Meehan and R. Jones). Canberra, Department of Prehistory, Australian National University, 1988, pp. 270–6.

19 E. Williams, 1988, op. cit.

20 H. Lourandos, 'Intensification: a Late Pleistocene/Holocene archaeological sequence from southwestern Victoria reconsidered'. *Archaeological and Physical Anthropology in Oceania*, vol. 18(2), 1983, pp. 81–97.

21 A. Ross, 1981, op. cit.; A. Ross, 1985, op. cit.

22 H. A. Martin, 1973, op. cit.

23 R. J. Lampert, 1971, op. cit.

24 R. J. Lampert, 'An excavation at Durras North, N.S.W.'. *Archaeology and Physical Anthropology in Oceania*, vol. 1, 1966, pp. 83–118.

25 J. V. S. Megaw (ed.), *The Recent Archaeology of the Sydney District. Excavations 1964–7.* Canberra, Australian Institute of Aboriginal Studies, 1974, pp. 1–12.

26 See references in S. Bowdler, 1976, op. cit.; R. Lawrence, *Aboriginal Habitat and Economy.* Canberra, Department of Geography, Australian National University, 1968.

27 I. McBryde, 1974, op. cit., pp. 284–92; *Coast and Estuary*, Canberra, Australian Institute of Aboriginal Studies, 1982, pp. 1–50.

28 See references in chapter 14 to Lourandos, Beaton, Ross, etc.

29 S. A. Sutton, 'Pleistocene axes in Sahul: a response to Morwood and Trezise'. *Queensland Archaeological Research*, vol. 7, 1990, pp. 95–109.

30 C. F. M. Bird and D. Frankel, 1991, op. cit.

31 J. M. Beaton, 'Evidence for a coastal occupation time-lag at Princess Charlotte Bay (North Queensland) and implications for coastal colonization and population growth theories for Aboriginal Australia'. *Archaeology in Oceania*, vol. 20, 1985, pp. 1–20.

32 R. Jones, 'Fire-stick farming'. *Australian Natural History*, vol. 16, 1969, pp. 224–8; S. Hallam,

Fire and Hearth. Canberra, Australian Institute of Aboriginal Studies, 1975; N.B. Tindale, 1959, op. cit.; R. L. Clark, 'Pollen and charcoal evidence for the effects of Aboriginal burning on the vegetation of Australia'. *Archaeology in Oceania*, vol. 18, 1983, pp. 32–7; T. Flannery, 1990, op. cit.

33 R. Gould, 1980, op. cit., p. 81.

34 ibid., p. 82.

CHAPTER SEVENTEEN

The Question of Agriculture

1 J. Golson, 'No room at the top: agricultural intensification in the New Guinea highlands', in J. Allen, J. Golson and R. Jones, 1977, op. cit., pp. 601–38; M. Spriggs, 'Pleistocene agriculture in the Pacific: why not?', in M. A. Smith, M. Spriggs and B. Fankhauser, 1993, op. cit., pp. 137–43.

2 D. Walker, 1972, op. cit.; J. Allen, J. Golson and R. Jones, 1977, op. cit.; D. Moore, *Islanders and Aborigines at Cape York*. Canberra, Australian Institute of Aboriginal Studies, 1979.

3 R. L. Vanderwal, 'The Torres Strait: prehistory and beyond'. *Occasional Papers of the Anthropology Museum, University of Queensland*, vol. 2, 1973, pp. 157–94.

4 R. V. S. Wright, 1971, op. cit.; G. N. Bailey, 'Shell mounds, shell middens, and raised beaches in the Cape York Peninsula'. *Mankind*, vol. 11, 1977, pp. 132–43; T. Stone, 1989, op. cit.; *Proceedings of the Australian Archaeological Association Conference 1993*, forthcoming, op. cit.; G. Bailey, 'Shell mounds in 1972 and 1992: reflections on recent controversies at Ballina and Weipa'. *Australian Archaeology*, vol. 37, 1993, pp. 1–17; R. L. Cribb, 'Getting into a flap about shell mounds in northern Australia: a reply to Stone'. *Archaeology in Oceania*, vol. 26, 1991, pp. 23–5.

5 F. D. McCarthy, 'Comparison of the prehistory of Australia with that of IndoChina'. *Proceedings of 3rd Congress of Prehistorians, Far East, Singapore*, 1940, pp. 23–52.

6 See articles by Moore, Wurm and Kirk in D. Walker, 1972, op. cit.

7 For a full account of the Macassans, see D. J. Mulvaney, 1975, op. cit.; C. MacKnight, 'Macassans and Aborigines'. *Oceania*, vol. 42, 1972, pp. 283–321.

8 J. Golson, 'Australian Aboriginal food plants', in D. J. Mulvaney and J. Golson, 1971, op. cit., pp. 196–238; J. Golson, 1977, op. cit.

9 N. Wace in D. Walker, 1972, op. cit.

10 R. Jones, 'The Neolithic, Palaeolithic and the hunting gardeners: man and land in the antipodes', in *Quaternary Studies: Selected Papers from IX INQUA Congress*. Bulletin 13, Wellington, Royal Society of New Zealand, 1975, pp. 21–34; N. Wace, 1977, op. cit.; B. Meehan, 'Man does not live by calories alone: the role of shellfish in a coastal cuisine', in J. Allen, J. Golson and R. Jones 1977, op. cit., pp. 493–53; B. Meehan, 'Hunters by the seashore'. *Journal of Human Evolution*, vol. 6(4), 1977, pp. 363–70; B. Meehan, 'Plant use in a contemporary Aboriginal community and prehistoric implications', in *Plants in Australian Archaeology* (eds W. Beck, A. Clarke and L. Head). *Tempus*, St Lucia, Anthropology Museum, University of Queensland, vol. 1, 1989, pp. 14–30.

11 R. Jones, 1980, op. cit., p. 23.

12 H. R. Allen, 'The Bagundji of the Darling basin: cereal gatherers in an uncertain environment'. *World Archaeology*, vol. 5, 1974, pp. 309–22.

13 T. L. Mitchell, *Three Expeditions into the Interior of Eastern Australia*. London, Boone, vol. 1, 1839, pp. 238–9, 290–1.

14 See references in H. Allen, 1974, op. cit.

15 F. R. Irvine, 'Evidence of change in the vegetable diet of Australian Aborigines', in *Diprotodon to Detribalization* (eds A. R. Pilling and R. A. Waterman). 1970, p. 280.

16 K. N. G. Simpson and R. Blackwood, 'An Aboriginal cache of fresh water mussels at Lake Victoria, N.S.W.'. *Memoirs of the National Museum of Victoria*, vol. 34, 1973, pp. 217–18.

17 R. Kimber, 'Beginnings of farming?'. *Mankind*, vol. 10(3), 1976, pp. 142–50.

18 R. Gould, 1980, op. cit., pp. 65–6.

19 C. Sturt, *Two Expeditions into the Interior of Southern Australia*. London, Smith Elder, vol. 1, 1833, pp. 54–5.

20 H. R. Allen, 1974, op. cit., p. 313.

21 R. Gould, 1980, op. cit., pp. 6–28, 68–9.

22 B. Meehan, 1977, op. cit.

23 R. Gould, 1980, op. cit., p. 64.

24 J. C. Beaglehole (ed.), *The Journals of Captain James Cook on His Voyages of Discovery*. London, Hakluyt Society, 1955, p. 399.

CHAPTER EIGHTEEN

The Last 1000 Years: Trade, Religion and Art

1 G. Aiston, 'The Aboriginals' narcotic pitcheri'. *Oceania*, vol. 7, 1937, pp. 372–7; P. Watson, *This Precious Foliage; A Study of the Aboriginal Psycho-active Drug Pituri*. Oceania Monograph no. 26, University of Sydney, 1983.

2 D. J. Mulvaney, 'The chain of connection', in N. Peterson, 1976, op. cit., pp. 72–94.

3 I. McBryde, 'Wil-im-ee Moor-ring: or where do axes come from?'. *Mankind*, vol. 11(3), 1978, pp. 354–82; I. McBryde, 'Kulin greenstone quarries: the social contexts of production and distribution for the Mt William site'. *World Archaeology*, vol. 16(2), 1984, pp. 267–85.

4 P. J. F. Coutts and R. Miller, *The Mt William Archaeological Area*. Melbourne, Victorian Archaeological Survey, 1977.

5 I. McBryde and A. Watchman, 'The distribution of greenstone axes in southeastern Australia: a preliminary report'. *Mankind*, vol. 10(3), 1976, pp. 163–74.

6 R. A. Binns and I. McBryde, *A Petrological Analysis of Ground-edge Artefacts from Northern New South Wales*. Canberra, Australian Institute of Aboriginal Studies, 1972.

7 G. A. Robinson, 1966, op. cit., pp. 600–1, 688, 903–5; G. Culican, Ochre sources and other recipes: a study of Aboriginal ochre production and distribution in Australia and Tasmania. B.A. Hons thesis, Australian National University, 1986.

8 Excavated by I. M. Crawford, Western Australian Museum (unpublished).

9 D. J. Mulvaney, 1975, op. cit., p. 114.

10 ibid., plate 78.

11 F. D. McCarthy, 'Catalogue of the Aboriginal relics of New South Wales. Part III. Carved trees or dendroglyphs'. *Mankind*, vol. 3(7), 1945, pp. 199–206; D. Bell, Aboriginal carved trees in New South Wales — a survey report. National Parks and Wildlife Service of New South Wales, 1981.

12 Australian Heritage Commission, *The Heritage of Australia*. Macmillan 1981 (subsequent State editions for W.A., S.A. and the N.T., Tasmania and Victoria) includes descriptions and photographs of Yuranigh's grave and many other significant Aboriginal sites. See also J. Flood, *The Riches of Ancient Australia*. Brisbane, University of Queensland Press, 1991.

13 R. Jones, 'The Tasmanian paradox', in R. V. S. Wright, op. cit., 1977, pp. 191–204.

14 R. Stead, Towards a classification of Australian stone arrangements. MA thesis, Australian National University, 1987.

15 See, for example, G. Walsh, *Australia's Greatest Rock Art*. Bathurst, E. J. Brill, Robert Brown and Associates, 1988; R. M. Berndt and E. S. Phillips, *The Australian Aboriginal Heritage*, Sydney, Ure Smith, 1973; F. D. McCarthy, *Australian Aboriginal Rock Art*. 1979; the journal *Rock Art Research*, passim.

16 B. J. Wright, *Rock Art of the Pilbara Region: North-West Australia*. Canberra, Australian Institute of Aboriginal Studies, 1968.

17 L. Maynard, personal communication, 1979.

18 R. Edwards, 1979, op. cit.; G. Chaloupka, 1977, op. cit.

19 M. C. Quinell, 'Schematisation and naturalism in the rock art of south central Queensland', in P. J. Ucko, 1977, op. cit., pp. 414–17; M. J. Morwood, 'Time, space and prehistoric art: a principal components analysis'. *Archaeology and Physical Anthropology in Oceania*, vol. 15(2), 1980, pp. 98–109.

Glossary

ABRADED GROOVE A continuous linear groove made by the repeated friction of rubbing a stone, bone or wooden tool to and fro across a rock surface.

ABSOLUTE/RELATIVE AGE An absolute date applies to a specific time in calendar or radiocarbon years, whereas a relative age only indicates whether an item is younger or older than other items. Absolute dating is also termed chronometric dating.

ACCELERATOR MASS SPECTROMETRY (AMS) 'A radiocarbon-dating method that utilizes an accelerator mass spectrometer to determine the actual numbers of ^{14}C atoms present in a sample, rather than the relatively small numbers of ^{14}C atoms that decay radioactively during the measurement time of the conventional beta-counting method. Both methods have about the same dating age limit of 50 000 bp. The greatest advantage of the AMS method is the sample size requirement of only 1mg of carbon.' (Bahn 1992)

ACTIVITY AREA An area within a site in which a specific activity, such as stone tool manufacture, was practised.

ADZE A small stone tool made on a flake and used as a woodworking 'chisel', usually mounted in a handle.

AGRICULTURE/DOMESTICATION The practice of cultivating the soil and bringing animals under human control.

AMINO ACID RACEMISATION 'A biological dating method that utilizes postmortem changes in indigenous proteins in carbonate shells of molluscs and bones, to estimate the time since death' (Bahn 1992). It can be applied to material up to 100 000 years old.

ANTHROPOLOGY The study of the human species.

ANTHROPOMORPH A figure of human form.

ARCHAEOLOGY The study of the material traces of the human past.

ARCHAIC/MODERN Early or primitive in contrast to late or recent characteristics.

ARTEFACT Any portable object made or modified by human agency (also spelt artifact).

ASSEMBLAGE Set of artefacts found in close association with each other at a particular time and place.

AUSTRALIAN CORE TOOL AND SCRAPER TRADITION A stone tool industry first identified in the late 1960s at Lake Mungo, characterised by hand-held, steep-edged flake scrapers, chopping tools and horsehoof cores. Assemblages of this type belong to the late Pleistocene and Holocene, and are found continent-wide including Tasmania, although by no means all Pleistocene industries fit this characterisation and there is considerable regional and temporal variability within this tradition. (See also chapter 3.)

AUSTRALIAN SMALL TOOL TRADITION A stone tool industry characterised by blade technology, the widespread use of hafting, and a range of small tools such as projectile points, Bondi points, geometric microliths, eloueras, and tula and burren adzes. This tradition emerged in the mid to late Holocene period, roughly 5000 years ago, and most elements were in use at the time of first European contact. The specialised small tools of this tradition were absent from Tasmania, and on the mainland their distribution varies significantly in time and space. (See also chapter 15.)

AWL A small pointed tool, usually made of bone, used for puncturing skins, hides, etc.

AXE-BLANK A stone shaped to the form of an axe, but not sharpened, flaked or ground.

AXE-GRINDING GROOVES The grooves left in friable stone, such as sandstone, by rubbing an axe to produce a ground cutting edge.

AXE/HATCHET A stone chopping tool, usually with a ground cutting edge.

BACKED BLADE A small stone blade with the margin opposite the working edge deliberately blunted to form a penknife-like back.

BAND A land-using group occupying a range; a small local aggregation of hunter–gatherers for economic, land-exploiting purposes.

BIFACIALLY TRIMMED An artefact worked on both faces.

BIPOINT A bone artefact fashioned to a point at both ends.

BIPOLAR ARTEFACTS Stone artefacts generally rectangular or squareish in shape, bearing marks of bruising or scaling at the two ends, more rarely on the four sides, resulting from manufacture by strong percussion using the hammer and anvil technique.

BLADE A parallel-sided flake, at least twice as long as it is wide.

BONDI POINT An asymmetric, small triangular blade with a thick, trimmed back.

BORA GROUND A ceremonial ground usually consisting of two earth-banked rings linked by a pathway.

BULB OF PERCUSSION The rounded swelling left on the inner face of a flake or blade directly below the point of impact on the striking platform.

BURREN ADZE A small, flaked, hafted stone adze with obtuse-angled striking platform resembling the *tula*, but with retouch and/or use-wear on the lateral edges.

CAIRN A pile of stones.

CALCRETE The superficial gravels cemented by deposits of calcium carbonate formed from solutions of calcium bicarbonate.

CAMP SITE/OPEN CAMP SITE An area in the open air showing a concentration of debris associated with human occupation. A surface scatter of stone and/or other artefacts lying exposed on the surface of the land.

CANOE TREE A tree scarred by removal of a large sheet of bark to make a canoe.

CARRYING CAPACITY OF LAND The number of people an area of land can support.

CARVED TREE A tree from which a slab of bark has been removed and with the exposed wood carved in geometric, curvilinear or other designs. Occasionally the outer wood is carved.

CATION-RATIO DATING (CR) The CR dating method for dating rock varnish within petroglyphs depends on determination of the ratio of calcium and potassium to titanium — (K + Ca)/Ti — concentrations within the rock varnish. The calcium and potassium ions are more mobile than titanium and are more readily leached from the surface; from this reaction the older the varnish, the closer the ratio approaches 1:1. The ion concentrations are determined by chemical analysis. Calibration is effected by accelerator mass spectrometry (AMS) dating of the varnish of samples from the same area. Cation ratios in rock varnishes on surfaces of known radiocarbon age are compared with the CRs of petroglyphs. Systematic changes which occur in the ratio of the cations in varnish over time are utilised in estimating ages. (See also chapter 11.)

CHENIERS Elongated low ridges of shell or shelly sand on tropical coasts.

CHERT A fine-grained crystalline aggregate of silica, with excellent fracturing properties, producing good cutting edges on stone tools. Similar to flint, agate, chalcedony and jasper.

CHIP A small stone fragment detached from a larger piece in the process of tool manufacturing or use.

CHIPPING/FLAKING FLOOR A workshop area covered in stone debris from the manufacture of stone tools.

CHOPPER/CHOPPING TOOL A large heavy core tool used for chopping.

CLAN A local land-owning or land-controlling descent group, membership of which is fixed by descent from shared ancestors. A clan has rights in an *estate* of land as ritual property. In a patriclan, membership is transmitted from father to child, in a matriclan from mother to child.

COMPOSITE TOOL An artefact consisting of two or more parts, such as small tools hafted onto a handle.

CONCHOIDAL FRACTURE Shell-like, curved surface with ripple marks formed in certain types of rock fracture.

COOLAMON An Aboriginal carrying dish, usually made of wood or bark.

COPROLITES Fossilised faeces.

CORE A lump or nodule of stone from which other tools are made; flakes are often removed by striking it with another stone.

CORE TOOL A core bearing trimming or use-wear, indicating its use as an implement.

CORTEX The natural weathered surface of rock, *not* resulting from human activity.

CULTURE The distinctive and complex system of technology, social organisation and ideology developed by a group of human beings to adapt to their environment. An archaeological 'culture' is an assemblage of artefacts which recurs consistently with a limited distribution in space and time.

CYCADS Woody, cone-bearing plants, 'living fossils' with many primitive characteristics; the poisonous seeds of cycads were detoxified and used as food by Aborigines.

CYLCONS Cylindrical stones tapering to a pointed or rounded distal end. They range from 15 to over 75 centimetres long, and are believed to have a ritual significance. Mainly found in far western New South Wales.

DESERT VARNISH/ROCK VARNISH A chemical crust of bacterial origin — usually brownish-black and glossy, consisting mainly of clays and oxides of iron and manganese — which builds up over the millennia on stable rock surfaces, particularly in arid environments.

DILLY BAG A woven bag used by Aboriginal people, especially women, for collecting food.

DINGO The wild dog of Australia, *Canis familiaris dingo*.

DIRECT PERCUSSION Percussion by a hand-held hammer.

DOLINE A conical depression in limestone, characteristic of karst scenery.

DRAWING A mark or picture made by adding dry pigment, often charcoal, to a rock surface.

DREAMING TRACK/SONGLINE A route taken by a Dreaming or Ancestral Being, along which a series of events occurred which are part of Aboriginal oral tradition and are marked by a series of sites and associated songs and stories.

DREAMTIME The time when Ancestral Beings — some human and some animal — travelled the country creating the form of the landscape. The era of creation. 'In Aboriginal mythology the time in which the earth received its present form and in which the patterns and cycles of life and nature were initiated.' (*Macquarie Dictionary*)

DUGOUT A canoe made of a hollowed-out log.

ELECTRON SPIN RESONANCE DATING (ESR) 'A radiogenic dating method that utilises residual effects of changing energy levels of electrons under conditions of natural irradiation of alpha, beta and gamma rays. The method is applicable to teeth, bone, heat-treated chert and flint ceramics, archaeological sediments, shells, spring travertine and speleotherms' from 1000 to several million years old. (Bahn 1992)

ELOUERA A triangular-sectioned stone backed blade, resembling an orange segment in shape.

ENGRAVING See petroglyph.

ESTATE The area or areas of land over which a clan has primacy in foraging rights.

ETHNOARCHAEOLOGY/LIVING ARCHAEOLOGY The study by archaeologists of the economy and material culture of living human societies to aid understanding of past lifeways and material culture.

ETHNOGRAPHY Study of a contemporary human society's way of life through first-hand observation.

ETHNOLOGY The comparative study of contemporary cultures.

EXPERIMENTAL ARCHAEOLOGY The replication by archaeologists of past artefacts and activities in order to gain a greater understanding of the past.

EXTRACTIVE TOOL A tool related to the direct exploitation of environmental food resources.

FIGURATIVE ART Art motifs which resemble objects familiar to the observer; representational or naturalistic art.

FIND-SPOT The place where a single artefact was found.

FIRE-STICK A smouldering stick carried by Aboriginal groups when travelling.

FLAKE A piece of stone detached from a core by striking the core with another stone.

FLUORINE ANALYSIS Fluorine analysis allows archaeologists to determine the *relative* age of buried bones. These progressively absorb fluorine from the ground water, so the fluorine content within bones increases with age. The fluorine content of bones from an archaeological site can be measured and compared, giving an idea of the relative age of the bones.

FORM (IN ROCK ART) The visual organisation of the components which make up a mark or picture.

FOSSILS The remains and traces of animals and plants found naturally incorporated in rocks. They comprise both the actual remains of organisms, casts and impressions thereof, and footprints of animals and humans.

GALLERY (ROCK ART) A major art site containing a large number of pictures.

GENE FLOW Change in genetic make-up due to the effects of intermarriage and migration.

GENETIC DRIFT Change in genetic make-up due to founder effects, bottlenecks and variation in population size.

GEOLOGY The science involving the study of the whole evolution of the Earth.

GEOMETRIC MICROLITH A backed blade less than 3 centimetres long and generally geometric in shape, often triangular, trapezoidal or crescentic, and usually less than twice as long as it is wide.

GEOMORPHOLOGY The study of present-day landscapes and explanation of their form and development.

GLACIATION The covering of an area, or the action on that area, by an ice sheet or glacier.

GLOTTOCHRONOLOGY A method of assessing the divergence over time of two languages based on changes in vocabulary (lexicostatistics), expressed as an arithmetic formula.

GRACILE/ROBUST Lightly built and thin-boned human in contrast to strongly built, thick-boned human.

GREENSTONE Altered volcanic rocks of Cambrian age, predominantly amphibole hornfels in southeastern Australia, widely used as material for ground-edge axes.

GRINDING Simple manual abrasion, as in rubbing an axe on sandstone to produce a ground cutting edge.

GRINDING GROOVE A tool-sharpening groove produced by manual rubbing of an artefact such as an axe to and fro on rock, particularly sandstone, to grind or re-sharpen its surface.

GRINDSTONE Grindstones or mortars are flat-surfaced stone blocks with a shallow oval or circular depression ground in one or both faces, used for the pounding, crushing or grinding of hard material such as seeds, fruits, other plant material or ochre.

GROUND-EDGE TOOL A tool with a sharp cutting edge at one end produced by grinding rather than flaking.

HAEMATITE A hydrated form of high-grade ferric oxide yielding a red pigment.

HAFTING The process of mounting an artefact in a handle or onto another artefact, for example, a hafted axe, a stone point hafted onto a spear.

HAMMER-DRESSING See pecking.

HAMMER-STONE A lump of stone or river cobble used in fashioning small stone tools or pounding up foodstuffs.

HEARTH The site of a campfire represented by ash, charcoal, discoloration and, possibly, hearth stones around it.

HOLOCENE Recent geological time period, covering the last 10 000 years.

HOMINIDS Both extinct and modern forms of humankind.

HORSEHOOF CORE High-backed, steep-edged stone core, dome-shaped like a horse's hoof, typical of the old Australian core tool and scraper tradition.

HUNTER–GATHERERS 'A collective term for the members of small-scale mobile or semi-sedentary societies, whose subsistence is mainly focused on hunting game and gathering wild plants and fruits; organisational structure is based on bands with strong kinship ties.' (Renfrew and Bahn 1991)

ICE AGE Period of cold climate and a series of glaciations separated by interglacials, spanning the Pleistocene Period.

INCREASE SITE A site where a ritual was performed to propagate the creative powers of an Ancestral Being and thereby increase the population of the natural species associated with that Being.

INDIRECT PERCUSSION Percussion by the hammer and chisel method.

INDUSTRY An assemblage of artefacts including the same tool types so consistently as to suggest that it is the product of a single society.

IN SITU Undisturbed from its original position.

INTERGLACIAL A warm interlude between two glaciations.

KARST A landscape which shows a pattern of denudation in limestone and dolomitic rocks. This topography is produced by percolating ground waters and underground streams.

KARTAN A large-tool industry characterised by horsehoof cores, hammer-stones, pebble tools and scrapers.

LIMONITE A hydrated form of ferrous oxide yielding a yellow pigment.

LITHIC SCATTER Two or more stone artefacts lying on the surface of the ground.

LUNETTE A crescent-shaped dune of sand or clay found on the lee side of some Pleistocene lakes.

MACASSANS Indonesian traders from Macassar and elsewhere in Sulawesi who voyaged to tropical Australia from about AD 1710 to 1906 to collect and process trepang, also known as 'bêche-de-mer' or 'sea cucumber'.

MACROPODS The animal family Macropodidae, meaning 'long feet', and including long-footed marsupials such as kangaroos and wallabies.

MANUPORT An unmodified object transported by human agency.

MATERIAL CULTURE The tangible objects produced by a society.

MEGAFAUNA Large extinct animals and birds, especially large variants of present kangaroos and wombats.

MELANESIA The geographical region comprising New Guinea, the Bismarck Archipelago, the Solomon Islands, Vanuatu, New Caledonia and Fiji.

MICROLITH A small stone artefact, less than 3 centimetres in its maximum dimension.

MIDDEN A prehistoric refuse heap, usually composed of shells.

MILLSTONE A flat-surfaced stone slab, usually of sandstone, with an all-over depression or from one to four shallow narrow grooves worn on one or both surfaces from use as the lower grinding surface in the wet milling of seeds. Millstones are the largest stone implements in Australia and range from 18 to 75 centimetres long and weigh up to 14 kilograms.

MOTIF 'A recurrent visual image which has a particular arrangement of components' (Maynard 1976:100). A mark or combination of marks of human origin which can reasonably be interpreted to have formed an individual or separate picture or design; a recurrent type of figure.

MOUND An artificial elevation formed by the deliberate heaping up of earth from the surrounding plain. Many such mounds have occupational debris in the surface layers and some have evidence that huts were once built on top of them.

MULLERS Upper grindstones, generally round or oval, used in the wet milling of seeds on millstones.

NEOLITHIC The period in which food production commenced.

OCHRE Soft varieties of the iron oxides haematite, limonite and goethite, used to make pigment (generally red or yellow) for painting.

OPEN CAMP SITE See camp site.

OPTICALLY STIMULATED LUMINESCENCE DATING (OSL) A dating method which measures the luminescence emitted by a mineral when exposed to visible light, for example green laser. OSL is a new technique, related to thermoluminescence (TL) dating. (See also chapter 6.)

OTOLITH 'Ear-stone; a calcareous body often of rhombic crystals found in the inner ear of vertebrates and some invertebrates. In fishes it is often of great size.' (*Oxford English Dictionary*)

OUTRIGGER A log or similar spar fixed parallel to a canoe to stabilise it.

OVEN A shallow depression in the ground, containing ash and charcoal, and often lined with stones or lumps of baked clay. Ovens were used for roasting large animals.

OXYGEN ISOTOPE ANALYSIS 'Isotopic analysis that examines the $^{18}O/^{16}O$ ratio of materials; changes in ratio are often interpreted as having palaeoclimatic significance, particularly in the analysis of deep sea cores.' (Bahn 1992)

PAINTING (ROCK) Mark or picture made by adding wet pigment to a rock surface.

PALAEONTOLOGY The study of the fossil remains of animals.

PALAEOMAGNETISM The study of fossil remnant magnetism acquired by ancient materials, such as baked earth and clay from prehistoric fireplaces.

PALYNOLOGY See pollen analysis.

PATINA 'In its lithological sense patina is a term loosely describing visually obvious surface laminae [thin plates, scales or layers] covering rocks. It differs in colour and chemical composition from the unaltered rock matrix, is the outcome of widely differing processes and . . . is a function of time.' (Bednarik 1979:23)

PEBBLE TOOL A chopping tool made by flaking one or both faces of a large river 'pebble' or cobble.

PECKING/HAMMER-DRESSING The production of small pits, nicks or indentations on the surface of a rock, usually by indirect percussion.

PETROGLYPH/ENGRAVING A mark or picture made on rock, made by pecking, pounding, abrading or scratching the rock surface.

PHALANGER An arboreal marsupial of the family Phalangeridae, such as the possum and cuscus.

PHOTOGRAMMETRY A method of making maps or scale drawings of sites or structures, or of determining measurements by a combination of photographic and surveying techniques.

PHYSICAL ANTHROPOLOGY The study of the biological or physical characteristics of humankind and their evolution.

PHYTOLITHS 'Microscopic biogenic opal silica bodies secreted or deposited in plants, that are incorporated into the soil upon decay of plants and often preserved. Different plants produce phytoliths with different characteristic shapes and sizes, although not all morphologies are unique to individual species; identification of phytoliths collected from stratified sections may indicate the character of past vegetation.' (Bahn 1992)

PICTOGRAPH/PIGMENTED ART A picture or mark in which pigment has been added to the rock surface, comprising paintings, drawings, stencils or prints.

PIRRI POINT A small stone point, trimmed on one surface, generally used as a spear tip.

PLEISTOCENE The glacial epoch preceding the Holocene, extending back from 10 000 years ago to about 1.8 to 2 million years ago.

POINT A small stone point, trimmed on one or both surfaces, generally used as a spear tip.

POLLEN ANALYSIS/PALYNOLOGY The study of fossil pollen and spores in connection with plant geography and vegetation history.

POPULATION DENSITY The number of people in a region, usually expressed as an average people/land ratio, for example, one person to 20 square kilometres.

POST-CRANIAL BONES The human skeleton except for the cranium (skull).

POTASSIUM-ARGON DATING This isotopic dating technique, based on the radioactive decay of ^{40}K to the stable isotope ^{40}AR, is used primarily to date volcanic materials such as lava, ash and tuff, aged between 1000 and 1000 million years old.

PRAU A Malay-type boat with a distinctive large triangular sail and canoe-like outrigger, used by Macassans.

PREHISTORY The story of human development before the time of written records.

PRESSURE FLAKING Shaping a stone by pressing off small, thin flakes with a bone or wooden tool.

PRINT A positive impression of a hand or other object on a rock surface, made by dipping the hand or object in wet pigment and pressing it against the rock.

PROJECTILE POINT A stone point mounted on a spear.

QUARRY A place where a source of raw material such as ochre and stone has been exploited, often consisting of pits and hollows where material has been dug out of the ground. Stone quarries are often identifiable by a dense scatter of broken stone, flakes, chips and roughly shaped artefacts or axe-blanks.

QUARTZ A common white stone with naturally sharp edges, but generally poor fracturing properties, varying from clear and crystalline to milky or reddish in colour.

QUARTZITE A hard, homogeneous, medium- to coarse-grained granulose metamorphic rock, representing a recrystallised sandstone consisting predominantly of quartz, with good conchoidal fracture excellent for tool-making. Red, brown, grey, buff or yellow.

QUATERNARY The period embracing both the Pleistocene and Holocene.

RADIOCARBON DATING The method of dating organic fossil remains based on their content of the radioactive isotope carbon 14 (C–14 or ^{14}C). 'Radiometric dating technique for determining the age of late Quaternary carbon-bearing materials, including wood and plant remains, bone, peat and calcium carbonate shell. The method is based on the radioactive decay of the ^{14}C isotope in the sample to nitrogen, with the release of Beta particles that is initiated when an organism dies and ceases to exchange ^{14}C with the atmosphere. After death the ^{14}C content is a function of time and is determined by counting Beta particles with either a proportional gas counter or a liquid scintillation counter for a period of time. The method yields reliable ages back to about 50 000 bp.' (Bahn 1992) (See also chapter 1.)

RANGE The area over which a band normally travels in pursuit of routine economic activities.

RESIDUE ANALYSIS See use-wear analysis.

RETOUCH (SECONDARY) The flaking or trimming of a stone artefact on detachment from a core, usually by trimming or resharpening the edges.

ROCK ART Marks or pictures painted, drawn, stencilled, imprinted or carved on a rock surface.

ROCK-SHELTER A naturally formed hollow or overhang in a cliff, outcrop or boulder, sheltering a floor area.

ROLLED ARTEFACT An artefact smoothed by water, sand and gravel action in a creek or river bed or on a river terrace or beach.

SACRED SITE Dreaming, mythological, traditional, ethnographic, story or living site, of particular religious significance to contemporary Aborigines; a place infused with the creative force of the Ancestral Being who created that element of the landscape.

SAHUL The land mass comprising Australia, New Guinea and Tasmania. At times of low sea level, the Sahul continental shelf was exposed as dry land.

SCARRED TREE A tree showing a scar caused by removal of bark by Aborigines for making canoes, shields, containers or other artefacts.

SCAT An animal dropping or faeces.

SCLEROPHYLL FOREST A eucalypt-dominated forest.

SCRAPER A stone tool made on a flake, with one or more working edges, generally used for chiselling, cutting, gouging or planing.

SECONDARY WORKING See retouch.

SEED-GRINDING PATCHES Patches of rock worn smooth by grinding by Aboriginal people, usually women, grinding grass, acacia (wattle) or other seeds into 'flour'.

SILCRETE A fine-grained rock with good conchoidal fracture.

SITE (ARCHAEOLOGICAL) A place where past human activity is identifiable. 'A distinct spatial clustering of artefacts, features, structures, or organic and environmental remains, as the residue of human activity.' (Renfrew and Bahn 1991)

STENCIL A negative silhouette of a hand or other item outlined by splattering paint on the rock surface. The paint is usually pigment mixed with water and sprayed from the mouth.

STONE ARRANGEMENT A human-made alignment of stones, consisting of circles, lines, piles or other designs, used for ritual or ceremonial purposes.

STRATIGRAPHY/STRATIFICATION The layering of sediments and/or occupational debris. A well-stratified habitation site has clear boundaries or breaks between successive horizons (layers) of superimposed occupational material, with older material overlain by younger deposits.

STRIKING PLATFORM The area on a stone core on which a blow is struck to detach a flake. The detached flake bears on its butt end part of the original striking platform.

STYLE 'A highly specific and characteristic manner of doing something', 'non-functional formal variation' (Sackett 1977). In rock art: 'The sum total of the technique, form, motif, size and character of a figure or group of figures' (Maynard 1976:143); 'combination of distinctive features of artistic expression or execution peculiar to a particular person, people, school or era' (R. Bednarik pers. comm.).

SUNDA/SUNDA LAND The enlarged continental region of Southeast Asia exposed at times of low sea level, which joined much of western Indonesia to the mainland.

SYMPATHETIC MAGIC The depiction or modelling of a desired event in order to make it happen.

TALLY MARKS A series of short, parallel strokes, usually vertical or diagonal in horizontal rows, painted or carved by Aborigines on rock.

TALUS SLOPE The slope at the foot of a cliff or below a rock-shelter, often covered with scree (rock debris).

TAPHONOMY 'Study of the transformation of materials into the archaeological record. The focus of taphonomic studies is the understanding of the processes resulting in the archaeological record *per se*.' (Bahn 1992)

TERTIARY PERIOD The period representing geological time from about 60 million to 2 million years ago, comprising the Palaeocene to Pliocene epochs, and preceding the Pleistocene epoch.

THERIANTHROPE A part-animal, part-human figure.

THERMOLUMINESCENCE DATING (TL) A scientific method of dating objects, such as those of baked clay, which have been heated to more than 400 to 500 degrees Celsius in the past, by measurement of their thermoluminescent (TL) glow. Applicable to materials up to several hundred thousand years old.

THUMBNAIL SCRAPER A microlithic discoidal or semi-discoidal *scraper*, resembling a thumbnail in size and shape. Most are end-scrapers, with the working edge on the distal end opposite the striking platform, but some have trimming on much or all of their edge.

TOOL, IMPLEMENT An artefact manufactured for use or showing clear signs of use.

TOOL KIT A set of artefacts.

TOTEM An animal, plant or other natural object used as the emblem or token of an individual or group, in a system of relationships providing spiritual linkages between people and the natural universe.

TOTEMISM 'The use of animal or plant emblems to stand for individuals or groups. The commonest forms of totemism in Australia are clan and personal totems. Clan totems were conferred during the creation period and are inherited. Personal totems are conferred at conception or birth, when the spirit of the unborn child announces its identity.' (Layton 1992)

TRACK A mark that looks like the tracks or traces left on the ground by a faunal species.

TRIBE The speakers of a single language or dialect. A major Aboriginal social and kinship group, made up of a number of clans, possessing a common language, identity and culture. A tribe's territory is the sum of its constituent clan estates.

TULA ADZE A hafted stone chisel used in arid Australia for working hardwoods such as mulga. It is made on a discoidal or semi-discoidal thick flake with obtuse-angled striking platform and a convex lower surface bearing the bulb of percussion. Retouch and use-wear occur on the distal end opposite the striking platform. Repeated resharpening of this convex working edge results in a distinctive steep-edged 'slug'.

TYPE An artefact class identified by the consistent clustering of attributes (characteristics such as form, size, raw material, decoration and colour).

TYPE/DIAGNOSTIC ARTEFACT An artefact with a wide distribution in space, but a restricted one in time, useful for correlating cultural sequences over large areas and for cross-dating.

TYPE SITE A site containing artefacts typical of a particular prehistoric phase.

UNIFACIALLY TRIMMED An artefact worked on only one face.

UNIPOINT A bone point worked at one end only.

URANIUM SERIES DATING A dating method based on the decay of radioactive uranium isotopes, particularly useful for dating stalagmites, bones and shells in the period from 10 000 to 250 000 BP.

USE-WEAR ANALYSIS Examination of the surface and working edges of artefacts for signs of use — either damage, polish or residues — usually by means of a high-powered microscope. The technique is used mainly in the study of stone and bone tools, which may suffer diagnostic damage or polishing when used to cut, saw, pierce, scrape or grind materials such as hides, plants or animals.

WASTE FLAKE A piece of stone detached from a core by striking the core with another stone, but lacking any further deliberate modification.

WEATHERING The alteration and decay of rocks as far down as the depth to which atmospheric agencies can penetrate.

X-RAY ART A style of rock art in which the internal skeleton and internal organs of humans or animals are depicted.

ZOOMORPH A figure of animal form.

Further Reading

Allen, H. and Barton, G. *Ngarradj Warde Djobkeng. White Cockatoo Dreaming*. Oceania Monograph 37. Sydney, Oceania Publications, University of Sydney, 1989.

Allen, J., Golson, J. and Jones, R. (eds). *Sunda and Sahul, Prehistoric Studies in South East Asia, Melanesia and Australia*. London, Academic Press, 1977.

Australian Heritage Commission. *The Heritage of Australia*. Melbourne, Macmillan, 1981.

Australian Museum. *Publication in Honour of Dr Fred McCarthy*. Records of the Australian Museum, Supplement no. 17. Sydney, Australian Museum, 1993.

Australian National Advisory Committee for Unesco. *Australian Aboriginal Culture*. Canberra, Australian Government Publishing Service, 1973.

Bahn, P. (ed.). *Collins Dictionary of Archaeology*. Glasgow, Harper Collins, 1992.

Bahn, P. and Rosenfeld, A. (eds). *Rock Art and Prehistory. Papers Presented to Symposium G of the AURA Congress, Darwin 1988*. Oxford, Oxbow Monograph 10, 1991.

Beck, W., Clarke, A. and Head, L. (eds). *Plants in Australian Archaeology. Tempus*, vol. 1. St Lucia, Anthropology Museum, University of Queensland, 1989.

Bellwood, P. *Man's Conquest of the Pacific: The Prehistory of Southeast Asia and Oceania*. Sydney, Collins, 1978.

— *Prehistory of the Indo-Malaysian Archipelago*. Sydney, Academic Press, 1985.

Berndt, R. M. and Berndt, C. H. *The Speaking Land: Myth and Story in Aboriginal Australia*. Melbourne, Penguin, 1988.

— *The World of the First Australians. Aboriginal Traditional Life: Past and Present*. Canberra, Aboriginal Studies Press, 1988.

Berndt, R. M. and Phillips, E. S. *The Australian Aboriginal Heritage*. Sydney, Ure Smith, 1973.

Blainey, G. *Triumph of the Nomads. A History of Ancient Australia*. Melbourne, Sun Books, 1975.

Bowdler, S. (ed.). *Coastal Archaeology in Eastern Australia*. Occasional Papers in Prehistory no. 11. Canberra, Department of Prehistory, Australian National University, 1982.

Brown, P. *Coobool Creek. A Morphological and Metrical Analysis of the Crania, Mandibles and Dentitions of a Prehistoric Australian Human Population. Terra Australis* Series no. 13. Canberra, Department of Prehistory, Australian National University, 1989.

Burnum Burnum. *Burnum Burnum's Australia*. Sydney, Angus and Robertson, 1988.

Butlin, N. G. *Our Original Aggression: Aboriginal Population of Southeastern Australia 1788–1850*. Sydney, George Allen and Unwin, 1983.

— *Economics and the Dreamtime: A Hypothetical History*. Melbourne, Cambridge University Press, 1993.

Connah, G. (ed.). *Australian Field Archaeology: A Guide to Techniques*. Canberra, Australian Institute of Aboriginal Studies, 1982.

Corke, D. *The First Australians*. Melbourne, Nelson (Young Australia Series), 1985.

Cowan, J. *Mysteries of the Dreaming: The Spiritual Life of Australian Aborigines*. Sydney, New edn. Prism Unity Press, 1992. See also other works by Cowan.

Dickson, F. P. *Australian Stone Hatchets*. London, Academic Press, 1982.

Dixon, R. M. W. *The Languages of Australia*. Melbourne, Cambridge University Press, 1980.

Dodson, J. (ed.). *The Naïve Lands. Prehistory and Environmental Change in Australia and the Southwest Pacific*. Melbourne, Longman Cheshire, 1992.

Edwards, R. *Aboriginal Bark Canoes of the Murray Valley*. Adelaide, Rigby, 1972.

— *Australian Aboriginal Art. The Art of the Alligator Rivers Region, Northern Territory*. Canberra, Australian Institute of Aboriginal Studies, 1979.

Elkin, A. P. *The Australian Aborigines. How to Understand Them*. Sydney, Angus and Robertson, 1964.

Flood, J. M. *The Moth Hunters: Aboriginal Prehistory of the Australian Alps*. Canberra, Australian Institute of Aboriginal Studies, 1980.

— *The Riches of Ancient Australia: A Journey Into Prehistory*. Brisbane, University of Queensland Press, 1990.

Frankel, D. *Remains to be Seen: Archaeological Insights into Australian Prehistory*. Melbourne, Longman Cheshire, 1991.

Gibbs, R. M. *The Aborigines*. Hawthorn, Longman, 1974.

Godden, E. and Malnic, J. *Rock Paintings of Aboriginal Australia*. New ed. Sydney, Reed, 1988.

Gould, R. A. *Living Archaeology*. New York, Cambridge University Press, 1980.

Haigh, C. and Goldstein, W. (eds). *The Aborigines of New South Wales*. Sydney, N.S.W. National Parks and Wildlife Service, 1980.

Hallam, S. J. *Fire and Hearth*. Canberra, Australian Institute of Aboriginal Studies, 1975.

Hayden, B. *Palaeolithic Reflections: Lithic Technology and Ethnographic Excavations Among Australian Aborigines*. Canberra, Australian Institute of Aboriginal Studies, 1979.

Henderson, K. R. (ed.). *From Earlier Fleets: An Aboriginal Anthology*. Hemisphere, 1978.

Hiscock, P. and Mitchell, S. *Stone Artefact Quarries and Reduction Sites in Australia: Towards a Type Profile*. Australian Heritage Commission Technical Publication Series no. 4. Canberra, Australian Government Publishing Service, 1993.

Horton, D. *Recovering the Tracks: The Story of Australian Archaeology*. Canberra, Aboriginal Studies Press, 1991.

— (ed.). *The Encyclopaedia of Aboriginal Australia*. Canberra, Aboriginal Studies Press, 1994.

Isaacs, J. (ed.). *Australian Dreaming. 40 000 Years of Aboriginal History*. Sydney, Lansdowne Press, 1980.

Jones, R. (ed.). *Archaeological Research in Kakadu National Park*. Special Publication no. 1. Canberra, Australian National Parks and Wildlife Service and Department of Prehistory, Australian National University, 1985.

Keast, A. (ed.). *Ecological Biogeography of Australia*. The Hague, W. Junk, 1981.

Kirk, R. L. *Aboriginal Man Adapting*. Melbourne, Oxford University Press, 1983.

Kirk, R. L. and Thorne, A. G. (eds). *The Origin of the Australians*. Canberra, Australian Institute of Aboriginal Studies, 1976.

Lawrence, R. *Aboriginal Habitat and Economy*. Canberra, Department of Geography, Australian National University, 1988.

Layton, R. *Australian Rock Art. A New Synthesis*. Melbourne, Cambridge University Press, 1992.

McBryde, I. *Aboriginal Prehistory of New England*. Sydney, Sydney University Press, 1974.

— *Coast and Estuary. Archaeological Investigations on the North Coast of New South Wales. Wombah and Schnapper Point*. Canberra, Australian Institute of Aboriginal Studies, 1982.

McCarthy, F. D. *Australian Aboriginal Rock Art*. Sydney, Australian Museum, 1979.

— *Australian Aboriginal Stone Implements*. Sydney, Australian Museum, 1979.

McDonald, J. and Haskovec, I. P. (eds). *State of the Art. Regional Rock Art Studies in Australia and Melanesia. Proceedings of Symposia C and D of the AURA Congress, Darwin, 1988*. Occasional AURA Publication no. 6. Melbourne, Australian Rock Art Research Association (PO Box 216, Caulfield South, Vic. 3162), 1992.

Maddock, K. *The Australian Aborigines*. 2nd edn. Ringwood, Penguin, 1982.

Massola, A. *The Aborigines of South-eastern Australia as They Were*. Richmond, Heinemann, 1971.

Meehan, B. *Shell Bed to Shell Midden*. Canberra, Australian Institute of Aboriginal Studies, 1982.

Meehan, B. and Jones, R. (eds). *Archaeology with Ethnography: An Australian Perspective*. Occasional Papers in Prehistory no. 15. Canberra, Department of Prehistory, Australian National University, 1988.

Meehan, B. and White, N. (eds). *Hunter–Gatherer Demography*. Oceania Monograph 39. Sydney, Oceania Publications, University of Sydney, 1990.

Mitchell, S. R. *Stone-Age Craftsmen*. Melbourne, Tait Book Co., 1949.

Moore, D. R. *Islanders and Aborigines at Cape York*. Canberra, Australian Institute of Aboriginal Studies, 1979.

Mulvaney, D. J. *The Prehistory of Australia*. Ringwood, Penguin, 1975.

— *Encounters in Place: Outsiders and Aboriginal Australians 1606–1985*. Brisbane, University of Queensland Press, 1989.

— *Prehistory and Heritage: The Writings of John Mulvaney*. Occasional Papers in Prehistory no. 17. Canberra, Department of Prehistory, Australian National University, 1990.

Mulvaney, D. J. and Golson, J. (eds). *Aboriginal Man and Environment in Australia*. Canberra, Australian National University Press, 1971.

Mulvaney, D. J. and White, J. P. (eds). *Australians: A Historical Library. Australians to 1788*. Sydney, Fairfax, Syme and Weldon Associates, 1987.

Peterson, N. (ed.). *Tribes and Boundaries in Australia*. Canberra, Australian Institute of Aboriginal Studies, 1976.

— *Australian Territorial Organisation*. Oceania Monograph. Sydney, University of Sydney, 1986.

Renfrew, C. and Bahn, P. *Archaeology. Theories, Methods and Practice*. London, Thames and Hudson, 1991.

Roberts, A. and Mountford, C. P. *The Dreamtime*. Adelaide, Rigby, 1965; *The Dawn of Time*. 1969; *The First Sunrise*. 1971.

Ryan, L. *The Aboriginal Tasmanians*. Brisbane, University of Queensland Press, 1981.

Smith, M. (ed.). *Archaeology at ANZAAS 1983*. Perth, Anthropology Department, Western Australian Museum, 1983.

Smith, M. A. *Puritjarra Rockshelter and the Prehistory of the Red Centre*. Terra Australis no. 14. Canberra, Department of Prehistory, Australian National University, 1994.

Smith, M. A., Spriggs, M. and Fankhauser, B. (eds). *Sahul in Review: Pleistocene Archaeology in Australia, New Guinea and Island Melanesia*. Occasional Papers in Prehistory no. 24. Canberra, Department of Prehistory, Australian National University, 1993.

Solomon, S., Davidson, I. and Watson, D. (eds). *Problem Solving in Taphonomy. Tempus* vol. 2. St Lucia, Anthropology Museum, University of Queensland, 1990.

Spriggs, M., Yen, D. E., Ambrose, W., Jones, R., Thorne, A. and Andrews, A. (eds). *A Community of Culture. The People and Prehistory of the Pacific*. Occasional Papers in Prehistory no. 21. Canberra, Department of Prehistory, Australian National University, 1993.

Stanbury, P. (ed.). *10,000 Years of Sydney Life: A Guide to Archaeological Discovery*. Sydney, Macleay Museum, University of Sydney, 1979.

Thorne, A. and Raymond, R. *Man on the Rim*. Sydney, Angus and Robertson, 1989.

Tindale, N. B. *Aboriginal Tribes of Australia*. Canberra, Australian National University Press, 1974.

Ucko, P. J. (ed.). *Form in Indigenous Art*. Canberra, Australian Institute of Aboriginal Studies, 1977.

Veth, P. *Islands in the Interior: Dynamics of Prehistoric Adaptations within the Arid Zone of Australia*. Michigan, Ann Arbor, 1993.

Walker, D. (ed.). *Bridge and Barrier: The Natural and Cultural History of Torres Strait*. Canberra, Department of Biogeography and Geomorphology, Australian National University, 1972.

Walsh, G. *Australia's Greatest Rock Art*. Bathurst, E. J. Brill, Robert Brown and Associates, 1988.

Ward, G. K. (ed.). *Archaeology at ANZAAS Canberra*. Canberra, Canberra Archaeological Society, Department of Prehistory and Anthropology, Australian National University, 1985.

Webb, S. G. *The Willandra Lakes Hominids*. Occasional Papers in Prehistory no. 16. Canberra, Department of Prehistory, Australian National University, 1989.

White, J. P. *Before the White Man. Aboriginal Life in Prehistoric Australia*. Sydney, Reader's Digest, 1974.

White, J. P. and O'Connell, J. F. *A Prehistory of Australia, New Guinea and Sahul*. London, Academic Press, 1982.

Wright, R. V. S. (ed.). *Stone Tools as Cultural Markers: Change, Evolution and Complexity*. Canberra, Australian Institute of Aboriginal Studies, 1977.

Index

Page references in *italic* type refer to illustrations.